Saint James Church

Worshipping in the Presence of the Past: 1720-2020

By Virginia Brown Bartels

To Bubba
Blessings!

Virginia Brown Bartels

DORRANCE
PUBLISHING CO
EST. 1920
PITTSBURGH, PENNSYLVANIA 15238

Dorrance Publishing Co
585 Alpha Drive
Suite 103
Pittsburgh, PA 15238
Visit our website at *www.dorrancebookstore.com*

ISBN: 978-1-6480-4597-4
eISBN: 978-1-6480-4620-9

Dedication

This book is dedicated
to all those who have worshipped
at Saint James Church,
James Island, South Carolina,
over the last 300 years
and to all those who have been
or will be blessed,
either directly or indirectly,
by Saint James' worshippers.

EXPLANATION OF THE COVER OF THE BOOK

The cover of this book is a 2019 painting—*Sea Island Glory*—by acclaimed Charleston artist Jim Booth. To honor the 300-year anniversary of Saint James Church, he painted a breathtaking image of the sixth sanctuary to be constructed on this site. His gift to our church will be a treasure to those who have worshipped here as well as a means of evangelism to draw others yet to cross its threshold.

The congregation, staff, and vestry are grateful for Jim's gift to the written history of Saint James. His artistic ability has captured the beauty of the church's architecture, its setting among huge moss-draped oaks, and the natural and spiritual light that has shone on this place of worship for three centuries. Self-taught, he has created lifelike realism, masterfully using color, detail, and lighting in a career spanning five decades. He completed thousands of paintings, most which depict the Low Country at its best—the harbor, marshes, wildlife, beaches, lighthouses, bridges, famous landmarks, and local college campuses. His works portray a variety of historic and current settings, diverse weather and seasons, nature's splendor and man's workmanship. He retired May 2018.

Saint James Church is special to Jim because he attended as a youth, he and his beloved wife Virginia were married here, and his parents—Lewis and Mae Booth—worshipped here. For many decades he has been a resident of either James or Johns Island.

We are also grateful to Jim's daughter Diana for her business expertise that she has shared to help the people of Saint James produce, advertise, and market her father's masterpiece, *Sea Island Glory*, a tribute to his Creator.

TABLE OF CONTENTS

FOREWORD

For three centuries, on several acres of land on an island just south of the Charleston peninsula, there lies a place first designated for worship of God in the early 1700s. The current sanctuary of Saint James is nestled among oak trees, some of which are probably older than the first of six churches built on this site. The earliest of the previous five worship buildings were known as chapels of ease, situated near a rural dirt road. Today Saint James is located at 1872 Camp Road, James Island, across from the Bishop Gadsden Retirement Community.

Much of Saint James' story can be told as one strolls through the expansive cemetery that extends behind and between the current traditional sanctuary built in 1959 and the newest building, the Ministry Center, built in 2003. Many people who have been dear to me, all former members of Saint James, rest in peace here. Buried there is my teacher, Frances "Frannie" Hayden, who taught me chemistry at James Island High—a brilliant educator who challenged all her students to learn more than we ever thought our brains could master. There is the grave of my friend and co-worker, Mary Bailey King, who taught Spanish at James Island High and served as a translator on many Saint James' medical missions. Moving reverently through the cemetery, I come to the grave of Sid Eason, my former classmate at James Island High, who married my friend Sharon. Sid lived long enough to give away his beautiful daughter Natalie in marriage, but he died much too early in 1999 of ALS. And there is the grave of my former pupil Raymond Tassin, who died in 1989 of an accidental gunshot wound. Nothing is more painful to a teacher than to return to the classroom after the death of a student and face his permanently empty desk.

As I walk through this memorial garden of sorts, I recognize other names of revered church members—that of Captain George Lisle, a retired Navy commander, who served our congregation so well as junior warden and died in 2009. Dr. Dan Ellis and his wife Kitty, both significant church leaders, share adjacent graves. This book quotes much of Dr. Ellis' research that he conducted prior to 1979. There is the grave of my long-time friend Kay Cupka, my fellow prayer warrior, who died in 2014. Using her culinary skills, sense of humor, and sensitivity for others, she, often with her husband David, served Saint James in many capacities—co-sponsor of the youth, vestry member, wedding coordinator, altar guild director.

Also buried here is William McLeod—Mr. Willie—who owned McLeod Plantation on Wappoo Cut. He worshipped at Saint James beyond his one hundredth birthday and gave the plaques with the Lord's Prayer and the Ten Commandments that hang on each side of the altar in the church.

Many tombstone epitaphs, comprised of poetic and scriptural inscriptions, testify to the service, faith, and love of those who have gone before us. Middle names, maiden names, and married names on the tombstones reveal how families on the island and at the church were intertwined for decades. Among the graves are the surnames of those whose families have lived for generations on the islands—James Island and Johns Island and Folly Island, Kiawah, Seabrook, Wadmalaw, Edisto, and Charleston itself. Oswald, Heyward, Dill, Rivers, Seabrook, Frampton, Jenkins, Meggett, Mikell, Creighton, Hinson, Welch, Royall, Grimball, Whaley, Lawton, and Legare are names of such families who were baptized, married, worshipped, and ultimately buried at Saint James.

A rural area for hundreds of years, James Island sustained its people, many of whom were gardeners, farmers, planters, and fishermen. Just as the land and rivers provided sustenance for life, these people drew the very earth and water into their being. In God's timing, they returned to the earth. Just as a mother swaddles her baby in soft blankets, Saint James swaddles its own in the protective covering of the graves overhung by limbs of ancient oaks and Spanish moss in its cemetery.

The land in front of Saint James was once filled with the horses and buggies of its Sunday worshippers. Then it was filled with Model T Fords and, decades later, the popular 1950 Chevys. In another decade, came the family station wagons, VW buses, and sporty Mustangs. Today the lawn and paved parking areas surrounding Saint James are filled Sunday mornings by modern sleek cars with air conditioning and computerized engines. But regardless of the modes of transportation, the churches were built. and the people have come… come to learn how to live and love because He first loved us.

Here the cycles of life for both man and nature seem more prevalent. Walking to the back of the church property, I can see Ellis Creek, which ebbs and flows with the changes of the tides. Viewed from the steeple or the ground, the four seasons bring changes with the azaleas, camellias, and landscaping. Sunrise and sunset, young and old, sorrow and joy, baptism and burial, sin and sanctification—the cycles of life teem here.

Whether the *Book of Common Prayer* was dated 1662, 1789, 1928, 1979, or 2019, His Word has been planted in the hearts of Saint James' people. Whether from the King James, New International, or English Standard Version of the Bible, the Gospel has been preached. This place of worship has survived fires, wars, hurricanes, politics, and mankind's folly. The three-hundred-year-old love story of the Father and His people at Saint James gives testimony to His goodness, greatness, governance, and grace.

People from all walks of life continue to flock to these holy grounds to grow closer to the Good Shepherd, their Creator and Savior. In worship, through the Liturgy of the Word—consisting of the readings, the sermons, the creeds, and the prayers—minds are cleansed and hearts are purified, resulting in spiritual renewal. The Holy Spirit breathes life into these worshippers, and they, in turn, go forth from our own Kingdom Community and even to the ends of the earth to be fishers of men. Coming individually, in pairs, or in families, God's people convene in this long-established place of worship truly to praise and adore the one and only God of all time, in faithful commitment to His immutable Truth found only in Holy Scripture.

Having been a member of Saint James since the early 1980s, I have witnessed many changes throughout the decades, but many things also remain constant. My study of Saint James Church's history emphatically reveals how God has raised up church leaders, both laity and priests, who have sustained and maintained this place of worship, decade after decade, generation after generation, leaving a spiritual legacy of grace through faith and redemption through Christ. One can only imagine how many songs and prayers have been lifted up from this one plot of sand and soil.

Today Saint James thrives in its modern world of both contemporary and traditional worship services, a world of new technology, a part of a world so vastly different from that of the 1700s and 1800s and 1900s. Nonetheless, it has stood the test of time. We worship in the present, yet we are also worshipping in the presence of the past.

Virginia Brown Bartels

PREFACE

History of Saint James Church: Worshipping in the Presence of the Past 1720-2020 documents the three hundred years of this church's existence in its present location. By no means is this book complete. How I wish that I could tell the story of each individual whose life on earth and in heaven was and is and will be enriched by this place of worship! Only God knows. Many times I have walked through the cemetery wishing the beloved departed members of our congregation could impart their unique stories and heart-felt testimonies in their own words, based on their own experiences, portraying their own viewpoints. How I wish that I could convey the place that Saint James has held and continues to hold in our local and worldwide community!

Surely the story of this three-hundred-year-old congregation is bigger and better than I have the ability to recount. Although gaps exist in this spiritual saga, details and depth also abound. At times, because of varied sources and accounts, readers might note inconsistencies, such as with spellings and dates. Readers unfamiliar with Saint James might find some details to be tedious; for those familiar with this church and its people, they will probably find that the names and events will evoke multiple memories and emotions. Here and there the narrative style changes depending upon the situation and the storyteller. I have included a bibliography to identify my sources and to provide readers a means to seek more information on their own.

Along with the timeless, unchanging Gospel, a church's history is intertwined with its geography, politics, culture, and current events; therefore, much of the content of this book includes details about these influences to provide a broader picture of the church's parish life and past. Sometimes I have merely reported facts, and other times my awe and admiration embellish the account being rendered. But Saint James' story consists of much more than facts; the faith of its people must be told as well. How I wish I could tell the story of all the saints of Saint James over three hundred years, but many of their stories have been lost over time, and one book of a few hundred pages cannot contain the countless stories of thousands of its parishioners and their priests.

When I began to sense that the story of Saint James needed to be told, God would not stop calling me to make an effort to capture these years and His people. And when He calls, He equips. The voices of the people of Saint James—those who have passed on to glory and those looking for that day to come—have spoken. As inadequate and imperfect as my account may be, I have tried to hear their voices and God's voice as well as I have attempted to honor both. Personal narratives, statistical accounts, oral histories, Low Country publications, newspaper articles, photographs, church records, diocesan periodicals, vestry minutes, and family diaries have all come together to tell Saint James' story, which is full of humility, grace, and glory. The history of this house of worship is complex, rich, and compelling.

In *Saint Philip's Church of Charleston: An Early History of the Oldest Parish in South Carolina*, Reverend J. Haden McCormick, the twenty-fifth rector of St. Philip's Church, said,

> I believe that along with Biblical knowledge, Church history is essential for the development of an understanding of God and gaining knowledge of His nature and His revelation through our Lord and Savior, Jesus Christ. Meditation and reflection on the sacrifices and hardships endured by those who have gone before us, sow in our souls seeds of courage and hope. (p. 229)

In summary, Rev. McCormick said that knowing the history of our church can help "equip us with the necessary tools to advance God's Kingdom." (p. 230)

Saint James' worshippers have been blessed recipients of a spiritual legacy of faith, hope, and love. Throughout the ages, diverse worshippers have been joined to each other as different parts of one body. As Romans 12:5 states, "In Christ we who are many form one body, and each member belongs to all the others. We have different gifts, according to the grace given us."

May this book inspire regular attendees who have found their places in the pews each Sunday at Saint James. May the children and grandchildren and great grandchildren of Saint James' members learn about their ancestors' spiritual roots. May this historical account inspire those who only read about it but live elsewhere. May it inspire those yet to be born and yet to walk through its doors to learn about and sustain this legacy of faith, hope, and love into eternity. To God be the glory!

REFLECTIONS BY REV. ARTHUR JENKINS

James Island is a Sea Island. Its history must be understood through that lens. This is the lens of tides and marshes, of ferries and bridges, of isolation and differentiation, and the edge-of-America mentality, and the culture of people who are drawn to live here. Even in this modern day with skyway bridges and the internet super-highway, there is still some of that residual culture that "We live on an island." From the Stono Indians, who probably inhabited the island as early as 600 B.C., to the current impact the medical, technical and manufacturing growth is having, there has been one constant: mankind's need for faith and fellowship.

MANKIND'S CONSTANT: THE NEED FOR FAITH AND FELLOWSHIP

In the midst of an ever-changing world and an ever-progressing history, there is one constant. This is our need for faith and fellowship. The faith we recognize intrinsically is, at the least, faith in someone or something greater than ourselves. The fellowship we long for deep inside is fellowship with someone other than just ourselves. We are this way because God created us this way. As Genesis chapter one tells us, "So God created man in his own image, in the image of God created he him; male and female created he them." (Genesis 1:27)

The early settlers of James Island and the ensuing plantation families acknowledged their need for faith and fellowship in establishing an Anglican presence of worship on James Island. Due to the realities of island isolation, these families brought the priest to the island rather than trying to bring the families to the priest. The first of these priests was the Rev'd

Mr. William Guy, who began sacred services here in 1719. Mr. Guy was the rector of Saint Andrews Parish, which we now know as "Old St. Andrews." He would row down the Ashley River (with the tide, of course) to hold worship for Saint James every fourth Sunday.

This Anglican presence of worship recognized the best of our Christian faith and Anglican heritage, based on the Reformation principles and the reclaimed Pauline revelation of "Justification by Grace as received through Faith." (Ephesians 2:1-10) This is known as "substitutionary atonement." Jesus Christ did for me what I could not do for myself. Jesus restored me to God-the-Father. This faith affirmed that the Bible, the Old and New Testaments, is "God's Word written."

The Anglican heritage begun here on James Island by Saint James Church was the faith in the Gospel of Jesus Christ as expressed in the Sacraments offered in worship. It was the heritage of liturgical worship as guided by the then 1662 *Book of Common Prayer*. It was the heritage of the affirmation and the proclamation of God's Word in sermons and by the Creeds, both the Apostle's Creed and the Nicene Creed.

This Christian faith and Anglican heritage offered to James Island a means of fellowship and continues as a fellowship that is not just composed of like-minded people. Rather, it is composed of people of many different likes and minds, but with one common bond, Jesus Christ as Lord and Savior. This Christian foundation of "fellowship" burst forth following the Day of Pentecost. "And they devoted themselves to the apostles' teaching and the fellowship, to the breaking of bread and the prayers... And all who believed were together and had all things in common" (Acts 2:42,44). It is this same inclusive/exclusive fellowship which the founders of Saint James brought to our island that has had a guiding, healing, nourishing effect for now 300 years.

The Change of History with an Unchanging God

The book you hold in your hands is the lovingly and faithfully compiled story of the life of an island and her people. It recaptures the response of a church of people who, in the midst of the ever-changing tides of time and events, offer the one unchanging need in life. This is our need for faith in and fellowship with an unchanging God.

It is my prayer that as you read this book and see the ever-changing church that is Saint James, you will also recognize the unchanging hand of God in her life. There are no coincidences in God's Kingdom. There is no "as luck would have it." God is never surprised. In God's promise of redemption fulfilled in Jesus Christ, we can see that in "...all things God works for the good of those who love him, who have been called according to his purpose." (Romans 8:28) I pray that as you see God's loving providential hand in the life of a people gathered, who continue to call themselves Saint James Church, you may also recognize His loving providential hand in your life.

CHAPTER ONE

Establishing a Low Country Anglican Community

In 1987 a history committee at Saint James published a document entitled "An Unfinished History of St. James' Episcopal Church." Following is the opening paragraph:

> Here on James Island, beginning in the late seventeenth century and far removed from the centers of civilization, a few families of hardy Christians and their later descendants had to struggle for survival not only against the threats of natural forces, but the destruction caused by a series of wars, famines, and pestilence as well as the tensions of living within a multi-racial community in which they were a decided minority. (p.1)

The Carolina Colony, extending along the coastline from Cape Hatteras southward, was originally claimed by early Spanish explorers. Eventually, this colony came to be regarded as the southernmost territory of the British Empire. King Charles II appointed eight Lord Proprietors to whom, in 1663, he gave land from Virginia to Florida.[1] Historian George Williams quoted from Rev. Frederick Dalcho's research, stating that the king wanted to "enlarge his dominions" and to propagate "the Christian faith in a country not yet cultivated or planted, and only inhabited by some barbarous People, who had no knowledge of God."[2]

When the first settlers arrived in this area, several native Indian tribes already occupied the territory. According to local historian Jim Hayes, the Cusabos, consisting of ten smaller tribes, lived along the coastline from Mt. Pleasant to Beaufort and inland as far as thirty miles.[3] Known as "Chicora," this area was home to natives from the Bohicket, Stono, and

Kiawah tribes, all names still familiar to today's James Island residents. The Stono Indians grew corn, fruits, and vegetables and hunted all animals, believing that everyone had a right to the wild life, thus causing dissension between them and the European settlers, especially regarding ownership of land.[4]

In the 1600s civil order on James Island was, for the most part, established by the disciplines taught by the Christian churches. However, many early settlers were lawless adventurers, unchurched debtors, former prisoners, and social outcasts. The Carolina Colony was established in 1670, but no organized religious group or religious leader existed for a decade. Finally, in 1680 an Anglican church was built on the Charleston peninsula—St. Philip's—with Reverend Atkin Williamson assigned; however, there was some question as to whether he had ever been properly ordained.[5]

According to Sidney Bolton in *Anglican Churches of Colonial South Carolina*, the colony had an estimated population of 8,300 settlers by 1703, half of whom were Europeans and the other half either African or other non-Europeans. Among the Europeans, approximately 1,700 were Anglicans; 1,300, Presbyterians; 400, Baptists; and 100, Quakers. [6]

In *South Carolina: A Synoptic History for Laymen*, author Louis Jones explained the Church Act (1704) in which the Anglicans attempted to do the following:

1 Support their church from colony funds

2 Legalize only those marriages performed by Anglican clergy

3 Bar from public office all Dissenters

4 Make the *Common Book of Prayer* the official form of religious service[7]

Outraged, the Dissenters appealed to the House of Lords, and in 1706 the Church Act was revised, recognizing the Anglican Church as the official church, granting Dissenters many basic rights, and establishing ten parishes to administer church laws and serve as election districts for local representations.[8]

Dr. Daniel W. Ellis, longtime member of Saint James, wrote the following opening to his eleven-page history of Saint James (completed in 1979) found in the *St. James Sampler II*, the congregation's cookbook published by The Quin Press on Broad Street:

> By an act of the assembly, November 1706, the sum of 2000 pounds was appropriated "out of the public treasury" for the establishment of six churches. One of these churches was St. Andrews and its parish included James Island. These churches operated under the supervision of the "Society for the Propagation of the Gospel in Foreign Parts" (SPG). Its ecclesiastical head was…the Bishop of London. Rectors of the several churches who were missionaries of

the Society made reports of their activities directly to the Society. There was no local bishop. A local clergyman held the title of "Commissary of Carolina."[9]

American rectors reported to the SPG. Dr. Ellis used these historical records for much of his own historical summary regarding Saint James. A "commissary" was a bishop-appointed male who could exercise ecclesiastical jurisdiction in a particular part of the diocese, but he was not allowed to consecrate churches, ordain priests, or administer confirmation.[10] The Church Acts (1704 and 1706) made the Church of England the official religion in Carolina, but other denominations (except for Roman Catholicism) were generally accepted.[11]

The SPG also worked to spread the Gospel to Native American Indians, slaves, and European settlers.[12] In 1712 the colonial legislature authorized baptism for slaves and native Americans but "such baptisms did not change the conditions of servitude of the baptized. However, baptism constituted membership in the Anglican Church."[13]

Gretchen Stringer-Robinson's research states the following:

> From the colonial period on, James Island hosted a large black population. They were brought in against their will from the Senegal-Gambia and Congo-Angola regions, Ghana and Sierra Leone. In 1720, Gov. James Moore issued a report showing 2,493 slaves in the St. Andrew's Parish, of which James Island was then a part…None [of the slaves] have last names, but records show first names such as "Fortune," "Delicate," "March," and "Brister."[14]

As explained in the Foreword in *St. Philip's Church of Charleston*,

> The colony of South Carolina [followed] the Barbadian…governmental system of ecclesiastical parishes as the political entities to rule the colony under the Proprietary and Royal governments…[T]he church's functions were partly exercised by commissaries appointed by the Bishop of London…The General Assembly… had representatives from the churches while passing laws for the colony.[15]

Non-Anglicans resented this empowerment of Anglicans in lawmaking; of course, these church/government ties were severed by the Revolutionary War.[16]

Commissioners, rectors, vestries, and churchwardens held roles that organized the early churches, such as Saint James. Commissioners handled church buildings, cemeteries, and priests' housing and glebe lands where priests could grow crops and raise livestock to supplement their salaries.[17] Rectors, paid from the public treasury, faced many hardships, including illness, poverty, difficult travel, and "disagreeable dissenters" (Scotch Irish Presbyterians, French Calvinists or Huguenots, Baptists, Anabaptists, and Quakers).[18] Vestries, elected by fellow church worshippers, were in charge of church business affairs and included a registrar who kept statistics about births, baptisms, marriages, and burials. Among churchwardens' duties of overseeing church affairs were apprehending those not attending Sunday services,[19] intervening in domestic affairs (particularly pertaining to marriage), fining parishioners for cursing in church, and fining vestry members who refused to serve when elected.[20] Parishes sustained their communities, taking care of the poor and orphans, maintaining a court system, serving as election districts, establishing free schools, and posting news on their church doors.[21]

In *Against All Odds*, Paul Porwoll states, "If Charleston is called 'the holy city,' …then colonial South Carolina was truly the 'holy province'… The names given to South Carolina's parishes were overwhelmingly ecclesiastical."[22] Many believe that Saint James of James Island was no exception, being named after the brother of Jesus and author of The Book of James of the New Testament. Other historians tie the name of Saint James to St. James Parish in Barbados.[23] Still others propose that James Island was named for James, Duke of York, brother and heir of King Charles II.[24] Another church also named St. James Episcopal was established in Goose Creek about 1713.

As a side note, in 1674 two boatloads of Dutch from New York, seeking escape from religious oppression in the northern colonies, settled along the Stono River. The Grand Council of the Colony authorized the new community to be called "James Town." However, according to Dr. Frederick Dalcho, the new establishment never fully materialized.[25]

Transportation over water was vital to the residents of "Boone's Island," as James Island was first referred to[26] or New Town, another name for the island, so the Wappoo and Elliott Cuts (channels) were dug to enable passage between the Stono River and Wappoo Creek. Ferries became available over the Ashley River, Stono River and over Charleston Harbor from Dill's Bluff on James Island to Oyster Point on the peninsula .[27] Since James Island actually is made of two islands (divided by what is known today as Dill Creek, Ellis Creek, and New Cut Creek [Bluff Creek or James Island Creek]), some residents in the past referred to the northern section as Little James Island and the southern section as Big James Island.[28]

Documents dated 1693 refer to the land as James Island, which was and is actually one of several barrier islands that extend from north of Charleston to south of Beaufort. James Island measures about nine miles long and varies from one to seven miles wide, encompassing over thirty-five square miles (approximately twelve thousand acres).[29] Having a triangular shape, James Island sidles up to Charleston Harbor, with Morris Island, Folly Beach, and Johns Island nearby, surrounded by marshlands and infiltrated by numerous creeks.[30]

More specifically, James Island is south of Charleston, inland of Folly Island, and east of Johns Island, with the Stono River separating James and Johns Islands. The intra-coastal waterway and the Ashley River to the north separate James Island from St. Andrews Parish and the city of Charleston.[31] The marshes of Ellis Creek are at the back of the church property. Saint James is slightly west of the geographical center of James Island.[32]

An excellent "geography lesson" regarding the early roads and regions of James Island can be found in the document "An Unfinished History of St. James' Episcopal Church":

> The earliest road on the Island, known as the Stono River Road, apparently began at a ferry landing on Wappoo Creek at what is now Riverland Terrace and ran southward paralleling the Stono River to a point about where the present Dill property is located. This entire section is now known as Riverland Drive. From there it turned eastward becoming known as the King's Way [Fort Johnson Road], crossing the high ground to what has been known for generations as Three Trees, where it turned northwest continuing on to Fort Johnson.
>
> Immediately after crossing the westernmost reaches of James Island Creek, where New Town Cut now crosses Riverland Drive, Camp Road took off to the east, eventually intersecting Fort Johnson Road about two-and-a-quarter miles to the northeast. St. James' Church is located on Camp Road just a short distance from the point where New Town Cut crosses Riverland Drive. Most of the early settlers were located either along these roads or their branches as …indicated on available maps of the Island.[33]

This geographic region, where Saint James Church originated, has an archaeological and historical richness pertaining to Native American inhabitants as well as English and Spanish explorers and Charles Towne settlers arriving in 1670.[34] Records from 1696 indicate that twenty-one families were listed as James Island residents.[35] As was typical in other parts of the parish, forests were cleared and transformed into farmlands and plantations. With its vast marshlands and proximity to the sea, James Island was not conducive for growing rice, [36] but much of the land was initially used for timbering [37]as well as raising cattle, hogs, and the lucrative crop of indigo.[38] There was also Dill's Bluff Shipyard from 1743 to 1772.[39]

In *A Brief History of James Island: Jewel of the Sea Islands*, author Douglas Bostick, states, "Early colonial South Carolina was a fascinating mix of Native American, West African, European and Caribbean cultures…Everything from food and housing designs was influenced by this 'melting pot'…James Island families had a diet based on fish, shellfish, beef, pork and corn. The island also had apples, plums, cherries, peaches, figs, pecans, persimmons and oranges."[40] Wild turkeys, woodcocks, and deer were hunted. Of course, the community from which a congregation is drawn makes up the character of its local chapel or church.

Characteristic of this geographical region and historical times were threats from fire and storms. Six powerful hurricanes damaged the area from 1698 to 1752, and six major fires ravaged the Charleston area from 1740 to 1861.[41]

Captain E. L. Rivers stated in his 1894 brochure "A History of St. James' Episcopal Church" (and revised and completed by Dr. Daniel W. Ellis in 1930) the following insightful words of introduction:

> The early history of Saint James' Church is, like that of so many of our older institutions, shrouded in the mist that invariably surrounds the activities of those who, in the formative period of our country, endeavored amid invasions of strife and pestilence to lay the foundations of our present social, political, and economic organizations. The information contained herein was assembled for the most part, by Capt. E.L. Rivers, and has been checked whenever possible by the present writer [Daniel Ellis]. It is to be greatly regretted that Capt. Rivers cited but few of his sources. It must be remembered, however, that many happenings which could be recalled by him and his older associates have now been obscured by the passage of time. Mindful of the care and thoroughness with which he performed all of the tasks of life, we accept those statements which cannot now be substantiated, as reliable information. Facts not set forth by Capt. Rivers have been gleaned from certain documentary evidence which is extant [private papers of W. G. Hinson, E. L. Rivers, and John Rivers].[42]

These words ring true for much of the church history today, representing what is and what is not available for modern researchers of Saint James. (Note: This publication was prepared for Saint James' bicentennial celebration in 1930. The second paragraph of this document begins, "The first Saint James' Chapel was built as a chapel of Saint Andrew's Church in or before the year 1730." More recent research documents Saint James as being a chapel of ease in 1720.)

J. H. Easterby, author of the introduction for Rev. William Way's book *The History of Grace Church, Charleston, South Carolina: The First Hundred Years* (copyright 1948), stated the following:

> The Church of England accomplished more in South Carolina than in any other of the thirteen American colonies....by 1698 it was receiving public support...in 1706 it was made the official church of the province. Therefore,

for a period of almost three-fourths of a century, it made the best of its privileged position, expanding from one to twenty-five parishes, maintaining the free schools, and dispensing the public appropriations for the poor.[43]

In the 1600s and 1700s, citizens of James Island, originating from several continents and living in a primitive wilderness, were blessed with missionaries and rectors sent abroad mostly from England to perpetuate the Christian faith as a new world was being established here. Today many churches in the Low Country, especially Saint James, now send missionaries and evangelists to spread the Gospel all over the world.

CHAPTER TWO

First Church and First Rector

Some entities—having become magnificent in modern times—are rooted in humble beginnings. In a simple eighteenth century sanctuary that could hold perhaps what eight or ten pews can seat in today's church, men of faith established their initial house of worship. In a seemingly primitive era, these early sea island worshippers could attend Sunday services approximately twelve to fifteen times a year. Thus, began the saga of Saint James.

Again, in Dr. Ellis' research, he wrote,

> Earlier historians have accepted the year 1730 as the date when St. James was founded. This year is mentioned by Dalcho as the first evidence of a congregation on James Island as a chapel was rebuilt at that time. More recent research indicates that the James Island congregation was active ten years earlier. In [a] report to the Society (SPG) on September 30, 1748, Mr. Guy [rector of St. Andrews for thirty-two years and part-time and first rector for St. James] states among other things "also (I) do constantly every fourth Sunday visit my chapel on James Island which I have hitherto done since my first settlement in this parish which is now near twenty-nine years". Thus, it is established that an active Anglican congregation existed on James Island in 1720. In an earlier report of January 15, 1721, Mr. Guy writes that since the previous August he had regularly, once a month, visited this congregation "in a very remote part of the parish", and in a report of August 1, 1722, he writes of plans made for the building of a chapel, "the

people finding the house where I generally preach at to be too little for the congregation."[1]

Dr. Ellis' reference to Dalcho pertains to Rev. Dr. Frederick Dalcho, who published *An Historical Account of the Protestant Episcopal Church in So. Carolina* (1820), a rich resource on the early churches in Carolina.[2] As a doctor, Dalcho (1769-1836) served in the medical department of the Army when assigned to Fort Johnson on James Island. He was also an editor, mason, and minister.[3]

A church document entitled "Missionaries, Curates, Ministers-in Charge, and Rectors of St. James Episcopal Church on James Island, Charleston County, South Carolina" lists significant dates and the priests from 1707 to 1960 (no publishing information available). This historical two-page resource lists Rev. Alexander Wood from 1707 to 1709 (died in service) and Rev. Ebenezer Taylor from 1711 to 1717 (retired from service) as the first two priests administering to James Island Anglican residents. Both ministers were provided by the SPG. Porwoll's research on Saint Andrew's Parish discusses both Rev. Wood and Rev. Taylor (pages 23-29). Their ministries precede the agreed-upon founding date of 1720, when Saint James became a chapel with an organized congregation led by Rev. William Guy.

Educated at Cambridge, Reverend Guy followed the liturgy, strove to convert those of other faiths as well as slaves to Anglicanism, was revered in the parish, and entrusted with important assignments.[4] He had initially arrived in Charles Town in 1712 and was hired as an assistant minister at St. Philip's and a schoolmaster in a free school where he taught Latin, Greek, and the Church of England principles of religion. He was charged "to take special care of the scholars' manners, both in and out of school, as well as teach the scholars to abhor lying and evil speaking. The need at St. Philip's was so great, however, that Guy gave up his position as schoolmaster."[5]

Later Rev. Guy, while rector at St. Helena's, barely escaped during the Yamassee War involving tribal nations that rose up to fight the white settlers over abuses regarding deerskin trade, enslavement, and land ownership.[6] Settlers of the Low Country sustained property losses, military defense costs, and deaths of 400 colonists.[7] Rev. Guy had been attempting to Christianize Native Americans in Beaufort, South Carolina, but in 1715 he fled from the Indians, escaping in a small canoe with another white man and three slaves, leaving behind his horse, and taking only his clothes, a Bible, and a *Book of Common Prayer*.[8] Rev. Guy made his way safely to his wife, who had a house on Tradd Street in Charleston.[9]

Rev. Guy replaced Mr. Taylor, rector at Saint Andrew's Parish, in 1719.[10] In August 1721 Guy then began to travel to James Island every third Friday. After a time in which he completed some duties at St. George, Dorchester, he changed his visits to every fourth Sunday because he thought the attendance would be better. Guy led services in a house on acreage he described as "extraordinarily good and well timber'd and very advantageously situated, being not above three miles by water from Charles Town, to which you pass over Ashley River."[11]

Dr. Ellis included the following summary regarding the first Saint James Chapel:

> Thus, it is established that an active Anglican Congregation, of island planters, holding regular services[,] existed on James Island in 1720 and that in 1722 a chapel was planned because the existing accommodations were too small. At this writing it is not known where the first "house" was located or whether it was a dwelling or a structure dedicated principally to worship. The exact date of the construction of the first chapel has not been established. The archivist of the Society says "probably in late 1722". However, it is the existence of the congregation, not the building, which is important.[12]

Guy's ministerial duties eventually took a toll on his health. In 1724 he wrote the SPG saying,

> I am oblig'd to acquaint you… that the extraordinary fatigue in riding thither, & in being forc'd sometimes to goe by water by reason of the badness of the roads, together with my being very often caught in the rain, has occasioned me such an ill habit of Body…it being so difficult a matter here to regain one's health.[13]

He reported having bouts of "Quinzey [inflammation of the throat] and a Distemper," making preaching difficult. Guy requested to return to London for a period of recuperation, and the SPG granted him permission to do so.[14]

Guy was married to the former Rebecca Basden, whose family had been some of Charles Town's early settlers. Guy and his beloved wife had ten children, but his second son Edward Basden died at an early age.[15] Guy reported regularly to the SPG and kept meticulous records, which can be found in H. Roy Merrens' *Colonial South Carolina Scene: Contemporary Views, 1697-1774*.[16] As part of his records on marriage, Guy entered the data regarding the marriages of four of his children, one being Mary, at age twenty-one, who wed William Chapman of James Island in 1741.[17]

Guy also kept records about burials. Life expectancy was not long then, about thirty-five years.[18] Many diseases, including diphtheria, dysentery, malaria ("country fever"), scarlet fever, small pox, typhoid fever, typhus, yellow fever ("stranger's fever"), and whooping cough were constant threats to health and life.[19] Children were especially vulnerable to early deaths, as were women in child birth.

Drownings were not infrequent because these early citizens were constantly drawn to the waters for passage, food, work, and recreation, without modern means of rescue. Travel on foot, on horseback, and in carriages along dirt roads—many of which were mere ruts through woods—made transportation on land arduous, so people often traveled by boat. Many were at risk while fishing from the marshes, rivers, and ocean. Raw materials, crops, and imported goods were transported by both blacks and whites working on the waters. Vessels, often small canoes made of cypress,[20] easily capsized. Unchartered waters, swift currents, and sudden storms created further hazards.

When Guy went to the James Island parish, the trip often took two days just to travel by land over primitive roads and by boat.[21] He probably followed what is now known as Ashley River Road southeastward for almost three miles to the present Wappoo Road where it turned southward for almost another three miles, crossing the old Savannah Road (US 17) and continuing on generally southeastward to the point where Wappoo Creek enters the Stono River.[22] Then, according to "An Unfinished History of Saint James," he would "make his way to the Wappoo Ferry and, after crossing, [followed] a rough road southward along the Stono River, to what is now Camp Road and the site of our present church, a distance of about twenty miles."[23] In 1724 Guy referred to Saint James as a "Chappel of ease," using this spelling and capitalization.[24]

Dr. Ellis noted, "The 1730 chapel is described as having 13 pews including 2 for negroes [slaves] and seating about 90 persons. In 1733, communicants reported 30." [25] Attached to this chapel were about seventy acres, which were then worth between forty and fifty dollars an acre.[26]

As with every era, the citizens had specific concerns. Because of a slave rebellion in 1739, male worshippers were required by Provincial law for several years to carry arms going to and from church services.[27] James Island Anglicans became worried when two more "dissenter meeting houses" were built on James Island by 1740. Along with his Saint James congregation, Guy was concerned that the Presbyterian minister would "seduce" their youth and convince them to convert to Presbyterianism. Therefore, islanders bought a 300-acre glebe (church property for the priest to farm) adjacent to the chapel and asked the SPG for their own priest.[28] So-called "dissenters" did not belong to the Church of England Protestants; they were Baptists, French Huguenot Calvinists, Quakers, Presbyterians, and Puritans.[29]

Dr. Ellis wrote the following about Saint James' loss of its first chapel and its replacement:

> In 1730 the first chapel was destroyed by a hurricane as reported to the Society by Mr. Guy. He later reports that a second chapel was completed on the original site in 1733. No further mention is made of the James Island congregation until Sept 1748 when Mr. Guy reported that he had been regularly holding

services once a month since 1720. It is to be concluded that he continued in this capacity until [1750] when his service in the provinces was terminated.[30]

Apparently, the second chapel was made of brick; however, records describe the interior as being "unfinished."[31]

Guy went on to become SPG's attorney in South Carolina, often handling wills, estates, and debts owed to the parish. He spoke out against one priest's performing a marriage that was against the wishes of the bride's legal guardians and suspended another priest for habitual drunkenness.[32] Guy served in an ecclesiastical trial in which he was one of the priests who had The Reverend George Whitefield suspended for using a charismatic preaching style; for causing listeners to weep, faint, and succumb to outbursts of emotion; for deviating from the *Book of Common Prayer* with extemporaneous prayers;[33] for criticizing the way slaves were evangelized; and for finding fault with other ministers.[34]

Rev. Whitefield drew thousands to hear his sermons in the colonies and England, preached the gospel in numerous places along the Eastern coast, was welcomed by Charles Town's Congregational Church, and encouraged people to examine their Christian beliefs and vocalize them. However, his revivals led to deeper division between Dissenters and Anglicans.[35]

Having seemingly boundless energy, Rev. Guy served as a temporary rector where there were vacancies and preached "charity sermons" to raise funds for rebuilding after the Charles Town fire of 1740 that destroyed over 300 houses, many warehouses, produce, wharves, and Guy's own house that he had recently built.[36] The fire had begun in a saddler's shop on Broad Street and destroyed every house south of Broad Street and others on the north side, burning about one third of Charles Town to the ground.[37] In *Against All Odds*, Paul Porwoll wrote, "Guy lost his material possessions three times, once to the Indians, then to pirates, and later in the great fire of Charles Town in 1740."[38]

In 1741 his wife Rebecca—mother of his ten children—died. Six years later Guy married Elizabeth Cooper of Goose Creek. In 1750, at the age of sixty-two, Guy died, but his gravesite at St. Andrews is unknown. Rev. Guy's obituary stated, "He lived the Life of the Just, and died the Death of the Righteous."[39]

Approximately one-fourth of the ministers who were sent by the SPG to the South Carolina region did not survive its climate for more than five years. Most parishes had frequent turnover of their clergy primarily because of sickness, transfer, or death. Rev. Guy had served as rector at St. Andrew's Parish Church for thirty-two years, with additional years served elsewhere.[40] He served Saint James from 1719 to 1750.[41]

What a marvel to see several churches' foundations rooted in this man's ministry—a man who did not let aggravating gnats and disease-carrying mosquitoes stop him…did not let muddy, dusty, rutted roads stop him…did not let choppy water to cross stop him…did not let humidity and heat and bitter cold stop him…did not let illness and exhaustion and personal losses stop him from spreading the Gospel throughout the Low Country and at the chapel of ease called Saint James.

CHAPTER THREE

Chapel of Ease

By 1751 Charles Town was the third-largest city in British North America, with only Boston and Philadelphia being larger. The city had 25,000 whites and 39,000 blacks. St. Michael's was to be built because St. Philip's could no longer accommodate the growing Anglican congregation.[1]

Charles Town and James Island were caught by surprise by a horrendous hurricane in September 1752, bringing a surge ten feet above average tides and swelling the creeks. Some city residents were up to their necks in churning water amid pieces of wrecked ships; others rode on a roof top floating in the Cooper River. Bridges, boats, wharfs, stores, houses, and the sea wall (now "The Battery") were severely damaged. Fifteen people in the city died during the hurricane, and additional deaths occurred on James Island and in Mount Pleasant.[2]

In spite of this natural disaster, services resumed at Saint James. Dr. Ellis recorded the following in his historical records: "On December 28, 1752, the Rev. Charles Martyn wrote that he regularly officiated once a month on James Island."[3]

In 1756 the chapel on James Island was officially established as a Chapel of Ease of St. Andrews parish by an act of the provincial legislature. This tardy official recognition of the James Island chapel probably accounts for the fact that it was omitted from a list of parishes, churches, ministers' houses, and chapels of ease as recorded by Mr. Guy in 1727. Despite mentioning four chapels of ease in his text[,] he lists only three.[4]

A chapel of ease was defined as an extension of a mother church.[5] Due to the difficulty of travel in this century, small churches were built throughout the Low Country for easy access, often in rural regions and often accessible by water. In 1831 Saint James Chapel of Ease became its own church.[6]

Replacing Rev. Guy after his death, Rev. Charles Martyn also held the rector's position at St. Andrews.[7] Beginning his ministry in the Low Country at the age of twenty-seven, Martyn was a strong advocate of Christianizing the Indian and slave residents. He reported to the SPG that the natives were shy and resisted instruction. In *Against All Odds*, Porwoll said that many white masters did not want their slaves to be baptized into the Anglican faith because they would "become lazy and proud, entertaining too high an Opinion of themselves, and neglecting their daily Labour."[8]

Martyn married Sarah Fuller from a wealthy family of the Low Country, and the couple had one son, Charles Fuller Martyn. They owned 250 acres of land on the east side of the Ashley River.[9]

According to Governor James Glen, the four socioeconomic classes at this time consisted of the following:[10]

Top 20 percent	Elite planters, merchants, professionals	"Plenty of the good things of Life"
About 40 percent	Small planters, overseers, artisans	"Necessarys of Life"
Next 20 percent	Some artisans, small merchants, shopkeepers	"Some of the Conveniencys of Life"
Bottom 20 percent	The poor	"Lived a bare subsistence"

Saint James was fortunate to have had Rev. Martyn conduct services every fourth Sunday; however, some other outlying chapels were plagued with infrequent visits by their assigned clergy. Therefore, an act was passed that if an assigned minister did not provide monthly church services, the churchwardens and vestries could file a complaint, and the minister could be charged a fee, which was roughly ten percent of a priest's annual salary in the mid-1700s.[11]

Rev. Martyn described the Saint James' chapel worshippers as being "…a considerable number of persons, educated in the Presbyterian way…and several of them produced Prayer Books, and made the Responses."[12]

Rev. Dalcho's book included the following: "Mr. Martyn wrote to the Society July 7, 1757, and stated his satisfaction at the success of his Ministry; but at the same time complained that, in the season of making Indigo, some of his parishioners profaned the Lord's day, by carrying on the usual work of the plantations."[13]

Rev. Martyn took up the cause regarding the calling and hiring of priests. At best, their positions were often tenuous as they served probationary periods before being elected as tenured priests. Ministers' jobs hung in limbo due to a circuitous career path involving a number of people, including Charles Town's merchants and England's church leaders. Meanwhile some clergy felt compelled to move frequently, seeking permanent positions, while other priests selflessly stayed with congregations that treated them unkindly. Likewise, the process was often hard on parishes if they were furnished with priests unsuitable for the job and the locale. Martyn and Governor Glen wanted the Bishop of London to select a commissary to handle the employment of priests and various church matters; however, that position was not filled.[14]

After traveling in the inland areas, known as the backcountry of South Carolina, Martyn was appalled at the lack of religious training and worship opportunities, so he had the SPG send Bibles and prayer books to distribute to these residents, many of whom were immigrants living in the most rural areas.[15]

Martyn inherited huge tracts of land and was financially well-to-do; consequently, he returned to the Society his annual salary equivalent to $600. This act of generosity impressed the Society but angered other Anglican ministers who feared it might look as if priests were being overpaid, and they already considered their salaries to be inadequate.[16]

According to a timeline entitled "Saint James Episcopal Church, James Island, Cemetery History," the church's graveyard dates back to 1769. The oldest tombstone is that of William Reynolds, which is located between the church and the parish hall. The second oldest tombstone is for Archibald Scott (1786), and the third oldest tombstone is John Woodberry's (1794).[17]

Saint James' cemetery booklet states that three old wooden markers have been preserved with fiber glass, but the names and dates are not known. The manuscript explains, "During Colonial Times wooden markers were used with a metal plate on which names and dates were inscribed. Over the years they deteriorated or were burned when the church was burned."[18] Grave markers of stone were more expensive than those of wood. With time, the stone engravings varied widely, one small stone simply saying "E.S. 1843" and others much larger with over twenty lines to honor the loved one's life.[19]

An historical video produced by Saint James members in the 1980s capably describes the churchyard, from the 1700s to the present:

> [On the markers are] names of …families [who for almost three] centuries
> have been the dedicated Christians primarily responsible for perpetuating
> the tenacious faith which has given this the present Church life. The faith

of its families has made this Churchyard among the most beautiful and revered resting places in the entire Charleston area and is a tribute to those who presently are responsible for its devoted care and protection. The live oaks are particularly beautiful and form a fascinating pattern of trunks, limbs, and branches especially when seen looking out through the clear-glass windows of the Church itself.[20]

Much of this churchyard remains the same, preserving the history of bygone eras, yet much of it has also evolved with passing years.

For his fledgling Saint James chapel, Rev. Martyn modeled that church leaders can become involved in political and social endeavors for the betterment of mankind and for the furtherance of God's kingdom. Although wealthy, he exhibited a heart for the poor and downtrodden. He did not shy away from difficult circumstances, even if those difficulties resulted in great disappointment and harsh criticism. He served Saint James well from 1752 to 1770.[21] However, much of Rev. Martyn's work and the chapel itself would be undone by the impending war.

CHAPTER FOUR

Mid to Latter 1700s

From 1720 to 1776, Charles Town prospered mainly because of its production and shipments of rice and indigo. By 1770 its seaport had strong trans-Atlantic trade with British and European ports.[1] However, these business relationships became more and more complicated as they became politically entangled, leading up to the Revolutionary War and ultimately impacting Saint James.

After Rev. Martyn's retirement, Rev. Thomas Panting preached occasionally at Saint James Chapel from 1770 to 1771. He was also the Headmaster of the Free School in Charles Town, which provided education to white students who came from homes that could not afford to pay for private schools or for tutoring.[2] Panting, the son of a doctor and graduate of Oxford, died in 1771 after serving as rector only two years. At his death, the *South Carolina Gazette* said that his passing was regretted by the public and all those who knew him—that "his virtue lives beyond his death."[3] [Note: Some sources state that Rev. Panting's ministry at Saint James was from 1771-1772; however, Porwoll's text states that it was from 1770 to 1771, with his death being recorded as September 23, 1771.]

Replacing Rev. Panting was Rev. John Christopher Ernest Schwab, a Bavarian who, before arriving in Orangeburg to work with Dutch settlers, had tutored the children of royalty.[4] Unfortunately, he contracted malaria and died after serving only nineteen months.[5] He had been at Saint James from 1771 to 1773.[6] Records of the following time period are sketchy, but Saint James might have been without an assigned priest from 1773 to 1787[7] after which Rev. Thomas Mills became rector in 1787 and preached at Saint James once a month.[8] According to Dalcho's research, Rev. Dr. Mills, while still living in England, had sympathized with the Whig Party in America and petitioned the king to cease with the war;

consequently, he felt persecuted for his political beliefs, left England, and arrived in Charles Town in June of 1786.[9]

During the American Revolution, parishioners expressed divided loyalties, with some remaining loyal to the Crown and others declaring allegiance to the patriots, thus creating dissension in families, businesses, and churches. The colonies' severance from England impacted the American church organization and structure that had existed for many years. About twenty percent of the priests returned to England.[10] Approximately sixty-six percent of the Anglican priests in South Carolina chose to support the cause of the colonists.[11]

In his history about St. Michael's Church, George Williams explained this complicated relationship between colonial Anglican priests and the King during the Revolution:

> Before coming to America [Anglican priests] had taken a special oath, the oath of the King's supremacy, which expressly forbade their toleration of any power, spiritual or temporal, contrary to that of the King. Conflicting allegiances constituted a problem singularly vexing to Anglican clergymen. Some believed in conscience that their duty lay with the Crown above the colony; others felt as genuinely the greater responsibility to [align them-selves] with the infant colonies. Clergymen of non-conformist denomina-tions, bound by no such oath, took every opportunity to rouse the colonists to resistance…While Dissenters both north and south were almost unani-mous for the patriot cause, the Anglicans were divided in a geographical fashion. In New England and New York Anglicans were assumed to be loy-alists. But from Philadelphia southwards there was a steady increase in the percentage of patriotic Anglicans. In South Carolina the Anglican clergy seemed to have joined the patriots in even larger numbers. Only five out of twenty-three Anglican clergymen became loyalists.[12]

Much of the church support had been from British government, so the church felt un-prepared regarding financial independence starting in 1778 when such support was with-drawn. Consequently, the Anglican community declined for about a generation.[13] Rev. Way explained in his historical research that the Revolutionary War was instrumental in leading to eventual separation of church and state. J. H. Easterby, author of the introduction of Way's research on Grace Episcopal, explained, "The result was that the South Carolina church, while in the processes of being severed from its roots in England, was cut away from its main source of sustenance... A period of bewilderment followed. Then came a gradual re-vival as the South Carolina congregations adjusted themselves to their new position with the Protestant Episcopal Church in the United States."[14]

British troops attacked Charles Town by sea on June 28, 1776. They initially suffered heavy losses and withdrew, mainly because of Fort Moultrie's walls of sand and soft palmetto logs, which did not crack when bombarded but instead absorbed the cannonballs.

In W.E. McLeod's "An Outline of the History of James Island, SC (1944)," he wrote the following:

> At the time of the siege of Charles Town…troops were placed on James Island to defend the town against Prevost, whose army had come up from Savannah and was advancing north across James Island. The defending Americans entrenched themselves near Wolfe Pitt Run in the center of the Island, on Camp Road one mile east of St. James Church and awaited the enemy there.[15]

In 1779 (some sources say 1780), the British redcoats crossed Johns Island and eventually James Island, capturing Fort Johnson and seizing cattle, horses, and food for their armies. The Battle of Stono was fought June 19-20, 1779, and a few weeks later along the Stono River another battle called "The Scrimmage at Matthew's Plantation" was fought.[16]

Ultimately, the British gained control of all ferries and crossings along the Stono River.[17] They set up headquarters on Peronneau Plantation, where Riverland Terrace is now located.[18] The British crossed alligator-infested Wappoo Creek and eventually seized Charles Town and plantations along the Ashley River, including Drayton Hall. The British not only destroyed Saint James Chapel and James Island Presbyterian Church; they also destroyed church bonds and financial records, inflicting even more monetary problems on churches.[19]

The British besieged the city in May 1780, forcibly occupying residents' homes, destroying and stealing belongings, and seizing slaves and livestock.[20] Their troops damaged and/or burned "dissenting" churches, mostly Presbyterian. For the most part, the British saw Anglicans as "less threatening to the royal cause."[21]

By January 1782 the British were trapped in Charles Town when militia and Continental soldiers surrounded and defeated them. By this time Southern colonists had become paralyzed by hunger, and food shortages for livestock were so limited that two hundred horses were slaughtered because there was nothing to feed them.[22] Planters suffered an economic depression. Some of the British soldiers had taken slaves as spoils of war; indigo crops no longer existed; fields once cleared for crops were overgrown once again.[23]

In *Sea Island Diary*, Beaufort historian Edith Dabbs wrote the following:

> The bloody years of revolution brought South Carolina face to face with bankruptcy…Generations of arduous struggle to establish the state had culminated in the heroic work of quite substantially aiding the founding of a

new nation. No other colony had given more than Carolina: the first two presidents of the continental Congress, four signers of the Declaration of Indepen[d]ence, many astute and well-trained politicians who stood ready with their diplomatic skills when most needed, numerous military leaders, and courageous, determined soldiers—all in addition to a vast area of blood-soaked home soil and people left homeless, facing financial ruin.[24]

Dr. Ellis's history made these comments about this time period:

> The second chapel was probably destroyed during the American Revolution, for in 1787 the Rev. Dr. Mills states that during his visits to James Island on the last Sunday in every month, he held services at the home of Mrs. Mallory Rivers, [which later became a part of the Grimball estate (p. xii)]. A few years later a third chapel was built. The funds for its construction were raised by popular subscription. However, services were discontinued a short time thereafter because the majority of the congregation were Presbyterians [or Independents] who now undertook the task of reorganizing their own church.[25]

Rev. Thomas Mills became Saint James' fifth priest from 1787 to 1816. Dr. Ellis wrote,

> Rev. Mills sought "asylum in the land of civil and religious liberty", after as he states "a political sermon exposed me to persecution and obscured my future prospects". As minister of St. Andrews[,] he preached at St. Andrew's Chapel of Ease on James Island once a month. During the Revolutionary War the chapel building (of 1733) was destroyed[;] the third chapel building was completed about 1787.[26]

The son of an Anglican priest, Mills was introduced in Charles Town by a letter from John Adams, Ambassador to Great Britain and later President; he was welcomed as a patriot by Gov. John Rutledge.[27] Rev. Mills' ministry was challenging because of the consequences of war, which had left the area impoverished, with many buildings and businesses destroyed.[28] Mills taught and served as master of the Grammar School in Charles Town to supplement his income.[29]

In the aftermath of the Revolutionary War, the Diocese of South Carolina was established in 1785, and four years later the Protestant Episcopal Church in the United States of America was founded.[30] It was difficult to get the Southern parishes to agree on the constitution and canons.[31] Before this change, most Anglican churches had relied on funding from the state or the SPG, but this new alliance required that parishioners learn to support their church buildings and ministers through their own independent and voluntary giving.[32] Another change eventually came about regarding the 1762 Church of England *Book of Common Prayer*: prayers for the royal family were deleted and replaced with prayers for the United States' President and Congress.[33]

Rev. Mills' first wife and mother of his six children, Honoria Knapman,[34] contracted yellow fever after she first arrived in Charleston and died four days later; his second wife, Eliza Timmons, with whom he had three more children, died as well, and he married two more times after that, the final time when he was eighty years old.[35]

Dr. Ellis reported that from 1787 to 1831 little is known about these forty-four years because of scanty records. His explanation follows:

> In 1831 the parish church, St. Andrews, was petitioned by members of the chapel congregation to transfer to them the chapel and the attached glebe lands. St. Andrews agreed to this proposal. St. James Church, James Island was incorporated and the chapel and glebe lands (about 70 acres) were deeded to the corporation with the provision that the church and glebe would revert to St. Andrews if at any time the congregation should be unable to support a minister for three consecutive years or if services other than those prescribed by the Episcopal Church be held in the church.[36]

Part of this period of Saint James' history can be metaphorically aligned with the Old Testament story of Moses and his people wandering in the wilderness for forty years. In war, death, and societal upheaval, even God might seem distant or silent. Nevertheless, He still maintains his omnipresence, and His Word remains alive and well. When human beings are called upon to do extraordinary feats, God works in extraordinary ways. Saint James' emergence from such a time period is assurance of such truths.

CHAPTER FIVE

Dormant in Early 1800s

Recovering from the Revolutionary War, residents and worshippers on James Island experienced an economic growth—re-establishing homes, businesses, and churches. Eventually rebuilding Saint James for a third time after a dormant period, the congregation once again strove to have regular services by 1833, even though they would be viewed as infrequent services by church members today. Lifestyles of the island's wealthy were enriched by retreats to summer communities; however, even the rich could not escape the impending factors that so often cut lifespans short in this era. Also, political and humanitarian views about slavery were becoming divisive throughout the nation. Issues supposedly apart from church had a way of becoming part of the church.

Clyde Bresee wrote a fascinating book entitled *How Grand a Flame* about three generations of the Lawton family who worshipped at Saint James and lived on their James Island plantation from the early nineteenth century until the 1940s. Much of this book is based on Cecilia Lawton's diaries as well as other historical documents.

One incident recounted in Bresee's text is set about three years before the War of 1812. Winborn Allison Lawton was a member of the Presbyterian Church, but some of their congregation had apparently reprimanded him for his swearing, dancing, and partying. Winborn supposedly came home inebriated after socializing with his Beaufort relatives and soon joined the Saint James Chapel "where the strictures on social life were less exacting."[1] Ultimately, Winborn became a founding vestryman at Saint James in 1831.[2]

Several island planters and their families, many who were members of Saint James, spent summers in the village called Johnsonville, near Fort Johnson, consisting of twenty-five homes, a schoolhouse, commissary, and meetinghouse. First established in 1825, it was a getaway for residents to escape mosquitoes and malaria and enjoy the waterfront breezes in hot weather.[3] By 1836 Saint James had built a chapel of ease in Johnsonville and hired an assistant priest.[4] For a few years Rev. Paul Trapier held services on Sunday afternoons from May to October.[5] Families often did not move back to their farms and plantations until mid-November.[6] The chapel and all other buildings of Johnsonville were destroyed in the Civil War.[7]

In the 1820s Elliot Cut was dug across the northern end of the island, connecting it with the Stono River about a half mile from where a ferry originally crossed Wappoo Creek. New Town Cut was dug by hand to connect the Stono River and James Island Creek [Ellis Creek].[8] Such channels provided easier access for islanders to local areas, including those traveling to and from church.

Saint James had become dormant during the early 1800s until in 1831 when an Episcopal revival swept over James Island, resulting in the reorganization of Saint James.[9] James Island residents had grown tired of traveling to St. Andrews Parish Church to worship. They wanted to select their own priest, elect their own vestry, and collect glebe rents.[10] Saint James petitioned, and St. Andrews agreed to the transfer of the James Island chapel and attached the seventy acres of glebe lands. The old chapel of 1787 was repaired and re-consecrated by Bishop Bohen on April 22, 1831.[11]

The following interesting paragraph can be found in an historical paper entitled "St. James, James Island":

> The only marriage recorded to have been solemnized in St. James Church was that of Mr. Edward Peronneau to Mrs. Anna S. Parker on 13th March 1834, the ceremony having been performed by Rev'd Paul Trapier. It was the usual custom on the Island to have this ceremony performed at the private residences of the inhabitants.[12]

Another custom of this time period included burials of loved ones on family property instead of in a church or community cemetery. Examples include the Scott Burial Ground at Orange Grove owned formerly by Mr. Joseph B. Hinson; Stiles Graveyard at Stile's Point owned by Mr. William G. Hinson; Harvey Burial Ground owned formerly by Rev. Stiles Mellichamp; and Sompson Graveyard by Mr. Croskeys Royall's place. (Note: This list reflects the spelling and punctuation used in Hinson's manuscript.) Slaves customarily buried their dead on the plantations of their masters.[13]

Dr. Ellis wrote the following about the seventeen families[14] worshipping at Saint James:

> In the period around 1831 an apparent surge of interest in St. James was obvious, not only as shown by the petition to St. Andrew's for transfer of

the chapel, but also the references note "summer services held in homes near Ft. Johnson, 17 of a total of 50 services in 1833." In 1836 Bishop Thomas state[d], "A chapel of ease was built of wood on government land at Johnsonville where a priest assisted Rev. Paul Trapier".[15]

According to "Historical Sketches: St. James' Church" that Mrs. M. S. Stackhouse wrote in 1947, Miss Eliza Dill presented a chalice and paten in 1833, and Captain John Rivers donated another chalice in 1856. His family also gave two chairs, presumably for the altar, in 1857. Later in 1909, Mr. Hinson gave a silver tankard to the church.[16]

In his records about Saint James' priests, Dr. Ellis reported on three pastoral leaders in this time period. From 1831 to 1837, Paul Trapier served as Saint James' priest.[17] Born into a long-standing prominent family on the Cooper River, he had attended Harvard and apparently joined the ministry to honor his parents' wishes; ironically, his religious upbringing had been weak.[18] As a young man in his twenties, who had never served as an assistant rector elsewhere, Trapier felt overwhelmed and inadequate regarding his ministry to the slaves, his delivery of his sermons, and his visits to parishioners.[19]

In speaking of his wife Sarah Dehon (related to the Nathaniel Russell and the Middleton families), Trapier wrote, "I secured a blessing second only to that of acceptance with my Saviour, who, I thank unceasingly for giving me such a wife."[20] Over the years, they became the parents of twelve children.[21] Rev. Trapier's first vestrymen at Saint James were Winborn Lawton, J.B. Hinson, J.R. Rogers, J.B.F. Minott, J.R. Harvey, John Rivers, and Abram Wilson—many surnames that reoccur in Saint James' records throughout generations.[22]

Trapier, serving at both Old St. Andrews and Saint James, focused more so on Saint James, for a while preaching on James Island about three times more often than at St. Andrews before eventually moving into the renovated parsonage at St. Andrews.[23] In addition to preaching at St. Andrew's Parish and at Saint James, he also began preaching in 1834 at St. Stephen's in Charleston.[24] Missing the conveniences of living in the city, Trapier then moved to Charleston and was elected the ninth rector of St. Michael's in 1840.[25] While there, he was assisted by his first cousin Rev. Paul Trapier Keith, the tenth rector. Later Rev. Trapier's younger brother Richard Shubrick Trapier became the eleventh rector at St. Michael's.[26] Rev. Paul Trapier went on to found Calvary Church, Charleston's first Episcopal church for blacks, and served as their rector for ten years. Trapier was devoted to the Confederacy and lost almost everything he had during the Civil War; when living in Camden, his home was plundered by Sherman's forces.[27]

Formerly a teacher and principal at the South Carolina Society Academy, Cranmore Wallace became a deacon and worked with St. Andrews' young, scholarly priest Rev. Jasper Adams, who had resigned his position as president of the College of Charleston and briefly served as rector at Old St. Andrews.[28] Becoming assistant to Rev. Paul Trapier,[29] Rev. Wallace conducted some of the summer services held in the chapel built on the government land at Ft. Johnson.[30] In 1837 Wallace became the head priest at Saint James and resigned his position in 1839.[31]

Sadly, in Saint James' Cemetery is a grave marker that states the following:

TO
THE MEMORY OF
JULIET
Only daughter of the
Rev. CRANMORE and J.F.
WALLACE
Who departed this life
The 24th MARCH 1840
AGE 5 YEARS and 6 MO, 14 DAYS[32]

In 1837 Mr. J.R. Harvey (some sources have the spelling Harley and Harbey—perhaps due to handwritten documents hard to decipher) donated a huge piece of property on James Island to create a fund to support "clerical leadership."[33] Mr. Harvey willed to Saint James forty-eight acres of beautiful wooded highland and fifty acres of marshland known as Parrot Point. (Note: Sources—maps, newspaper articles, vestry notes—throughout decades have recorded numerous spellings, including "Parrott," "Parrots," "Parrotts," "Parrotts'," and "Parrot's." The spelling in this book's quotations has been left unchanged. Current addresses for property in this area use the spelling of "Parrot.") The will stipulated that the land would be used for support of the church's rector.[34] This property became significant over upcoming years as vestries designated various uses of the land and in much more recent years when most of it was sold to build what is referred to as The Ministry Center at Saint James today.

Josiah Obear served as rector of Saint James from 1839 to 1842. Dr. Ellis wrote, "In addition to Rev. Obear, Bishop Gadsden and 'others' preached at St. James."[35]

Stiles Mellichamp, who was studying for orders, was a lay reader, beginning an association of about thirty-three years with Saint James. According to Dr. Ellis' records, from 1842 to 1851 Mellichamp was head rector, and under his leadership, "Much attention was give[n] to 'nurture and admonition' of the negroes."[36] In some of Mellichamp's reports dated 1853, he recorded "conducting 147 services reaching 250 negroes."[37] Many of these services were held in the McLeod Plantation's barn on Sunday afternoons.[38] In the pamphlet entitled "Historical Sketch of St. James' Parish," "In 1844, the Sunday School had 15 white and 20 colored children. A parsonage was purchased in 1845. In 1851, Mr. Mellichamp removed to St. Helena's in Beaufort, but continued to hold some services at St. James'. He returned to St. James' in 1853."[39]

In 1837 The Episcopal Diocese of South Carolina produced "A Catechism to Be Used by Teachers in the Religious Instruction of Persons of Color." By 1845 most diocesan leaders saw religious instruction of slaves as a duty as well as a policy.[40]

One interesting 1840s record reveals that plantation owner W.W. McLeod moved a slave named Hardtimes Dawson from St. Paul's Parrish to James Island to plant cotton. Hardtimes and his wife Mary were married by Rev. Mellichamp at Saint James Episcopal Church. After the Civil War, Dawson and his family were given a small plot of land on James Island that he farmed.[41]

According to Paul Porwoll's research, most priests worked within the day's culture of slavery and not to change the plantation system.[42] For humanitarian, political, and spiritual reasons, most encouraged slave ministry and religious instruction, hoping to encourage the enslaved to be obedient to their masters and to seek eternal salvation. Rev. Frederick Dalcho, author of *An Historical Account of the Protestant Episcopal Church in South Carolina*, was an advocate for slaves to worship with their masters at churches where trusted pastors were expected to preach a message of salvation consistent with the existing political and economic order, tolerant of chattel slavery.[43] In the 1840s, there were eighteen black Episcopalians and three hundred black Presbyterians on James Island. Many plantations started building Episcopal slave chapels, particularly in rural areas.[44] In the following decade, citizens, including those at Saint James, grew increasingly concerned over the nation's political and philosophical conflicts pertaining to tariffs, states' rights, and slavery.

Eugene Frazier, Sr. is the author of both *A History of James Island: Slave Descendants and Plantation Owners* and *James Island: Stories from Slave Descendants*. These books, often based on oral histories and interviews, give more insights into the James Island farms and plantations with names of multi-generational owners, many of whom worshiped at Saint James: Dill, Grimball, McLeod, Hinson, Mikell, Seabrook, Clark, Rivers, Legare, Ellis, Lawton, Royall, Mellichamp, Lebby, Hill, and Nungezer. Several long-time residents of James Island, both black and white, have ancestors who worked these properties and still reside in this area today.

The Episcopal Church grew substantially throughout South Carolina under the leadership of Bishop Christopher Gadsden. The number of clergy increased from forty-six in 1840 to seventy-one by 1850. Within this decade parishes increased from thirty-seven to fifty-three; white communicants rose from 2,936 to 4,916; black communicants increased from 973 in 1840 to 2,247 in 1850.[45]

As Rev. Mellichamp served from 1853-1863, Saint James' third chapel building was razed and the fourth chapel built about 1853. Rev. Mellichamp's son described this church as follows: "It was wooden, tastefully built in Gothic style, surrounded by a splendid grove of live oaks. It was a few yards south of the Church taken down....the graveyard dated back to 1769."[46] Some records state that the church was able to seat two to three hundred people, but Dr. Ellis wrote that he thought that that was a questionable number.[47] The need to seat such a large congregation on such a sparsely populated area would not likely have been the case.[48] It had galleries for the slaves attending with their masters. (handwritten addition by McLeod in Mrs. Stackhouse's history dated 1947)[49]

Rev. Mellichamp "preached three to four times each Sunday to both white and black congregations on "The Glorious Cause."[50] Planters and slaves often worshipped together but sat separate from one another. Records indicate that baptisms, confirmations, weddings, and funerals were held for slaves at both James Island Presbyterian Church and Saint James Episcopal prior to the Civil War.[51] In 1862 services were discontinued during the war.[52]

Along with Rev. Thomas Girardeau and Joseph Lee, Rev. Mellichamp also taught the white children in an antebellum-era school that was said to be near the Freer family store; however, the school building was destroyed during the Civil War.[53] Notes based on William G. Hinson's 1888 interview include the following:

> The Free School for white children was prosperously kept by Mr. Baldwin and afterwards by John Edward Rivers, Esq., who became a lawyer at the Charleston bar. Rev. Stiles Mellichamp took it from 1845 to 1851. Then the Rev. Thos. J. Girardeau who was succeeded by Mr. Joseph Lee of Edisto Island. Since the war it has been under the direction of Miss Jacobs and Miss Freer. There are now [1888] three free schools for blacks, one at Three Trees, another at Society Corner and a third at New Town Cut Bridge.[54]

In South Carolina the "free schools" of the 1700s and early1800s were often reserved for the families who could not afford tutors or parochial or private schools for their children. Some free schools were even derogatorily labeled as "pauper schools." It was not unusual for clergy also to be teachers.

Historically speaking, ministers were well known throughout their communities, having far-reaching and long-lasting impact theologically, socially, politically, and geographically. Interestingly, several places on James Island today still honor Rev. Stiles Mellichamp and members of his extended family through their names: Mellichamp Drive, Stiles Drive, Stiles Point Subdivision, and Stiles Point Elementary.[55]

In 1860 James Island had about 1700 residents, 89 percent of them being black. It had twenty-one plantations, two churches, and two stores.[56] In *A Brief History of James Island*, Bostick wrote about the white males at this time, listing them as being sixteen planters, "two merchants, two mechanics, two clergymen, three overseers, two physicians, a clerk, a cotton factor (broker), a boatman, a ploughman, a sailor, a lazaretto (quarantine station) keeper and one 'Gentleman'."[57] These men, along with their families, likely worshipped either at what was then Saint James Episcopal or James Island Presbyterian Church.

One of many grave markers in Saint James Church's cemetery portrays a personal pain all too common to the people of the Low Country in that time. Embedded in the right side of the church is the engraving of the following memorial stone:

SACRED
TO THE MEMORY OF
MRS. ANN McCANTS BURCH
WHO DIED 26th JUNE 1826
Aged 22 years 11 mo & 15 days
ALSO OF

GEORGE RIVERS BURCH
SON OF EDWARD CHRISTOPHER
& ANN McCANTS BURCH
WHO DIED 10th SEPTEMBER 1826
AGED 3 YEARS 3 MO. and 23 DAYS

This frail memorial is created to them
By a bereaved
Husband and fond Father
T. Walker[58]

Children in particular were vulnerable to early deaths, often with more than one child dying in a family. For example, Constant H. and Mary E. Rivers lost a son, William Edings Rivers, at age one year, three months in 1854; they lost another child, Susan A. Rivers, at age six months, eleven days. Susan C. and John B.F. Minott lost a daughter Margaret Ann at age one year, three months, nine days; another daughter Eugenia Perry at age six months, nine days; and a third daughter, Eliza Dill, at age six, eight months, twenty-five days. Their mother died at age thirty-nine.[59] Lack of modern medicine brought death early and frequently, thus leading people to mark each day of life as being significant and valued—something to carve in stone to preserve and honor.

Just as history and culture are entwined in the Biblical stories of the Old and New Testaments, history and culture were evident in the lives of those worshipping at Saint James. Although shifting political, social, environmental, economic, and scientific conditions influenced the congregations of those decades, man's permanent need for unwavering worship was also a part of the congregation where laymen and ordained leaders spearheaded that worship. Calling priests from various walks of life and with diverse spiritual gifts, God provided for the people of Saint James Church in the early to mid-1800s as the church evolved from having closed doors to having doors open to the community once again.

CHAPTER SIX

During the War Between the States

Prior to the War between the States, nine plantations were owned by the following families on James Island: Harrisons, Mikells, Bees, Seabrooks, Grimballs, Lebbies, Rivers, Ellises, and McLeods.[1] However, war broke out, wreaking havoc not only on the island's plantations but also on its other residences, businesses, schools, and churches.

On December 20, 1860, South Carolina voted to secede from the union, and within six months, several more states seceded. The Civil War broke out on January 9, 1861, only a few miles from Saint James when Citadel cadets fired on the Union steamship *Star of the West* steaming off Morris Island towards Charleston Harbor and Fort Sumter. Confederate forces on James Island fired on Fort Sumter on April 12, 1861. St. Andrews' warden William Izard Bull, leader of his church vestry, offered his services to General P. G. T. Beauregard, commander of the Confederate forces in the Charleston area. Bull later served as a colonel with General Johnson Hagood on James Island.[2] In June 1861 the Diocese of South Carolina left the Protestant Episcopal Church of the United States of America and aligned with the Protestant Episcopal Church in the Confederate States.[3]

Bostick wrote in his history on James Island, "Following the surrender of Fort Sumter, all but one of the white James Island men of age enlisted for service in the Confederacy. Wallace Lawton [member of Saint James] initially declined to serve, noting that he had 'important matters to attend to'."[4]

In May 1862 Brigadier General Gist ordered that James Island be evacuated. Beef, cattle and sheep were to be left on the island for the Southern troops.[5] When Wallace Lawton refused to leave the island, the provost marshal threatened to arrest him, so he initially moved just across the river to another one of his residences on Rutledge Avenue in Charleston.

William Wallace McLeod, Saint James member, took his family to Greenwood.[6]

In *How Grand a Flame*, an historical novel based on facts drawn from letters, diaries, and interviews, Clyde Bresee wrote that in an attempt to escape Sherman's troops in 1863, Wallace Lawton left his plantation called 100 Pines and took ninety-nine slaves, his possessions, mules, and sheep and went down to Beaufort where he bought 3,000 acres. As Bresee put it, "Well, what [Lawton] did was walk right into Sherman's way."[7] Hayes noted in his history *James and Related Sea Islands* that four members of the Lawton family entered the Civil War. Ironically, Captain William Sherman had been friends with the Lawtons prior to the war and, as a young soldier, occasionally visited at Lawton Bluff.[8] Among enlisted men from Saint James were also Rev. Stiles Mellichamp and some of his relatives.[9]

In Saint James' Cemetery is the following headstone:

JAMES PERRONNEAU

ROYALL

PALMETTO GUARD

2nd S C L

BORN ON JAMES ISLAND

24th OCT'R. 1840

FELL AT MALVERN HILL

1st JULY 1862

WHILE IN THE FAITHFUL

DISCHARGE OF HIS DUTY

Erected by Comrad.[10]

Because of the war, services at Saint James ceased in 1862.[11] Rev. Mellichamp arranged with the Presbyterian minister to hold services every other Sunday. After Saint James had replaced its building with a fifth structure at the end of this century, many Episcopalians and Presbyterians on the island continued to worship together, alternately attending one denomination's service on a designated Sunday and attending the other's service the next Sunday. This custom continued until 1951.[12]

Battles at Sol Legare Island, Grimball Plantation, Secessionville, and Morris Island followed.[13] McLeod Plantation, used by Confederate forces for their headquarters and hospital, was later seized by Federal troops in 1865.[14]

Dr. Ellis wrote,

> Bishop Thomas reports that the church burned in a woods fire started when confederate soldiers, hunting rabbits, accidently set grass on fire. St. James' records, which had been removed [in 1862] to Winnsboro by treasurer, Con-

stant H. Rivers, were lost when Sherman's troops burned that town. After the war only the silver service and two chairs remained of the church and its furnishings.[15]

Elaborating on the fire that burned the fourth church of Saint James in 1864 are Mr. Willie McLeod's handwritten notes preserved on microfiche in the Charleston County Library on Calhoun Street:

It is said that some Confederate soldiers who were then on the Island set fire to the field adjoining the Churchyard in order to run out the rabbits for a hunt. Stationed on the Island at that time several miles from the Church was Col. Ellison Capers, who later became Bishop of the Diocese of South Carolina. (The Diocese then embraced the entire state.) Upon receiving information that the church was endangered by the fire, Col. Capers sent some of his men to the scene to extinguish it. That night, however, a strong wind sprang up and started the fire again. This time it swept through the Churchyard, completely destroying the Church.

Writing more generally about this era, Ellis said the following about the period of the Confederate War:

Then ensued the period of war, devastation, and reconstruction. All communicants left the island in 1862. The church was destroyed by fire in 1864. The majority of the dwellings on the island suffered the same fate. Only spasmodic religious activity was possible under these conditions. Several ministers held services once a month at various times either in the Presbyterian church or in the homes of communicants.[16]

One confederate soldier, W. G. Hinson, who later joined Saint James and became a prominent leader within the congregation, escaped death a number of times. On December 27, 1853, he was accidently shot in a hunting accident. Later Dr. Ogier saved him from lockjaw. Then he was shot during the Civil War and survived that wound as well.[17] Among Saint James' historical records is a manuscript attributed to Mr. Hinson (dated 1888) and cited numerous times in this text.

People of James Island and the surrounding areas struggled as the Civil War dragged on. Beginning in July of 1863 Union armies moved onto Morris Island with the intent to surround Charleston. Confederate President Jefferson Davis declared August 21, 1863 to be a day of fasting, humiliation, and prayer, and Southern troops attended church services in masses. After 586 days of artillery bombardment, lasting until February of 1865, Charleston was overtaken by Union forces.[18]

The Episcopal churches on the peninsula of Charleston suffered destruction and disruption of services. According to Dorothy Anderson and Margaret Eastman's research,

> The congregation continued to worship at St. Philip's after the bombardment of Fort Sumter until it was hit by enemy fire on Thanksgiving Day 1863. Thereafter it worshiped uptown at St. Paul's. Bursting shells also drove the congregations of St. Michael's and Grace Church away, and the combined congregations worshiped in St. Paul's until Union forces entered the city.[19]

At the end of the war, St. Philip's was "in deplorable condition. During the constant bombardment during the Siege of Charles Town, ten shells entered the walls, the chancel was destroyed, the roof was pierced in several places and the organ pipes were hauled away."[20] Most communicants of Saint James were familiar with these Charleston churches, had worshipped in them with friends and family, and grieved about their destruction with fellow Episcopalians just as they grieved about the loss of their own church.

In *A Brief History of James Island*, Bostick wrote, "In the spring of 1865, James Island was in a state of almost complete destruction. Of the planation homes, only six houses were left standing."[21] In *How Grand a Flame*, Bresee wrote about Wallace Lawton's return to the island: "His commodious plantation house, which had stood at the end of a row of trees, was now only seven blackened chimneys and a pile of ashes. The gin house, the mule barns, the whitewashed fences, the poultry house, and the carriage house were charred boards and ashes. Not one of his sixteen outbuildings remained…All the trees were gone."[22]

Mr. William Hinson's 1888 manuscript states,

> The Island was put under martial law and thousands of Confederate soldiers were garrisoned, it doing great damage to buildings and other property in the most wanton manner…All public buildings too, churches, Club houses, Free School for whites and the public library, all had disappeared under the ruthless hand of war. At Fort Johnson not a vestige of a house was to be seen, but this at least was done by the Confederate Engineers to make room for the fire of guns.[23]

Near the closing of Hinson's recorded recollections from 1888, he states:

> All of the young men enlisted on the side of Southern Liberty in the war of 1861 with but a few exceptions who remained inactive. As far as can be re-

membered, the following are the names of those who joined the Provisional Army of the Confederate States, necessarily incomplete:

- W. Rivers—2nd Regt. So. Caro. Volunteers; served in Virginia
- C. H. Rivers—Benbow's Reg't.
- W. A. Clark—Signal Corps
- Stiles M. Hinson—7th SC Cavalry; killed in Virginia
- Wm. G. Hinson—7th SC Cavalry; promoted to Lieut.
- Campbell Holmes—Killed in Virginia
- Starling Lebby—Capt. of Privateer *Sally* and blockade runner *Hattie*
- Dr. Robert Lebby—Surg. Gen. Talliaferro's (Taliferro's) staff [different spellings on different lists]
- Walker Lebby—Engineer; drowned in blockade runner *Cecile*
- Paul Lockwood—Killed in Virginia (had married Sarah Hinson)
- Edward T. Legare—Signal corps
- John C. Minott—1st regular infantry; lieutenant; wounded at Bentonville, NC
- W.W. McLeod—Charleston Light Dragoons; died in service
- Dr. J. H. Mellichamp—Sur. on Gen. Drayton's staff at Battle of Port Royal
- E. H. Mellichamp—Engineer Corps; captured at Ft. McAllister, Ga., died at Point Lookout (?) while prisoner [Note—Another copy of this list says he died at Almira, N.Y. while prisoner.]
- Jos. M. Mellichamp—25th SC infantry; captured at Ft. Fisher, NC; died in prison [Note: This entry is on the Hinson's original list but not on the 1919 list.]
- W.S. Mellichamp—27th SC Infantry; died in hospital in Charleston from exposure on walls of Fort Sumter
- St. Lo. E. Mellichamp—Washington Artillery; served on coast of SC
- Stiles Mellichamp—Signal corps; served at Battery Wagner, Morris Island
- R. E. Mellichamp—Co. "A" SC Siege Train (2nd lieut)
- W. Lawton Mikell—7th SC Cavalry
- James Peronneau Royal— 2nd SC Infantry; killed in Virginia

- A. W. Rivers—[Rollins or Rawlins Rivers?]—2nd SC Infantry; killed in the West

- Elias L. Rivers—Promoted to Capt.

- Constant Rivers—Capt. 1st Regular Infantry

- Wm. B. Seabrook—Lieut; Benbow's Regm't Evan's Brigade

- J.C. Seabrook—[Saul or Julius Constantine?]—2nd SC Infantry; killed in Virginia

- J.M. Holmes

- J.F. Lawton

- B. M. Leighty—Surgeon

- W. A. Mellichamp—Engineer Corps

- S. R. Mellichamp—Engineer Corps

- R. & J. L. Girardieu

This is a combined list recorded by William Hinson, as he wrote it, one initially dated 1888 (pages 9-11 with handwritten notes added) and the other dated 1919 (page 13). One can readily note that many of these names are also names of Saint James' parishioners.[24]

By1865 fourteen men from James Island had been killed or died as a result of the war, many with last names historically known on James Island and some to Saint James—Stiles M. Hinson, Lt. Campbell Holmes, Walker Lebby, Joseph Mellichamp, W. S. Mellichamp, Captain Paul Seabrook, J. C. Lawton, J. Mikell Lawton, Sandiford Bee, William Wallace McLeod, James Peronneau Royall, Julius Constantine Seabrook, Rawlins Holmes Rivers, and Edward H. Mellichamp.[25] Many of their families were active at Saint James for generations, and many of their descendants continue today with ties to the church.

William Godber Hinson was recognized on a Saint James plaque that still exists in the sanctuary at Saint James: "Brave Confederate, Wise Reconstructor, Progressive Planter, Faithful Warden."[26] In memory of William Wallace McLeod, a tombstone was placed in Saint James Cemetery with the following inscription: "died in Confederate service; rests in unknown grave." His death left his three children as orphans to be cared for by an uncle, and the family property was not returned to the McLeod family until 1869.[27] In Walter Edgar's *South Carolina: A History*, the author states that thirty to thirty-five percent of South Carolina males of age to enlist died fighting for the Confederate cause.[28]

On November 27, 1870, Rev. C.C. Pinckney of Grace Church delivered a reflective discourse on the effects of the Civil War. His words are relevant not only to his own church but, in a universal sense, to all churches and mankind suffering from war:

Not only the material interests of a nation, its agriculture, its commerce, its manufactures, its arts, its whole industrial life, but its moral and spiritual being, is touched in every point by that bloody hand. Schools, colleges, churches, are scattered by its discordant voice. Every benevolent, and moral, and missionary, and social agency...is paralyzed by its breath... Pestilence, and famine, and cruelty, and consuming anxiety, and every moral and physical evil which blasts human life and human happiness, is included in that one word—war. Hasten the time, thou Prince of Peace, when men shall learn war no more.[29]

Whatever is in a worshipper's head and heart ends up in the church sanctuary, whether he or she occupies a pew or the pulpit. Losing their land and lifestyles and livelihoods, losing limbs and the lives of loved ones, the congregation of Saint James and neighboring churches longed to reestablish some sort of order and security in what seemed to be a wasteland. Many who were hungry and homeless at the end of the war felt a need for God more than ever as they struggled to obtain food and shelter. Surely the people of Saint James implored God for miracles and mercy as they read the Book of Psalms in the King James Version: "My soul melteth for heaviness; strengthen thou me according unto thy word" (119:28).

CHAPTER SEVEN

Following the War Between the States

After the start of the Civil War, the states that had seceded formed "The Protestant Episcopal Church in the Confederate States of America" and withdrew from the union's national church. After the war the Episcopal Diocese of South Carolina postponed its convention in 1865 because there were not enough clergy to form a quorum. Only six of the fifty-two diocesan churches that had been vibrant prior to the war could be represented.[1]

According to Clarke's *Anglicanism in South Carolina*, in 1868 a committee of the Diocese of South Carolina reported the following to the Protestant Episcopal Convention:

> Three churches had disappeared; ten had been burned to the ground; twenty-two parishes were suspended; no church between the Savannah River and Charleston…had been left intact; from Georgia to North Carolina only four parishes, all in Charleston, were holding services; practically every church had lost its communal silver; eleven rectories, including the ministers' libraries, had been destroyed by fire; clergy were sustaining themselves and their families as best they could by farming, fishing, and the mechanical arts.[2]

John Kershaw, author of his book published in 1915 about St. Michael's Church, wrote about the hardships of this historical time period, stating that "no free people were ever subjected to an ordeal more severe and bitter than were our people during the ten years following upon 1868…Such experiences could not but leave their mark upon the Church and the State alike."[3]

Adding additional statistics, Porwoll reported, "The fragile state of the diocese a quarter century after the Civil War was sobering: only sixteen of ninety-five parishes and missions across the state were self-supporting."[4] For several years following the War Between the States [Saint James' parish] was inactive except for occasional weddings, funerals, baptisms, and confirmations.[5]

The post-war years were difficult for Saint James members and their community. Most, but not all, of the James Island residents returned in 1866.[6] Stated in Bostick's research, possibly based on W.E. McLeod's "An Outline of the History of James Island, SC" (1944), was the following information about existing residences: "Only six of the island's plantation houses remained at the conclusion of the war: McLeod, Stiles Point, the Heyward-Cuthbert House on Lawton Plantation, White House, Secessionville Manor, and the home of Edward Freer at Sessionville."[7]

Because of the Emancipation Proclamation and the Thirteenth Amendment, the slaves were freed, vacating the fields of the workforce that planters had depended on prior to the war. The deaths of their elders and soldiers left voids in leadership and stability. Land on James Island diminished in value, creating financial hardships for farmers. Those who had survived the war often suffered from lack of agricultural knowledge, available cash, and organized government.[8]

The James Island Agricultural Society, established in 1872, organized white Sea Island farmers and planters to address labor management policies, crop problems, and general community matters. Growing market vegetables, called "truck farming," became significant in the post-Civil War years.[9] These crops often included melons, okra, tomatoes, peas, beans, squash, cabbage, turnips, and both Irish and sweet potatoes.[10]

Following the Civil War, separation of worship for the blacks and whites came about. Black churches often became charismatic in worship, with services characterized by a display of emotion, dancing, and even mysticism, influenced by intuition and meditation. They hosted all-day gatherings on Sundays and served as centers to meet the social, educational, political, and welfare needs of their members.[11] Rowland's *History of Beaufort County* makes note of the black evangelical services, which infused African music and language—characteristic of the Negro churches throughout the Low Country of this time.[12] William Hinson reported that five black churches of different denominations were built on James Island after the Civil War.[13]

Historian Porwoll stated that "the Episcopal Church of South Carolina lost its national identity with the defeat of the Confederacy."[14] Many churches had been destroyed by fire and shelling. Some churches had been temporarily converted by Union forces into headquarters, hospitals, stables, commissaries, and bridge-building materials.[15] Following the war, the average pledge per communicant for the forty-three diocesan churches was fifty-one and a half cents.[16]

In spite of the devastation brought about by the War between the States, Dr. Ellis reports, as follows, on positive strides made by two devoted churchmen:

> During the post war period (from 1865) in spite of minimal church activity in the form of formal services, valuable work was done by two wise and energetic Episcopalians of the island; namely, W.G. Hinson and E. L. Rivers. Property was available and income from the glebe land and Parrot's Point was wisely invested in land. As these holdings were added to, there was a proportionate increase in the income. Much of the progress made by St. James in the future years was to be made possible by the wise foresight of these gentlemen. One of the first fruits of their wisdom was the erection of the fifth church building in 1899.[17]

Another positive fact in this dark period of history was that Rev. William Bell White Howe became the sixth Bishop of the Diocese of South Carolina. Remaining in this leadership position for twenty-one years, he ordained forty-four men and confirmed 6,700 people.[18]

In Saint James cemetery, visitors can still see a very unique grave marker in the Lawtons' family plot where Wallace and Cecelia Lawton's young son and daughter are buried. Although records are not precise, the children probably died of diphtheria, a disease that spread quickly and was especially life-threatening to children in the late 1800s. Clyde Bresee describes this grave stone well: "…two sculpted lambs in white marble resting on a granite base, a monument that must tell us all we can know at this far time of little Herbert and his sister. Herbert died on December 2, 1876, and little Cecilia died five days later. On the granite base are words that read almost like a stifled sob: Cecilia—Herbert—Our Darlings. Thy will be done."[19] Their father Wallace died November 30, 1906. After a church funeral, attended by his loyal black employee Peter Brown and his wife Emma, Wallace was buried in the family plot near his children's graves and his own father's tall grave marker.[20]

Author Nell S. Graydon, writing about the barrier islands of the South in the 1800s, stated the following:

> All of the planter's wealth could not protect his children from the "malignant fevers" and "summer complaints" about whose cause and cure he knew so little. In all of the Low Country graveyards one sees numerous small headstones, topped by little angels or lambs—mute testimony to the fact that many a prosperous planter lived to find more of his children in heaven than on earth.[21]

Two other significant Saint James gravestones belong to sisters, Eleanor C. Dill and Mary Hayes Rivers. According to records entitled *St. James Episc. Church, James Island (SCHS 50-94 RNC)*, one sister died suddenly, and when the other one heard about it in the same house, she died suddenly also. One headstone reads as follows:

ELEANOR C.
WIFE OF JOSEPH T. DILL
DIED 11 MARCH 1878
AGED 52 YEARS, 11 MO'S, 27 DAYS
Hence forth there is laid up for us
a crown of righteousness.
"With us her name shall live,
Through long succeeding years;
Embalmed with all our hearts can give,
Our Praises and our Tears."

The other sister's tombstone reads as follows:

MARY HAYES RIVERS
DIED 11 MARCH 1878
AGED 66 YEARS, 6 MOS., 26 DAYS
"I shall be satisfied
When I awake with thy likeness."

On the 11th March 1878
The Reaper gathered, at a breath,
these Sisters, whose lives had long been
Devoted to the service of the Master.[22]

According to Porwoll's research, "It was during this time in 1884 that the glebe was claimed by St. Andrews under the reverter clause in the original deed to St. James. After much negotiation, St. James paid St. Andrews the sum of $708.60 in satisfaction of the claim."[23]

Still reeling from the recovery of the War Between the States and Reconstruction, the Charleston area suffered the Great Earthquake in August of 1886, beginning exactly 9:15 PM,[24] sending tremors across 2.5 million square miles.[25] Hitting at night and consisting of repetitive shocks for over a two-hour period, the earthquake was estimated to have been between 6.6 and 7.3 on the Richter Scale. In several James Island locations, it caused hot springs to erupt from the ground.[26] Bostick's research states, "The violent shaking left hundreds of places on [James Island] where the earth opened in long 'rivers' of cold water mixed with sand and pluff mud. Many people on the island reported a sensation of nausea throughout the quake and the aftershocks."[27] Bringing about new damage on some buildings recently repaired and rebuilt after the war, the destruction included five to six million dollars of damage, the immediate deaths of twenty-seven people, and another forty-nine dying of injuries in the Charleston area.[28]

At the end of the nineteenth century and the beginning of the twentieth, natural disasters on and surrounding James Island involved storms, floods, and crop-eating insects, such as caterpillars, that devastated acres of produce.[29] A hurricane, which destroyed about fifty buildings on August 26, 1885, added to the hardships. In 1893 another hurricane ripped off roofs, damaged homes and churches, washed away livestock, and destroyed both the quarantine station at Fort Johnson as well as the Baptist Church of James Island.[30] In 1894 hail as big as plums did further damage.[31]

By 1893 James Island was producing some of the finest black-seed or long-staple cotton in record-making amounts, thus increasing the plantation owners' profits.[32] Sea Island cotton produced a silky fiber twice as long as that of upstate cotton, so it sold for at least six times as much, making land on the Sea Islands some of the most valuable property in South Carolina.[33] Captain Elias Lynch Rivers (whose son John—1869-1941—is buried in Saint James' Cemetery[34]) developed what was called "Rivers Cotton" or "Centerville Cotton," which was resistant to wilt disease.[35] However, in 1918 boll weevils wiped out cotton crops, which never became the "king crop" of the island again.[36]

James Islanders produced sweet potatoes, corn, peas, beans, butter, wool, and hay.[37] Islanders also lived off the land by hunting partridges, doves, woodcock, and turkeys and off the waters by fishing for bass, black drum, whiting, and sheepshead. They also ate shrimp, oysters, conch, clams, "yellow-bellied cooters" (terrapins), and "palmetto cabbage."[38]

Another sad but interesting note found in Dr. Ellis' research regarded the gender of Saint James membership following the Civil War—Mr. William B. Seabrook was the only male communicant. W. G. Hinson and E. L. Rivers attended and later joined and became prominent leaders of the congregation. In 1866 W. W. and J.P. Lawton returned to James Island; however, some other residents never returned to the island after the War Between the States.[39]

In spite of problems arising from conflicts with both man and nature, Saint James began acquiring land from island residents. Gradual financial recovery and large amounts of land available at low prices enabled the church to purchase property. The far-sightedness of churchmen, especially W. G. Hinson and E. L. Rivers, enabled Saint James to invest income from the glebe land and Parrot Point into business transactions, such as the following:[40]

- 1887—97 acres on James Island purchased from F. P. Seabrook
- 1893—97 acres on James Island purchased from Rev. J. McL. Seabrook for $2600
- 1895—103 acres purchased from Mrs. Martha Love Seabrook Walpole for $1200
- 1895—3.25 acres purchased from Caesar Smith for $35[41]

Having accepted a call to a church in Orangeburg, Rev. Mellichamp preached there briefly and then agreed to return to Saint James; a parsonage was built in 1872 for him at Parrot Point.[42] However, he died in 1872, and Saint James was listed as a "suspended mission."[43] Nonetheless, Saint James had vestry members: W. B. Seabrook, J.T. Dill, W.W. Lawton, E.L. Rivers, and Mr. W. G. Hinson.[44] No regular services were held again until 1887 with Rev. Prentiss[45] preaching "occasionally" or once a month.[46]

James Island Presbyterian Church had also been destroyed during the Civil War and rebuilt in 1867-1868.[47] During a couple of transitory decades, Saint James had a series of priests who served relatively short periods of time: W.O. Prentiss from 1867 to 1869; Stiles Mellichamp returning briefly in 1870 and called again in 1872 but died; S.E. Prentiss from 1887 to 1888; John L. Egbert for only three months (January through March of 1896); and Andrew Ernest Cornish for one year—April 1896 through April 1897.[48] Sporadic religious services were sometimes held in homes of communicants. James Island residents held alternating Presbyterian and Episcopal services, with Rev. W. O. Prentiss preaching at the Presbyterian Church once a month in 1869 and Rev. Stiles Mellichamp holding services once a month in 1870. Then Episcopal services were not held regularly again until 1887-1888 with Rev. S. E. Prentiss. For the next seven years no regular Episcopal services were held.[49] Then in 1898 Saint James became an organized mission again.[50]

Thomas' book *Protestant Episcopal Church in South Carolina* includes the following interesting anecdote: "St. James' received…from the famous Plowden Weston St. Mary's Chapel, Hagley, in All Saints' Parish, the gift of a Bible, prayer book, altar service book, and oak book-rest. The [Bible] was used until [lay readers found the font too difficult to read and] a more modernly printed Bible was secured and given as a memorial to Mr. Cornish."[51]

In the late 1880s Rev. A. E. Cornish ran a mission farm "Sheltering Arms," which provided farming jobs and thus helped to curb hunger that was so prevalent throughout the South after the Civil War.[52] First located facing Morris Island, Sheltering Arms was also an orphanage and school. Adding to Rev. Cornish's worries about on-going shortages of funds was an incident when another official embezzled what little money they had at the time.[53] Sheltering Arms was moved in about 1900 to a location known as "Three Trees," which was supposedly named by the Indians who went there to resolve any disputes among themselves. Three Trees was located near what is now the entrance to the subdivision called Lighthouse Point.[54] This same location was also where the Francis Rodgers family distributed government food staples (rice, flour etc.) to the impoverished during the Great Depression and operated a landscape nursery for many years.[55]

In Saint James' historical records is a copy of what is entitled "Bishop's Journal," with the date 1903 written on it. The following excerpt gives one an idea of the "farm":

> I [the bishop] visited "Sheltering Arms," Mr. Cornish's home-farm, where we had a service for the children...There were eighteen children present..., all of them under the faithful care of the Misses Grenaker, others of the children being too young to attend the services or by permission away with friends for the day....Everyone here who can work is at work...Mr. Cornish showed me forty acres of promising cotton and twelve acres of beautiful corn, for the most part the work of the larger boys.[56]

During March of 1893, when some former Union soldiers were touring Charleston, they found a lone grave of Pvt. John F. Cook on Cole Island (elsewhere spelled *Coles* and *Cole's*) on the west end of Folly Island. The visitors noticed that the grave was in danger of washing away. Charles C. Soule of Boston reported this to General Huguenin of the Survivors Association, and he, in turn, reported it to W. G. Hinson and E. L. Rivers. These men went to Cole Island, removed the remains and stone, and had this former confederate soldier buried at Saint James.[57] His grave stone reads:

IN
MEMORY OF
JOHN F. COOK
WEE TEE
VOLUNTEERS
1st REGT. S C V
BORN IN
WILLIAMSBURG
Who died in the service of his
Country, on Coles Island
14th Nov. AD 1861
Aged 32 years, 2 months,
24 days[58]

In the *Saint James Cemetery Booklet*, one may note the death of Joseph T. Dill on January 3, 1900.[59] In those times, when a vestryman died, a loving tribute was written on his behalf and included in the vestry minutes. A copy of the tribute was shared with the deceased member's family in honor of his service. The vestry's secretary inserted a blank page into the next meeting's minutes to represent the empty chair and the silenced voice of that serving vestryman. The following, typical of other such eloquent tributes, was in the April 16, 1900 vestry minutes (Note: Punctuation has been added for clarification in the text):

> Whereas since our last meeting in the Providence of God, Mr. Joseph T. Dill, the chairman of this vestry, has been called from time to eternity, and Whereas by this sad occurrence this vestry has lost its oldest member, and this Parish one of its chief supporters.

> Whereas this vestry deeply sensible of the great loss that has thus befallen it, is desirous of recording its appreciation of the services which the deceased has ever rendered to this church. Therefor [sic] be it

> Resolved that in the death of Mr. Joseph T. Dill, this church has sustained a loss which we cannot contemplate without a feeling of the deepest sorrow.

> Resolved that we extend our heartfelt sympathy and condolences to his bereaved family.

> Resolved that a blank page in the minutes of this vestry Be inscribed to his memory.

> Resolved that a copy of these resolutions be forwarded to his surviving family.

Mostly due to the efforts of W. G. Hinson, E.L. Rivers, and Rev. Cornish, construction was begun on the fifth Saint James church in 1898, and it was consecrated June 30, 1902 by Bishop Capers.[60] William G. Hinson brought wood (chestnut and walnut) from Saluda, North Carolina, to build the chapel.[61] Dr. Ellis described the church as follows: "The new building was a wooden building of gothic design. The interior had exposed cypress beams and the outside was painted white with a steep red shingled roof. Its seating capacity was about one hundred people."[62] This church's design resembled that of the Church of the Transfiguration in Saluda.[63]

Saint James member Frances Hayden included this detailed paragraph in a newspaper article that she had published in 1953:

Of particular interest to islanders is the walnut altar rail given by Dr. D. W. Ellis made from walnut trees that grew on the island. Mr. W. G. Hinson also gave the memorial glass window above the altar and the circular glass window high in the front gable; also he built the brick and iron gateway and planted azaleas and shrubbery. Mrs. E. S. Thayer, sister of Capt. E. L. Rivers, gave the prayer desk and Miss Hattie Howe and Miss Annie Waring gave the wooden alms basins.[64]

Mrs. Hayden's article also says, "The altar and other ecclesiastical hangings were the handiwork of the Misses Louise Heyward and Julia Dill. Mr. Hinson gave the vases and font as an Easter offering. Mr. Elias Rivers had the choir stalls built. Later the Woman's Auxillary [sic] gave two silver alms basins in memory of Mr. W. G. Hinson and Capt. E. L. Rivers."[65] Parishioners placed significance on gifts of time, labor, and money.

Dr. Ellis went on to say:

> The consecration of the new building occurred in 1902. Thus began a new era in the fortunes of the Anglican faith on James Island. As we have seen, during the first 182 years of its history it was necessary to construct five buildings. The island had been devastated by two major wars when hostilities occurred on its soil. There had also been hurricanes, an earthquake, and pestilence. The congregation was almost nonexistent from the revolution to 1831. Immediately following the War Between the States, there was only one male communicant. However since 1902 there has been no interruption in worship. Services were held, at times only once a month or twice a month, until 1960.[66]

A "Certificate of Incorporation" granted by the State of South Carolina was signed by William G. Hinson, Elias S. Rivers, D. W. Ellis, St. J. Alison Lawton, and W.R. Jenkins, stating that they were "agents appointed to manage the affairs of St. James Church, James Island, May 14, 1903, … [and] the said organization holds…property in common for a Religious, Educational, Social, Fraternal, Charitable or other eleemosynary [benevolent] purpose…and is not organized for the purpose of profit or gain to the members."[67]

The Rev. A. E. Cornish formerly of Saint John's Chapel was the first rector of this new church;[68] John Henry Brown served as the assistant minister.[69] In 1907 Rev. Cornish preached on the second Sundays in each month (vestry minutes in 1909) and reported six families and thirteen communicants in Saint James' congregation. Bishop Thomas attributed the dire situation to the fact that the church had not recovered from the war.[70] Episcopal services were held once a month up until 1913, and then Sunday services were offered twice a month.[71]

From 1907 to 1913 Rev. H.C. Mazyck served as rector of St. John's Episcopal and minister-in-charge at Saint James.[72] St. John's Episcopal, founded in 1734 with its first building completed in 1742, was built on Johns Island near Church Creek and Angel Oak.[73] The vestry notes from a meeting on April 8, 1912 stated that Saint James' vestrymen would ask Rev. Mazyck to preach in addition to every second Sunday also every fifth Sunday, adding four more services a year. In May of 1913 Saint James was readmitted to the Convention of the Diocese as a parish.[74]

In May of 1913 Rev. P. H. Whaley, a beloved pastor, succeeded Mr. Mazyck, but he died at the age of sixty-two in 1915.[75] Known as an author with scholarly attributes, he was in Minnesota collecting material for a history of the Episcopal Diocese at the time of his death. He was buried on Edisto Island.[76]

In 1914 Saint James' status changed from that of a mission to that of a church. [77] In the vestry minutes from April 5, 1915, the secretary recorded the following:

> Some discussion was entered into regarding the inadequacy of the present seating capacity of the church and there seemed to have [been] some confusion on this point because of the fact that a few people had at times found their accustomed seats occupied when they came to church, and the Rector was therefore requested to state that all were welcome, that all pews were free and that if any found their accustomed place occupied, they must not feel embarrassed and should proceed to the next most convenient seat.

Many current readers will chuckle when seeing that this sense of ownership of certain pews existed decades ago and sometimes still exists today. Modern readers will also note the secretary's dignified tone laced with tactfulness and courtesy.

In 1917 Rev. Cornish returned as rector, and vestry minutes indicate that the church was able to offer him a salary of $600 per annum. His wife died after a long illness.[78] Her headstone in Saint James Cemetery reads, as follows:

SARAH CATHERINE

BELOVED WIFE

Of

A.E. CORNISH

FEB. 11, 1858 JAN. 6, 1918

So shall we ever be with the Lord.[79]

After being a widower for two years, Rev. Cornish married Miss Katie Waring Simons in 1920, but he died later that same year.[80] His headstone in Saint James' cemetery reads as follows:

REV. ANDREW ERNEST
CORNISH
DEC. 4, 1861
OCT. 12, 1920
Pure and undefiled
before God the Father
is this:
To visit the fatherless and
widows in their affliction and
to keep himself unspotted
from the world.[81]

In July 1921 the Rev. Wallace Martin became the rector and served through 1944.[82]

Saint James' Cemetery has gravesites of the following parishioners who served in World War I: William Clyde Easterling (1892-1962), Burmain A. Grimball (1895-1957), Carl W. Prause (1893-1970), Calhoun Clark Royal (1886-1944), and Thomas Cooper Welch (1891-1975).[83] Again, these names are among those whose families have been long-time James Island residents and long-time Saint James worshippers.

Many messages can be drawn from this period of history. The greater the struggle, the more important are tenacity and devotion. What might be more important than how long one serves is that he manages to serve at all. From month to month and year to year, these priests, doing the best they could considering the circumstances, served Saint James and its neighboring people intermittently and occasionally, receiving minimal salaries from a financially struggling congregation; nevertheless, they served, thanks be to God. Surely these faithful leaders and followers implored, "Veni Sancte Spiritus"—"Holy Spirit, come to us."

CHAPTER EIGHT

1920s—Clyde Bresee's *Sea Island Yankee*

Regarding Saint James Church, one of the best first-hand accounts of the time period from 1921 to 1929 is recorded in Clyde Bresee's *Sea Island Yankee* published in 1989 by Algonquin Books of Chapel Hill.[1] He recalls his childhood when he and his family moved from Pennsylvania to James Island where his father managed the Lawton Dairy Farm. Clyde's father had been hired by St. John Alison Lawton, a prominent citizen of James Island and a member of Saint James Episcopal Church. The move brought huge cultural and climate changes to the Bresee family. Bresee reflects, as follows:

> This phalanx of James Island planters [and dairy farmers] could have pre-sented a formidable obstacle to our social progress in the community, but in fact it did not. Overtures of friendship came from all sides. These school families were also the church families; the parents of my friends were pillars in the Presbyterian or Episcopal churches, which the Bresees began to at-tend on alternate Sundays of the month, as was the James Island custom. The same group belonged to the newly formed PTA, of which my mother soon became president, and her friends belonged to the Ladies Auxiliary of the Southern Presbyterian Church. The James Island Agricultural Society, the Parent Teachers Association, and the little churches were one. For us youngsters, the overlap of the James Island Grammar School, the Sunday school, and the Christian Endeavor Society was almost complete.
>
> Experts in social psychology could not have devised a setting that could more speedily have transformed a Yankee boy into a Southerner—or at least

the James Island version of one. I fell in love with grits and red rice at first taste."[2]

In another chapter Bresee comments about the teas and social gatherings among the church members, as follows:

> A custom of our planter friends on James Island that could no doubt be traced back to "the departed elegance" of their forbears was Sunday evening tea…This charming James Island custom certainly had no counterpart in our Northern farming routine, but we took to it as easily as birds to air…
>
> The invitation usually came as we stood under the trees in the church yard after the sermon, making our farewells for the week. "Won't you-all come over this evening for tea?" We never refused.[3]

Bresee dedicates Chapter 6 "Remember Now Thy Creator" to his church experiences on James Island. Following is a long excerpt:

> There was no Methodist church on James Island—for white people, that is—but there was the James Island Presbyterian Church and the St. James Episcopal Church. I think the Presbyterians got to us first, but as things turned out it would not have mattered. Most of the James Island families were Presbyterian one Sunday and Episcopalian the next. The problem could be stated simply: no one wanted either of these historic churches to close its doors, and there weren't enough planters for both. Loyalty to tradition and community prevailed over doctrinal differences.
>
> There was, indeed, a Presbyterian church complete with deacons and elders, and an Episcopal church with priest and vestry. Both had small Sunday schools. Neither could afford a full-time preacher, the Presbyterian preacher serving also on Wadmalaw Island and the Episcopal priest serving at the Seamen's Home in Charleston.
>
> "Which church today, Mom?"
>
> "The Presbyterian."
>
> "I thought we went there last Sunday."
>
> "We did but this is the fifth Sunday. We go to the Presbyterian church every first, third, and fifth Sunday."
>
> "That cheats the Episcopalians. Do they mind?"
>
> "No, because their minister has a service in town on fifth Sundays."[4]

...

As a child, I found switching churches rather enjoyable. If the word "enjoyable" sounds startling, it should be remembered that the option of nonattendance did not exist in my family. Alternating between the two churches offered a pleasant change. My Sunday school class in the Presbyterian church was held in two short pews at the rear of the church, and in St. James in a nook behind the reed organ.[5]

...

The Episcopalians had their strong points. The rector wanted a choir for each service and gladly accepted children as well as adults. Martha Rivers, the organist and my teacher in public school, knew that my sister and I could sing acceptably, and soon had us outfitted in robes and marching down the aisle behind the crucifer. The rector, although saddled with a small church—actually half a church—leaned toward High Church liturgy and included as many formalities as he could manage with his limited resources. I found the pageantry and movement a pleasant contrast to the plain, colorless Presbyterian service. I liked the divided chancel, the candles, the robes.[6]

To reward the choir and keep up morale, the rector had a charming custom at Christmas time. At the end of the Christmas service he gave each choir member, right down to the youngest, a pound of Norris's chocolates. There is no way by which I could make anyone today comprehend what that pound of chocolates meant to us. First of all, it was a grown-up gift; this was not a box of suckers or candy canes. I remember clearly the Sunday my sister and I brought home two pounds of chocolates.

"Did the preacher"—he was never the rector to my father—"give a box to everyone in the choir?" he asked.

"Yup, everyone. And he had some left over," we said.

"Twenty-five boxes of candy on his salary? He must have a friend in the wholesale business!"

"Seems like one box per family would have been enough" my mother observed. There she went again—my mother and her penchant for moderation. Why couldn't we just revel in candy? Box after box of it! But my mother found it hard to revel in anything.

"It wasn't you folks who did the singing," we reminded her. "*We* did the singing."

The situation put our Sunday school lessons about sharing to the test in a most annoying way. Of course we could and would pass it around, but when do our proprietary rights get recognized? My sister and I had earned this candy, we maintained.

"There were kids singing today who are no older than Kenneth [their younger brother]," my sister and I told them. "He's supposed to have such a sweet voice—let him sing next Christmas."

"We'll see," my mother said. "That's a long way off."

The next year our Christmas Sunday came off just as we had planned. Miss Rivers welcomed us with a smile and helped us to adjust our robes. We formed on the church porch, the children leading—including three Bresees. A long procession extended behind us—halfway around the side of the church. There were some new faces in our choir from the Folly Beach area, and I thought I knew the reason for their sudden interest in singing. The service went off without a hitch, including the anthem and the new Christmas responses. While we were removing our robes, the rector came back to the choir room with his arms full of boxes. He handed one to each of us with a big smile and a "Merry Christmas." Just then my mother came by the choir door to hurry us along. She faced three grinning children, each with a box of chocolates. This was too much for my proud, honest mother. This was excessive pay for doing the Lord's work and, besides, the situation looked rigged. "This isn't right. I'm going to see the minister." As she walked away, we could only watch and hope; the matter was no longer in our hands.

"These children do not deserve three boxes," my mother said. "Our family has much more than our share."

"Oh, no, there is a box for everyone who sings in the choir on Christmas Sunday." My mother started to speak. "Now, Mrs. Bresee, you wouldn't want to deny me the pleasure of giving Christmas presents, would you?"

My mother smiled in a sweet, defeated way and turned to us, "I hope you thanked him for his kindness."

In a chorus: "Oh, yes, we have!"

We raced over to the blue Dodge parked under the oak trees, and climbed triumphantly into the rear seat. Three pounds of candy!

Yet as the months passed, we began to think of ourselves as more Presbyterian than Episcopalian. There were two reasons: there was a stronger Sunday school influence in the Presbyterian church, and my father had trouble with the liturgy of the Episcopalians. The formal prayers, the choral responses, "all the fuss about candles and bowing" were a long way from his brand of Methodism. He sang in the Presbyterian choir and was, of course, asked to sing with the Episcopalians. He declined. He wasn't about to get rigged out in a robe and surplice. Particularly distasteful to him was the time when the rector, on special Sundays, turned his back to the congregation and intoned a solo chant.

Our friends, however, switched back and forth easily. My Sunday school teacher, Mrs. King of Stono Plantation and a loyal Presbyterian, would sing "Love Lifted Me" in her church one Sunday, and just as enthusiastically the next Sunday proceed up the aisle of St. James with book held high singing "The Son of God Goes Forth to War."

Perhaps we moved toward the Presbyterians because they did a little more urging and inviting. While the people at St. James were cordial enough, and you always knew that you were welcome, I used to feel that either you were born an Episcopalian or else you might decide in the privacy of your own mind to request to become an Episcopalian. But there would be no unseemly tugging at your sleeve.[7]

In yet another paragraph, Bresee tells about the organist at Saint James:

Miss Rivers played the reed organ in the St. James Episcopal Church, and it was hard work. A reed organ works on a vacuum; wind is sucked in over the little reeds, not blown as in pipe organs. A wooden arm stuck out from the side of the organ, and a boy could grasp it and work the bellows to produce the suction. But Martha Rivers preferred to pump the bellows with her feet. She played, slightly bent from the waist, swaying a little from side to side, not unlike a bicyclist pedaling up a hill. Part of her problem was leakage from the bellows. We could hear it as a sort of quiet gasp, especially when she worked up a strong suction to handle the responses between commandments. We sang, "Lord have mercy upon us and incline our hearts to keep this law" ten times, and she had to be ready.[8]

…

Martha Rivers was the daughter of Elias Rivers, a captain in the Confederate army. St. James Episcopal Church had been their church, and it was the one I attended on alternate Sundays. It was a little Gothic structure, made of wood with an interior of highly polished tongue-and-groove boards. It looked and felt like a church. The bond with the past was stronger here than with the Presbyterians—or at least I felt it so. It may have been the liturgy and the timeless expressions in the Book of Common Prayer that linked me to history in a way that the Presbyterians could not.[9]

…

I think that I knew the things Martha Rivers was remembering as she heard these prayers, and I found myself remembering them, too. Somehow I felt that I belonged in this procession of history; I could even be proud to step up and take my place.[10]

...

There was a certain cold Sunday morning in Advent. This was not Christmas Sunday, when everyone turned out and the church was warm, and there was an overflow choir. It was a day when someone had forgotten to start a fire, and that task had just fallen to the first comer. The little group who gathered for Sunday school that morning kept their coats on and shivered. At ten o'clock Miss Rivers started up the organ with "O Little Town of Bethlehem, How Still We See Thee Lie." I whispered to the boy beside me that I *thought* I was getting a steam engine for Christmas. Then we sang, "The First Noel" and huddled around the stove for our Sunday school class. Miss Rivers stopped by to say that she was counting on us for the choir, and went off to a back room to lay out the robes.

Why did they do it—Miss Rivers, my Sunday school teacher, and the people who shivered on that Sunday in Advent? Was it an unthinking response to "the pressures of ancient folkways"? A little exercise that made them feel better—but still an exercise in futility? If that was so, why do I remember it?

I know why now, and I did then. The reason was never uttered—it didn't have to be; we know without being told. They did it for us.[11]

One passage in particular demonstrates how intertwined the community and church were. The Lawton family needed a new storekeeper for their property and ultimately a young man named Charlie Mack got the job. Clyde Bresee shares his adult understanding on the interconnectedness of the island's people of work and worship. In his explanation, Bresee writes:

In retrospect, I see a shifting set of circumstances which seemed predetermined to fall into the precise pattern that brought Charlie to the Lawton plantation toward the close of our stay on James Island. If the tramp steamer *Doric Star* had not developed engine trouble and put into Charleston dry-dock for repairs; if Charlie had not, in boredom and loneliness, gone that evening to the Seamen's Home; if he had not had a long talk with the Reverend Stanley Martin, chaplain of the home; if the Reverend Martin had not also been Alison Lawton's pastor at St. James Church; if Lemuel Knight, our storekeeper, had not that week decided to return to his little farm near Jamestown...

During the family discussion regarding the hiring of this new employee, Clyde's father went on to explain:

> Reverend Martin got to know him at the Seamen's Home and took a liking to him. That's the place the Episcopal church runs to be a sort of "home-away-from-home" for sailors who don't want to spend all their time in those taverns on East Bay.[12]

As a part of this story, Father Martin of Saint James asked Mr. Lawton if he could hire Charlie, and Lawton did, demonstrating how the island priest and island parishioner trusted one another in matters beyond the church grounds.

When Clyde's brother Kenneth developed tuberculosis, the Bresees decided to leave James Island to return to their family's home state. Clyde's childhood in the 1920s became a permanent part of his treasured past, much of which was influenced by Saint James and its people.

The jacket of *Sea Island Yankee* says this:

> *Sea Island Yankee* is a sensitive beautifully-crafted account of a time and a place that today seem utterly lost; subdivisions now flourish where the old Lawton's Bluff dairy herd grazed. Yet Clyde Bresee's narrative is no merely nostalgic lament for a romanticized past, but a perceptive, moving, and by no means uncritical look at a remarkable sea island community as experienced by a highly observant child, remembered and, with the insight that time and change alone can provide, now truly understood.[13]

Mr. Bresee ultimately obtained his Ph.D. at Cornell University, served in World War II, and became a director of guidance for public schools in Athens, Pennsylvania. He and his wife Elizabeth had two children.[14] In spite of these achievements in his adult life lived far north from James Island, he remained attached to his childhood years of wading barefoot in the marshes, observing a Southern agricultural society, and worshiping in a gothic-style Lowcountry Episcopal Church—all which he honored in his historical memoir. Well past his retirement, Bresee continued to return to James Island to visit Saint James Church and reconnect with the members of its congregation. In fact, Rev. Arthur Jenkins recalled that in 1991 Bresee spoke as part of a Wednesday evening Lenten series when Rev. Paul Zahl was rector at Saint James. Dr. Bresee was "worshiping in the presence of the past" and grateful for how the past had shaped his future.

NOTE: Bartels paid a fee to the University of SC Press for permission to include Bresee's excerpts.

CHAPTER NINE

More about Saint James in the 1920s and 1930s

Saint James' worshippers, along with their community members, saw many changes occur with the ushering in of a new century. The worldwide changes brought industrialism, electricity, telephones, and cars. In 1905 W.W. McLeod drove the first vehicle over the James Island Bridge (just east of today's Wappoo Bridge),[1] and the wooden Stono Bridge connecting James and Johns Island opened in 1931.[2] Folly Road became the first paved road on the island about 1930.[3] Local residents became participants in organizations such as the Confederate Veterans, James Island Agricultural Society,[4] the James Island Yacht Club, and the Riverland Terrace Riding and Driving Club.[5] Some worked on local dairy farms, such as that run by the Lawton family. Some became residents in the new subdivision called Riverland Terrace laid out in 1925.[6] Many continued to farm the land, producing truck crops such as corn, peas, and potatoes.[7]

During this time period, minutes of Saint James' vestry and annual meetings demonstrate a necessary frugality. A specific example pertains to the need for new carpet for the church. On April 24, 1916, the minutes state, "Dr. Ellis then brought up the question of a new carpet for the church and upon discussion offered a resolution that Mrs. Bee and Mrs. Lawton be appointed a committee of two ladies to look into the matter and should they agree that a new carpet was necessary, they call upon the treasurer for the amount necessary to buy it. This motion was lost." Almost a year later in the April 21, 1917 minutes, the following is recorded, "The question of a new carpet was then brought up by Dr. Ellis and it was determined to start a personal subscription to try and raise money for this purpose. Thirty-five dollars was raised at the meeting. Vestry members agreed that the present time was not the proper time to buy but that the money could be held until prices were more reasonable." In April 5, 1920, minutes say, "The carpet question next came up," and since only $179 had been collected and $300 was needed, vestry members were again "compelled to delay buying until the remainder of the $300 was raised." In this same meeting it was "determined we could not continue our present schedule of church finances…as there was no money put aside to provide for repairs to church property nor to meet any extraordinary expenses," so the vestry voted to raise the rent on land belonging to the church to $7.00 per acre. Vestry minutes from March 28, 1921, indicated that the church could not count on much money being earned from rental farm land due to boll weevil problems and low prices of farm products.

In John Rivers' minutes from April 17, 1922, the vestry wanted to beautify the grounds with azaleas, but there were no funds available; Dr. Ellis offered to do some of the labor on the grounds at no cost to the church. April 21, 1924 vestry minutes reveal concerns about heating for the church building, a fence around church property, a church shed, and a sign put up on Folly Road to guide visitors to the church; still, funds fell short, and apparently the vestry often made up the difference out of their own pockets for needed improvements.

Rev. Wallace Martin was named rector at Saint James on July 1, 1921, and was serving at the church during the bicentennial celebration in 1930.[8] The Women's Auxiliary of the church gave a Bible in memory of Reverend A. E. Cornish, former rector. Several members of the parish gave an altar service book. Mrs. P. C. Coker gave a pair of Eucharistic candlesticks in memory of her husband, Priestley Cooper Coker. On Easter 1930 a brass processional cross was given as a memorial to Lila Rivers Means, sister of Miss Martha L. Rivers, organist.[9]

Albert S. Thomas' *Protestant Episcopal Church in South Carolina* provides the following detailed summary:

> In 1922, the Reverend Wallace Martin, coming from Montrose, Pennsylvania, became Rector in connection with his duties as Chaplain and Superintendent of the Seamen's Home (in Charleston). He continued in charge until his resignation in January, 1945. In 1922, the wardens were John Rivers and St. J. A. Lawton; the secretary and treasurer, John Rivers. During the period, the membership of the Church only increased slightly, from 37 to 41, but the Sunday School went from 16 to 55. The music was much improved by the introduction of a vested choir, Miss Martha Rivers being the efficient organist. On September 9, 1930, the Church celebrated its bi-centennial; Mr. Martin conducted the services, Bishop Thomas preached a historical sermon. A sketch of the Church by Capt. E.L. Rivers, revised and completed by Daniel W. Ellis, was published.[10]

Although the bicentennial was celebrated in 1930, more extensive historical research would indicate that the two-hundredth birthday should have been in 1920.

On a statewide level, the Diocese of South Carolina divided into two dioceses due to the growth of the diocese (the number of communicants had doubled) and the demands on the bishop, who had been trying to visit each Episcopal church in the diocese annually. In 1922 the General Convention of the Episcopal Church added the Upper Diocese.[11]

Many of the vestry minutes of the 1920s pertain to the most ethical use of the financial gain from the land that had been bequeathed to the church or bought for the church by former parishioners. On April 5, 1920, Mr. Bee proposed that the vestry consider trading Parrot Point for a forty-acre tract of land known as "The Farm," but the vestry did not do this because they determined that Parrot Point was worth more. Also, they might confront legal issues since the will of Mr. Harvey indicated that the land "should not change hands at all." In July 1932 the vestry decided to lease Parrot Point for a ten-year period to Tudor Chisolm.

Many of the vestry minutes recording meetings from the 1920s and 1930s address policies pertaining to the church's cemetery. In April 17, 1922, vestrymen expressed the concern that "strangers" might buy in the "enclosure," meaning the cemetery. Creating this concern was their perception that James Island was growing and that newcomers might see the church's cemetery as a community cemetery open to everyone. Vestry members decided that the existing enclosure should be reserved for those who had been members of the community and parish. They extended the fence to the back embankment, and if any "stranger" applied for burial rights, he could apply for the new track and possibly be assigned a spot in the rear of the present enclosure, at a charge of $10, but the rector was the one to whom applications must be made. In April 1932 the vestry established a committee to "superintend" the erection of all monuments to be placed in the cemetery. In actuality, many members of Saint James Episcopal are buried in James Island Presbyterian cemetery, and, likewise, Presbyterians are buried at Saint James because they often worshipped in both churches and often wanted to be buried with family members, who might technically be members of the other denomination.

September 9, 1928's vestry minutes indicate that the men decided to order what were called "duplex envelopes," with the offering put in the "red side" set aside for missions and the offering put in the "parish side" set aside to pay for Sunday school expenses and the future growth of the parish.

If someone stands facing north, looking at the front of the sixth church built in 1959, he can still look east and west over his shoulders and see huge oaks that once outlined the original dirt road. It came up close to the brick pillars, wrought iron gate, and chain-link fence that ran along the road-side property line of the fifth church building. Marked by a thin line on a map dated 1932, the dirt road curved up to the church and then curved slightly back out, extending through a wooded area not far from James Island Creek. The foresight of the vestrymen enabled them to determine that any future expansion of the facilities would be blocked by this dirt road running so close to the front of the fifth church building. Thus, through a gift by William McLeod and through the vestry's negotiation with the highway department, a new dirt road was set about 150 to 200 feet away from the current church, and the original dirt road was abandoned as a public thoroughfare. Ultimately, this replacement road became Camp Road, a two-lane paved street, connecting Folly Road and Riverland Drive. What was once the original dirt road has been absorbed into an expanded lawn in front of the church with an avenue of live oaks leading out to the new Camp Road. The parking area is set on both sides of the old avenue in front of the parish hall. Gone with the original dirt road are also the front chain-link fence setting off the cemetery and the wrought iron gate leading up to the church. The current church and the Ministry Center would have been impossible to build, as they are today, without this relocation of the road passing in front of Saint James.[12]

Saint James struggled financially in the 1930s, as much of the nation did during the Depression. According to records of receipts by the parish treasurers during this period, "Even as late as the 1930's, financial support was limited and a pledge of fifty cents a week was apparently considered munificent [very generous] by the relatively few supportive parishioners."[13]

In spite of limited incomes during these two decades, proper decorum was maintained through acceptable dress of the day for Sunday services. Many of the ladies donned gloves and wore large hats, frequently decorated with artificial flowers and fruit, held in place with hat pins often pushed through their hair styled in buns. Their Sunday skirts and dresses were likely to be few in number, modest in style, and homemade. The ladies of this era never even considered wearing pants to church.

In the 1920s, if in Charleston on Saturday, a man might get a shoe shine for a dime, a haircut for a quarter, and a shave for fifteen cents more so he would look good for Sunday worship. Men's church suits sold for as little as $12.50; others were made at tailor shops. They were often sold with two pairs of pants, the reason being that pants wore out before the jacket. Formerly, men's shirts had unattached collars, which were fastened in place with buttons, enabling a man to change a dirty collar before he had to have the whole shirt washed. A gentleman wore a hat, which he tipped to ladies and removed in buildings. Unlike other public buildings, which often provided a place for a man to hang his hat, churches made no provisions for the hanging of hats, so men usually placed their hats on the pews beside them. For the boys, a coming-of-age event was discarding their knee-length pants "knickers" and getting full-length pants.[14]

Many additional fashions and guidelines have come and gone over the decades, such as when to wear black and white and how long hem lengths had to be for a woman to be "ladylike." Today's church attire has lost much of this formality, embracing a much broader acceptance of variety and much more casual clothing.

Several vestry minutes address issues pertaining to the music of the church. Limited funds made it challenging to vest a choir, replace worn hymnals, and hire an organist when

Martha Rivers became ill. Two front pews were changed to right angles so that the choir would not have their backs to the congregation during worship.[15]

On June 25, 1938, the bishop consecrated two seven-branch candelabra, which were memorials to Miss Anna Keim Stauffer and Mrs. Rose Perry Posey.[16] In light of the economy of this time period, such a costly gift was even more significant.

The closing paragraph of "A History of St. James' Episcopal Church" is as follows:

> The property of Saint James' church has been of major importance in its history. From the time of the first charter, 1831, rents derived from the church lands have provided a none too large but yet steady income which, wisely handled by the vestry, has enabled it to accomplish much that would have been otherwise impossible. In fact, it is highly improbable that the present building could have been erected had not the accumulated proceeds of the church lands been at the disposal of the vestry.[17]

The so-called "Lost Generation," that followed World War I, labeled many "lost" in the sense that they had lost their faith, family ties, long-term goals, and moral codes. Then came the "Roaring Twenties," the onset of industrialism, the crash of the Stock Market, the Depression—all these impacted the worshippers of Saint James and worshippers elsewhere in the 1920s and 1930s. Yet in these daily living experiences was the living presence of the Holy Spirit, enabling those faithful to Him to cope with changes, survive throughout an unstable economy, appreciate the resources entrusted to them, and sustain a sanctuary to worship their Creator and Provider.

CHAPTER TEN

1940s—A Decade of Stewardship and Outreach

On March 10, 1941, long-time Saint James parishioner Mr. John Rivers died.[1] He had been the vestry's secretary and treasurer since 1905, totaling a service of thirty-six years in this role. Taking over these duties, Mr. William Ellis McLeod served in this same capacity from March 1941 until February 1961. Their copious pages of handwritten vestry notes indicate their conscientious endeavors to record accurate minutes for Saint James' vestry meetings and annual parish meetings. These minutes portray politeness, formality, graciousness, and gratitude as well as a good balance of details and summaries.

Parishioners' gifts were appreciated during this era. For example. F. W. Clement, vestryman and superintendent of the church school for a number of years, bequeathed $200 to help maintain the church yard. Later the vestry received permission from Mrs. Clement to set aside this $200 for plans of a contemplated parish house.[2] In 1942 the McLeod family donated a brass altar cross in memory of William W. and Hallie E. McLeod.[3] In December 1943 the congregation received a monetary gift of $25 from Rev. Dr. C. A. Jessup of Buffalo, New York, a former winter resident of Charleston and guest preacher at Saint James each year during Lent. On January 23, 1944, the congregation decided unanimously to utilize Rev. Jessup's gift to purchase a silver wafer box to be used at communion.

For decades the vestry minutes indicate that about the same dozen churchmen served as faithful vestry members. At the April 11, 1944 parish meeting, these minutes were recorded: "Election of the vestry for the ensuing year was then entered into and this touched off a somewhat heated discussion of the qualifications of vestrymen and the interest they should take in the church as well as the example they should set. When this flurry was over, …the same vestry [were] elected."

From 1922-1944 Rev. Wallace Martin served as the priest for Saint James. Porwoll included a significant paragraph in his book *Against All Odds,* summarizing the priesthood of Rev. Martin:

> As the parish changed from country to suburb, Wallace Martin led its Episcopal church through twenty-three years of ministry. His sudden death on Good Friday 1946 was a blow not only to St. Andrew's...but it was felt throughout the Lowcountry. While serving at St. Andrew's, Reverend Martin also cared for other distressed parishes—all while serving full-time as chaplain of the Harriott Pinckney Home for Seamen in Charleston. Nearly every year from 1923 until 1946, Wallace was not only chaplain of the Seamen's Home and priest in charge of St. Andrew's, but he was rector of St. John's, Berkeley, and St. James's, James Island, and either St. John's, Johns Island, or Trinity, Black Oak, Pinopolis. For his twenty-five years at the Seamen's House, Martin was remembered for his tenacity in the face of daunting conditions: He was "often in the face of great discouragement due to failure of support, often forced to the necessity of 'making bricks without straw'."[4]

The following touching tribute was offered in honor of Rev. Wallace Martin in April 1946:

> Coming from the North to a section of the country which clung to the history of the Sixties [1860s], he was called upon to meet situations requiring great tactfulness. His love for his fellow man and his ability to see the other point of view enabled him never to offend...He was guided by a Higher Power...We mourn...in losing one whose life on Earth should ever be to us an inspiration to follow in the footsteps of our Maker as he did. He followed Him daily doing good unostentatiously, and on Good Friday afternoon he was called [by] his Master to the higher life beyond sunset's radiant glow.
> Signed by J. A. Lawton, Senior Warden, and William H. Mikell, Junior Warden[5]

Rt. Rev. Albert S. Thomas, a retired bishop of the diocese, acted as *locum tenens* from January 1945 until April 1946.[6]

The 1940s were turbulent during World War II. In the minutes from an annual parish meeting April 26, 1943, a report from the Women's Auxiliary shows "considerable interest and activity by the small group in spite of the shortages of gasoline and tires caused by the war." In some 1944 vestry minutes, the following is recorded regarding the gift ordered with

Rev. Jessup's Christmas offering: "The sterling silver wafer box was ordered on the 24th of January, 1944, but, due to scarcity of silver and the restrictions placed on silver by the government on account of the war, there was some delay in getting this piece. However, it finally arrived and was consecrated by the rector, the Rev. Wallace Martin, at the Easter communion service on the 9th April 1944."

Even the property called Parrot Point was impacted by the war, according to the vestry minutes:

> There was some complaint about undue trespassing at the Parrots Point property. Three of the group of four who lease this property are now in the armed service of the nation and, although the place is supposed to be sub-rented, it seems that it is all but abandoned except that its rent is paid regularly. This is not only an undesirable condition but it involves depredation and constitutes a risk of fire, especially since the property is growing up in a thicket. The rector appointed [vestrymen] to see the renters and ask their cooperation in remedying this situation.[7]

Many of Saint James' veterans who served during World War II in the Navy, Army, Coast Guard, Air Force, and Marine Corps are buried in the church cemetery. They are listed, as follows:

> John S. Brinson (1924-1999), Robert A. Dickerson (1921-1999), Edward R. Faulkner (1926-1993), Louis C. Fischer, Jr. (1911-1985), Joseph E. Flint (1924-1980), Frank Freeman (1916-1985), Ralph L. Gelhken (1920-2001), Herbert B. Getsinger (1921-1971), Edward L. Grimball, Jr. (1913-1984), Clifford T. Hampson (1917-1983), Floyd R. Harper (1911-1978), John W. Haizlip (1924-1996), Joseph H. Moody (1938-1978), Edward W. Murray (1917-1975), William P. Musgrove (1920-1970), Royal G. Powless (1925-2001), J. Lynn Rhodemyre (1908-1995), Lemuel C. Sansbury (1917-2003), Donald S. Smith (1914-1982), Edmond D. Taylor, Sr. (1920-1996), and Croskeys R. Welch (1920-1993).[8]

Often times a citizen interested in buying some of Saint James' land would approach a vestryman, and after a thorough discussion, the vestry member provided an answer to the potential buyer. Usually the response was, "The vestry is not interested in selling that piece of property at this time." Obviously, they were good stewards of the church's land, weighing the intended purposes of the purchasers as well as profit gained for parishioners' best interests. Records demonstrate that they were more likely to sell land for the benefit of local schools and other churches. The vestry consisted of astute businessmen who could "drive a deal," yet they also demonstrated a sense of fairness and integrity for both the buyers and sellers.

Another land issue arose on April 11, 1944. Vestry minutes include the following:

> The secretary [McLeod] stated that he had been approached by a committee from the colored Methodist church on the Island, who said they would like to buy the land on which their church stands. This lot and considerable body of adjacent land belong to St. James' church. The colored church holds a long-term lease on the lot which expires on the first of January 1967, the rental being one cent a year. After considerable discussion, a motion was carried that the secretary be instructed to inform the colored Methodist committee that the vestry of St. James' church does not wish to sell the lot in question.

Vestry notes from September and November of 1946 record discussions with the Sanitary and Drainage Commission in regard to building a right-of-way to give access from the relocated road to the church grounds. Saint James also requested the right to obstruct other side roads in the vicinity that had been gradually used without permission. The vestry asked the Commission for a deed and title to that part of the road, which had been abandoned when the new road had been relocated a few years earlier.

Pertaining to the November 8, 1946 vestry meeting, minutes stated the following:

> [A] discussion followed concerning the question of selling to the colored Methodist church on the Island the piece of land on which their church is located and enough adjacent land for their congregation to use as a burying ground. Finally, on motion of Mr. Mikell, duly seconded, a vote was taken to ascertain whether or not the vestry really wished to sell this piece of land…The vote was six to one in favor of selling. However, no further action was taken in regards to price, terms, etc. The colored congregation are very anxious to buy the land in question.

These minutes go on to say that because of the Methodist church's need for this property, the Saint James vestry felt that it would be non-Christian to refrain from this sale. In February 1947, the vestry voted that the Methodist church be sold the land that was the site of their church building and adjacent land for burials. The deed stipulated that the property was to be used only for religious and burial purposes. Vestry records from December 1947 specify that the selling price was $2,000. Records from February 27, 1947 indicate that the purchaser was Payne's Chapel, R. M. U. E. located at 1560 Camp Road.

Bishop Carruthers anticipated the Civil Rights Era with his advocacy for representation of black congregations in the Diocese of South Carolina. In 1945 the Upper Diocese of South Carolina voted to give membership to black churches in their diocese, but the Diocese of South Carolina defeated the vote for equality for the black Church, making that diocese the only one in the nationwide Protestant Episcopal Church to exclude any group. Carruthers described this stance as being "indefensible" and said that this decision must change.[9]

The vestry discussed selling timber from church property to generate much-needed funds. A forester had estimated that there was a little over 300,000 board feet of pine of fair quality and about 17,000 board feet of hard wood of somewhat poor quality.[10] Minutes of the congregational meeting on July 28, 1946 reported that the church had earned $1,000 from the sale of timber in 1945. In additional meetings, the vestrymen discussed environmental issues regarding their entrusted property, taking care not to over-cut the forested land and to replant where foresters had removed trees. The vestry notes from May 26, 1948 include details regarding re-seeding of pine and not cutting oak.

According to Mrs. Stackhouse's historical records and some handwritten notes reserved on microfiche (slide 462), "In 1946 electric lights were installed in the church with city current." In 1947 Miss Wilhelmina W. McLeod and Mr. William E. McLeod presented an electric motor for the organ, giving more volume to the music and relieving the organist of the hard work of pumping by her feet.[11]

Often times in this decade, information about those elected to church vestries was considered newsworthy, so in the archives at the Charleston Library, Calhoun Street, one can find articles in the local newspapers listing names of the newly elected men and wardens for Saint James as well as the outgoing vestry.

In August 1946 the vestry minutes report a new plan for election for vestry: "Several … suggestions were made with the idea of bringing the younger men of the Parish into more active participation in the work…of the church." The vestry laid out a three-year, two-year, and one-year rotation plan, stating that "the rotation system is used in many parishes in order to give more of the male communicants of the parish the privilege and experience of serving on the vestry, and…we believe that this procedure will be beneficial to the welfare of our parish." When a vestryman completed his term, he would be ineligible for re-election for one year.[12]

The vestry received a letter written on January 17, 1947, from senior warden St. J. A. Lawton, who was resigning due to poor health. He stated,

> My deep love for the church with which I have been identified for so many years, and my desire that all should be done to promote the proper functioning of the official body, makes me know that someone in good health and able to attend the meetings should be elected in my place to carry on

this sacred work…It is not easy to do this as my love for the church and all that concerns its welfare is very profound but often we should offer up ourselves for the good of the great work.

When Mr. Lawton's letter was read at the January 1947 Annual Parish meeting, the congregation unanimously voted to refuse to accept Mr. Lawton's resignation, and when Mr. McLeod informed Mr. Lawton of the congregation's request that he continue as their warden, he felt honored. However, Mr. Lawton died the next month.

The May 8, 1947 vestry minutes include a tribute as well as a biographical sketch regarding Mr. Lawton:

On the 14th day of February, 1947, Mr. St. John Alison Lawton was called from this life to eternity. He was born in Charleston and was graduated from the Virginia Military Institute where he was esteemed highly by the faculty and cadets…He was a great reader of good literature…In his early manhood he was engaged in architectural work and civil engineering. Later, however, he moved to The Bluff, the ancestral plantation on James Island. Here he grew sea island cotton and truck [crops] and also developed one of the finest herds of Holstein dairy cattle in the state. Some years ago Clemson College awarded him a certificate of merit for "his contribution to agriculture." He was a man of high honor and morality, modesty and refinement and of a retiring and unselfish nature. He loved his home, his fellow man and his church…He served as vestryman and as senior warden in St. James' Church for many years and held other positions of honor and trust in the community. His memory will be cherished by all who knew him as one who had been faithful in all his relations in life…

Included in the vestry notes from November 8, 1946, is a copy of Josiah R. Harvey's will pertaining to Parrot Point. Since the intent of this will would be debated for about the next sixty years, it is included, as follows, to provide specific detail:
Probate Judge's office, Charleston County, Will book H. Page 395

WILL OF JOSIAH R. HARVEY. JAMES ISLAND. ST. ANDREW'S PARISH
I do hereby give and bequeath unto my sister, Mary G. Keely, all my Estate both real and personal, etc.…except my Point Plantation, commonly known or called Parrott's Point, containing fifty acres of high land or thereabouts with all the improvements and appurtenances thereunto belonging which said tract as before mentioned I do give unto her during her life to her use

and benefit to act as she thinks proper and after her death I do give it unto the Episcopal Church of James Island, the said land to be rented out, the proceeds to be applied for the purpose of raising a fund for the support of a minister to perform the duties of said church and no other denomination but the Episcopal Church and the aforesaid land is vested in the charge of the Vestry and the Wardens of said church forever and I do hereby order if any attempt should be made to have said property sold by anyone, it is my will that said property should be taken by the commissioner of the Orphan House to the sole use and benefit of that Institution forever and ever.

Dated August 22, 1837

Dr. Dan Ellis, in his history of Saint James, noted that this fund was earmarked for "clerical leadership," and that it was to revert to the church upon the death of his sister Miss Keely, who died in 1864.[13] In 1946 the vestry discussed whether selling the land to apply proceeds to a rectory would honor the intention of the will to support the rector of Saint James Church. Legal counsel was sought pertaining to quit claims involving both Saint James and the Orphan House. In February of 1947 the vestry conferred with the chancellor of the diocese, Col. Barnwell, who advised against selling the Parrot Point property because such an action could be legally viewed as "a breach of the conditions of the will which would result in a reversion of the property or its proceeds to the heirs of the testator." Col. Barnwell went on to say, however, that there was nothing illegal about the church making a long-term lease on the land. For decades yet to come, the will and the property led to different prospects and proposals, as described in upcoming chapters.

Vestry notes from as early as September 1926 indicate that there had been discussion of the possibility of Saint James sharing a priest with St. John's Episcopal Church. January 1946 vestry notes state that both Saint James and St. John's had been without a rector for a full year, so Bishop Carruthers proposed that the two churches extend a call to World War II army chaplain Rev. Edward Brailsford Guerry, who ultimately served as priest at Saint James from 1946 to 1960.[14] He was born in Atlanta. His father was the Right Rev. William A. Guerry, the eighth bishop in South Carolina. Maj. Gen. William Moultrie, a Revolutionary War hero and former South Carolina governor, was one of Rev. Guerry's ancestors. Rev. Guerry graduated from the University of The South, University of Pennsylvania School of Law, and Virginia Theological Seminary. After a career as a lawyer, he served as a priest in Virginia, North Carolina, and South Carolina.[15]

Guerry's first service at Saint James was on Palm Sunday of April 14, 1946. That Easter he held a united church service with the congregations of James and Johns Island. Both churches soon hosted a combined supper to honor the men of the two parishes who had served in the armed forces during World War II.[16] For years the two congregations remained close, sharing events such as Laymen's League supper meetings, Sunday school picnics at Seabrook Beach, Young People's League's activities, and Thanksgiving services. The two vestries often had joint meetings with both churches' representatives and their shared priest, Rev. Guerry, and then split into separate vestry meetings for their own churches. The minutes of these joint meetings often include the names of Saint James' Episcopal leaders working and worshipping alongside those representing St. John's Episcopal, with surnames known on Johns Island for generations, including Sosnowski, Whaley, Jenkins, Rivers, King, Seabrook, Ashe, and LaRoche. In 1952 St. John's was larger, with 228 communicants. St. James had 136 but would grow significantly in years to come.[17] Dr. Ellis wrote, "In the post World War II period under the able and dynamic leadership of the Rev. Edward B. Guerry, things were beginning to happen."[18]

St. John's of Johns Island and Saint James built a rectory—a house serving as the residence for the priest and his family—on land given in 1947 by the McLeod family (Miss Wilhelmina W. McLeod, Mrs. Rose McLeod Barnwell, and William E. McLeod).[19] This lot was approximately three-fourths of an acre and at the time appraised for $1500.[20] Many of the vestry notes from the 1940s and 1950s have details regarding the annual inspections of the rectory, noting how well it was maintained by the Guerrys and at the same time what improvements (painting, landscaping, water service, etc.) were needed. All costs for the rectory were shared fifty-fifty by the two churches.

During the 1940s the vestry often met in the homes of members as well as at the churches. Sometimes the vestries of Saint James and St. John's met in the Guerrys' home where Mrs. Guerry entertained the wives upstairs while their husbands and Rev. Guerry held their joint meetings downstairs. One may safely assume that even though the women could not serve on the vestry at this time, they made their views known through their husbands and had an impact on the churches' decision-making. Then, as recorded by Mr. McLeod, the men and women came together afterwards for refreshments, and he often concluded the minutes with the statement, "A good time was had by all." Other minutes indicate that annual parish meetings were preceded by covered dish suppers. The historical records of both parishes demonstrate the strong bonds between the two churches in the 1940s.

At a congregational meeting in July of 1946, Saint James parishioners considered the building of a parish house to provide space for offices, Sunday school rooms, and common meeting areas. W. H. Mikell, chairman of the committee, went to Pinopolis to examine a parish house, was pleased with much of the design, but considered the rooms to be too small for Saint James' anticipated growth. Vestry minutes from August 1, 1946 state, "The parish house project was then discussed and argued in a friendly way." The vestry decided to hold a campaign, asking the congregation to donate $3500 to add to the amount of $2,559.76 that E. C. Morrison, Sr., had reported earlier as being in the account for this building. In 1948 construction began for a parish hall, a cinder block structure covered by stucco, costing about

$12,000 to $15,000.[21] On the outside walls of the parish house were monuments to the Minott and Rivers families.[22] A bronze tablet bearing Rev. Guerry's name as well as the names of W. H. Mikell and W. G. Meggett, wardens for 1948, was placed near the door.[23] Mr. and Mrs. E. C. Morrison donated an "electric refrigerator and an electric range."[24]

Having completely paid for the parish house, the congregation held a dedication ceremony on October 30, 1949, with about one hundred twenty-five people in attendance and the Bishop of the Diocese, Right Rev. Thomas N. Carruthers, officiating in the ceremony.[25] Dr. Ellis wrote in his church history, "In 1949 the first construction of any sort in the past fifty years occurred with the building of the parish house."[26]

On May 8, 1947, Mr. W. Gresham Meggett, who was also one of the public school trustees, presented a letter to the vestry in regard to the school board's proposition to purchase fifteen acres of church land for a centralized and consolidated school with space for an athletic field. In September the vestry had a survey made of the fifteen acres on the south side of Camp Road, a short distance west of Folly Road, and then proposed to sell each acre for $200. However, a legal issue regarding a will first had to be addressed. Minutes from the vestry meeting on January 18, 1948 state the following:

> The Deed to the tract of land of which the 15 acres is a part had been conveyed in 1895 to W. G. Hinson as Treasurer and not to St. James Church itself which had not been incorporated….the Church was later incorporated but …the property had never been legally transferred to the Church as a Corporate Body…Saint James Church…[was proven to be] the true owner [of] the tract of land containing 103 acres more or less which [had been] conveyed by Martha Love Walpole to William G. Hinson as Treasurer of its church.

Ultimately, fifteen acres were sold for $3,000 to School District #3, Charleston County, for the location of James Island High School, where teens on the island were educated for decades until the original James Island High merged with Fort Johnson High on Fort Johnson Road and was renamed James Island High. What had been the location of the original island high school became the site for Fort Johnson Middle. Currently, it is the site of the modern Camp Middle, where the two island middle schools were merged in 2017.

A note among the women's church records from November of 1948 tells about Mrs. Wilson reporting that her committee had purchased the china for the parish hall—100 dinner plates, 100 bread and butter plates, and 100 cups and saucers, all at a cost of $25. They had placed a down payment of $10.00 and earned the balance due of $15 at their bazaar. These limited sums might amuse a modern reader. Yet these women servants made ends meet with their fundraising and frugality to provide fellowship within a family of worshippers.

The vestry minutes of January 6, 1949, include "Rules and Regulations Governing Burials in St. James Episcopal Churchyard," stating what funds would be appropriated to the cemetery, that burials had to have the consent of the wardens, and that fees were raised from $10 to $15 for members, and $50 for non-members. Persons born or reared on James Island and whose families were members of Saint James Episcopal Church or the James Island Presbyterian Church and/or whose families were already buried in Saint James churchyard could be buried there as well. Those members who had moved away, such as to make a livelihood or due to marriage, would still have the privilege of burial in the churchyard upon application to the committee and approval of the vestry. More details address the clearing of plots, the size of plots, and the necessity of presenting sketches of all tombstones to be erected beforehand to get the cemetery committee's approval. Based on previous years of vestry notes, one can assume that African Americans were also buried in or near the Saint James Episcopal Cemetery; however, on December 19, 1950, the vestry voted that no more burials be allowed "in the colored burying ground north of the church yard."

As one reflects on this decade of the 1940s, he is made all the more aware that Christian faith is not limited to Sundays in the sanctuary. Acting on their faith, the priests, parishioners, and vestrymen conducted legal transactions with integrity, interacted with other parishes as brothers and sisters-in Christ, honored those who went to Glory before them by providing a place of burial, exhibited God's gift of hospitality in their homes and community, served as good stewards of natural and manmade resources, and even risked their lives and sometimes made the ultimate sacrifice in service to their country when called to war. What a legacy!

CHAPTER ELEVEN

1950s—A Decade of Growth

Vestry minutes of the 1940s and 1950s are reminders of how rural James Island still was. For example, on September 29, 1948, the vestry discussed the need of paving Camp Road in front of the church (less than one mile) and voted to go before the county legislature delegation in Charleston to recommend the paving. At the January 28, 1951 meeting, they discussed asking people living within the vicinity of Saint James to keep their hogs and cows from roaming around on the church grounds. As late as September 1958 the vestry voted to send the South Carolina State Highway Department a letter requesting a "traffic control light (red, green and yellow) to be installed at the intersection of Folly Road and Camp Road." Copies of the letter were sent to other James Island civic and religious organizations, asking them to likewise make this same request. As for technology, vestry minutes from July 1959 state, "The matter of installing a telephone in the Parish House was brought up but after some discussion, the cost of the service was considered high, and the matter was dropped."

Minutes frequently reveal how Saint James' vestrymen sought ways to use the church's natural resources to meet budgets and to sustain the church's facilities. For example, on January 20, 1950, minutes state that the state highway department wanted to remove earth from about ten acres of church land to mix with asphalt for road surfacing. The church was offered $300 per acre, with the highway department having ten years to complete their operations. However, soil samples indicated high amounts of clay, making the soil unsuitable for the highway project.

Vestry minutes repeatedly demonstrate how parishioners themselves completed jobs on behalf of the church either at no cost or at a reduced fee. For example, in May of 1948

Read and Read Realtors volunteered to handle the sale of a piece of land for no financial compensation. In October 1950 Mr. McLeod paid for the new flooring on the porch of the church.

Even non-parishioners helped to support Saint James. In December 1953 the vestry discussed the details of Miss Wilhelmina McLeod's will in which she had designated funds for Saint James' cemetery, campus, and buildings. Miss McLeod was actually a member of First Scots Presbyterian Church in downtown Charleston. Minutes state, "Her beautiful Christian character has profoundly influenced the life of this Parish, being a generous supporter of St. James, even though not a member, but she was a resident of James Island."

At the January 28, 1951 congregational meeting, William Hinson Mikell was referred to as "the moving spirit in the church...served faithfully, devotedly, and most ably as junior and senior warden." In spite of his being seriously ill in a Charleston infirmary, he was elected by acclamation as senior warden. However, he died "greatly lamented" on February 23, 1951. During the March 13, 1951 congregational meeting, all stood in silence in his honor, and his son, William Hinson Mikell, Jr., was unanimously elected to the vestry.

Realizing the value of church surveys, wills, and other liturgical documents as well as their communion silver and other treasured items, the vestry decided on March 14, 1952 to purchase a safe.

On August 13, 1952, the house that had been built in 1872 on Parrot Point was totally destroyed by fire, presumably, according to vestry minutes, because of lightning. No one was there at the time that the eighty-year-old house burned. At a following meeting in May the vestry appropriated $6500 to build a new house in which a caregiver of the property could live.

The vestry made several decisions on behalf of the young people at Saint James. In May of 1950 they voted to allocate $10 to help defray the expenses for the daily vacation Bible school. Ten dollars paid for much more decades ago. In July of 1950 Sunday school was temporarily closed due to an outbreak of poliomyelitis. At the congregational meeting January 28, 1951, Mr. Meggett urged parents not just to send their children to Sunday school but also to attend with them. In January of 1953 the church started a nursery for infants, toddlers, and preschoolers. Donations were given to what was then called Porter Military Academy, a private, local Episcopal-sponsored boys' school, and to York Orphanage. In March of 1954 Mrs. E. T. Brown requested that Saint James sponsor a Brownie troop—#38, which remained active for years.

Rev. Guerry was the first to hold regular Sunday services at Saint James since 1861.[1] In the November 12, 1952 minutes from a joint meeting of Saint James and St. John's, the vestrymen discussed what a huge undertaking it was for Rev. Guerry to serve as rector to what was then "the biggest territory in the diocese," which included James Island, Johns Island, Folly Beach, and Wadmalaw Island. At that time Saint James alone had sixty-four families and one hundred forty-nine communicants. For the most part, vestry minutes state that Rev. Guerry's salary was increased about $100 annually by Saint James members.

As a trustee of Porter Military Academy (now Porter-Gaud School), Rev. Guerry was credited with keeping the private Charleston school viable. Within the diocese he took on many leadership roles including the Board of Directors of the Church Home on Bee Street, the board for Camp St. Christopher, and historiographer of the diocese.[2]

The October 4, 1953 issue of *The News and Courier* published an article by Frances Hayden, a long-time member of Saint James, entitled "St. James Church to be Included in Garden Tour." The opening paragraph states, "St. James Protestant Episcopal Church is one of the four homes and churches included in the tour of Historic James Island and Fall Flower Show of the Riverland Terrace Garden Club to be held Friday from 3 to 6 p.m. Tea is included in the tour and will be served at the parish house of St. James Church."[3] Her article goes on to include much of the information given chronologically in this book.

When William H. Simmons, Jr. first became a member of Saint James, he recalled the fifth church structure, as follows: "Saint James…at that time [1953] was a small quaint structure which seated eighty people. The organ was pumped by an old vacuum cleaner motor… Many times, when the pews were filled…we would sit on the front porch or steps."[4]

More significantly, on the national scene, Separate but Equal initiatives and Civil Rights were being debated, with major legal cases being decided by the Supreme Court, especially regarding the integration of public schools. In 1954 Bishop Thomas Carruthers again reprimanded the diocese and reminded churches in the Diocese of South Carolina that "the canons state that any baptized or confirmed Episcopalian is eligible to attend services at any Episcopal church."[5]

Reflecting the political stance held by the majority of Southern white residents of the 1950s, Rev. Guerry issued a letter in May 1954, stating why he and his congregations opposed these rulings, calling them "unrealistic and unfortunate" in the title of his letter. Among reasons that he gave were the following: these movements were splitting opponents into "quarreling factions" and causing "discord, confusion, and a sharp conflict of views." He felt that the Supreme Court had "gone beyond [its] judicial function" and had taken on authority that should be reserved for the individual states. In spite of his strong stand against integration of schools, Rev. Guerry ended his published letter, as follows:

> Here we are, two great…races living on the same soil. The leaders of the two races must now work out this grave educational problem in such a way that the welfare of both races will be preserved. May the two races remain calm, exercising toleration and restraint, and continue to live together in Christian charity, in mutual courtesy and respect so that in the world to come, which is our real destiny, we may possess life everlasting through

faith in our Lord and Savior, Jesus Christ. (letter is preserved in Saint James' historical documents)

In February 1959 the vestry held an informal discussion, suggesting that their church should survey their facilities and give some thought to establishing a parochial school in case an emergency with racially integrated schools on the island should arise.

Just as the inside of the church was cared for, so was the outside. Foundations were rebuilt for four of the very old horizontal marble gravestones in the churchyard, "as they were unsightly and gave the appearance of neglect." Reports included that "six more such tombs…are in very bad condition and mar the beauty and the peaceful air of the churchyard."[6] The cemetery has required ongoing work throughout three centuries.

While household budgets are often limited, so are church budgets. In the December 6, 1954 vestry minutes, the vestry debated whether they could afford to buy a used adding machine, and in September of 1957 vestrymen proposed that Saint James and St. John's buy a used typewriter to share. However, an expensive purchase was made in November 1955 when the vestry bought a Wurlitzer electric organ for $4800 with a forty-watt tone cabinet.

Saint James sold 7.4 acres to School District #3 of Charleston County for $9,480. This transaction had been initiated by Mr. Meggett because a new "white graded school" was needed. This tract of land was described as being located on Camp Road and adjacent to an African American Methodist church (Payne Church).[7] In years to follow this school became known as James Island Middle.

The communicant membership had increased to 157 in 1954.[8] By 1959 Saint James had 102 families, thirteen individuals, and 245 confirmed members.[9]

As was to become the custom at Saint James pertaining to sponsoring deacons and priests, on March 9, 1954, John Rivers was admitted as a candidate for Holy Orders. Later Dr. Ellis wrote, "In 1956 occurred the ordination of John Rivers to the Deaconate. This was the first such occasion to be celebrated at Saint James, and the Rev. Mr. Rivers is the first priest to emanate from the St. James congregation."[10]

At the close of the decade, as much time and energy were being put into designing, building, and paying for a new—the sixth—church on the site, the congregation was also weighing what to do with the old church—the fifth building on the site. As early as April 1957 the vestry considered but rejected a proposal to move the old church to a new mission sponsored by St. Michael's Church some distance north of Charleston above Remount Road. At a March 1958 vestry meeting, the rector read canons of the church on the de-consecrating of churches in order to inform vestrymen about that process if they decided not to keep the fifth building as a sanctuary. On December 10, 1958 the vestry decided to move the fifth building to the east of the front of the new church. A gift of $3,000 from Miss Martha Rivers enabled the vestrymen to move the little church.

In the same year the Baptist denomination wanted Saint James to sell them a site for a new Baptist church on Camp Road. Initially the vestry "gave sympathetic consideration to this proposition but deferred action to a future meeting."[11] Eventually, in November of 1957, the vestry agreed to sell to the James Island Baptist Church not less than four but not more than five acres of cleared land. In January of 1958 the vestry discussed the price they had set on this land and considered Mr. Wilson's views that they had set "too high a price." He told the vestry that "this is a body of Christians we are dealing with and that St. James Church should govern itself accordingly." Therefore, at the next January meeting the vestry decided to sell to the Baptist church three acres for $3,000 per acre and a fourth acre for $2,000 if they wanted it. In March of 1958 the vestry decided to sell a little over eighty-four acres to Ernest Sterling for $127,260. Vestry minutes and attached documents reveal a body of church leaders who were ethical, astute businessmen familiar with drafting contracts consisting of formal and legal phrasing.

In 1959 a plaque was presented in honor of W. G. Hinson and Captain E. L. Rivers for sustaining Saint James Church, especially when funds were meager and their management of resources and finances was so wise.[12]

By 1958 the vestry had made some important decisions regarding the building of the sixth church. The Colonial style was chosen instead of the gothic style.[13] The vestry studied thirty-one sheets of plans and drawings of the proposed church.[14] In March of 1959 they determined the inscription on the cornerstone: "Established A.D. 1730, 6th church on this site: 1730, 1733, 1787, 1853, 1898." (More current research indicates that the congregation which became Saint James was worshipping as early as 1720.) Copious details were addressed pertaining to floors, doors, pews, paint, colors, and furnishings. Plans had to be made for the proper re-interment of human bone fragments and coffins that were exhumed in making the excavation for the foundation of the new church.[15] Hours of discussion pertained to what land could be sold to help fund the building of this new church.

The steeple of Saint James' church is a significant part of its structure. The architect recommended steel reinforcing rods in the steeple for safety and strength.[16] A steeple pointing its congregation to the heavens is testimonial, serving as a symbol of man's fidelity to a cause from above. An illuminated steeple bears witness to God, a light shining in darkness.[17] Saint James' steeple is a theological icon.

In a *News and Courier* newspaper article published on Sunday, May 10, 1959, the opening paragraph states, "The cornerstone will be laid today, the first Sunday after Ascension Day, for the new St. James Protestant Episcopal Church on James Island."[18] The rest of Marjorie Campbell's article is so rich in information and detail that it deserves quoting:

> The brick and steel structure now taking form is the sixth church to occupy
> the site amid moss-draped oaks on Camp Road. Nearing completion beside
> it is the remodeled and enlarged parish house.

Both the church, designed to seat 332 persons, and the parish house enlargement, more than doubling church school classroom space, were necessitated by the steady growth of membership in the suburban church which was organized as a chapel as early as 1730 [1720 according to other reliable sources].

The cornerstone for the new edifice will be laid in ceremonies set for 4 o'clock this afternoon. Afterward, a reception and open house are planned in the parish house.

The church is being constructed by Dawson Engineering Co. for $134,792 and is expected to be completed by Sept. 1. The parish house was remodeled at a cost of $58,852 by Suburban Construction Co. and is scheduled to be completed in a matter of weeks. Simons, Lapham and Mitchell of Charleston were architects for the combined project.

The Rev. Edward B. Guerry, rector of St. James Church, will officiate at this afternoon's service. The cornerstone will be laid in place by the Right Rev. Thomas N. Carruthers, bishop of the Protestant Episcopal Diocese of South Carolina.

Also participating will be the Right Rev. Albert S. Thomas retired bishop of the diocese; a number of communicants of the church and other clergymen of the diocese. Bonum S. Wilson, senior warden, will deposit a copy of the Holy Bible; William H. Simmons Jr., junior warden, a *Book of Common Prayer*; William E. McLeod, secretary, a roster of officers, vestrymen and communicants of the parish; the Rev. W. R. Haynsworth, executive secretary of the diocese, the last Journal of the Convention of the diocese; the Rev. Franklin Martin, managing editor of the Diocesan publication, *The Diocese*, a copy of the magazine; a representative of the architectural firm, the elevation and floor plans for the new church; and the Rev. John Rivers of Hampton, a history of the church.

There also will be deposited in the copper box to be sealed in the cornerstone a copy of the Constitution of the United States, today's issue of *The News and Courier*, a paper dollar bill and some coins and a copy of the order for the laying of the cornerstone.

The first church building to occupy the site was known to have existed as early as 1730 [1720] and was a chapel of ease to St. Andrew's Parish Church. It was destroyed by a hurricane but was rebuilt by 1733. The second building was thought to have been destroyed during the War of the Revolution. A new chapel was erected about 1787 and in 1831 St. James Church was incorporated and the chapel and the glebe land were transferred to the corporation by the St. Andrew's church.

On or about 1852 the old church was taken down and a new one was built, but it was accidentally burned by a wood fire which had been started by Confederate soldiers. The present church was built in 1898.

The church is located in a rapidly growing residential area. Its communicants, which now number about 250, were only 56 strong in 1945 and 120 in 1950.[19]

Rev. Guerry's remarks made at this ceremony included the following:

> Certain books, historical documents, and other evidences of our American way of life will now be deposited in this copper box, which will be sealed and placed inside the Cornerstone. Thus they may possibly be preserved…in order that the living of some generation of the far distant future may know the ideals, the beliefs, and the fundamental convictions of the people of this Parish, and of our fellow Christians who are with us on this occasion. They will also be benefited by the historical data which we desire to perpetuate.
>
> The life and worship of the people of this Parish constitute a microcosm or small example of the larger life of the people of this State and Nation. The sacred site which the sixth Church is being erected symbolizes this. Furthermore, there are many parishioners here this afternoon who are descendants of the Colonial families of our beloved Low Country of South Carolina.[20]

In a church program entitled "The Order for Laying the Cornerstone of St. James Church James Island, Diocese of South Carolina, The Sunday after Ascension Day, May 10, 1959," the following words were read—some read individually, some read in response, and some read in unison (and some passages omitted):

> *We are gathered together here to lay the Foundation stone of a building which we humbly trust may in due time be consecrated as a House of God.*
>
> *…Let us praise God's Holy Name for the mercy and goodness with which He has so far prospered our work; and let us further devoutly pray that He will… bless all who…help forward its completion, that He will protect from danger those who may be engaged in the building; that He will send his blessing upon our undertaking.*
>
> *…Almighty Lord God, …dwell with Thy Church here on earth; Visit…with Thy loving kindness, this place whereon we lay the foundations of a house to the praise and honor of Thy Holy Name. Let it not be profaned by impiety or put to*

common use...grant that...Thy servants may see Thy work, and their children Thy glory...

Then the bishop, laying his hand upon the stone, prayed the following:

Lord Jesus Christ...the one Foundation, and the chief Cornerstone; Bless what we do now in laying this Stone in Thy Name, and be Thou...the beginning, the increase, and the consummation of this our work, which is undertaken to the glory of Thy Name...

Instructions and blessings in the program for this ceremony read, as follow:

Then, all things being made ready, he shall lay the Stone, striking it three times, with these words: *In the faith of Jesus Christ we place this Foundation Stone, in the Name of God the Father, God the Son, and God the Holy Ghost. Amen.*

Then the bishop continued:

Here let the true faith and fear of God with brotherly love, ever abide; and by this place now set apart with prayer, and with the invocation and praise of the Most Holy Name, be evermore the Temple of the Most High God...Amen.

The service continued with the following prayers:

Almighty...God, ...Receive our supplications and prayers...for all Estates of men in Thy Holy Church, especially for those who have given of their substance to this good work; that every member..., in his vocation and ministry, may truly and godly serve Thee...O God,... be ever at hand...to protect... the builders of this house; keep them in their labour from all sin and profaneness, and shelter them from all accident and peril, that the work, which, through Thy mercy, hath now been begun, may by their labour be brought to a happy end through Jesus Christ our Lord. Amen.[21]

These are profound words for a profound event, reminding the congregation not to take lightly the solemnness and sacrifices involved in building a place of worship where the sacraments would be shared and souls would be saved.

Saint James reached a milestone when the vestry held their December 16, 1959 meeting in the new church as they sat on boxes and lumber; however, the building was already warm and well lit.

Earlier in his years at Saint James the vestry had asked Rev. Guerry to consider becoming their full-time rector. On October 19, 1959, Mr. Guerry shared this gracious statement of resignation:

> After much indecision, great distress of soul and mind, and weeks of intense thought and fervent prayer,…facts and circumstances indicate that it is God's will for my ministry to continue my Rectorship of St. John's Parish. This decision has not been reached on the basis of personal preference for one Parish over the other….This has been one of the hardest decisions of my life, and I can only hope and trust in God that it is what He wants me to do…My experience in the Army during World War II taught me that indecision is the road to catastrophe.

With great respect, Saint James' vestry accepted Rev. Guerry's resignation, and he became St. Johns' full-time rector in August of 1960.[22] The Rev. Robert M. Watson, Jr., from Durham, North Carolina, was eventually called to Saint James to be the new rector[23] and served from 1960-1962.[24]

Reflecting on this decade of the 1950s, one is awestruck by the leadership of Saint James' clergy and parishioners in conjunction with congregations of other churches, as well as with the citizens of James Island. Laymen and leaders operated on what they perceived to be not just logical and legal guidelines but also Godly principles upon which they based both secular and ecclesiastical decisions. In financially difficult times, they used various resources that had been provided to them, yet they remained considerate of and generous to others. In times of political and societal upheaval, they sought discernment through prayer, counsel, Scripture, and the power of the Holy Spirit. Dealing in the broken world of their day, they still knew that Christ was the head of the church, that Christ loved the church and gave Himself up for her (Ephesians 5). They loved their church. They loved Saint James. Much is to be learned about how to worship and serve today by studying how these men and women worshipped and served before us!

CHAPTER TWELVE

1960s—A Decade of Change

Dr. Ellis' words, which lead up to the conclusion of his history of Saint James, can also introduce this chapter's records of the 1960s, as follow:

> In 1959 the laying of the corner stone of the sixth building took place. The gothic building had become too small and the construction of a new church became the Herculean task of the vestry and the rector. The writer [Dr. Ellis] remembers vestry meetings lasting until 1 A.M.; the problems of funding the project together with decisions as to the design and furnishings seemed endless. A large portion of the money came from sale of lands belonging to the church…About forty thousand dollars was pledged by the congregation.
>
> The year 1960 again marks the end of one era and the beginning of another with the benediction of the new church building, the sixth to occupy the same site. For 240 years St. James had served what was essentially an agricultural community. At best services were held no more than twice a month and pastoral work was limited. In the period 1946-1960, the community was undergoing a progressive change toward suburban status.[1]

Among historical records filed at Saint James is a sermon written by Rev. Robert M. Watson, Jr. addressing a social issue that also became an ecclesiastical one in the 1950s and 1960s. In his sermon he cites the power of the Supreme Court, declares that he must obey the law of the land, and says that his decisions must be based on the premises of righteousness. He emphasizes the Christian doctrine that all men are created and sanctified by God. He goes on to identify himself as a "gradualist." He refers to integration as a human problem so vast in its dimensions, involving the welfare of millions of people living over a wide expanse of territory, that it is far from a simple matter yielding to a quick solution. It requires a massive psychological adjustment, affecting basic attitudes and traditions centuries old, that for good or for evil, make up the pattern of modern society. Rev. Watson says that only Christ can handle something of this magnitude. "Gradualism" involves movement toward a solution; inaction is morally indefensible.

Watson shares that he could trace his ancestors to one great-grandfather who had owned slaves and another who had commanded Confederate troops in Mississippi. However, as a teenage corporal in the army in World War II, Watson found himself on a crowded, dirty troop ship in the Pacific, short on rations. His bunk was by that of a Negro sergeant who shared half of his highly-treasured store of chocolate bars because he knew that Watson was hungry. Reflecting on legal and societal issues as well as his ancestral accounts and personal experiences, Watson states that it is our God-given duty to preserve as well as add to the spiritual riches of our progenitors, gradually shifting to more humane and godly views of mankind.

Since this sermon is dated May 15, 1960, and vestry notes state that Rev. Watson was called July 24, 1960, one can assume that this sermon, based on its introduction, was given in response to the integration of a boys' camp in North Carolina and not given at Saint James. The significance of this sermon is that it reveals this priest's character, insight, and sensitivity to a complex moral and spiritual matter dominating this time period.

While seeking discernment regarding the needs of such complex racial matters, parishioners addressed more church-specific needs, often with gifts. The following church furnishings were made in memory of loved ones:

- Altar, re-table (raised shelf above the altar for the cross, candles, flowers, etc.), reredos (wall behind a church altar) in memory of Ms. Wilhelmina McLeod
- Communion rail in memory of Mr. and Mrs. John Fripp Meggett and Miss Martha L. Rivers
- Pulpit in memory of Mr. Louis de Saussure Chisolm[2]

More gifts were given in January 1966, as follow:

- Alms basin by Mrs. J. R Jeffries
- Funeral pall by Mr. and Mrs. E. L. Grimball, Jr.
- Baptismal font by Mrs. W. H. Langford

Church members Clark and Louise Morrison saved the church brochure for the first service in the sixth new church. The date is given as Sunday, August 28, 1960. In addition to the rector (The Rev. Edward B. Guerry), senior and junior wardens (Mr. W. Gresham Meggett and Mr. William Henry Simmons, Jr.), and secretary/treasurer (Mr. W. E. McLeod), were the following vestrymen: Mr. James S. Baynard, Mr. Daniel L. Jenkins, Jr., Mr. Floyd I. Dovell, Jr., Mr. John A. Keith, Mr. Francis M. Harleston, Mr. E. Clark Morrison, Jr., and Dr. Charles J. Smith. The superintendent of the church school was Mr. Floyd I. Dovel, Jr.; vice-president of the Laymen's League of St. James and St. Johns, Mr. S. S. Bee, Jr.; President of the Women of St. James, Mrs. Wm. C. Easterling; President of the Y.P.S.L., Miss Margaret Rudd; Choir Director, Mrs. Daniel W. Ellis; Director of the Junior Choir, Mrs. John A. Keith; and organist, Hinson L. Mikell, Jr. Many of these names were well known throughout James Island, and many of their descendants have worshipped at Saint James in the decades since.

"The Order of the Benediction of a Church" was led by retired Bishop of South Carolina, The Rt. Rev. A. S. Thomas, formerly of Wadmalaw Island and then resident of Columbia. The sermon was given by the President of the Standing Committee of the Diocese of South Carolina, Rev. Thomas S. Tisdale of Orangeburg. Clergy assisting with the administration of the sacraments were Rev. William M. Kirkland and Rev. John Rivers. The flowers on the altar were given in loving memory of the late Mr. W. H. Mikell, a former senior warden of the parish, and his granddaughter Harriet Lebby Mikell.

In the *News and Courier* newspaper published Sunday, August 28, 1960, was an article entitled "New St. James Church Opens Its Doors Today." It describes the church as follows:

> The new church, of Colonial design with a graceful steeple rising above the wooded setting, is the sixth church to be erected on the site. It—and the enlarged parish house which was occupied last year—are valued at nearly a quarter of a million dollars. The church building includes an auditorium, sacristy, choir rooms and a robing room.

The closing paragraph of this article states,

> The church has shown rapid growth during recent years, with subdivisions [being developed] on James Island. Although the church rolls still contain family names that appear in the first vestry records, many new residents now claim St. James as their church home.[3]

This sixth church building was consecrated by Bishop Temple September 28, 1964.[4] With its mortgage marked "paid in full," it had cost $165,000 and seated 330 worshipers.[5] Prior to this service of consecration of the new church building, Dr. Daniel Ellis and Matthew Townsend, senior and junior wardens, announced to the congregation that the mortgage was satisfied and had been given to the church. Instead of celebrating by burning the mortgage, the wardens preserved it as an historical record.[6]

When the service began, the bishop knocked on the church door, and the two wardens opened it. William E. McLeod, senior warden emeritus, appointed to do so by Bishop Temple, spoke the "sentence of consecration." Rev. Edward Guerry, who had overseen the building of this sixth church before becoming head priest at St. John's, preached the sermon, and the Rev. Charles F. Duvall was currently the priest. At the time of this service Saint James still had its original seventy acres of glebe land given by the King of England.[7]

On the wall of the library in today's parish hall hangs a framed copy of the "Sentence of Consecration," dated and signed, which is as follows:

> In the name of the Father and of the Son and of the Holy Ghost. Amen. For as much as it has pleased Almighty God to put it into the hearts of faithful men and women to erect this Church in the City of Charleston, James Island, and State and Diocese of South Carolina to the Honor and Glory of God to be named and known as St. James Church and it being certified that the building is without lien, debt, or any incumbrance whatsoever. Now, therefore, we …set this Church apart from all unhallowed, ordinary and common uses and do Consecrate it to God's Great Name, and do dedicate it to His Service, for reading His Holy Word; for celebrating His Holy Sacraments; for offering to His Glorious Majesty the Sacrifices of Prayer, Praise and Thanksgiving; for blessing the people in His name; and for all other Holy offices of His Church according to the use and ritual of the Protestant Episcopal Church in the United States of America. In testimony whereof we have set our hand and seal this Monday being the 28th day of September in the year of our Lord One Thousand Nine Hundred and Sixty-four and in the Fourth year of our Episcopate. Signed Gray Temple, Bishop

As a continued overview of Saint James' history, Dr. Ellis wrote the following:

> A new full time rector began the second era on September 12, 1960. There has been a rapid increase in all phases of church activity since that time. The present schedule shows some type of religious activity almost every day in the week as well as three services on Sunday. The number of communicants has increased to the point where the present building appears at times to be inadequate. The budget has increased approximately fifty

times since 1945. In 1964, all debts having been paid, the church building was consecrated by the Rt. Rev. Gray Temple.[8]

The ordination of the Rev. Edmond D. Campbell, Jr. occurred in 1965. Rev. Campbell was the [third] priest [following Mellichamp and Rivers] to be sponsored by and to go forth from St. James. The capital improvement program was accomplished in 1968. This $100,000 project included doubling the size of the parish house, building the church office and the Sunday School building, and the installation of the pipe organ. While contributions of the congregation were very significant, the back bone of this progressive effort was again funds derived from income from church property.[9]

According to vestry records, the early1960s demonstrated transitions not only with property but also with policies, programs, and leadership roles. Having followed in the footsteps of Rev. Guerry, Rev. Robert M. Watson, Jr. led his first vestry meeting at Saint James on September 8, 1960. After taking care of the cemetery for fifteen years, Raymond Grimball retired from those duties.[10] Mr. Weston sent a letter of resignation as organist and choir director.[11] Mr. Willie McLeod resigned as treasurer after holding this position for twenty years and was made warden emeritus.[12] Also Edmond D. Campbell began seminary.[13] After serving as rector of Saint James for two years, Rev. Watson, Jr., resigned to enroll in Duke University to seek a higher degree.[14] Commander Van Leer went before the vestry June of 1962 about promoting Boy Scout Troop #44 on the church campus. In September of 1962 the vestry voted to call Rev. Charles Duvall as rector. A change in church policy was also brought about when Mr. William Bailey, long time vestryman and senior warden, moved that smoking be eliminated during Sunday school classes.[15] Mr. Bailey handled the church while the congregation was without a rector for four months.[16]

Still on the church property was the fifth church building of Saint James. Rev. Paulwyn Bolick, who had been authorized to organize a Lutheran mission on James Island, asked if he and his fledgling congregation could use the old church. The vestry responded that they would be happy to work with them and by November had written a contract.[17] The congregation of Martin Luther Lutheran Church continued to use the old church until they vacated the building in the fall of 1963 and moved to their new sanctuary at 1605 Harbor View Road on James Island.[18]

Many vestry notes pertain to the men's discussions about the use of and repairs to the 1899 church. In March 1963 termites were found in the little church. Of course, the vestry had to consider costs of maintenance and repairs, which were estimated in April 1964 to be $3,316. Thought was given to using the small church as a chapel, classrooms, and offices.

In June of 1964, 160 letters were mailed to the households of the congregation, asking them for their input. Thirty-three voted to remove the church, four to repair it, fifteen to convert it to classrooms, and three not to convert the sanctuary to classrooms. Consequently, the decision was made to dismantle the church, and it was de-consecrated in September of 1964.

Plans were made to take the memorial windows and plaques from the old building and place them in the parish house or eventually inside the new classroom building scheduled to be completed within two years. Holy Trinity Church on Folly Road, The Crescent, was given the pews for their choir,[19] and the furnace was sold. Rev. Edward Legare of Johns Island offered to tear down the church building in exchange for the materials he could salvage.[20]

During the decade of the 1960s Saint James negotiated with the YMCA, which was seeking a location to build a facility. In August of 1962 officials from the YMCA contacted the vestry about purchasing seven acres of their land on Camp Road. The vestry was "sympathetic to the plea" but not interested in selling the land at that time. However, in February of 1963 the vestry drew up a contract to sell to the YMCA four acres on Camp Road at $2500 per acre, plus the lease of six more acres with the right to purchase in two years. When an appraiser said that the land was worth $3,500 per acre, the vestry paused in the meeting for prayer and meditation and then decided not to sell the land. In April of 1963 the YMCA bought ten acres on what is now Quail Drive in Lawton Bluff Subdivision.

From 1963 to 1965, just as in previous years and ones to come, the vestry fielded requests regarding both the lease of or purchase of Parrot Point on James Island. These requests came from individual citizens such as Robert Clement, church organizations such as Episcopal Church Home for Men and Women, farmers such as Judson Tucker and George Oswald who wanted to graze cattle, realtors such as James Island Realty Company, and business organizations, including West End Dairy. The vestry turned down most of these requests. The vestry's Land Committee consulted with the Orphan House Commission to obtain a quit claim deed for any interest they may have had in Parrot Point. In response, the Orphan House said that if Saint James wanted to sell the property, they would give a clear title, provided they received up to half of the proceeds for the sale.[21] In August of 1967 Mr. Louis E. Lane, who became the property manager at Parrot Point, offered to lease the land at $300 per year to use a portion of it, including an acre on the creek. He also offered to rebuild the house, so the vestry prepared a ten-year lease for Mr. Lane in August of 1967.

Ordained as a deacon in 1960 and priest in 1961, Rev. Charles Farmer Duvall was hired after Rev. Watson resigned. Duvall served as rector at Saint James from 1962 to 1970. A native of Bennettsville, he grew up in Cheraw, South Carolina. A graduate of The Citadel, Rev. Duvall attended Virginia Theological Seminary, earning his Masters in Divinity. Before coming to Saint James on October 30, 1962, he had served at Holy Trinity in Grahamville and The Cross in Bluffton.[22]

In December of 1964 vestry members were concerned about Goucher College's Episcopal chaplain, who gave a sermon "Sex with the Created Order," implying sanction of pre-marital sexual relations. Consequently, Rev. Duvall wrote Rev. Frederick Wood of Baltimore, stating the vestry's strong disapproval of the chaplain's sermon. Rev. Duvall asked for those in authority to take steps to correct this position and for this viewpoint not to be taught as doctrine in the Episcopal Church.

At the January 1965 annual parish meeting, the congregation became all the more aware of how Rev. Duvall had become devoted to many Christian endeavors in his 345-member church as well as the community. He was chairman of the Division of Youth Work, chaplain for the Episcopal students at the College of Charleston, board member for Camp Saint Christopher and Vorhees College, treasurer for the Charleston Ministerial Association, among other roles and duties. In March he acted as spokesperson on behalf of the church's youth who sought the vestry's permission to include some American folk music written by a minister to be played in lieu of the organ music during the communion service. As rector, he helped to host the 175th Annual Convention of the Diocese of South Carolina at Saint James on May 4 and 5, 1965. Vestry notes of this decade also indicate that he periodically "swapped pulpits" with other ministers, allowing him to preach to other congregations and allowing different clergy to preach at Saint James.

When the vestry became aware of a situation in which four children living with their grandparents needed more room, a member—a contractor—of Saint James offered to build onto the grandparents' house at cost. This example is one of many indicating the vestry's and congregation's compassion and concern regarding others within the community.

March 14-17, 1966, Rev. Joseph R. Horn of Florence came to Saint James to conduct a week's Lenten mission. In the latter 1960s he assisted the first Sunday of each month and conducted services while Rev. Duvall was away. Later his son and namesake Joseph R. Horn IV served as assistant priest at Saint James, and his daughter-in-law Martha McGougan Horn was sponsored at seminary by Saint James. Joseph R. Horn III (1921-1971) is buried beside his wife Jean Hayden Horn (1926-1998) at Saint James. Likewise, Rev. Martha Horn (1952-2015) and her son Joseph R. Horn V (1981-1999) are buried in the cemetery.[23]

In September 1966 the vestry began discussing the cost of air conditioning the church. Those familiar with the heat and humidity of the Low Country's geographical area know the need for this provision. In July 1967, four vestrymen voted for air conditioning and two against. At that time the church needed funds to hire a full-time secretary, a Christian education director, an assistant priest, and a trainer for lay people. The cost of installing air conditioning was $12,988, so the action was deferred. However, in the summer heat of August, the discussion led to yet another debate, and this time the vestry voted to install air conditioning.

In 1967 the vestry wanted to buy an "addressograph machine" designed for rapid, automatic labeling and addressing of mail in large quantities. An Elliott #880 Electric Addressograph was indeed approved for purchase in 1967. Current readers might be taken aback regarding technology differences within a span of a few decades.

By June of 1967, because of the expanded congregation at Saint James and the fact that other denominations often had more than one church of their denomination on the island, the vestry began discussing the establishment of a mission church on James Island. In July of 1968 the vestry proposed a possible mission site in Lawton Bluff near a shopping center and 1,000 feet from the fire station. It consisted of three acres worth $5,000 per acre. The vestry planned to borrow $10,000 to buy land "for religious purposes" in Section 12 of Lawton Bluff Subdivision.[24]

In November of 1967 the vestry reviewed a proposal to move the rectory from the Maybank address where the Guerrys had resided and possibly rent or sell that property or provide the rector with a housing allowance. The next year Read and Read Realty sold the rectory for $20,178.59.[25] The vestry voted to purchase a house for $31,500 to serve as a new rectory for the priest and his family on Burning Tree Road in Country Club #2.

Rev. Duvall was instrumental in enabling the congregation to grow in numbers, leading to doubling the size of the parish house to provide office space and Sunday school rooms.[26] For years vestry notes in the 1960s discuss the need for and design of this addition. In September 1967 Lucas and Staubes Firm was hired to prepare plans and obtain bids for modifications to the sanctuary to accommodate the Shantz pipe organ (purchased in 1966 for approximately $30,000) and to remodel the parish house for office space and a church school. In spring of 1968 the vestry was busy working with architects, contractors, bankers, lawyers, realtors, and landscapers.

On May 5, 1968 a groundbreaking ceremony to celebrate plans to expand the parish house was held in which the rector and wardens turned the dirt and prayed, "Forasmuch as devout and faithful people have taken in hand to build on this ground, a building to be used to the glory of God and the education and wellbeing of God's people, therefore We break ground for this building." The closing prayer was as follows: "O God who by thy Holy Spirit has made us all members of fellowship of thy Holy Church, Bless the work begun on this educational building and grant that all who enter here, whether to teach or to learn, to work or to play, may be bound together in thy love, through Jesus Christ our Lord."[27] Having struck an earlier deal with Simmons Realty for the sale of church property, the vestry anticipated the full $60,000 remaining balance to be paid on what was called the Lynwood property—the subdivision developed off of Camp Road.[28]

An historical "marker" is evident in the minutes of the January 14, 1968 annual meeting when nominations for male *and female* candidates could be made. Mrs. Daniel W. Ellis ("Kitty") was nominated but not elected. At this same meeting diocesan rules stipulated that delegates to the Diocesan Convention *must be male* since the canon only stipulated that women could be elected to the vestry. Consequently, no women from the congregation were nominated to be delegates to that upcoming convention.

Saint James' vestry minutes for November 7, 1960 stated, "After much discussion on the matter of racial integration in the services of the church...a motion was made that colored people not be admitted to the services [at Saint James]. After more discussion a vote was taken with the following results: three in favor of the motion, two opposed, and three abstentions. This [motion] was barely adopted." No records were found indicating that any guests were turned away based on race, skin color, nationality, or socioeconomic status.

Indicative of a time when many racial issues were changing on James Island and elsewhere in the South, the October 17, 1965 Sunday church bulletin included the following blurb: "The Rector [Rev. Duvall] and Vestry invite any interested members of the congregation to an informal discussion of the Church and Race Relations this evening in the Parish House at 8 o'clock."

On the diocesan level, churches of the Low Country were still wrestling legally and morally with segregation matters, especially pertaining to schools, transportation, restaurants, hotels, and churches. Although the Supreme Court case known as Brown vs. the Board of Education of Topeka essentially declared "separate but equal" schools to be unconstitutional, violating the rights of blacks, white communities fought opening their school doors to students of color. Many Southern congregations feared that if this court ruling required them to open their church doors to all races, they might have to deal with possible scenarios involving sit-in's, protests, sectioning off pews for black guests, and handling offended white members during worship.[29]

Also during the 1950s and 1960s many local Episcopalians grew in resentment of the National Council of Churches in Christ in the United States of America (NCC), which included the Episcopal Church. Contributions from local parishes went to the Diocese, and ultimately some of that funding went to the NCC. Throughout the Low Country many Episcopalians viewed the NCC as an organization pushing social reform that smacked of communist philosophies, socialist agendas, and unsubstantiated political stances.[30] Integration and civil rights activities were two of the many controversial factors.[31]

Revision of the *Book of Common Prayer* was cause for debate as well, as many viewed proposed changes in the long-established liturgy to be yet another intrusion from the national church.[32] The intent was to modernize worship, but such departure from the beloved 1928 *Book of Common Prayer* to a newer version created controversy throughout the Diocese of South Carolina and with some of the members at Saint James.[33] Objections included the change to the Creed, from "*I believe*" to "*We believe*" and the omission of the "Prayer of Humble Access."[34] Another addition that brought some resistance was the passing of the peace after the confession of sin.[35] For generations worshippers had embraced the 1928 prayer book for not only their Sunday worship and Holy Eucharists but also for sacraments, including marriages, baptisms, and burial rites. After a series of trial liturgies, the *Book of Common Prayer*, listing 1979 for its copyright date, was placed in the pews at Saint James. (The *Book of Common Prayer 2019* was recently published by the Anglican Church of North America.)

Rev. Duvall served at Saint James for eight years (1962-1970) before accepting a position as rector of the Church of the Advent in Spartanburg. On April 11, 1981, in Pensacola, Florida, Rev. Duvall became the Bishop of the Central Gulf Coast Diocese.[36] In 1987 the Rt. Rev. Charles Duvall was the guest speaker for the "Episcopal Series of the Protestant Hour," which was broadcast on more than 400 radio stations across the country. His twelve programs, entitled "Love Songs and Blues of the Soul," were based on the twelve best-known psalms.[37]

Throughout this decade of rapid growth, many vestry minutes address budget concerns. In fact, in September of 1968, the vestry sent a letter to members of the congregation regarding pledges. Stating that since church expenses were being met on a "month-by-month basis," Saint James was dependent on the members' offerings. To remind communicants of their pledges, the treasurer mailed quarterly statements and appealed to those who were in arrears in their giving.

At the same time, many 1960s vestry minutes demonstrate the generosity of its people within and beyond the church. Mr. Fabin donated wine from his store for church Eucharists. In November 1968 the church gave their old organ to Porter Gaud School. In 1969 Miss Lily Seabrook Rivers bequeathed a portion of her estate to help maintain the church yard and cemetery. In February 1969 when Rev. Mackey told the vestry that St. Andrews Mission needed a baptismal font, Saint James donated the one that they had formerly used.

As more women entered the work force, the church realized an opportunity of outreach and in 1969 hired Mrs. Joan Seel as director of a kindergarten. Registration for children was $15, and the monthly fee was $20. In exchange for the use of the church facilities, Mrs. Seel pledged $50 per month from kindergarten funds to Saint James. The first class in September 1969 consisted of eleven preschoolers, with enrollment dropping to as few as eight as families underwent changes, such as moving.

A church bulletin dated May 18, 1969, reveals names of parish leaders and activities. Rev. Duvall was the rector, Dr. Daniel W. Ellis was senior warden, Mr. Matthew T. Townsend was junior warden, and vestry members were Floyd I. Dovell, Jr., Henry McManus, E. Clark Morrison, Jr., Philip D. Pinckney, Dr. William M. Rambo, Thomas L. Read, and William H. Simmons. The bulletin, with a beautiful photograph of the church, listed activities involving Junior EYC, Boy Scout Troup #44, Brownie Scouts, vacation church school teacher training, cub den meeting, and junior and senior choir rehearsals. This particular service was designated as a "Youth Sunday Service: An American Folk Song Mass and Talks," leading off with the song "Lord of the Dance," and Lou Costa serving as acolyte. In this same year Mr. Duvall became a dean and was appointed Dean of the Charleston Deanery.[38]

Yet another church bulletin dated November 23, 1969 lists the names of twenty-seven youth and eight adults who were welcomed into the parish life of Saint James through the Order of Confirmation. Announcements included an invitation to a joint Thanksgiving service for all the churches of James Island to be held at the James Island Presbyterian Church. This community bonding of James Island churches, blending different worship styles and music, has continued for decades. Food offerings were collected on behalf of the agency HELP. Another announcement was entitled "Advent Corporate Communion and Breakfast" for men and confirmed boys of St. James. (In upcoming years Saint James formed a brotherhood of men who would meet for the weekly Friday Morning Men's Breakfast from 7:00 to 8:00.) This "corporate communion" breakfast for males in 1969 was first held at St. John's Episcopal on November 30, 1969, indicative of the ongoing connection of the two island churches sustained throughout the years.

Although Saint James was thriving, for the most part, throughout the 1960s, America was, to a great extent, in a state of dramatic transition on major issues. Music, movies, literature, and hair and clothing fads reflected deeper societal shifting in the decade. Significant changes regarding women's roles, recreational drug use, court cases addressing equality, and anti-establishment movements left most looking upon an unrecognizable world. The assassinations of President John Kennedy, Senator Robert Kennedy, and Rev. Martin Luther King, Jr., as well as the mounting American service members' deaths in Southeast Asia, led to national grieving and protesting. Normative values regarding God, family, life, and faith— all on which a peaceful, Godly, and productive American society had been built—seemed to be eroding nationally. Saint James observed and interacted with the trembling national scene, yet faithfully, this island community and church congregation held fast to those norms in obedience to a Triune God. Despite national circumstances, Saint James remained a body of believers focused on building more Sunday school rooms, supporting scout troops, donating to neighboring churches, evangelizing on college campuses, sustaining community charities, and worshipping an unshakable God in a world badly shaken.

CHAPTER THIRTEEN

Saint James: 1970s—A Decade of Harmony and Discord

In the conclusion of his history of Saint James, which ends in 1979, Dr. Ellis wrote, "During the past ten years, all activities of the church have grown considerably both in variety and scope. Young people particularly have become involved in diverse phases of church participation and have undoubtedly exercised an influence upon our destiny."[1] This decade indeed demonstrated harmony amid change, yet discord eventually erupted, splintering the church into sub-groups in opposition to one another.

Clearly each generation has had its parishioners step forth to take on leadership roles that have sustained the church. Listed in the April 5, 1970 bulletin are names familiar to many who lived on James Island and worshipped at Saint James during this period:

- Senior Warden: Thomas L. Read; Junior Warden: Matthew T. Townsend

- Vestry: Lloyd M. Ash, Thomas P. King, Henry B. McManus, E. Clark Morrison, Jr., Philip D. Pinckney, Joel P. Porcher, William H. Simmons, Jr.

- Receiving Treasurer: Edward L. Grimball, Jr; Disbursing Treasurer: E. C. (Joe) Morrison, Sr.

- Clerk of Vestry: Francis M. Harleston

- Organist and Choir Director: J. Wyman Frampton

- President of Men of the Church: Thomas P. King

- President of Women of the Church: Mrs. Vernon W. Weston
- Parish Secretary: Mrs. W. H. Simmons, Jr.
- Sexton: Cornelius Fleming

Another interesting event to note in this church bulletin from April 5, 1970, is the following, which is a tribute to Charleston being known as "The Holy City":

> THE ENTIRE CHARLESTON AREA will mark the influence of religious faith on our heritage...by a mass Service in the Johnson Hagood Stadium, beginning at 7 PM... Bishop Paul Harding of the United Methodist Church will be the official speaker, and there will be a 300-voice Choir, and a procession of clergy and lay leaders, which is hoped to represent over 300 congregations in this area.

Other details that reveal a thriving church of faith include the following announcements:

- Picnic on church grounds immediately following the Family Service
- Junior and Senior EYC [Episcopal Youth Council] to go to "Festival of Faith" at Johnson Hagood Stadium
- Spanish Class at the Parish House
- St. Martha's Chapter to meet at the home of Mrs. L. G. Booth in Clear View
- Delegates and alternates to the Diocesan Convention to have pre-Convention meeting at the Cathedral

During this time the church was very pro-active in designating committees and vestrymen with clearly defined responsibilities, activities, and goals. Church leaders were conscientious about making home visits both to potential new members as well as long-standing parishioners.

Vestry minutes include a letter dated November 5, 1970, calling Rev. Richard F. Dority to Saint James, and his first Sunday with the church was January 13, 1971. A graduate of Coker College and the University of the South (1958), Rev. Dority had previously served churches in Summerton, Pinewood, Manning, Columbia, and Darlington.[2]

The following is well said on Saint James' website regarding this era:

> The 70s were a time of spiritual renewal in the US and a fresh experience of the Holy Spirit. The Toronto movement, John Wimber, the Jesus Movement,

and many more expressions of the Spirit hit the church. Saint James was not exempt from this, and every member of the church was influenced to one extent or the other by what God was doing. Under Rev. Richard Dority (1971-1979) the Holy Spirit breathed a new experience of God's power into Saint James. God was propelling the Church out of the buildings and into the world.[3]

More and more funds were needed, especially in meeting the salaries of a growing staff. Many of the vestry's minutes of this decade include lengthy conversations about budgets and parishioners' pledges. In the early 1970s vestrymen even discussed publishing the monetary contributions promised by individuals and families, but others insisted that that information be kept confidential, with only the vestry having access to those records for the sake of financial planning. They considered dropping from the church roll those not pledging or pledging a "pittance." However, Rev. Dority preferred a more positive approach, choosing to emphasize what parishioners *were* giving. Some members held back pledges due to issues with the National Church; consequently, members were informed that they could stipulate that none of their money would go to the National Church.[4]

Balancing the church finances was an ongoing concern. Often the vestry researched needs to select a "most-for-the-money" solution. An example representing the tight budget can be noted in the vestry minutes from January 1973 when the members voted to install a rotary telephone service because having only one phone for the entire church had become problematic.

W. G. Meggett, chairman of the Land Committee, provided a report, summarized as follows:

- Tract B—remainder of glebe land (49.4 acres)—consideration given to possible use for public cemetery, private school, extension of Jamestown Estates, or future playground (10 acres)

- Tract C—tip of land necessary for drainage of Tract D

- Tract D—about 15 acres (some on the marsh) where church, church school, cemetery, and parking lot are currently located

- Tract E—Walpole Tract—retained for parking

- F.P. Seabrook and J. M. Seabrook Tracts (purchased as an investment in 1887 and 1893) equal to 87.8 acres of high land and 27.5 acres of marsh. There is a marsh creek running through this land just to the rear of James Island Elementary [to become James Island Middle] and extends to deep water leading out to the James Island Creek.

- Parrot Point Tract—48 acres of high land and 50 acres of marsh (The will stated that if the church attempted to sell the whole tract, the property would automatically go to the City of Charleston Orphan House; however, as of September 1, 1971, the Charleston Orphan Home was no longer in existence, having been relocated and renamed the Carolina Youth Development Center.)

As in previous years, much of the church's focus pertained to the sale of land to sustain church endeavors. In January of 1971, vestrymen addressed a proposal to sell approximately eighty-seven acres of highland and about twenty-seven acres of marshland, all known as the Seabrook Tract, which had been leased out to farmers, on the north side of Camp Road. The sale of this property was to enable Saint James to set aside 25% for a mission site to become a second Episcopal church on James Island, 25% for property maintenance, 15% for development of a proposed cemetery across from Saint James on Camp Road, 15% for the development of the Parrot Point property, and 20% to be given to outreach beyond the parish.[5]

However, William Brown, Bonum Wilson, Sr., and W. E. McLeod were against selling the Seabrook Tract. Mr. Wilson, Sr. stated that if the church continued to sell land—instead of parishioners' making personal financial sacrifices, thus creating a deficit budget and foolishly wasting resources—the congregation would decline materialistically and spiritually. On the other hand, Mr. Henry McManus asked, "What is stewardship but using what has been given to us for the work of God and the Gospel of Jesus Christ? The willingness to sit tacitly on a piece of property, which is doing nobody any good, is a question that each person has to answer for himself." Mr. Brown suggested that the vestry submit to the congregation at special meetings any proposals of selling church land. Mr. Thomas Read stated that the congregation elects the vestry to carry out the business of the church, and if they had to bring everything they did to the congregation, the vestry would be about useless.[6] Thus, one can see that the varied viewpoints created lively discussions.

Again and again throughout the 1970s, the vestry and congregation wrestled with complicated issues and proposals regarding the sale and use of church land. The vestry decided to sell the rectory on Burning Tree Road because Rev. Dority preferred to have a housing allowance and purchase his own house. Read and Read Realty handled the sale, listing the house at $44,500.[7] William S. Brown offered to buy the Seabrook Tract, putting in the only bid of $310,000.[8] Over the next few years the vestry held many discussions regarding the payment and interest fees regarding Mr. Brown's land purchase; ultimately, they sought legal counsel, sorted out misinterpretations, and set up contracts to handle the complications associated with this land transaction. Vestry minutes periodically mention receiving Creek Point Limited checks from Mr. Brown such as $82,380 (sale price plus interest) for thirty acres of the Seabrook Tract in June of 1972[9] and $71,604 in April of 1973.[10]

Mr. Louis E. Lane, who had a long-term lease on part of the Parrot Point property, died, and his wife requested to remain on the land. She signed a contract to assume responsibility for the duration of the lease.[11] At that time the Parrot Point property was valued at $3,000 per acre.[12] The vestry turned down a proposal from the Optimist Club, interested in a long-term lease (as much as twenty-five years) for eight to thirteen acres to build a playground, camp, and club house, spending as much as $10,000 on the facilities.[13] In May of 1973 the vestry passed a motion to go before the Court of Common Pleas in an effort to clear the title on Parrot Point.

A 1970s handout entitled W.H.O. (We Help Others) indicates that Saint James, in coordination with other island churches, met multiple community needs: day care centers, emergency shelter, food, clothing, children's toys, furniture, Bible school, school shoes, blankets, heat, and more. This island-based humanitarian endeavor seems to be a forerunner of the James Island Outreach, established in 1989. It was eventually housed on Saint James' campus in 2018 and supported by many churches of various denominations throughout the island.

Much of this decade focused on the plans to build a second Episcopal church on James Island. In 1972 the vestry discussed what to do with the land that had been purchased for the mission site, but no consensus was reached.[14] In 1973 the vestry expressed concern that the mission site was depleting church funds and proposed the possibility of it becoming a gathering place for civic groups.[15] In 1974 vestrymen discussed the idea of establishing a counseling center manned by a priest and counselors, but the cost of erecting a building and paying additional salaries seemed financially daunting.[16]

Church leaders in the early Seventies placed an emphasis on increasing the attendance for Sunday school. Rev. Dority asked that every member of the vestry attend Sunday school every Sunday and that parents bring their children.[17] Parishioners considered various proposals to reward Sunday school participation by having a contest to see which age group had the greatest increase in attendance, sending out "You were missed" cards for members who were absent, and having classes give two-minute presentations about their lessons.[18] At the time four hundred families appeared on the Saint James roster, with 200 of these families pledging, and twenty persons paying over half of the church's annual budget.[19]

Miss Bet Boykin, who had been the Christian Education coordinator since 1968, resigned in 1971. Miss Lynda Owen was hired, but only after the vestry and Rev. Dority had a disagreement about whether he had indeed been given permission to hire her. Apparently, some vestrymen were making a distinction between the phraseology of "seeking" someone to handle the Christian Education and "hiring" someone. Nevertheless, Miss Owen was hired as the parish assistant to begin work in September of 1971. She proposed that the Sunday school use the "Gospel Light" curriculum. She taught senior high school students, handled young people's confirmation classes, and met with the Sunday school teachers to discuss teaching materials.[20] She began training teens to teach the younger-aged Sunday school classes.[21] By the fall of 1972 Miss Owen had classes for ages three through adults and an active EYC with about thirty students at each meeting.

In May of 1973 the young people requested a bus for transportation, and in May of 1974 Lloyd Ash (vestryman, Boy Scout leader, lay reader) submitted costs and needs for the purchase. A used school bus was eventually bought. Many subsequent vestry meetings address the use and cost of the church bus, including the young people painting it and often Lloyd Ash's repairing it, replacing part after part.

Some parishioners raised eyebrows, disapproving of choices made on behalf of the teens in particular. For example, the vestry grew concerned about an all-night party being planned for high school graduates at Saint James. Such a party, they believed, could take away from the dignity of the church. Ms. Owen explained to the vestry that the church party was to protect the young people, giving them a wholesome environment different from some teens' unchaperoned and potentially problematic all-night house parties.[22]

Church members expressed conflicting opinions about additional issues with the youth. Although Miss Owen was praised for the success of the Lenten Missions 1972 Program that she spearheaded, others expressed concern about a "lack of formality, clapping in church, and packing of pews."[23] Rev. Dority reported that Miss Owen had been working with many youths who had drug problems, which had become a more escalated and widespread crisis among high school and college-aged students.[24] By December of 1974 the vestry formed a troubleshooting committee to deal with several members' complaints about some of the Sunday school materials and youth services. In April of 1975 when Rev. Dority hired Mr. Shannon Hebert as the music director for the Sunday night praise services, Rev. Dority encouraged the vestry to attend one of the services to "form their own opinion."[25]

The church's oldest silver chalice, which had been given in memory of Miss Eliza Dill in 1833, as well as the baptismal shell, had been stolen, so the insurance company issued a check October 5, 1972 for $125 to replace the stolen communion cup.[26] In November, 1972, Saint James received a letter from Christine's Antiques in Birmingham, Alabama, saying that they thought they had a chalice belonging to Saint James. When that cup was shipped to Saint James, members realized that the chalice was merely a reproduction of their original chalice. As a follow-up, they wrote to Geissler Company, which had been commissioned to make the reproduction, in hopes of finding out how this fake had come to be and how it got to Alabama.[27] A letter on file among church records explains that Saint James had written to Geissler, asking that "Copy of" be added to the engraving on the replacement chalice. When the reproduction was created, the words "Copy of" were mistakenly omitted, so Geissler had sent the duplicate chalice back to the engraver. In route, the chalice was lost or stolen and never recovered by Geissler Company. That first reproduction was apparently the item that ended up at Christine's Antiques in Birmingham. Geissler made another replica of the chalice, had that one engraved, along with "Copy of," and sent to Saint James. Mr. Thomas Read, Sr. also gave an additional silver chalice to the church.

Several vestry minute entries record the generosity and good will of parishioners both within and beyond the church. Mrs. D. A. Stevens III purchased one hundred prayer books and one hundred hymnals in memory of her mother Mrs. Anne Street Maxwell.[28] The vestry helped a woman in need of a dialysis machine[29] and assisted a couple who ran a laundry/dry cleaning service on Folly Road while they were hospitalized.[30] Members of Saint James believed that islanders were to be loved as neighbors. In 1975 when Elizabeth "Betty" Simmons died, the vestry was eager to honor her service to Saint James. She had initially taken on the position of part-time parish secretary without pay in 1960 and then served diligently as full time-secretary from 1967 to 1975.[31]

Rev. Dority ushered in several new activities that brought about changes. Instead of the vestrymen attending their meetings at church or a member's home, these elected church officials and their wives held some of their meetings as retreats at Bonnie Doone Plantation. Another one of Rev. Dority's new proposals was to make a variety of books available on a table by the church's front door. Each book was free, provided the taker promised to read it. He advocated a "school of practical learning" as a service to the community to promote good will and fellowship; parishioners were to teach their own skills—home repairs, typing, art— for a six-week period one night a week. The Blood Mobile was scheduled to come to the church for parishioners to donate blood. The church planned father-son camping trips as well as family picnics at Camp St. Christopher.[32] Rev. Dority provided daily devotionals on a local radio station, WNCG.[33] Considering the benefits of a smaller church, he was in favor of founding the additional Episcopal church on James Island.[34] Unfortunately, the kindergarten closed due to low enrollment.[35] The vestry discussed the need of a Parish Council Chairman to coordinate church organizations and activities.[36]

This decade reflects how societal shifts were impacting church policies and procedures. Changes were made with the vestry, deleting the word "male" and replacing it with "members," and increasing the number of vestry members from nine to twelve. Vestry members decided that junior and senior wardens would be elected from and by the vestry.[37] Rev. Dority used the black 1928 prayer book for morning family services and the green prayer book ("Services for Trial Use 1971") for communion services.[38] The Worship Committee sent out questionnaires to the congregation regarding these trial services, but few were returned, and those that were sent back indicated that the responders were against the use of the new green prayer book.[39]

Although many records indicate a cohesiveness that was spiritually rich, records also indicate friction among parishioners and vestry members. Vestry minutes do not specify specific concerns at this time, but the fact that a Parish Council was organized so that Rev. Herb Gravely from St. Alban's Church, Kingstree, could meet with Saint James' council signifies conflict. He was often sent by the bishop to parishes that needed to address discord. Some vestry meetings had become contentious; thus, minutes from November 15, 1972 include a request that vestrymen not interrupt fellow members who were speaking. A cross-section of twenty members of the congregation was selected for the first meeting with Rev. Gravely on November 21, 1972, and five courses of instruction were planned, giving special attention to laymen's ministry.

In September of 1974 the minutes included the following, indicating the need for more effective communication vital for relationships:

> Mr. Lucas [a vestryman] said that because of past observations by some members of the vestry, they felt reluctant to express themselves because of fear of criticism or consequences. He asked the vestry to consider carefully what other members felt and, at the same time, express their own feelings in such a way as not to hurt other members. He said there is an urgent need for the vestry to regroup and work together.

Records from upcoming years in this decade indicate repeated efforts to do exactly as Mr. Lucas requested, yet troubles persisted.

In the January 1973 annual parish meeting, Rev. Dority presented his report, noting that he had never been in a parish where there had been more activity in personal Bible study, prayer, witnessing, and personal ministry. He commended the parish assistant Lynda Owen on her work in creating much of the interest and enthusiasm in those areas. Rev. Dority said he would be trying more experimental worship services and asked the congregation to keep an open mind and follow the lead of the Holy Spirit. For example, he planned a "chancel drama" for Lenten services, in which the trial of Jesus would be enacted, and the congregation would play a part.

Rev. Dority requested permission from the vestry members for a trial basis for lay readers and vestrymen to assist in Communion by administering the chalice. The church began a six-month trial run of allowing vestrymen to administer the chalice, with William Bailey, Frank Lucas, Joel Porcher, Bonum Wilson, Sr., Jack Cranwell, Jr., and P. Maynard Grooms being the first to do so.[40] Parishioners were invited to share their feelings with Rev. Dority. In spite of respected parishioners carefully chosen to take on this new role, Mr. William McLeod wrote a letter to the vestry, expressing his viewpoint on laymen administering the chalice:

> I am opposed to this innovation because I believe that a service as solemn, sacred and holy as this should be performed by a priest. However, in a case where there is a large congregation, and only one priest, the service is apt to be unduly long and some practical means must be devised to relieve this

condition. In a situation such as this, I would reluctantly and conditionally give my approval. I do not believe that persons selected for this service should necessarily be vestrymen or lay readers but laymen from the congregation at large who are regular attendants at services, baptized, contributing communicants in good standing and who are known to be well qualified for this sacred duty. It is my opinion that those worthy men of this type be recommended to the Bishop for his approval. (letter dated April 16, 1973 in church records)

For several decades, trained lay readers, chalice bearers, and patens [those who administer the wafers at communion] have taken on Eucharistic roles once performed only by priests.

Minutes from the summer of 1974 portray a very active youth: twenty-seven enrolled at Camp St. Christopher, ten worked as counselors at Camp St. Christopher, some went to Kanuga, and children of all ages attended the two one-week vacation Bible schools.[41] In March of 1975 Lynda Owen proposed an upcoming summer program of three months filled with activities for the parish youth, and Robert Horn was hired at $50 a week to assist. He proposed that the youth hold a "Rock-a-Thon" to raise funds for the summer youth program.

However, not all the reports on youth in this time period were favorable. In October of 1974 the vestry addressed the fact that some youth (not necessarily church members) had been horseback riding on the church property, so they obtained the names of the young people and called their parents. In November, "No trespassing" signs were posted on property directly across from Saint James after junior warden Matt Townsend dealt with a problem of young people (again, not necessarily church members) shooting their guns in the area and worrying local residents.

Some vestry minutes reveal opinions about the leadership of Bishop Temple during this decade. In January of 1973, the Bishop apparently publicly stated that he was against the proposed James Island Bridge across Wappoo Cut. Upset by this stance, the vestry wrote him to express their feelings, and Bishop Temple immediately clarified his viewpoint, indicating that he was not against the bridge, just the proposed connector.[42] In another instance, when St. Thomas Church of North Charleston shared a joint venture with Baptist, Presbyterian, and other Episcopal churches to form a Planning Council Committee, Bishop Temple expressed enthusiasm about a similar program for James Island churches working together.[43] In 1974 the vestry discussed Bishop Temple's letter stating his disapproval of women deacons wanting to become ordained priests.[44] Parishioners voiced various levels of agreement and disagreement with Bishop Temple's views.

Vestry decisions often pertained to the church property. In June of 1975 a committee was formed regarding the installation of a steeple bell, which led to several years of planning before it was finally installed. The vestry voted to keep the air conditioning on throughout the summer to prevent mildew and moisture problems that could damage the paint, organ, and furnishings.[45] A committee was established to design wooden panels or plaques to be placed on both sides of the altar for aesthetic and spiritual purposes. Members proposed that inscriptions, such as the Apostles Creed and/or the Lord's Prayer, would be appropriate. Estimated costs were $2,000 each.[46] These plaques were created and hung a few years later. Another issue pertained to more frequent break-ins on the church property, so burglar alarms were installed, additional lighting was placed outside, and new locks replaced the old ones.[47] In May of 1977, at Rev. Dority's request, a "spy glass" was installed in the door of the vesting room to enable him to see parishioners being seated in the sanctuary before services. Some of the vestry's discussions brought about immediate changes, and some came to fruition in the next decade.

Vestry minutes abound with details throughout 1976 with the youths' activities. Teens hosted breakfasts with speakers, presented a "Feast of Lights" pageant with thirty performers and 200 attendees, and traveled to "Fishnet '76" in Virginia. Blending fellowship with faith-building activities, they went to movies, games, dances, picnics, and Camp St. Christopher. They went bowling, camping, skating, and backpacking in the mountains of North Carolina. They planned activities for the younger children, including Easter egg hunts and vacation Bible school.

The vestry debated increases in salaries for Ms. Owen and Rev. Dority. Throughout the lengthy discussion, members proposed various motions, voted on and passed them, then changed or retracted them, indicating dissension among vestry members and taking the meeting to 12:15 AM. Then they disputed how to relay their decision to the congregation.[48] In March and April of 1976, many parishioners wrote letters [saved in vestry records] to the vestry and sent copies to Bishop Temple voicing strong disapproval of raises the vestry had voted to give to both their rector and youth leader. Among other problems mentioned in these letters were dissension among the parishioners, conflicts between Rev. Dority and wardens, and more charismatic worship styles interpreted to be "disruptive."

In light of embezzlement problems that other churches had faced throughout the country, Saint James generated some procedures after receiving input at the Diocesan Treasurers Conference in April 1976. New regulations required that at least two persons be present to count money taken up each Sunday before donations were removed from the church premises. The church treasurer's books were to be updated weekly and audited annually.

Also pertaining to church funds was an impassioned presentation given by Dr. Dan Ellis to the vestry. After a discussion regarding investments, budgets, and stewardship, Dr. Ellis stated the following, applying history to the 1970s:

> We of St. James need to realize that these…funds…constitute a Trust, the
> stewardship of which we are responsible. We are responsible just as the

people a hundred years ago were responsible. Had they not been good stewards, it is doubtful if we would exist now as St. James Church…We should carry this responsibility, remembering that we are responsible to those people who have been responsible for over two hundred and fifty odd years when we first had a little piece of land which had a building on it…It is our responsibility to carry on with the same caliber of responsibility exhibited by our ancestors, which allows us to have today our physical assets which proclaim the glory of God…[49]

In September of 1976, Rev. Dority called Robert "Bob" L. Oliveros, rector of St. Frances in Greenville, to serve as assistant priest at Saint James. Rev. Oliveros was particularly interested in starting the mission church the vestry had been considering, which would have been located near the Harbor View Road Shopping Center. However, after a brief but positive stay, he resigned as of December 1 of that year to seek a secular position.

In his congregational report on January 16, 1977, Rev. Dority referred to "continued progress" at Saint James, with ninety-six new members and 1,199 baptized members. Throughout 1976 the vestry had invested much time and expertise to establish clear, ethical guidelines, with the help of professional organizations, regarding the use of legacies, stocks, bonds, trusts, and budgets to honor wills and maximize investments.

More history was made at Saint James in January of 1977 when it elected its first female, Kitty Ellis, as senior warden, replacing William "Bill" Bailey after his service as senior warden had been completed. The vestry voted not only to allow but to encourage females to become acolytes.[50]

In May of 1977, as an attempt to unify and renew Saint James which was becoming more fragmented, the following proposal, or plea, was issued on behalf of the vestry to the congregation:

> Whereas, the members of the Vestry believe that the Holy Bible contains all of the ingredients for life, salvation, and matters for dealing with a person's relations with others…may it be resolved that in the spirit of Unity and for the good of its members, each member of the Vestry agrees to read the Bible on a daily individual basis for the next thirty days and asks the members of St. James Church to join with them in the hope that at the end of the thirty day period each member of the vestry and each member of the Church would find themselves committed to continuous reading and study and will have a renewed spirit with the Father, Son and Holy Spirit, and will enjoy a feeling of unity and oneness with each other, their families, and with all others.

In July of 1977 Rev. Dority hired Mr. Fielder Israel as assistant priest. He soon established new Bible study groups and prayer groups and led a youth group on a camping trip to Oconee State Park. His ordination was held on May 27, 1978,[51] and the vestrymen gave him a vestment (clerical robe).[52] That September Rev. Israel accepted a call to a church in Marion, South Carolina.

In 1975 Robert Horn went before the vestry and received their support when he asked for them to recommend to the bishop that he be allowed to begin the process of ordination. In November of 1977 Saint James completed an "Endorsement of Application for Postulancy," stating that the vestry testified that Joseph Robert Horn, IV is "sober, honest and godly, and that he is a communicant of this Church in good standing. We do furthermore declare that, in our opinion, he possesses such qualifications as fit him to be admitted a POSTULANT FOR HOLY ORDERS."

In May of 1978 Rev. Dority called a special vestry meeting to inform members that he had asked for the resignation of Lynda Owen as Director of Christian Education. When Mrs. Ellis, senior warden of the vestry, asked for reasons, Rev. Dority replied that they were no longer functioning as a team and could not work together. Mrs. Lillie McGougan, volunteer youth director assisting Ms. Owen, read to the vestry a summary of accomplishments due to Miss Owen's leadership with the young people.

In 1978 Rev. Chip Nix, who had considerable experience in youth work, was hired for an assistant priest's position.[53] Aware of the strife at Saint James at that time, Rev. Nix encouraged the staff, vestry, and congregation to strive towards better communication. He took particular interest in forming committees to visit church members and potential members to nurture harmony and build membership. After serving at Saint James a little less than a year, Rev. Nix announced that he had accepted a call to St. Alban's Church, Columbus, Ohio.[54]

By September 1978 several families had chosen to leave Saint James because they were dissatisfied with a variety of issues—changes from long-held traditions; matters pertaining to programs for the youth; leadership styles of Rev. Dority, Ms. Owen, and the vestry; to name a few. Consequently, Jack Thorp spearheaded a committee to reach out to these people, share their responses with the vestry, and seek a means of reconciling them with the church. The vestry passed a motion, stating that they pledged to work towards a more positive, prayerful unity in Saint James.[55]

Church records from the close of this decade include "Report of Rector to Vestry" and "Report of Special Committee to the Vestry," both of which are professional and tactful in tone and detail. Rev. Dority's report includes an apology if he spoke in defensiveness or carelessness or failed to be open about current problems. He addressed a point of contention between Miss Owen and himself, saying that he encouraged parishioners to take on positions of teaching and leadership whereas she felt that some of his decisions put into positions of authority people who were not "totally committed to Jesus and Saint James."

"The Report of Special Committee to the Vestry" numbered the following four categories of concern: (1) doctrinal problems—inconsistencies in sermons, theology, authority (2) untruthfulness (3) divulging confidences (4) saying unfair and un-Christian things about people and mishandling people. Some of the doctrinal problems were centered on the Sunday night praise services, viewed by several to be spiritually rich and viewed by others as an unbecoming mode of worship characterized by nontraditional church music and clapping. The committee concluded this portion of their report by saying, "If you don't like this form of worship, you can merely go to the other regular forms of services held here at St. James." Rev. Dority's sermons were criticized by some as being elementary, lengthy, and inconsistent; however, this report validated his sermons. In addressing issues of confidentiality and abrasiveness, the committee expressed an overall faith in their priest but also recognized his fallibility. This report ends in a plea for forgiveness, positiveness, and getting on with the Lord's work in unity. After reading both reports, Bishop Temple explained that his policy was to refrain from interceding in these types of problems, emphasized the roles of the rector and vestry to govern the parish in accordance with the Canon Law of the Church, and stated that it was his hope that he would not eventually have to intervene according to regulations set forth by church government.

On February 2, 1979 Rev. Dority shared with the vestry that he had accepted a call to nearby St. John's, Oakland, of West Ashley. With Rev. Dority's leaving Saint James, some parishioners transferred with him to St. John's Episcopal, located on Savannah Highway. Plans were made to host a reception for the Doritys and give him parting gifts of vestments and candlesticks.

In the next decade of his ministry, on May 21, 1987, Rev. Dority wrote Rt. Rev. C. Fitzsimons Allison to state that he was resigning from St. John's and submitting his renunciation of the Episcopal ministry according to the provision of Canon 108, with no canonical offense of misconduct or irregularity. He then went on to help found the James Island Christian Church just off of Folly Road.

In 1979 Rev. Sidney Holt served as *locum tenens*, meaning that he was temporarily fulfilling the duties of a priest until one was hired on a permanent basis. He was called, especially to conduct a program in which the vestry did self-evaluations and the church could seek redirection. The congregation agreed that they would not hire a new rector until this study, indicating their strengths and needs, had been completed. After conducting interviews with many of the parishioners, Rev. Holt presented his report to the vestry July 8, 1979 in an all-day session, based on twenty-two hand-written pages, culminating in ten typed pages, and outlining six steps for unification. Bishop Temple conducted a follow-up meeting, outlining a nine-step procedure to select the next rector.

Having fulfilled his duties as *locum tenens*, including an exhaustive report to redirect Saint James on a path of unification, Rev. Holt submitted his resignation. On July 15, 1979, the Sunday church bulletin stated, "We regret that Rev. Sidney Holt is leaving us after today.

We have grown to love him and indeed are most grateful to him for the work he has done at St. James. We trust he will observe in us the fruits of his labors in the months to come. Thank you, 'Sid.' We hope you will come back and visit us."

Senior Warden Kitty Ellis mailed a heartfelt letter to parishioners in August 1979, some which is quoted, as follows:

> Over the past few years, heightened by events of the past several months, very serious troubles have developed in St. James Church, creating factions, tensions, distrust, hurt, and general discord within its membership. The slow build-up of these factors has culminated in the resignation of the rector and the transfer of more than a score of families from the roster of St. James.
>
> Every avenue must be exhausted in an effort to heal the wounds of the recent past. Every effort must be expended to reunite the membership into a truly Christian family. Every means must be employed to prevent a repetition of this very painful experience.
>
> Accordingly, the attached document has been drafted in a sincere effort to satisfy the foregoing dictates. It comprises a statement of the characterization of St. James Episcopal Church, James Island, its intended direction, goals and missions. It sets forth the major objectives, guidelines, and latitudes for its functioning in the basic areas of Worship Service, Christian Education, Fellowship, Outreach through Service to others, and Evangelism…

Attached to this letter were two pages of specifications and clarifications, approved unanimously by the vestry.

After giving consideration to several candidates for the new rector's position at Saint James, the vestry issued a call to Rev. Rodney Caulkins; however, he did not accept the offer.[56] Rev. Sidney Holt agreed to return as interim, working three days a week until a full-time rector could be hired.[57]

In 1979 the Diocesan Canons assigned the following duties of vestry members:

- To be the official representation of the parish (ex. parish life)
- To be in charge of all temporalities of the parish (ex. property, money)
- To carry out all duties assigned by the Diocese or General Convention (ex. participation and constructive decision-making, reaching decisions by a democratic process without rancor or bitterness, compromising where possible, always striving for solutions)

Church records reveal how many changes occurred from 1720 when Saint James, as a chapel of ease, served a small gathering of worshippers once a month, at most. By the mid-twentieth century, this suburban church was reaching out to a community of believers, offering them multiple activities and services throughout each week within parishioners' homes, the parish hall, the church itself while additional downtown and diocesan events were occurring elsewhere. Clearly, seeds of faith had fallen on fertile ground many years earlier and taken root.

Nonetheless, with growth comes change, and with change comes dissension rooted in fears of giving up what is known and loved and venturing into uncharted waters. Change, for better or worse, can create a disequilibrium that is unsettling. In this decade, transformations and disparities threatened the unity of this body of Christ. One can hope and pray that by knowing the church's past, we can better understand the present and prepare for the future.

CHAPTER FOURTEEN

Vibrant Youth Ministry in the 1970s

The decade of the 1970s holds the distinction that from its youth ministry evolved six ordained priests and a full-time minister with the organization Jews for Jesus. Many others have dedicated their lives as worship and church leaders in lay minister positions. Rev. Richard Dority, youth director Lynda Owen Cole, and assistant youth director Lillie McGougan played key roles in this extraordinary outpouring of spiritual leaders.

Mrs. Cole stated that when Richard Dority was the priest at St. Matthew's Church in Darlington, South Carolina, she met with him to discuss ministry, and in one of those conversations, he said, "One day I see us ministering together." When Rev. Dority became the priest at Saint James, he telephoned her to interview for the position of Christian Director. She was hired, and they worked together for several years.[1]

Volunteer assistant to Mrs. Cole was Lillie McGougan, who began attending Saint James with her family when she was five years old. In fact, her father, Cosmo E. Brockington II (1910-1959) was on the committee that built the sixth church on its site, and he is buried in the church cemetery alongside his wife Marguerite (1915-1987).[2] After moving frequently due to her husband's military career, Lillie returned to the island and to Saint James and became involved in one of the most active periods of the church's youth ministry. Her daughter Martha, who eventually married Robert Horn and was also ordained a minister, was a part of this vibrant youth worship.

The junior high, high school, and college members were in age-based groups called "Fire Escape," "Salt and Light," and "Disciples." Having been spiritually inspired in Saint James' college-aged group, several members took different paths to priesthood. Robert Horn, Martha McGougan Horn, Creighton Evans, Chris Huff, Mark Cooke, and Suzy Mc-

Call were all eventually ordained. Biographical sketches on these six men and women can be found in the chapters entitled "Female Priests with Spiritual Roots at Saint James" and "Male Priests with Spiritual Roots at Saint James." A seventh member, Paige Saunders, made a career working for "Jews for Jesus," a national Christian organization in California.[3]

The young people formed a group called the "Hallelujah House," which sang scripture songs and praise music locally and even nationally. Most of the time they traveled in their old school bus purchased for $300 that had over 600,000 miles on its odometer. The youth repainted it a bright yellow, with a dove on the back, "Jesus Is Love" scripted on the front, and "Saint James Episcopal Church" down the side. The young people treasured their "hippy-like" means of transportation that took them places like the Canterbury House, Camp St. Christopher on Seabrook Island, and many other churches. They parked the bus at Middleton Gardens where people could walk through the bus to see various Biblical displays that they had created.[4]

Traveling on the bus could have been considered a "leap of faith." Vestry member Lloyd Ash volunteered his expert mechanical skills to save money and keep it running, yet there were problems with the bus on a 1976 trip to Atlanta,[5] and it broke down again a month later in Florence, South Carolina, on a trip home from Virginia. Vestry minutes stated, "Several cars were driven up to meet the stranded young people and bring them home. The bus has been towed home." The vestry authorized up to $1,000 to be funded for repairs, and parishioners donated an additional $1,000.[6] Typically, in May 16, 1977 vestry minutes is the following: "The bus had to go into the shop for repairs."

Mrs. Lynda Owen Cole shared the following story:

> On one of our trips to Florida, our bus broke down, so we gathered together to pray for God's help. A Baptist pastor noticed our bus and stopped to see if we needed help. He told us that he would have our bus fixed, provide us with shelter, and feed us if we would do the Sunday night service at his church. Everyone thought that that was a wonderful trade. The worship team led the congregation in several songs and then some of the young people gave testimonies about their relationships with Jesus and how knowing Him had changed their lives. It really turned out to be an amazing service.[7]

Not all of Saint James parishioners loved this youth bus. A few were aghast, saying "the bus is just too Baptist" and "the music just too charismatic," and felt not only embarrassed but also repulsed by the attention-getting jalopy. When the teens wanted to include guitars in their worship, some of the parishioners indicated to them that "organs were the holy instruments" of the church. Some were uncomfortable with the questions, "Are you saved?"

and "Have you been born again?"[8] Ultimately, the bus was sold for $200 to Victory Baptist Church in December of 1981.[9]

Some parishioners also worried that the youth groups were bringing in others who were not Episcopalian or were "unchurched." Years later, when reminiscing about his Saint James youth group of which he was a part, Rev. Robert Horn talked about a troubled young man who started to participate in their activities. At first the group did not know how to include him. Then one time this teen shared with the others about having an abusive father, a depressed mother, and a mentally troubled brother. The youth group experienced a wave of repentance and shifted their attitude from "You can come along" to "You belong." This young man from a dysfunctional family, but embraced by this nonjudgmental youth group, became a minister.[10]

As a young vestry member, Robert Horn stated to fellow vestrymen that one of the main purposes and strengths of the youth group was that members were being trained in how to minister to their peers. Youth were also being trained to provide services to their church, such as setting up for large meetings, babysitting in the nursery, stuffing envelopes for mailing, assisting with picnics and meals, cleaning up the church grounds, singing in the choir in the summer to allow choir members to sit with their families during worship, and much more.[11]

Other churches observed Saint James to examine its draw on the younger generation. Some families joined the church so their children would be members of such an active youth program where it was not unusual to have over one hundred children and teens in Sunday school and over one hundred participants in vacation Bible school. Three evenings a week were set apart for the three different age groups to meet.[12]

Although notes from vestry and congregational meetings repeatedly include Rev. Dority's praise of and appreciation for Mrs. Cole's work as the Director of Christian Education for over seven years, he asked her to resign in May of 1978 for reasons stated in the previous chapter. As a result of Mrs. McGougan's resignation from the vestry, Mr. Grooms was asked to be the chairman of the committee entitled Christian Education and Youth. Rev. Dority's decision pertaining to Mrs. Cole's dismissal ultimately contributed to the schism that occurred at Saint James in the late 1970s and played a part in Rev. Dority's leaving for St. John's Episcopal on Highway 17.

Rev. Suzy McCall recalled, "Those years at Saint James (1975-1980) were lifechanging for me, and I have often told people that the solid foundation of discipleship from Lynda Owen Cole and Lillie McGougan has held me steady through many a storm. Lillie has been a spiritual mother to me. It blesses me so much that my connection with Saint James remains strong. God is so faithful to hold us together."[13]

While attending the College of Charleston, Mark Cooke was very active at Ashley River Baptist Church, which also had a vibrant youth group. He became friends with a score of

Christians from Saint James on the college campus and found them to be just as passionate about Jesus as he was. Realizing that they had a deeper expression and awareness of the Holy Spirit than he had experienced with other college-age believers, he began to attend the Bible studies at Saint James. Rev. Cooke stated, "I didn't know it then but realized later that at the altar in the old church, I encountered the real presence of Christ in Communion for the first time."[14]

In *Saint James' Lenten 2019 Booklet*, which includes 500-word entries by parishioners and staff, Rev. Cooke wrote about attending a Wednesday Lenten breakfast at Saint James in 1976. Rising early as a college sophomore, Cooke, unfamiliar at the time with the term "Lent," joined Rev. Dority, some of the men of the church, and the other Salt and Light members at 7:00 AM for a meal and worship. Cooke wrote the following:

> The depth and rhythm of the historic Church Calendar resonated in my soul in a profoundly new way. The idea of preparing oneself for forty days for Holy Week, and then moving purposefully through the days leading to Christ's Passion, felt as if I had stumbled into a whole new, yet ancient world…I …found a stirring for more that has never ceased and became forever hooked on the cycles of our historic faith.[15]

Dating his future wife Jane Leigh Meredith of James Island, Cooke often took her to worship there where he first participated in an Episcopal Eucharist. He sensed a call to ministry in August 1977 while he was on staff at Camp St. Christopher on Seabrook Island.[16]

At age sixteen Chris Huff began to attend EYC [Episcopal Youth Council] at the invitation of two of his cousins. He said that his initial primary interest in attending was to meet girls, but he found a vibrant faith in Christ being taught in the group. He has always said that it was at Saint James where he not only was re-introduced to Jesus, but he also was introduced [in 1972] to his future wife, Kim Yeager. He explained, "In attending services at Saint James, I was deeply impacted by the depth and mystery of the liturgy and sacrament of the Episcopal Church. It was quite a contrast to the Presbyterian focus on 'word only,' nearly to the exclusion of the sacrament." Rev. Huff added the following:

> As a member of the youth group, I began to lead worship on a music team for the Sunday Night Praise Service at Saint James. During that time I learned much in the way of discipleship and Bible study from Lynda (then Owen) Cole. Eventually, the group that grew into our young adult Bible study of around thirty-five members began to travel around the Southeast leading contemporary worship at conferences and retreats.

The "Hallelujah House" even rented Winnebagoes to travel to the Church of the Redeemer in Houston.[17]

Martha McGougan Horn had been mentored and taught the value of discipleship through the ministry of Mrs. Cole. This mentorship, bestowed individually and modeled collectively, built a spiritual foundation, enabling Martha to serve faithfully in the roles of the wife of a priest, a gifted Bible teacher, and eventually a priest herself.[18]

When reminiscing about her participation with these youth groups from the 1970s, Lillie McGougan says that for over four decades these participants have remained close, like family, attending each other's and their loved one's ordinations, weddings, funerals—meeting spontaneously if one comes to town or has a crisis or has something to celebrate. These strong bonds have even been carried into the following generations. Scads of pictures remain of these youth, testifying that they traded their hip garb of the 1970s—their tie-dyed T-shirts and bell-bottom pants—for the black shirts and white collars they wear today. As Ms. Mc-Gougan declares, "They became disciples for Christ for life."[19]

CHAPTER FIFTEEN

1980s—Renewing, Restoring, Reflecting

The new decade brought renewed hope for Saint James. Feeling that the staff, vestry, and congregation were functioning effectively and that he had completed his agreed-upon purposes in returning to Saint James as interim, Rev. Holt notified the vestry of his second resignation to take place April 30, 1980.

Rev. Morris J. Lent, Jr. accepted a call to Saint James on May 15, 1980, stating that he would begin his role as rector August 1. The bishop installed him on September 7. Although reared as a Presbyterian, he was later confirmed as an Episcopalian. After his graduation in 1964 from West Point, he joined the infantry and went through airborne school and ranger school, both of which demanded physical endurance. He called them "confidence-building exercises." He completed a tour in Korea and then in Vietnam where he worked as an adviser to a Vietnamese ranger battalion.[1]

Then he enrolled in the University of Virginia Law School, and after graduation, he worked in Washington, D.C. in the Judge Advocate General's Court. While there he took courses at Virginia Seminary. Rev. Lent also taught law classes to undergraduates at West Point and decided that teaching in a minister's position was indeed his calling. He was sponsored by the bishop of East Carolina when he went to seminary, and in 1975 he began his study for the ministry at The South at Sewanee, Tennessee. Rev. Lent received his first call to St. Michael's Episcopal Church in downtown Charleston, South Carolina, where he was an assistant to the rector for two years.[2]

Reporter Elsa McDowell's article about Rev. Lent states:

[His congregation] likes the down-to-earth way he communicates...They like [his] inspiring sermons... they particularly like [his] caring counseling... One way he communicates is through story-telling. In his sermons, he weaves in everyday stories to illustrate the Gospel...he uses vignettes to provoke thoughtful discussion. And in his counseling, his observations come alive with practical applications.[3]

He, his wife Harriett, their son, and their Vietnamese foster son were loved by the congregation as the church regained a unity and new direction.

Much discussion throughout this decade preceded what would eventually result in the establishment of the Bishop Gadsden Episcopal Retirement Community. In the summer of 1980, the vestry started discussing what would be best to do in regards to the Bee Street Retirement Home for the elderly, which would be closed and replaced by a new building. Interestingly, the following were sites initially considered for the location of the retirement home: Porter-Gaud School, Seabrook Island, Parrot Point, land next to Saint James, and land across Camp Road from Saint James. The Very Rev. Lynwood McGee, Dean of the Cathedral, and The Rev. Canon Edward Guerry proposed building a retirement home on Saint James' property. Diocesan representatives gave several reasons why property near the church would be best.

A letter among vestry minutes dated October 20, 1980, signed by Rev. Lent and Senior Warden William Bailey and addressed to Bishop Temple, states that the vestry was "inclined to work with the Diocese on the transfer of property to be used for a home for the aging... not [yet] a firm commitment. That can obviously come only after we are more aware of specific plans for the project." Of course, this was part of the initial planning to establish the Bishop Gadsden Home, with Rev. Lent serving on the board that initiated this retirement center.[4]

The Land Committee, chaired at the time by Clark Morrison, also agreed that the property where Bishop Gadsden was ultimately built was the best location. The land originally designated for donation was five acres, with eventually two additional five-acre tracts that could possibly be added in the future.[5]

In 1984 the vestry sent a letter to Mr. Thomas Myers, Chairman of the Bishop Gadsden Board, stating, "It is the intention of the Vestry that the entire 50 acres across the street will be available for the Bishop Gadsden Episcopal Community. The availability will be in the form of staggered options and right of first refusal to be determined at the time of the exercise."[6] This amount of land to be granted incrementally was certainly more than the original proposed gift of five acres.

Parishioners wrote letters in support of this initiative. On December 4, 1980, Jennie Olbrych wrote to Rev. Lent about the "possibility with relocating the Bee Street Home across the street from St. James....I believe that ultimately it may be the duty of the Church to raise consciousness…in respect to honoring our fathers and mothers. I can also see St. James growing tremendously in many ways as a result of this ministry." Her letter goes on to say that this undertaking will require a huge commitment from Saint James' parishioners and priests.

In a letter dated December 6, 1980, Dr. and Mrs. David Egleston wrote, "Scripture certainly commands us to care for the 'widows and orphans,' and it seems this would be a means of ministering to many who are often neglected." This home "will increase our church family." (Both letters are saved with vestry notes.)

Directing their attention to another matter, the vestry and staff examined current policies pertaining to parishioners taking on leadership roles in church services. Approval of those requesting to be lay readers was still a matter to be seriously considered and voted upon before they were able to serve in this capacity. The inclusion of women filling this role was a major historical change from the all-male lists of lay readers for centuries. As of May 1981, four new lay readers were named: Mac Rhodes, Kitty Ellis, Jennie Olbrych, and Sally Vale. By November Miriam Keeler had also been added to the certified lay readers.

On July 26, 1981, a Dedication Service was held on St. James' Day. The church bulletin expressed much of the belief upon which this book's historical account is based:

> Our hope is that today's service will give us a deeper sense of our heritage, and that this new appreciation of <u>who we have been</u> will enable us to become even more <u>who we are</u>—God's children and God's servants. We want to specifically thank several people who have made this day possible: Mr. Willie McLeod, Mary Allen Ravenel and Frances Hayden for the memorial gifts; Amarylis Cranwell and Trudy Ketcham for many hours spent collecting and displaying parts of our history; all the people who have loaned us items from that history; Jennie Olbrych and Harriett Lent for designing and making the new Saint James' banner (Jennie dedicates her work on this banner to the memory of her great-grandfather, The Rev. Andrew Cornish—former rector of this parish—and his wife, Sarah Catherine Cornish); and Dr. Dan Ellis, our Parish Historian, for sharing his knowledge and insight about our history.

In this July 26, 1981 Sunday service, on behalf of the McLeod family, Mr. William E. McLeod presented a chalice, which was dedicated to Rev. Edward B. Guerry. Prayerful words regarding the chalice were "Grant that all who receive the holy Mystery from this vessel…may be sustained by His presence and enjoy forever His heavenly benediction." A lectern Bible was presented by Mary Allen Ravenel in memory of her husband Arthur Ravenel, Sr., and dedicated by Rev. Morris J. Lent, Jr. who said, "May we so diligently search Your holy Word that we may find in it the wisdom that leads to salvation." A picture of the stained-glass windows (as they hung in the former church building) was presented by Frances Hayden in memory of her husband, James G. Hayden, and dedicated by Rev. Lent, including these words, "O Lord God, the whole world is filled with the radiance of Your glory: Accept our offering of these windows which we now dedicate to You for the adornment of the Parish Hall and the inspiration of Your people. Grant that as the light shines through it in many colors, so our lives may show forth the beauty of Your manifold gifts of grace."

Records show that Rev. Lent made several important decisions regarding personnel. He hired Brenda Albinger as Saint James' new organist. Ms. Albinger was a music teacher at Harbor View Middle School and later Fort Johnson Middle. She had been the organist at Ft. Johnson Baptist on James Island.[7] He hired Cindy Taylor, a seminarian, to work throughout the summer of 1985.[8] He also hired Rev. Keith Burns to do part time preaching and teaching and Mrs. Polly Sosnowski to be the youth director for high schoolers.[9]

Vestry minutes from September 1982 address a proposal to convert two Sunday school rooms in the parish hall into a chapel for meditation, prayer, smaller services, and kindergartners' daily worship. Costing $7500,[10] the chapel was named Saint James Memorial Chapel. The first service was held May 1, 1983. Senior Warden Vic Burrell reported the following in the *Congregational Report 1984*: "The new chapel came into being largely through the efforts of Henry McManus and his dedicated committee. It adds not only its beauty to our physical plant, but adds much to the flexibility of our services."[11] Its uses included weekly midday Eucharists, baptisms, weddings, and special services, such as one held for expectant parents in the parish family. An Anniversary Eucharist was held the second Thursday of each month for married couples.[12]

Because Rev. Lent was still on Army Reserve duty in the spring of 1982, Rev. James Donald and Rev. Sidney Holt filled in for him. Greg Prior was on staff as a seminarian the summer of 1982, became assistant rector in March of 1983[13] and was ordained at Saint James in June of 1983. A former native of Providence, Rhode Island, Greg Prior, with his wife Anna Gray and their four children, had moved to Charleston where he had worked for the *News and Courier* before deciding to go into the ministry. He had received a Masters in Divinity from Sewanee in 1983.[14]

At the 1983 Diocesan Convention, clergymen over fifty were encouraged to get an annual physical to be paid for by their congregations—ages forty-three to fifty, physicals every other year; ages forty and under, every three years. If the priest agreed, medical results would be forwarded to the bishop, and the clergyman would have lunch and conversation with the bishop during the rector's birthday month.[15]

Fellowship and educational programs were vibrant in this decade. An intergenerational group gathered Sunday mornings in the parish hall for a spiritual message, music, and sometimes a skit. Then the youth would disperse to classrooms for age-specific lessons while adults stayed to hear messages from the priests and guest speakers. In March of 1982 the children of Saint James were encouraged to collect and contribute dollars to "Heifer Project International," a mission program that purchased farm animals to be donated to needy families in other countries.

New and varied worship services were added. A "Lessons and Carols" service was included in Advent, and a New Year's Eve service was held December 31, 1983.[16] In 1984 the vestry voted to reinstate an Epiphany Sunday service (usually an evening prayer service) done by candlelight and ending with the congregation carrying lighted candles, filing out of the sanctuary, forming a circle under the oaks, singing the closing hymn, followed by the benediction.[17]

Susan Watkins, education coordinator, filled over two single-spaced pages in the *Congregational Report 1984* about a huge variety of activities for both children and adults with Sunday school and youth group events. Mrs. Watson's 1985 report includes details about several plays and programs—"Geraldine and the Church Mice," "Saints at St. James," and "Alternatives at Christmas." Vacation Bible School was entitled "Summer Celebration '84: Celebrating God's Family." The Christmas pageant continued as an annual seasonal event, involving costumed children reenacting the Christmas story. At that time the Episcopal Youth Group (EYC), led by David and Kay Cupka, was very active. One example was their Rock-a-Thon to raise money to contribute to the Ronald McDonald House downtown. The youth would solicit pledges from sponsors beforehand and then earn the donations per hour that they rocked in rocking chairs during a church "lock-in." A technological introduction was made to the parish, a VCR used for a study of six video series "Old Testament—Greatest Adventures."[18]

Using the Rose Barnwell funds ($50,000 earmarked "to be used as needed"), the vestry modernized the parish hall kitchen, refurbished the parish hall, constructed a ramp between the parish hall and the church, and erected a new sign in the front of the church. The balance of the fund was to be invested, the interest to be spent on persons, projects, or programs outside of Saint James.[19] In July of 1984 the vestry was informed that Saint James would receive an additional $20,000 from Mrs. Rose Barnwell's fund.

In 1984 Boy Scout Troop 44 had thirty members, Cub Pack 44 had thirteen cubs, and the Girl Scouts had twenty members, with reports of the boys going to Camp Ho Non Wah on Wadmalaw Island and High Adventures Camp in Virginia, and the girls going to the home of Juliette Gordon Low, founder of the Girls Scouts, in Savannah.[20] The congregational reports for this decade are filled with details about their camps, trips, jamborees, service projects, merit badge opportunities, community undertakings, and participation in Low Country events, such as the Piccolo Spoleto Festival.

The *Congregational Report 1985* is particularly interesting regarding the adult education activities, many of which were organized by Jennie Olbrych, an active parishioner who went on to be ordained. Some members attended a series on "Stress and Stress Reduction." Morey Lent and Greg Prior provided programs on liturgy. Bishop Temple taught a Bible study on First Corinthians. A professor at Sewanee, The Rev. Christopher Bryan, conducted a "Teaching and Preaching" weekend as part of the Lenten activities. Other studies were entitled "Our Gifts and Ministries," "Stewardship," and "Preparing for Resurrection" (a series about wills, grief, funeral planning, and talking with children about death).[21]

In May 1985 Rev. Prior was called to St. Paul's in Conway where he served for eight years and then received yet another call to All Saints' Church in Hilton Head in 1993.[22] He was called to St. Andrew's-by-the-Sea in 2002, completed his Doctor of Ministry degree from Sewanee in 2005, and retired from St. Andrew's in 2009.[23]

In November of 1985 Rev. Frederick Sosnowski was hired as priest associate. He had graduated from Virginia Theological Seminary, been ordained a deacon at St. Johns (Johns Island), and was ordained in 1956 to the priesthood at Trinity Cathedral. After having served as rector in Henderson, Texas, he returned to Bugby Plantation on Wadmalaw Island to farm for a while with his father. At Saint James he offered to parishioners professional Christian counseling on numerous issues, including marriage, family, separation, divorce, careers, depression, and abuse. He assisted parishioners in making connections with additional counselors. He also did many home and hospital visitations.[24]

Carol Shue, director of Christ Kindergarten, reported that by 1985 enrollment was up to one hundred children with eight staff members emphasizing reading and math skills. This large enrollment contrasted the fledgling programs that had struggled some years before to maintain an adequate number of children to sustain a kindergarten.[25]

Brenda Albinger, organist and choir director, at this time had twenty-six members in the adult choir and involved them in musical programs, such as the Diocesan Choir Festival at the Cathedral in downtown Charleston. They performed three special anthems written by choir director emeritus Vernon W. Weston.[26] Ms. Albinger referred to the "launching of our fleet of the new *Hymnal 1982*" in the *Congregational Report 1987*. The Saint James choirs performed well beyond the church's campus, including the Kanuga Arts Conference and the Children's Choir Camp at Saint Christopher. The "Young Episcopal Choristers" were often accompanied by a harp, recorder, and Yamaha digital piano.[27]

The Outreach and Evangelism Commission was created in 1983 to support ministries outside the parish community and to reach and bring people into the life of the parish.[28] They hosted "Guest Sunday," extending invitations to the unchurched to become a part of Saint James. In 1985 this group erected the two directional signs to help people locate the church, one at the Folly and Camp Road intersection and the other where Riverland Drive and Camp Road meet. Members delegated monies to overseas projects, the Soup Kitchen, the Good Samaritan Mission of North Charleston, and other Christian organizations. Monies were sent to missionaries Beth and Chuck Boardman for Project Uganda where they pro-

vided crutches, wheelchairs, and other equipment in their school for the physically handicapped. Parishioners worked with the Florence Crittenton Home for unwed mothers, provided food for the needy, helped a family who had lost their home in a fire—and the list
goes on.[29] The *Congregational Report 1987* stated, "We are able to contribute financially to
many worthy programs through the money made available for this purpose in the Rose
McLeod Barnwell Trust." Details abound about assisting with the Star Gospel Mission, James
Island Senior Citizens Center, My Sister's House, World Food Day, Bishop's Fund for World
Relief, and Carl Green's prison ministry.[30]

Headed by Kimberly Gibson, the Pastoral Care Commission sent church members to
visit shut-ins and the hospitalized. They created a "Welcome Booklet" to provide information
to potential new church members.[31]

The Evangelism Commission was very proactive in inviting new members and visitors
to feel welcome at Saint James. Rev. Lent conducted classes about the customs, beliefs, faith,
and goals at the church and, with his wife Harriett, held receptions for these incoming
members. Walter and Martha Ameika hosted a party in their home to welcome new participants. A phone chain issued personal invitations to church activities, such as the parish
picnic.[32] Royal "Chip" Gibson, stewardship chairman in 1986, reported forty new pledges
in that year.[33]

An interesting historical detail in January 18,1985 vestry minutes pertains to a letter from
the City of Charleston that a 911 emergency call system was being put into place under the
leadership of Mayor Joseph P. Riley, Jr. The letter was mailed with a map to verify the address
of the church. Also, in 1986, panic bars were installed for the Parish House doors, emergency
lights were installed in the parish hall and school area, a new phone system was purchased,
and exit signs required by the fire department were posted.[34]

During the Sunday church service on February 3, 1985, a Service of Dedication marked
a significant addition provided for the sanctuary of Saint James' Church. Mr. William
McLeod, in memory of his sister Rose McLeod Barnwell, dedicated two plaques, one on either side of the altar, the Lord's Prayer and the Apostles Creed. As explained in the church
bulletin, the committee who oversaw the design and installation of the two tablets, made
by Wippell Company, were Katherine Burrell (chairman), Kay Cupka, Frank Freeman, Au-
drey Hall, Francis Harleston, Dorothy Huff, Clark Morrison, and Anne Read. In absentia,
The Rev. H. Pierce Middleton of Annapolis, Maryland, served as a consultant to the committee. Rev. Middleton was a member of the National Church's Commission on Religious
Arts and Architecture.

Rev. Lent prayed,

> We bless Your Name, O Lord, because it has pleased You to enable Your ser-
> vant, Mr. Willie, to offer this gift for Your worship. Remember him for good,

and grant that all who benefit from this gift may show their thankfulness to You by living their lives in accordance with Your will; through Jesus Christ our Lord. Amen.

Then Mrs. Ella Guerry and Mrs. Harriett Lent unveiled the two plaques that had been placed parallel from each other on the side walls of the altar. Rev. Lent offered the following prayer:

O God, whose blessed Son was sanctified and transfigured the use of material things, receive these tablets which we offer, and grant that they may proclaim Your love, benefit Your Church, and minister grace and joy to all who worship here, through Jesus Christ our Lord. Amen.

Almighty God, we remember before You today Your faithful servant, Rose McLeod Barnwell, and we pray that, having opened to her the gates of larger life, You will receive her more and more into your joyful service, that, with all who have faithfully served You in the past, she may share in the eternal victory of Jesus Christ our Lord. Amen.

O Lord, watch over Thy servant, Mr. Willie, as his days increase; bless and guide him wherever he may be. Strengthen him when he stands; comfort him when discouraged or sorrowful; raise him up if he falls; and in his heart may the peace which passeth understanding abide all the days of his life; through Jesus Christ our Lord. Amen. (recorded in church bulletin February 3, 1985)

Organist Dr. Wyman Frampton, Jr., played a hymn on bagpipes and wore the McLeod tartan. An insert about bagpipers in the Sunday's service bulletin, dated February 3, 1985, stated, "The greatest of all hereditary pipers were the MacCrimmons, pipers to Clan McLeod of McLeod, the clan from which Mr. Willie is descended."

By the mid-1980s plans were becoming firm regarding the Bishop Gadsden Retirement Community, named after the fourth bishop of the Diocese of South Carolina (1840-1852) and grandson of the Revolutionary patriot General Christopher Gadsden. Bishop Gadsden had led the initiative in 1850 to establish a home for women and for orphans at 55 Laurens Street, the first institution of its kind in the area. In 1896 this Laurens Street house was combined with "House of Rest" and housed on Ashley Avenue. In 1906 the Diocese assumed responsibility for the church home and orphanage. In 1909 children were moved to what is today known as York Place. In 1937 the women were moved to a fine old three-storied mansion at 12 Bee Street. When that property was sold in 1983, plans were coming about for the Bishop Gadsden Retirement Community. Thus, due to Bishop Gadsden's initial passion and historical accomplishments to provide special-care residences, this retirement facility bears his name today.[35]

Those involved in planning for Bishop Gadsden received information regarding various levels of care, standards in the retirement home industry, financial options, and federal regulations. By that year Saint James had plans to donate a minimum of fifty acres to the home.[36] Mr. William Bailey served as co-chair of the fund drives at Saint James on behalf of Bishop Gadsden, reporting pledges at $222,291 in mid-1984.[37] Interestingly, the March 17, 1986 vestry minutes state that if the property were sold to a third party, Bishop Gadsden would be appraised and would pay Saint James for the appraised value of the church home. Also, any liability suit of any injury would be the responsibility of Bishop Gadsden.

On April 27, 1985 the vestry interviewed Rev. Clark Wallace Paul Lowenfield and voted unanimously to offer him the position of assistant rector. He and his fiancé Miss Tricia Keller were welcomed. They were married October 4, 1986 in El Paso, Texas.[38] A graduate of Amherst College with majors in political science and economics, Rev. Lowenfield had earned a Master of Divinity at the University of the South—School of Theology in Sewanee.[39]

The February 1987 *Jubilate Deo* included a lengthy article introducing many of its readers to initial information pertaining to Bishop Gadsden, built on the land granted by Saint James. The following are three paragraphs taken from that report:

> The first phase…consists of a cluster of eight buildings connected by enclosed corridors, and includes seventy residential living units, dining room, group gathering rooms…parlors, activity areas, and a courtyard and other beautifully landscaped areas…
>
> [It] offers a supportive environment for those individuals who are still active and independent, but feel the need to be relieved of some of the burdensome, and often very stressful, daily routines. A variety of services will be provided which will allow our residents to conserve their energies for the activities they enjoy…These services include three meals daily, nurse/assistants on duty daily, weekly housekeeping service, linen service, security supervision, planned social activities, scheduled transportation, and all maintenance of buildings and grounds.
>
> Future phrases of the Community will include a comprehensive health care facility and apartments and cottages. When all phases are completed, the Bishop Gadsden community will be a continuing care retirement community [with] options to meet individual needs and preferences. The Community will have apartments and cottages for those who are totally independent[;] congregate living for those who are also independent, but need additional services[;] and intermediate and skilled nursing care for those needing comprehensive medical supervision.[40]

A land tract of 2.09 acres, added to four more acres, was deeded by Saint James to Bishop Gadsden to accommodate ten more rooms to their original plans and comply with zoning requirements for utility and drainage facilities.[41] In late October, 1987, the first residents moved into the Bishop Gadsden. In 1988 the vestry voted unanimously that Saint James could be designated as an emergency evacuation site for use in any emergency rendering the Bishop Gadsden facilities unsuitable for habitation. The word "Episcopal" became an official part of the whole name: Bishop Gadsden Episcopal Retirement Community.[42] After the Bee Street home closed, the silver, which had been used in the chapel there, was consigned to the chapel at Saint James; however, at the request of Rev. Guerry, the silver was given to Bishop Gadsden to be used in its chapel.[43]

In a letter dated December 14, 1989, and addressed to Mr. William Trawick, administrator at Bishop Gadsden, Vic Burrell wrote,

> The Vestry does feel that Saint James', as a growing neighbor alongside a growing Bishop Gadsden Community, needs to be involved explicitly in your long-term thinking. We are parallel entities. As the years go on, it will be important for us to have a continuing one-minded relationship of service to our respective and common community.

Of course, over the years initial buildings have been completely renovated, and many new structures have been built, multiplying the facility in size and enabling Bishop Gadsden to earn the reputation of being one of the finest retirement homes in the country.

Well up in years, Rev. Guerry continued to have a high profile in the diocese. The March 1987 *Jubilate Deo* stated that at age eighty-three, he asked to be relieved of his position of the Diocesan's historiographer who organizes the many resources that chronicle the history and work of the diocese.[44] In an excerpt from "Tributes to Canon Guerry," Rev. Fred Sosnowski wrote the following:

> Mr. Guerry almost single-handedly saved Porter Gaud School when the wisdom of the day was to let it go. The huge property which now houses St. Christopher was given to the Diocese by the Morawetz family. This wonderful gift was a direct outgrowth of their relationship to Ed Guerry and their conversations concerning a vision of that beautiful spot as a vehicle for the growth and nurture of children.

The Sosnowski family affectionately called Rev. Guerry "the parson," and many referred to his wife as "Miss Ella."[45] When Mrs. Guerry was asked if she had any advice for a young minister's wife, her response was to love the members of her husband's church...to be as loyal to the church members as she'd be to her own family.[46] In yet another tribute, Rosamond and Sandie Bee said, "He may have been short in stature but to us, he was a giant of a man."[47]

Rev. Guerry and his wife eventually moved to Bishop Gadsden. On October 18, 1992, he died at the age of ninety, his funeral was held at The Cathedral of St. Luke and St. Paul on Coming Street, and he is buried in St. Philip's Churchyard in downtown Charleston.[48]

This decade reveals several transitions regarding women's roles within the church. Rev. Lent expressed a desire to appoint Kitty Ellis as a Lay Eucharist minister. A proposal at this time to appoint a female to this role required vestry approval, which she received unanimously, thus paving the way for more female parishioners to take on this privilege.[49]

The 1987 publication entitled "An Unfinished History of St. James' Episcopal Church" ended with this paragraph:

> The History of St. James' has yet to be written by its…coming generations. For almost ten generations the people of St. James', James Island, have brought this present, vibrant and growing Episcopal Church from the wilderness to a world of superhighways, split-levels, condominiums, televisions, and word-processors. What is to come next is still to be seen. In the past, their enemies were Indians, pestilence, starvation, and a constant struggle for existence. Today, the enemies are perhaps more insidious and difficult to identify. Can the values of Christianity, as our fathers knew them, survive the assaults of these present enemies? By knowing more about our past, we can find strength for our future—in St. James' on James Island.[50]

Presently, parishioners, even more aware of extreme examples of modernism, continue to reflect on these same concerns regarding Christian values in a complex culture that often seems contradictory to Biblical mores.

Saint James held a dedication service in which two alms basins were gifted to the church. One was in memory of Ruth Carter and Eugene Clark Morrison, Sr., by Eugene Clark Morrison, Jr. The other was given in memory of William Stevens Brown by his mother Margaret Schaffer Brown, his sister and brothers Margaret Brown Buck, Frederick Henry Brown, and Edmonds Tennent Brown III.[51]

Regarding communion, the vestry discussed the use of bread vs. wafer and the use of the "common cup" in light of the AIDS threat. They decided to use the wafer, which was easier for those who chose intinction, which involves the communicant dipping the wafer in the wine so that he receives both together. After several dioceses of the Episcopal

Church examined the use of the shared cup, the consensus supported the continued use of it. The vestry also wanted to honor the longstanding custom of using the wafer and communal cup.[52]

A *Jubilate Deo* article entitled "St. James to Host Convention" shares an account of the 197th Diocesan Convention. Rev. Lent and his colleagues prepared a four-page insert sharing the history of Saint James and the plans and progress for Bishop Gadsden Episcopal Community.[53] The article concludes with the following paragraph: "The story of the buildings of Saint James' is…to inform you of the people of Saint James' and their struggle and determination to keep the faith alive on this island. These people have been, and still are, people of the land. We value earthiness and simplicity…"[54]

Rev. Lent resigned effective August 1, 1987, after seven extremely busy years, much of which had been devoted initially to crisis management of restoring a discordant congregation and then ultimately to rapid growth at Saint James. Senior warden R. Eugene Miller sent a letter to parishioners, stating, "We must applaud [Morey] and pray that the Lent family will always be blessed the way they have blessed us. We love and respect [Morey] and will be forever grateful to Our Lord and Savior for having lent us Morey Lent." According to vestry minutes, a farewell reception was held in honor of the Lents on July 26, 1987.

Rev. Lent accepted the chaplain's position at Porter-Gaud School where he could make good use of his skills in storytelling, instructing, and counseling. According to a 1987 *News and Courier* article, Lent was hired to "teach Old Testament, New Testament and Ethics, lead worship services; and serve as counselor and spiritual adviser for the school—students, staff and parents."[55]

Rev. Lowenfield served Saint James as rector, locum tenens (meaning "one holding a place") while the church's search committee sought a rector to replace Rev. Lent. In his letter to the congregation on January 15, 1988, Rev. Lowenfield wrote, "The Family of Saint James', as families do in times of change, has pulled together, realizing that the Lord is opening the door to a new and exciting era built on the firm foundation of what has gone before." Replacing Rev. Lowenfield as rector, locum tenens, Rev. Knud Anthon Larsen III ("Father Kal") served at Saint James as interim rector until September 4, 1988, his last Sunday at Saint James.

September 8, 1988, Rev. Lowenfield was installed as the thirteenth rector of the Church of the Holy Communion in downtown Charleston. In years to come, he did mission work in Rwanda and became Anglican Bishop of the Diocese of the Western Gulf Coast, which incorporates parts of Louisiana and Texas.[56]

Saint James' Congregational Report 1988 contains some impressive statistics: 728 members at the end of 1987; average Sunday school attendance between 150-160; the Boy Scouts, 52 members, and cub scouts, 68 boys; 800 sandwiches that the ECW Kitchen Committee prepared for the Diocesan Convention; and the donation of land to the Bishop Gadsden Episcopal Community for the addition of a 44-bed nursing facility.

In Saint James' church bulletin for May 1, 1988, an insert entitled "Parish of Saint James' Church, James Island, Resolution" named Dr. Daniel Wordsworth Ellis as Senior Warden Emeritus due to his faithful service for over seventy-nine years—a repeatedly elected vestryman always serving with "energy, dedication, wisdom and distinction."

An interesting insert, as follows, is in the vestry minutes of September 19, 1988:

> Rev. Edward B Guerry had discovered that old records of the Parish not burned by General Sherman were in badly deteriorated condition as a consequence of acidification of the papers, ink, and storage containers...Ms. Jane M. Brown, a conservator, had examined the documents and determined that deacidification by gas under pressure is required but not yet available to non-governmental entities in this area. In the interim, she recommends acid free storage containers and future use of acid free paper.

These same vestry minutes contain yet another interesting historical detail indicating the longstanding ties between Saint James Episcopal and James Island Presbyterian churches:

> ...the trustees of the Estate of Pauline R. Dill had decided that the monies designated for the perpetual care of Dill plots at St. James' and the James Island Presbyterian Church could be divided between the two churches and deposited into their respective general investment accounts, provided that each agree to provide perpetual care.

The Charleston Museum website states the following about the "Dill Sisters' Estate":

> The Dill Sanctuary, located on [Riverland Drive] of James Island contains assorted habitats for wildlife and numerous cultural features including three earthen Confederate batteries and prehistoric, colonial, antebellum, and postbellum archaeological sites. The Dill Sanctuary has been protected for purposes of preservation, wildlife enhancement, research and education.[57]

Another source states, "Where Meridian and Queensboro subdivisions are now...a section of the Dill Plantation ...was called Turkey Pen and Cut Bridge."[58] Saint James' cemetery booklet includes information about the gravestones of Eleanor C. Dill (died 1878); Regina Alison Dill (died 1896); Joseph T. Dill (died 1900); Frances Adeline Hinson Dill (died 1916); Julia Rivers Dill (died 1970); and Pauline Rivers Dill (died 1985). These two relatively current vestry entries show how the church's and the island's recent histories are constantly intertwined with more modern times.[59]

On September 11, 1988, Rev. Paul F. M. Zahl (37) was welcomed as Saint James' new rector. Born in New York City, he graduated from Harvard and received his theological degree in Nottingham, England. Having left his rectorship at St. Mary's Church in Scarborough, New York (1982-1988) to come to Saint James, he said that he was "building on a firm, strong ministry," with a desire to provide "warm, classic pastoral care," spiritual leadership, and support for the growing parish ministry to youth. He was identified as a "prolific writer," having contributed frequent columns to the *Episcopal New Yorker*, *Jubilate Deo*, *The Anglican Digest*, the *Virginia Seminary Journal*, and the *Episcopalian*.[60]

Rev. Zahl shared in a letter, dated September 11, 1988, to the congregation that he had three initial goals: (1) be a pastor to the parish, comforting and visiting and listening and loving, (2) be a teacher and preacher of the scripture, seeking to help the old story come alive and speak to our real lives, (3) and attend to the young people of St. James'. He and his wife Mary, a professional garden designer, had three sons—John, David, and Simeon.

Rev. Zahl wrote a book entitled *Who Will Deliver Us?: The Present Power of the Death of Christ*. The back cover of the book states the following about this text:

> Drawing on the classic teaching of the atonement as it is presented by St. Paul and other Christian thinkers, Paul Zahl unfolds its meaning for this generation. He then applies it to the problems of spiritual malaise and meaninglessness which afflict us today: problems of depression and despair, of loneliness, of broken relationships. Throughout, the Good News of Christianity—forgiveness, reconciliation, new life—is presented in terms which contemporary readers can easily understand and apply to their lives.[61]

Rev. Zahl had an encyclopedic knowledge of music, books, and movies, to which he often referred in his sermons. An article about him in the *News and Courier* stated, "Rock music is more than a hobby to the self-described conservative, even orthodox priest. His in-depth knowledge of [rock music] has opened lines of communication with many a troubled teenager who otherwise never would have talked with a priest." When some gravely concerned parents approached Rev. Zahl about their son, who had become noncommunicative and stayed in his room playing heavy-metal music, Zahl said to them, "Ask him what he thinks of Motorhead." That question led the young man to go to Rev. Zahl's office, initially to discuss the legendary rock group. The teen found that his priest knew the group's members by name. That introduction enabled Zahl to reach a young man dealing with suppressed anger. Rev. Zahl often peppered his sermons with song lyrics that incorporated moral themes, such as redemption, love, and grace. At the same time, Zahl acknowledged that some song lyrics can have negative influences.[62]

According to vestry minutes of February 1988 and the *Congregational Report 1989*, the scouts, EYC, and other volunteers worked on two grounds projects, one which was to create twelve stations of the cross and a trail to an outdoor chapel where Ellis Creek runs along the back of Saint James' property. This area is still used today for small weddings, annual services for blessings of the animals, and a quiet getaway for personal reflection and prayer. With unanimous support from the vestry, this work on church grounds also included moving a back fence to encompass the old graves belonging to black James Island residents.

Additional plans included the building of an elevated concrete walkway connecting the parish house to the right side of the church (when facing the front). However, vestry members argued as they hired architects, wrangled over various potential designs, considered the location of oak trees and their root systems, and wrestled with the cost, which was between $25,000 and $30,000.[63] Finally plans for a functional, attractive ramp were selected. With steps and railings placed alongside, this new walkway gave easier access to those physically disabled and was beneficial to everyone in inclement weather. Decades of users have appreciated this ramp.

Returning to a topic that was in Saint James' historical records for over a century, more negotiations took place regarding Parrot Point. In 1983 the Charleston Orphan house made an offer to sell their reversionary rights. They testified that they needed financial support rather than land support and were eager to sell their rights to the property. Senior warden Gene Miller, as the church's attorney, represented Saint James in 1988, with parishioners Vic Burrell, Thomas L. Read, and W. McLeod Rhodes as witnesses. The *Congregational Report 1989* had this to say about Parrot Point property, submitted by Mac Rhodes, then Land Committee Chairman:

> The church in 1988 initiated legal action to clear the title of the Parrott's Point property. This matter has been concluded in the following fashion: Saint James Church will pay $50,000 to the Charleston Orphan House, the Orphan House will sell its reverter rights in said land to Saint James Church, subject to the proviso that the Orphan House will have the right for five years after said sale to join in equally the proceeds of any sale of Parrott's Point, less the $50,000 After the five year waiting period, the Orphan House will have no interest in the property and the property will be subject to no reverter.[64]

In January of 1989 Dr. Ford M. Lallerstedt, who had earned a doctorate at the Juilliard School of Music, became the director of music at Saint James. Flying back and forth, he continued to teach part time at the Curtis School of Music in Philadelphia.[65] Inviting guest vocalists and musicians, he coordinated several impressive music programs and organ recitals open to the public. He was featured in a newspaper article entitled "Churches Attract Serious Musicians."[66]

Called to serve as an associate rector, Rev. Frank Limehouse joined the staff at Saint James to work with Rev. Zahl beginning in August of 1989. Rev. Limehouse had an interesting pathway to the priesthood. Although reared in a Christian home, he eventually held agnostic beliefs. While attending Wofford College, he was married. He and his first wife had a daughter but eventually divorced. Having grown up in Orangeburg, he worked as a haberdasher for twenty years in his family's clothing store that had been established in 1922. While married to his second wife Jane Mewborne, a devout Christian, they had a son, Frank Limehouse IV, who was baptized in their home. Reverend Bill Snow, pastor of the Church of the Redeemer in Orangeburg where Jane worshipped, invited Frank to play golf with him. At the ninth hole, he asked Frank what he had against Christianity and posed this question: "Is it the resurrection?" Initially annoyed, Frank, however, began reflecting on this question, made an appointment to talk with Rev. Snow, and started studying the history of Christianity.[67]

St. Helena's publication entitled *Amazing Grace*, explained the following significant moment in Frank's life when he went to New York on a buying trip for his father's business:

> Frank Limehouse found himself outside St. Patrick's Cathedral and felt compelled to go in. Not knowing what he was doing there, he felt lifted down the aisle and got down on his knees to do something he had not done since he was a little boy in his grandmother's lap: he prayed. *'God, I don't know how to pray. Just tell me. Was He or wasn't He? Is He or isn't He? Did He or didn't He?'* Frank began to feel a love he had never felt before.[68]

From choir member to chalice bearer to vestry member to a retreat at an Episcopal monastery—Frank was led to attend seminary. He shared an inspirational story from his past about his father and his clothing business, which had a five-year lease to be honored. His father at the time was seventy-five years old and retired. In learning about his son's desire to go to seminary, his father said, "Although I've never been a particularly religious man, perhaps this is a way I can participate in your ministry. You go to seminary and I'll ride the lease out," so he went back to work full time until the lease expired. On June 29, 1989, Rev. Limehouse was ordained deacon at the Cathedral of St. Luke and St. Paul by the Right Reverend C. FitzSimons Allison, the twelfth Bishop of the Diocese of South Carolina, who continued to serve as Frank's mentor.[69] Limehouse was ordained into the priesthood June 17, 1990 at Saint James.

Weather brought a dramatic end to this decade. During the night between September 21 and 22, 1989, Hurricane Hugo came roaring into Charleston County's coastal area with high winds and storm surge, threatening the oaks, sanctuary, parish house, and cemetery at Saint

James. It was a category five storm with winds at 138 miles per hour.[70] Several parishioners weathered out the hurricane in Saint James' parish hall, not only to seek shelter but also to be able to attend to the property immediately after winds and rain had subsided.[71] The church ceiling was inspected during the eye of the hurricane, a leak was noted, but the repair was deferred. Although located not far from tide-water marsh, flood waters did not invade the church buildings. Unlike many gravesites that were opened in other cemeteries, Saint James' burial sites remained sealed. Elsewhere, commercial and residential buildings had roofs ripped off, but not at Saint James. However, there was some roof damage, which caused the vestry concern regarding repairs, especially since the shingles contained asbestos. One of the custom-made windows in the steeple, as well as the copper on the steeple, had to be replaced.[72]

The grounds were littered with tons of debris caused by broken tree limbs, scattered Spanish moss, and an assortment of remnants ripped from nearby properties. Some large trees on the land where the Ministry Center is now located were snapped off or uprooted by the powerful winds. According to Vic Burrell's 1990 senior warden report to the congregation, a crew of parishioners went to the church on Saturday and Sunday after the hurricane to begin the task of clearing paths. Worship services resumed before all of the island had its electricity restored and before all roads had been completely cleared. A fallen tree damaged the air-conditioning and heating unit for the first floor of the Sunday school building. The replacement cost was $5,000. Initially, $11,000 was spent for clean-up, with an additional $4,000 to $5,000 needed to complete the work.[73] Because the hurricane destroyed so many pine trees on the back of the church property, much of that land was cleared, expanding the size of the cemetery.[74] Vic Burrell wrote that junior warden Matt Townsend "worked with adjusters, building contractors, roofers, loggers, and tree experts" to get Saint James repaired and restored. As parishioners struggled to deal with cleanup of their roads, houses, schools, and businesses, they also struggled to restore some order to church property.

According to vestry minutes, church staff and members made decisions pertaining to matters other than property following Hurricane Hugo. The stewardship drive that had been scheduled for October was postponed. Francie Egleston coordinated a telephone survey to contact members to identify special needs and problems and to keep the priests abreast of these matters.[75]

Helen Schatz, the ECW Kitchen Chairman, reported the following in the *Congregational Report 1990* to the congregation:

> When Hugo came along, …the tomatoes we had frozen were made into soup and chili along with food from various parishioners' freezers. With Carol Galbraith's help, soup, rice and chili and 450 sandwiches made by the EYC [Episcopal Youth Council], we served food to residents of Folly

Beach [which had sustained extensive damage] and Hugo relief workers. We also fed volunteers working in the church yard and the congregation after Sunday service. We twice served meals to Mennonite groups from Pennsylvania here doing Hugo aid on James Island.[76]

Much of the November/December *Jubilate Deo* 1989 reported on the aftermath of the hurricane throughout the Diocese. In an article entitled, "The Day after Hugo...Destruction Everywhere," one of the paragraphs stated, "At an emergency meeting of St. James' on James Island, two days after Hugo struck, the vestry offered a large sum from its hitherto sacrosanct endowment [a principle usually regarded as too important or valuable to be interfered with] for immediate interest-free loans."[77] Vestry members voted to take $100,000 from the investment capital for interest-free loans for those members of the Saint James family with pressing financial needs. Although individual loans were capped at $1500, a parishioner could appeal for more funds, if necessary.[78]

Help came from within and outside the community. For example, a letter dated September 27, 1989 was sent by Lena Honnberger, secretary and treasurer of St. Mary's Episcopal of Templeton, Pennsylvania. In the letter was a check for $400 to be used on behalf of hurricane victims. This donation was remarkably generous because it was from the smallest church in the Diocese of Northwestern, Pennsylvania, a country church that had a total membership of eighteen people.

Junior warden Matt Townsend invested much time and thought into how to use insurance proceeds to pay for much needed repairs and renovations, mostly due to Hurricane Hugo. His accomplishments were listed, including replacing roofs, painting inside and out, enlarging the parking lot, repairing fencing, refurbishing the nursery, purchasing furniture and appliances, and doubling the size of the cemetery.[79]

Surely, many parishioners were relying on the comfort from the old hymn's words: "O God, our help in ages past, our hope for years to come, our shelter from the stormy blast, and our eternal home."

In *How Grand a Flame*, Bresee ends his three-generation account about the Lawtons on James Island with a profound epilogue dated 1989. He said that he asked Creighton Frampton, a retired Charleston County Schools superintendent who had grown up on a James Island plantation, to visit Saint James with him. He describes this reflective venture as follows:

> Turning onto Camp Road a few minutes later, we saw the steeple of St. James over the trees—no longer the little Gothic building of pine and cypress presided over by an itinerant preacher every other Sunday, but a church faithfully modeled after St. Michael's in Charleston, its tower a diaphanous white, floating over the treetops, the whole edifice exuding re-

finement and elegance. The doors were open for a children's service that was in progress, and mothers in cars were waiting under the trees.

How could this grand building have been fitted between the arms of the cemetery that had nestled close to the sides of the old church that I knew? It did not fit, Creighton told me, and the bones of many had to be reinterred. There was a formal service when it was done, the rector in his ecclesiastical robes standing beside the new earth, prayer book in hand.

The Lawton graves did not have to be moved. They were in the precise plot of land that Winborn had selected nearly a century and a half ago, a rectangle of earth enclosed by an iron fence. Creighton and I stood by the enclosure in silence, our thoughts receding to other days.

The three generations were together at last, I thought, chief players in a story that lasted 160 years. Winborn's stone was the tallest, an eight-foot obelisk mounted on a granite base. Next, the graves of Wallace and Cecilia; for their children who had died six days apart, two marble lambs were nestled on a low stone above the inscription "Our Darlings."

"And here are the two we remember," Creighton said, "St. John Alison Lawton, V.M.I.—'91, and Ruth Jennings Lawton, President Regent, U.D.C."

The fence enclosed the graves neatly—no need for extra room, for there are no more Lawtons of that line to join them.

"Alison, you know, had no brothers and sisters who survived infancy and he had no children," Creighton continued. "There have been no Lawtons—at least of that branch of the family—on James Island for many years now. I feel a little bad about that."

This little tract of earth, it occurred to me, is all that remains of the lands of a family who, for a century and a half once owned a goodly portion of James Island—lands brought to fruition by human slavery, fought over by two invading armies, destroyed, restored, and now become city. The forces that were played out on their fields and marshes—forces that once troubled the whole nation—have now subsided. They will be replaced, I thought, by other struggles that future historians will have to name.

We turned away from the little rectangle of earth and monuments, brought abruptly back into the present by the singing of tires on the Folly Island Highway and the laughter and bright faces of children now leaving the church.[80]

When reflecting on these ten years (1980-1989), one sees a giving, growing church. While some of these details might seem tedious, they are recorded for two purposes: to honor how

God was working through His people at Saint James and to provide examples that might be implemented again at Saint James and elsewhere. One is reminded of James 2:26: "As the body without the spirit is dead, so faith without deeds is dead." Throughout this decade, faith was very much alive as indicated by the work and deeds, demonstrating a vibrant Spirit. Changes were interwoven as rectors accepted different callings, a huge tract of land was donated to Bishop Gadsden, and a hurricane wreaked havoc—with God sustaining His people all the while.

CHAPTER SIXTEEN

1990s—Rectors, Real Estate, and Faith in Action

The next decade continued the growth of the 1980s, building on that foundation and expanding in many ways. Sunday school attendance, Bishop Gadsden facilities, and music programs reflect some of this growth. Also change characterized these years, particularly pertaining to land issues, priests' careers, and fund-raising.

By 1990 Saint James had grown to the point that Rev. Zahl's "Rector's Report on the State of the Parish" noted that space was a challenge. Zahl asked the question, "How do we find room for all that is going on, within our present physical limits?"[1] For several years the staff and congregation worked to find answers to this question.

In that same report, Rev. Zahl also made some prophetic remarks regarding the national Episcopal Church:

> Our church nationally (though not in South Carolina) is in poor shape.
> Many dioceses are closing churches, part-time priests now serve hundreds
> and hundreds of churches that once supported a full-time rector, and the
> mood is one of confusion and uncertainty…The world needs our message.[2]

In his assistant rector's report in the *Congregational Report 1990*, Rev. Limehouse said, "[Saint James] is a solid, 'Christocentric' parish, i.e., in this parish, Jesus Christ is the focal point. Don't be misled. This is not the case in many Episcopal churches where often times the objective truth about Jesus Christ takes a back seat to the…fringes of Christianity." Rev. Limehouse emphasized that Saint James was a "caring, loving parish," creating "a perfect place to begin [his] ordained ministry."[3]

In that same *Congregational Report 1990*, Susan Watkins, Christian Education director, said that Saint James had twenty-two Sunday school teachers, ten church school classes ages three years to high school, a nursery with four attendants, 175 Sunday school participants on roster with an average Sunday attendance of 126 and expanded to 250 when the number of adult attendees were added—all impressive statistics for a church the size of Saint James.[4] In 1991 Ann L. King became director of Christian education, building on Susan Watkins' programs, incorporating many hands-on activities, and emphasizing the power of Bible stories told in a loving, supportive environment.[5] Julia Marshall coordinated music and worship for younger members.[6]

As in the 1980s, Saint James' vestry members and director of Bishop Gadsden Episcopal Retirement Center Bill Trawick often conferred with one another. In April 1990 Bishop Gadsden's board of directors stated that Saint James' senior warden would be a voting member of the board.[7] In May of 1990 Bishop Gadsden's board requested that Saint James deed them approximately eight more acres needed for a skilled and intermediate care nursing wing. The vestry agreed but first wanted to examine an existing fifty-foot access road to land not affected by this gift for expansion.[8] June 10th vestry minutes state that the retirement home annexed thirteen acres given by Saint James.

In April of 1990 the vestry voted to give $5,000 to their "mother parish," Old Saint Andrews Episcopal Church on Highway 61, which had sustained over $100,000 of damage during Hurricane Hugo.[9]

As with previous years, Saint James was noted this decade for its exceptional music. On May 5, 1990, Saint James hosted the Annual Festival Service of Music that included choirs from all over the Diocese. Dr. Ford Lallerstedt, director of music at Saint James, led choristers in anthems by Brahms, Rutter, Verdi, and Mendelssohn. Chaired by former Saint James organist Brenda Albinger, the Choir Festival was a project of the Diocesan Division of Church Music.[10] January 5, 1992 Pat Gould was hired as Saint James' new director of music.[11]

On June 17, 1990, the ordination to the priesthood of Frank F. Limehouse III took place at Saint James where the celebrant was The Right Reverend Edward L. Salmon, Jr. In the front of the ordination's program was "A Word from Frank," in which he wrote the following:

> I used to think Jesus Christ was a kind of adult Santa Claus and that Christianity was helpful, but nevertheless undergirded by sentimentality, myth, and human need for religion. Religion, I thought, was "a personal thing."
>
> My wife, Jane, says that she used to pray that one day I would really understand who Jesus of Nazareth really was (is). Many years later, after asking her if she would consider uprooting our family to go to seminary, she said, "I didn't mean to pray so hard!"

I thank God for the many people who encouraged and supported me along the way. With their help, we made it, and now, "Here I stand."

But what I feel compelled to say at this very special, personally wonderful moment, is that the focus of attention does not belong on me, but on the "awesomeness" of God's Grace. For I come to this moment fully aware that I am not worthy of it. And yet, I believe that I am, at the same time, justified because of the work of the Son…

Please join me tonight in thanking God for the life, death, and resurrection of Jesus Christ. This is what Christianity is all about. He is the only reason I am being ordained, and He is the only reason we are here.

In August of 1990 the vestry voted to double the size of the cemetery, providing for 1,200 more grave sites. The cost of grave sites was also increased.[12]

The land referred to as the Madden property, located on Mellichamp Drive, adjoining the northern boundary of Saint James' property, was desirable for enlargement of the present parish house and day school. After several previous attempts to negotiate a purchase, the church prepared a contract for $94,000. Realtor Fred Wichmann assisted in this business transaction.[13] However, in September 1990 Mr. Madden stated that he was not interested in selling the property.[14] Vestry notes for several years to come revisit the church's attempts to negotiate the purchase of this land.

In May of 1995 Saint James again drafted contracts for purchasing this property, which had a 1500 square foot house on it. Fred Wichmann reported, however, that the Madden family had conflicted feelings about selling the property. Also, some of the neighbors expressed growing concerns about how Saint James would use the land. Thus, these business deals did not materialize either.[15]

At the same time, the vestry addressed details regarding disputed boundary lines of church property adjacent to that of Mr. Richardson. Legal research indicated that Mr. Richardson (to the left of the church when facing it) actually did not own the land in question. The Richardsons had used this piece of land for fifty or sixty years, but Saint James had been paying taxes on it.[16] Ultimately, Saint James gave Mr. Richardson permission to continue to use the property.[17] However, the vestry needed to resolve the issue legally since there [were] "two recorded plats, each showing different ownership of the area."[18]

The vestry also debated the issue of some choir members being hired to fulfill positions not filled by volunteers from the congregation. Some argued that this approach was setting a bad precedent, but others felt that the minimal pay some choir members received addressed the vacancies which needed to be filled for the sake of the quality of the music.[19]

In September of 1990 Rev. Zahl went on a trip sponsored by an inter-faith group headquartered at the Cathedral of St. John the Divine in New York and met with government leaders, scholars, and religious leaders (Protestant, Roman Catholic, Jewish, Muslim) in East Germany, Poland, Czechoslovakia, Hungary, and the Soviet Union. In Eastern Europe, the visitors wanted to observe the "spiritual dimension," which had undergone profound political change.[20]

Even with his extraordinarily busy schedule, Rev. Zahl still continued with his publications, writing "Censorship in the Fine Arts" as well as several articles in the *Anglican Digest, Episcopal and Anglican History*, and *St. Luke's Journal*.[21] He taught a course entitled "Introduction to Religion" two evenings a week at the College of Charleston.[22] Rev. Zahl also talked to the vestry about the possibility of Saint James publishing a quarterly magazine or journal as a means of evangelism.[23]

The brochure "Welcome to St. James' Episcopal Church," published while Rev. Zahl was the rector, stated, "Worship at St. James' is both vertical and horizontal. Vertical, as we praise God and thank Him, hear His Word as help and strength, and meet with Him in the sacraments. Horizontal as we come together as family, seeking to grow in love and outreach." Rev. Zahl described Saint James as "an historic country church that is now a suburban church, with a large, active congregation and … is a focal point in the community." He said, "We must build on our inherited strength."[24]

In his associate rector's annual message in the *Congregational Report 1991*, Rev. Limehouse wrote the following:

> I consider St. James' Church to be one of the strongest churches I have ever known (which, incidentally, includes some churches with mighty fine reputations!). In the relatively short time that I have been here, I have seen… that many people have come to know who Jesus of Nazareth really is and have come to understand what He has done for them.[25]

The McLeod and Barnwell estates necessitated that churchmen devoted time and attention to the many important details of these wills. Initially, Mac Rhodes fulfilled these legal duties. As of August 13, 1990, Walter Ameika, Jon Anderson, and Thomas Read, experts in law and real estate, oversaw the transactions. The vestry discussed an unrestricted gift of $170,000 from the McLeod estate, primarily placed into a building fund, and $10,000, designated for scholarships.[26] In March the vestry received an additional $45,000 from the McLeod estate for scholarships. The vestry considered a proposal from the Historic Charleston Foundation to buy the McLeod estate from contingent beneficiaries for $215,000 for Saint James.[27] On November 16, 1992, Saint James received payment of about $107,000. The church also received $10,000 from Mrs. Rose Barnwell and $67,000 from Miss Wilhelmenia McLeod. These proceeds represented Saint James' portion from the sale of the McLeod property on Maybank Highway.[28] Saint James also received $63,000, the last item to be inherited from the McLeod estate, which was set up in a trust.[29]

In his January *1991 Congregational Report*, Rev. Zahl revisited a proposal that had encouraged the congregation to reconsider starting a mission—a second Episcopal church—on James Island. He wrote the following:

> We need to ask ourselves, "Is it possibly the time for St. James to start a mission on James Island?" The timing would seem apt: The bridge [connector from the city of Charleston to James Island] is soon to be finished, and development of James Island will continue. The church owns an ideal parcel of land along Harbor View Road across from the entrance to Stiles Point [Plantation Subdivision]. A large unrestricted legacy has recently come to the church, which could allow development of this concept to begin. Bishop Salmon's policy for the Diocese of South Carolina is intentionally oriented to mission, and he has asked us to complete by April 1st [1991] a self-study towards new work...[30]

On March 6, 1991, the congregation received a heartfelt resignation letter from Rev. Limehouse. He wrote,

> If I have correctly perceived His voice, God is calling me away from this wonderful place to another church—as rector of St. Bartholomew's in Hartsville, South Carolina...I never imagined that such an honored challenge and joyful anticipation could be so heavily mixed with pain...I am absolutely positive that it is God who sent me to James Island and to this church. I wasn't close to being "ready" out of seminary. True, except in the "Day of the Lord" I will never be fully ready, but it is here that I have received an avalanche of finishing touches, as this frail and fragile man seeks to fulfill God's call...A part of my heart will never move away...I remind myself that our lives are much like mystery novels in which the pages and chapters are the passing days and years. But the wonderful thing is that God has already revealed the ending (John 14: 1-3).

Three years later Rev. Limehouse accepted another call, this time to the Parish Church of St. Helena in Beaufort.[31] Addressing structural problems in the historic church of St. Helena's, he led the congregation through a costly but necessary restoration and construction on his campus. In 2005 Rev. Limehouse accepted a call to be dean of the Cathedral Church of the Advent in Birmingham, Alabama.[32]

The vestry voted on April 29, 1991 to begin construction for a new sign for the front of the church. A plaque was to be placed on the sign saying "In Memory of Bonnie Gallahorn" as money donated in her name paid for the construction of this sign.

Bishop Gadsden Community received a $185,000 grant from the Duke Endowment's Hospital Division and thereupon conducted a capital drive to add a $3.2 million 44-bed skilled and intermediate care nursing facility. At that time plans were being made for many more expansions for the fifty-acre campus.[33] In 1993 the celebration of the fifth anniversary of Bishop Gadsden's founding was held during which the new Health Care Center was dedicated on November 12. The Board Chair at the time was Thomas Read, a long-time member of Saint James.[34]

The vestry announced that Mr. Arthur Jenkins would join the staff as assistant rector at Saint James on July 1, 1991.[35] Mr. Jenkins had graduated with high honors from Virginia Theological Seminary and was to be ordained to the Diaconate on July 15 at Trinity Church, Scotland Neck, North Carolina. As assistant rector, Rev. Jenkins was especially effective in building up the youth program (EYC), conducting small-group Bible studies, and conducting Wednesday evening services that included a simple supper, Eucharist, and small group meetings.

On February 16, 1992, Rev. Zahl, on his last Sunday service at Saint James, wrote the following in the church bulletin:

> The people of St. James' have been so kind to us. So loving, in fact. So true. And especially so now, as we prepare the new phase in our ministry, doctoral study at Tubingen [Germany]. Mary and I, with John, David and Simeon, are deeply grateful to you. Your love has touched us right to the heart…I feel I am leaving on the "wings of a dove"…St. James and the Zahls will be separated geographically…But God's grace is the great bond of life because it promises reunion forever. That is our Hope, and I embrace it.

Saint James' website states that Rev. Zahl, rector at Saint James from 1988 to 1992, "brought a deep and profound understanding of grace as well as an appreciation for life long Christian formation. His tenure was one of great intellectual growth in the congregation. He later became the Dean of Trinity Seminary."[36]

On June 6, 1992 Arthur Mack Jenkins was ordained into the priesthood at Saint James with the celebrant The Right Reverend Edward L. Salmon, Jr. In the program for this event was "A Word from Arthur," as follows:

> …I know there must be a God when a pig farmer can come to the foot of the Cross as a minister in God's Church. There must be power in a gospel which changes lives so dramatically…
>
> I can only be thankful to each of you who have been used by our Lord so abundantly and gracefully to bring me to this day. Your encourage-

ment, your patience, your prayers have been a great source of provision for me.

There are three people for whom I wish to offer a special note of thanksgiving. They are the three women in my life, Kay, Kate and Lawson [his wife and two daughters]. Kay responded to God's call before I had the courage to say "maybe." She loved me, put up with me, and prayed for me for many years to bring us both to this day. Kate responded to a loving Jesus when, as a young girl, she spoke words which struck this hardened heart. Lawson continually gives me the same gift of love of which I believe our Lord was speaking when He said, "for such belongs the Kingdom of God."

In his leadership role, Arthur Jenkins, then assistant rector, was instrumental at Saint James for nine months until a new rector could be called.[37] Rev. Fred Sosnowski remained the counselor associate, helping fellow priests, staff, and parishioners.[38] In 1994 Father Sosnowski accepted a call to work with Rev. Chris Huff at St. Peters but remained available to provide counseling one day a week at Saint James.[39]

In September 1992 Rev. Samuel Johnson Howard, known as John, was called to be the senior rector at Saint James and served until 1998. His first Sunday at the church was November 29, the first day in Advent. He was a native of Raleigh, North Carolina, and a graduate of Williams College and Wake Forest Law School (1976). He and his wife Marie had two sons. From 1976 to 1986, he was Assistant U.S. Attorney for the Eastern District of North Carolina, heading up the Task Force responsible for Organized Crime Drug Enforcement from 1981 to 1985. He became a federal public defender and also served as an attorney on the staff of the United States Senate Commerce Committee. He received a Masters of Divinity degree in 1989 at Virginia Theological Seminary, was ordained in 1989, and was the assistant rector of the Church of the Holy Comforter in Charlotte, North Carolina.[40]

In his message in the *Congregational Report 1993*, Rev. Howard wrote that his initial emphasis would be on Christian stewardship, endowments, church facilities, membership, and "shepherds' groups" fostering pastoral care, worship, and Bible study in neighborhood clusters.[41] Also in that report, Ashby Taylor and Anne Read, in their Christian giving account, stated that pledges were down, probably due to the transition between rectors and the current financial times.[42] Mary Porcher, chairman of the Memorials and Gifts Committee, reported the vestry had started a fund to place a bell in the steeple.[43] Assistant rector Arthur Jenkins thanked the staff and parish leaders, spoke frankly about his multiple duties and being hampered by time restraints during the search for a rector, and asked for more involvement by the parishioners in church services, Bible study, and prayer groups. He concluded, "We come to worship in order to transcend our current situation. We come to 'touch the hem of His garment'."[44]

One of the key changes Rev. Howard brought about was the introduction of the 9:00 AM service, which was less traditional, had communion each Sunday, and included contemporary praise music.[45] The 8:00 AM and 11:00 services remained unchanged, and Sunday school was held between the 9:00 and 11:00 services. He also established the "2:42 small groups" (based on Act 2:42) that met periodically in parishioners' homes for Bible study, prayer, fellowship, and evangelism. In addition, with the vestry's full support, Rev. Howard requested that those in lay leadership positions resign after three years of service in a particular capacity to promote more and varied participation from parishioners.[46]

In the late summer of 1993, Rev. Jenkins, after being at Saint James almost three years as an assistant pastor, was called to Christ Church in Fitchburg, Massachusetts. The congregation hosted a farewell reception on his behalf.[47]

In March of 1994 Mrs. Carol Shue resigned from her position of Director of Christ Kindergarten, and the vestry began a negotiation process with Mrs. Sharon Eason.[48] In August of 1995 the vestry was also working with Mrs. Wooten to establish policies regarding Christian training as well as use and care of space.[49] In 1998 the lease of the day care was temporarily discontinued.

During this time the vestry struggled with deficits in the budgets. Although attendance was increased, parishioners were behind in their pledges. Eighty members who usually pledged had not done so. The vestry simply did not have the monies to fund their staff, programs, and campus. Much of the vestry minutes throughout 1993 address these dire concerns.[50]

The vestry was proactive with outreach, fellowship, and communication. Rev. Howard proposed a "Bring-a-Friend-to-Church Sunday." A team of parishioners visited newcomers. A small notebook was placed in each pew for members and visitors to sign and pass to one another, thus facilitating the learning of one another's names and providing contact information for those visiting.[51] Anne Read reported that 120 home visits had been made by her membership committee. About 250 families were photographed for the church directory. Nearly 400 nametags were printed for parishioners to wear and return each Sunday. A greeters' committee was active in welcoming visitors.[52] A newcomers' reception was held in Rev. Howard's home in 1995, and another was hosted in Jenny White's home in 1996.

Also documents and contracts were revised to establish clearer guidelines with the church's constitution, weddings, copy machine use, income from the church day care, childcare during church weekday functions, alcohol sales at church events, and much more. A list of chalice bearers was submitted to the bishop for approval. A Long Range Planning Committee of seven parishioners was established.[53]

The vestry approved the establishment of a bell fund in 1992 and began making specific plans for the installation of the bell in Saint James' steeple in 1994. The vestry considered various options, including a single cast bell with a rope pull for $15,000, a single cast bell with push button controls for $20,000, a combination of three bells for $37,000, an automatic electronic carillon consisting of tapes with an amplifying system, and a microchip system with unlimited capabilities.[54] By December 1994 Mr. Slip Haizlip, Chairman of the Bell Committee, reported that they would purchase one cast bronze bell, which seemed to be most in keeping with the traditional setting of Saint James.

After more fund-building and decision making regarding the bell, Mrs. Egleston reported that a contract with Van Bergen Bell, Inc. was signed for a 198-pound cast bronze bell for the cost of $20,400. Roy Prescott furnished the men and equipment to build the infrastructure.[55] David Barns, Eddie Porcher, and other men of the congregation were instrumental in getting the bell hung.[56] Plans to dedicate the bell on October 3, 1999 included the addition of a traditional bell rope and an automatic clock that controlled electric striking. The bell was displayed for a few Sundays so parishioners could see it before it was installed.[57]

In April 1994 Rev. Jeffrey Scott Miller was called to be assistant rector at Saint James. Having grown up in a Christian home in Pennsylvania, Rev. Miller went to Geneva College in Beaver Falls, Pennsylvania. One of his professors invited him to attend St. Stephen's Episcopal Church in Sewickley, Pennsylvania, where the rector was Rev. Dr. John Guest, an English evangelist known for his music and ministry that especially drew youth to Christ. Within a year Miller was confirmed as an Episcopalian and began praying intensely about possibly being called to the priesthood. He graduated from Indiana University of Pennsylvania and then went to Virginia Theological Seminary.[58] An endorsement for ordination to the priesthood from the Diocese of Pittsburgh was signed by the vestry on November 6, 1994 on behalf of Miller, and he was ordained at Saint James on January 15, 1995. He took on duties such as leading Bible studies, the youth groups, and confirmation classes.[59]

To facilitate vestry meetings, members agreed that prior to being presented to the vestry for approval, proposals relating to policy and other significant matters should first be given full consideration by the appropriate committee or committees. Also, a thorough, but brief written description of each proposal should be provided to each vestry member in advance of the meeting at which action by the vestry was to be taken.[60]

Because of national social awareness regarding child protection, the vestry discussed the "Sexual Misconduct Policy Manual" prepared by the diocesan staff and the Church Insurance Company. The church required a background check on all employees.[61] By September 1995 the vestry had drafted a manual on sexual misconduct to prevent such problems from occurring with Saint James' staff and volunteers.

The church sanctuary had an ongoing problem with peeling paint, especially on the ceiling. Parishioners with expertise, such as Eddie Porcher and Gene Morrison, worked to diagnose the problem. The vestry realized that they would need $10,000 to $20,000 to paint the entire interior of the church. Peeling problems were rooted in moisture control issues as well as previous improper paint applications and deteriorating roof conditions.[62] This problem occurred again in consecutive years. Finally, in 1996, the sanctuary was repaired and painted.

Bishop Terence Kelshaw, a renowned scholar and teacher from the Rio Grande Diocese, was invited to lead a revival at Saint James during Lent in March 1995. A detailed three-day program "to share the Good News" was prepared. Invitations were extended to members at other Episcopal churches, flyers were placed in Christian bookstores, and ads were posted in the local newspaper.[63]

Four main goals were established by the vestry in the summer of 1995: (1) enhance the youth program and hire a full-time youth director (although funding was a great challenge), (2) increase lay ministry outreach through projects and activities to promote participation in church endeavors, (3) participate in foreign missions work and plan both mission trips and funding and (4) focus on small groups and allow unique growth for each.

In June of 1995 the Long Range Planning Committee's statement spurred action to build an additional place of worship referred to as the Ministry Center. Their report stated that the current physical plant was inadequate to meet Saint James' present needs in several respects: kitchen, offices, storage, nursery, meeting spaces, and gathering area for families for weddings and funerals. Insufficient space was a problem for the music and youth programs as well as for fellowship and small groups. The committee met with five architectural firms to seek advice regarding remodeling and maximizing areas to meet these needs. Nine additional proposals resulted. Using a topographical map, a tree survey, and an extensive analysis of the buildings and the land, Dan Beaman of Cummings and McGrady Architects served as a consultant to the vestry.

In August 1995 Karen Majors, Richard Tassin, and Melissa Ward were the recipients of the scholarship awards from the McLeod Scholarship Fund, with a total of $7500 being disbursed.[64] Two years later additional scholarships were given to Allison Durgee, Christina Fair, Melissa Ward, Eliza Cone, and Ann Morrison. The McLeod Fund allowed the vestry and chairman David Cupka to grant scholarships for years.[65]

In the fall of 1995, the vestry appointed an ad hoc committee of vestry members and parishioners who were charged with considering changes to various administrative and election procedures. Seven standing committees received clarifications regarding their duties: finance, buildings and grounds, cemetery, land, investment, memorials and gifts, and stewardship.[66] In March of 1996 the vestry voted to revise the 1990 by-laws, especially regarding the Finance Committee and Investment Committee.

In June of 1996 Rev. Miller left Saint James to become the rector at St. David's Church in Cheraw, South Carolina.[67] Then in 2000 Rev. Limehouse extended a call to Rev. Miller to join St. Helena's as an assistant rector.[68] After Rev. Limehouse accepted the call to Alabama, Miller took over as the rector at the Parish Church of St. Helena October 2005.[69] Rev. Miller also hired Patricia Gould, former organist and choir director at Saint James who had retired, to become Director of Music.[70] May 2016 Rev. Miller was called to be the rector at Saint Philips Church in Charleston.[71]

In August 1996, David Cupka, senior warden, announced that after an extensive search, Michael McIntyre was being hired as a full-time youth director, and Kit Stubbs was named the Sunday School coordinator. Within a couple months Mr. McIntyre was working with the junior and senior EYC, conducted Tuesday night Bible studies with the senior EYC, planned an EYC trip to Fripp Island in October, and coordinated youth volunteers to take on chores on the church campus and assist with younger children in the church.[72] He wrote a monthly newsletter entitled *Youthnet* for youth group members. Mr. McIntyre also involved other young adults to help him lead church retreats and train other youth leaders around the Low Country. He joined students on the front of their school campuses for "See You at the Pole"; there students could gather for prayer before school one morning a week during this world-wide event. Throughout the upcoming years, he involved youth in annual field trips, multiple community services, worship opportunities, Bible studies, and relational ministries.[73]

In 1995 the property on Affirmation Boulevard appraised for $64,000, and the property at Parrot Point appraised at $1,674,000 in mid-1995.[74] Ending a rather lengthy period of discernment about whether the church should start a mission on James Island, Saint James obtained permission from the Bishop and Standing Committee of the diocese to sell four acres on Affirmation Boulevard for $75,000 in 1997.[75] In another transaction, David Cupka, as senior warden representing Saint James, signed over thirty-one acres of land to the Bishop Gadsden Retirement Community so it could expand its facilities.[76]

In September 1997 the vestry approved $155,000 in repairs for the organ. Initially, a contract was signed with Ontko and Young to refurbish the organ, which had not had extensive repairs in several years. However, vestry notes from March 1998 indicate that four other companies also bid. In May of 1998 Knowlton Organ Company in Davidson, NC, was hired to do the work at $173,000. However, many delays with the repairs followed,[77] and finally in 2000 the organ was restored.[78]

Vestry minutes of the 1990s include details about various trainings for parishioners. Rev. Howard taught a thirteen-week course entitled "DivorceCare" as a means of support for people who were separated or divorced. About half of those who attended were not Saint James members.[79] Also a three-day course in June 1997 entitled "A More Excellent Way" was offered for leadership training.[80]

As in previous decades, parishioners and priests sought ways to honor fellow church and family members. At the November 21, 1994 vestry meeting Rev. Howard proposed that a marble plaque be placed in memory of Mr. Edward Guerry for his contributions to the parish and diocese and displayed on the wall inside the church. A new processional cross was given as a memorial to Kitty Ellis.[81] In 1994 Chris Gehlken constructed a tract rack so that parishioners could have access to Christian materials.[82] In 1996 he made and donated a table for the sanctuary to be used for funeral urns at cremation services. He dedicated the table to the memory of his father.[83] In memory of his wife Lorraine, Herman Daniel gave a wafer box designed to assist rectors in counting wafers for the altar.[84] In 1999 the Memorials and Gifts Committee purchased two Charleston benches in memory of Mr. and Mrs. Henry McManus.[85]

In 1997 Saint James built a Memorial Prayer Garden in the church cemetery and erected a large granite cross and stone inscribed as follows:

This Memorial Garden is dedicated
TO THE GLORY OF GOD
And in loving memory of
THOSE DEPARTED THIS LIFE
With thanks to all who
Contributed to its realization
ESPECIALLY CARL GUNNAR JOHNSON
MAY 18, 1997[86]

The Episcopal Church Women (ECW) contributed money for landscaping.[87] Additional funds came from the monies set aside for maintenance of the cemetery. Jane Horne was also instrumental in bringing this project about successfully.[88]

From 1996 until 2003 Rev. Floyd W. Finch, Jr., served as pastoral associate at Saint James. A descendent of Benjamin Franklin, Rev. Finch earned a master's degree in education at Appalachian State University and a Master of Divinity at Virginia Theological Seminary. He was ordained a deacon in 1954 at Calvary Church in Fletcher, North Carolina, married Leona Sutherland, and became an ordained priest in 1955. Rev. Floyd served churches as rector and as a headmaster in dioceses of North Carolina, South Carolina, and Georgia.[89]

Several of Rev. Finch's sermons addressed the history of Saint James. On Saint James Day July 25, 1999, Rev. Finch based his sermon primarily on the Gospel of Matthew, tying the story of James, the brother of John, to the name of Saint James, connecting Biblical history and Saint James' history. Rev. Finch explained, "James was killed by the sword, and his symbol, seen on the banner of Saint James Church, is the sword and the scallop shell—the sword as the symbol of how he died and the scallop shell as a symbol of his earlier vocation as a fisherman."

In the fall of 1996, Rev. Finch made home visits for both church members and newcomers.[90] Giving one a sense of his work in 1997, Finch reported one month on twenty-nine baptisms, twenty-three confirmations, sixteen letters of transfer in, forty-eight private communions, three ministrations at death in the parish, three new babies, and thirteen possible candidates for confirmation.[91] In October of 1999 the congregation gave Floyd and wife

Leona Finch a "Pilgrimage to the Holy Land and Jordan," a venture and blessing that Rev. Finch referred to as "exquisite, high quality continuing education…[where] our faith deepened and expanded."[92]

In November of 1997 Rev. Howard accepted a call to Trinity Wall Street Episcopal Church and Saint Paul's Chapel in New York City. His last Sunday at Saint James was November 23, 1997. When the Twin Towers were brought down by the terrorist attacks, he became a spokesperson and leader in the redevelopment of the World Trade Center. Rev. Howard was elected bishop coadjutor [a bishop assisting a diocesan bishop] of the Episcopal Diocese of Florida on May 16, 2003, and was consecrated at St. John's Cathedral, Jacksonville, on November 1, 2003. He became the bishop of the diocese on January 29, 2004.[93]

When Bishop Salmon met with the vestry to discuss hiring an interim priest, supporting Father Finch as pastoral associate, and searching for a new rector, Salmon said, "St. James has been fortunate in that the last two Rectors have been two of the finer clergy of the Episcopal Church and have moved on to positions of significance." The Bishop encouraged the vestry to conduct an exit interview with Rev. Howard, participate in a self-study, and appoint a search committee. In January of 1998 Bishop Salmon again met with the vestry and outlined thirteen observations and suggestions addressing the vestry's leadership role.[94] In February 1998 the vestry asked Rev. Jack F. Nietert to serve as the interim rector to prepare the church for its new rector and lead the church until that time.[95]

In June of 1998 a search committee selected by the vestry of Saint James printed a parish profile to help in their search for a new rector to succeed Rev. Howard. It began with this paragraph:

> St. James' is a family-oriented parish located on a South Carolina sea island, adjacent to the historic peninsula of Charleston. Our current membership is 721 communicants, with an average of 317 in combined attendance at our three Sunday morning services. We have several strong programs including Christian Education, Music, Outreach and Missions, Youth Ministry, and Bible study. St. James was founded in 1730 [now declared to be 1720] and our parish sanctuary reflects our history with its traditional colonial style structure, located on fifteen acres, shaded by majestic oaks.[96]

Of thirty-four nominations, the following were elected to be on the search committee: David Cupka (chairman), Jimmy DuPre (vice-chairman), Robert Barber, Ann L. King, Jack Cranwell, George Martindale, Bill Elmore, Bill Read, Mary King, Bill Huff, Virginia Ward, and Gunnar Johnson. Bishops Salmon and Skilton served as consultants.[97] On July 20, 1998 the vestry issued a call to Rev. Arthur Jenkins to return to Saint James as their rector. Accompanying him were his wife Kay and daughters Kate and Lawson.

When parishioner Greg Leighton, suffering from a terminal illness, could no longer physically communicate with his family, the vestry voted to purchase a computer device for Greg's use. They also invited the congregation to contribute meals and to a fund on his behalf. His wife Ellen served on Saint James staff for many years following the death of her husband in February 2000.[98]

June 1, 1998 the vestry approved spending up to $25,000 for a van to be used primarily by the youth—as requested by Michael McIntyre. Ultimately, a 1997 Ford fifteen-passenger was purchased for a little under $19,000.

In 1999 Saint James began a fundraising campaign called "Faith in Action" to help pay for the new Ministry Center that was scheduled for completion in 2004.[99] This building was to be a place for the following: contemporary worship, instructional settings, Christian events (banquets, conferences, diocesan meetings, etc.), community gatherings compatible with Saint James' vision and faith, activities other than worship (bazaar, youth activities), and a room for Saint James' entire congregation to be able to come under one roof and build unity.

According to the *Congregational Report 1999*, Saint James' Land Committee further investigated the sale of Parrot Point, forty-eight acres of waterfront property zoned for single-family development, in the subdivision Lighthouse Point, located off of Fort Johnson Road. As the property was readied for sale, controversy arose regarding the stipulations by which the land had been donated and whether the development of the land would erase a nature preserve. Saint James had requests from some nonmembers to leave the land undeveloped. Some parishioners were not at all in favor of selling the property. To honor the wishes of Josiah Harvey, who had willed the Parrot Point property in 1837, a portion of the proceeds from the sale of the land was to be invested in support of the church's ministers. Funds generated from the sale of the land were needed to expand the buildings and ministry at Saint James.[100]

According to vestry minutes dated January 23, 1999, Bill Read made a motion to build a Ministry Center at Saint James, Bobbie Galbraith seconded it, and the motion passed unanimously. Another motion passed unanimously that the sale of Parrot Point property would fund this building initiative. In spite of naysayers, the vestry was unified in this mission. Many details had to be addressed, including seeking permission from Bishop Salmon and the diocesan Standing Committee to sell the land. Decisions had to be made regarding a possible waterfront lot and/or building a rectory. Surveys, title searches, a building committee, a capital campaign, a vision for the use of the new building, notification to Mrs. Lane (a long-time resident and caregiver at Parrot Point) regarding the sale of the property—all this and more became part of the vestry's "to do" list. Much discussion centered on how to communicate these transactions to the congregation. On April 26, 1999 the following were selected to serve on the Building Committee: Bobbie Galbraith (chairman), Ben Horne (deputy chairman), Lillie McGougan (chaplain), Michael Spivey, Lois Jenkins, Virginia Ward, Anna Coe (who was replaced by Becky Williams when Mrs. Coe resigned to dedicate more time to the church's youth program).

In March 1999 Rev. Jenkins proposed that Saint James bring Rev. Marc Robert Paul Boutan onto the staff. Having first served as a deacon and assistant at St. Andrew's in Mount Pleasant, he was ordained on March 18, 1992 at Saint Andrews, with the Right Reverend Edward L. Salmon, Jr. serving as bishop. Rev. Boutan was hired as an assistant rector between September and October of 1999. Throughout that year and the next he led a ten-week Sunday school series based on I Corinthians 13, orchestrated Wednesday evening educational offerings, and led the contemporary music while choir director Pat Gould was ill.

At the June 21, 1999 vestry meeting, Mr. Galbraith reported that architectural firms were to submit formal proposals for the Ministry Center. On July 26, three presentations were made, and the building committee was given permission from the vestry to pick one.[101] All proposals had to take into consideration huge oaks and gravesites. Art Field presented a budget and menu for a special event for the Faith in Action Campaign designated to raise funds for construction.[102] By August 2, 1999, the Building Committee had selected Craig, Gaulden and Davis as architects for the Ministry Center.

In a letter dated September 1, 1999, the vestry provided updated information regarding the sale of Parrot Point property, which was "likened to a talent buried in the ground. The vestry felt that the time had come to convert this dormant, though appreciated asset into a more liquid form to put it to work and significantly support our mission to 'Proclaim God's Grace in Jesus Christ'." The following paragraph went into detail about expenses and payments:

> After the repayment of the loan to finance some $110,000 of the costs of our organ, an amount to support, but not totally pay for, our new Ministry Center was considered. It was felt that a total amount of $2,000,000 would get the initial limit of support from endowments. This would be made up by $1,700,000 from land sale and $300,000 from the invested building fund, being largely from the McLeod estates...As to remaining proceeds of sale, these will be retained and invested for future ministries or phases. We are serious about honoring the faithfulness and generosity of our past, while at the same time moving with faith into the future.

In order to sell Parrot Point, the vestry advertised in the *Charleston Post and Courier, Wall Street Journal,* and *The New York Times.* Initially the asking price was 3.5 million dollars.[103] By December 13, 1999 the vestry received ten offers ranging from 2.2 million to 4.2 million.

In 1999 Mark Barwick was hired as the new Christian Education Director. The vestry struggled to find meeting spaces for all the needed Sunday school rooms. They considered plans perhaps to partition off room(s) in the parish hall and to use some meeting rooms at Bishop Gadsden.[104] In November of 2000 Mr. Barwick began discernment to enter the ordination process, but these plans did not materialize.[105]

In December of 1999 the vestry approved mailing a Christmas card to approximately 6000 households on James Island, costing $1600. The intent was to invite more people of the community to consider attending Saint James.

A great summary passage for the last decade and a half is included in the 1998 Parish Profile, as follows:

> God has blessed St. James' through our last three Rectors, who renewed the spiritual journey of our Parish. The first [Rev. Morey Lent] of these Rectors led us out of division and into healing; the second [Rev. Paul Zahl] helped us to focus on the Gospel of Jesus Christ and sparked a hunger for the knowledge of God's will for us; the third [Rev. John Howard] and most recent Rector continued the focus on the teachings of the Gospel of Jesus Christ, and strengthened our movement towards more outward demonstrations of our faith through ministry and missions.[106]

The many changes of this decade, including those of land and leaders, are reflected in the third chapter of Ecclesiastes: "There is a time for everything, and a season for every activity under heaven…a time to plant and a time to uproot…a time to tear down and a time to build…a time to embrace and a time to refrain…" In their constant seeking to serve the Lord, the people of Saint James were flexible, resilient, and forthcoming with modifications, variations, and transformations.

CHAPTER SEVENTEEN

2000 to 2010—Expanding Ministry

In Saint James' 2000 congregational report, Rev. Arthur Jenkins wrote, "One of the signs of the Kingdom of God is when the dissimilar are united. Remember, in Jesus, heaven and earth are united." (Psalm 85) This decade was indeed one of uniting different styles of worship, different buildings of worship, and different opinions regarding transitions and decisions at Saint James.

The mission statement for this time period was "Proclaiming the Grace of God in Jesus Christ." Accompanying this mission statement was a six-page grid, with 119 boxes, listing all the committees, groups, and activities in the categories of worship, discipleship, outreach, fellowship, and service. This information preserved in vestry records of this decade is indicative of an active and organized church.

Much of the first half of this decade focused on the financing and building of the new Ministry Center, which had an estimated cost of approximately $3.7 million. In order to fund it, a main focus during the first couple years of this decade was on the sale of Parrot Point.[1]

To finance this construction and remodeling, Bishop Salmon gave his consent to sell Parrot Point. The Diocesan Standing Committee provided its formal consent as well. Mr. Harvey's will stated that Parrot Point was to be rented out, "the proceeds to be applied for the purpose of raising a fund for the support of a Minister to perform duties" at Saint James. However, in the Court of Common Pleas Case No : 00-CP-10-2268, reports based on leasing the land for farming had generated "sums insufficient to support a minister." It was deemed that Mr. Harvey's intent to use the land to support a minister was, by extension, honored by supporting continued growth of the church as a whole.

Ford Development Corporation, with Rex Robertson as purchaser, submitted contracts April 3 and May 15, 2000 and applied for a dock permit from South Carolina Department of Natural Resources. Initially, Ford Development's site plan for Parrot Point was not approved by the Charleston County Board of Zoning Appeals due to the tree ordinance (the proposed roads were too close to some grand trees).

In 2000 Mr. Kenneth C. Krawcheck, attorney, needed a summary of the plans for the use of the proceeds and the sale of Parrot Point to get clearance from the State Attorney General's Office in preparation for the selling of the land. One can see that the multiple steps made the procedure complex.[2] As the details were determined for the Ministry Center, they were also being determined for Parrot Point. What would be the plan for house placement in this new subdivision? Would this property be incorporated into the City of Charleston? Complicating matters were four lawsuits filed by the James Island Public Service District regarding zoning endorsement issues. Reflecting on this time, Rev. Jenkins stated in the 2002 congregational report regarding Saint James' announced intentions to sell Parrot Point for development, "We were appropriately questioned by some and maliciously maligned by others. We had to pray. We prayed for God's direction."[3]

In the spring of 2001, Ford Development offered to reduce the proposed development to twenty-eight lots in an effort to acquire approval from the Zoning Board and to be sensitive to concerns regarding density and traffic.[4] Rev. Jenkins discussed with Mr. Robertson the possibility of his canceling his contract, with perhaps another buyer—Gary Davis or Crump and Miller of Cornerstone Builders—taking over with the negotiations and construction of Parrot Point.[5]

Rev. Jenkins wrote a letter on May 30, 2001 to the Lighthouse Point residents, who lived on property adjacent to Parrot Point, and issued a press release to address concerns and to remain transparent on business transactions and development plans. In addition to the fewer but larger lots, it was agreed that approximately fourteen acres of high land on the periphery of the 48-acre tract would be left in an undisturbed natural state to maintain a diverse wildlife habitat. Other changes included realignment of a main street and preservation of more grand trees on the property. The sale price was changed to $4.2 million, with the grantee being named Parrot Point LLC. The letter also addressed the will of Josiah R. Harvey and the legalities of "changed circumstances" pertaining to the sale of the land.[6]

Also, according to September 17, 2001 vestry minutes, Saint James had to give consideration regarding Battery Haskell on the Parrot Point property. On Schooner Drive in Lighthouse Point an historical marker, erected on the remaining earthworks, reads, in part, as follows:

> This two-gun Confederate artillery battery and magazine is all that remains of Battery Haskell, a large fortification built on Legare's Point in 1863 to

help defend James and Morris Islands. This two-gun battery was just behind the left flank of Battery Haskell, named for Capt. Charles T. Haskell, Jr., of the 1st S.C. Infantry, mortally wounded on Morris Island July 10, 1863.

Battery Haskell, "a massive open work," was built for twelve guns…It and the rest of Charleston's defenses were evacuated February 17, 1865. Battery Haskell was gradually demolished from the 1920s to the 1960s for farm use and later for residential development.

Senior warden Ann L. King and Rev. Jenkins conferred with the South Carolina Battleground Preservation Trust. In November of 2001, Ann L. King met with the City of Charleston Subdivision Board. The historical marker website that posts information about Battery Haskell states that "St. James Episcopal Church donated Battery Haskell to the So. Carolina Battleground Preservation Trust."[7] If the Trust were to close, the property would revert to Saint James.[8]

Another interesting historical note about Parrot Point is found in the booklet *Historic Sites of James Island*, which includes the following passage about this land that was in Saint James' possession for well over a century:

> Archaeologists believe Native American shell rings mark occasions when people came together to celebrate and feast. Researchers found three shell middens and evidence of several houses at Parrot Point. They believe the people who lived here were part of a community that lived around Charleston Harbor 4,500 years ago. In addition to hundreds of pounds of oyster shells, researchers found thousands of artifacts including pieces of pottery, bone pins, whelk tools, and shell beads.[9]

The authors of this booklet state, "Sometimes the only information we have about people or an event is preserved in the ground …Most of the history of the United States happened before there were written records."[10] If an archaeological dig were conducted on the land where Saint James has been established for three hundred years, what additional information would be unearthed? One could add that many of Saint James' records—oral and written—have been lost over time.

Mrs. Margie Lane, a tenant and caretaker for forty years on Parrot Point, was saddened about having to move upon the sale of the land and hesitated on leaving, thus requiring legal negotiations about a departure date and delaying negotiations with Ford Development. At the time Mrs. Lane was dealing with serious health issues, and the vestry authorized financial assistance to aid her in her transfer to another residence.[11] She and her family had loved this property, and the staff and vestry were committed to help her make this transition with grace and a monetary gift.[12]

In the fall of 2001, the long debate on how to use the proceeds from the Parrot Point property and still honor Mr. Harvey's nineteenth century will was determined. Vestry minutes gave the following details: organ note to Wachovia of $110,000, endowment $950,000, Building $2,600,000, Loan (CRT) $400,000, and Mission/Outreach of $140,000, for a total of $4,200,000.[13]

By the spring of 2002, many of the problems surrounding the sale of Parrot Point had been resolved, and senior warden Ann L. King, in a letter (dated March 24) to the congregation, stated, in part, "The process of selling the property has brought the message of Christ to this community. The prayerful discernment process to do Christ's work and remain a faithful people continuing to love one another, even in the midst of disagreement, is a great blessing." In her report for the 2002 congregational meeting, she stated that selling Parrot Point had included five buy-sell amendments to the contract that had begun in the fall of 1999 and ended in the spring of 2002.[14]

In September 2000, the vestry was told that the Building Committee had interviewed three contractors and, of the three, Trident Construction was selected. Trident was the largest and had presented the strongest team insofar as input in planning with the architect for design and construction.[15]

By the year 2002 plans for building the Ministry Center were underway. The congregation welcomed Bishop Haynsworth to ask God's blessing on the ground, the building, and the ministry it would support. In his letter to the congregation for the 2002 congregational meeting, Rev. Jenkins stated:

> We are building more than a new building. We are building more than a church here. We are building a Community of Christians...We are building a community of believers where people may come for celebration, healing, transformation, and encouragement. We are building a safe, spiritually intimate fellowship where all are welcome. Where all are invited to meet Jesus Christ personally. Claim Him as Savior and follow Him as Lord. A Community [where...] we serve each other because that is how we show our love for Jesus.[16]

Also, the Faith in Action Capital Funds Campaign ultimately raised $1.2 million through "not equal gifts, but equal sacrifice," as Rev. Jenkins stated, for the church to grow and be available to more people in the community, to be a "mission-focused ministry as opposed to a maintenance-focused ministry."[17] Committee members who were wise with financial knowledge provided valuable advice regarding loans, investments, expenditures, budgets, and resources.

A great deal of thought went into the location and design of the Ministry Center. Bobbie Galbraith and Ben Horne met with the Diocesan Architectural Review Committee, which expressed a concern about the distance between the current church and the proposed building. However, if the distance were lessened, it would necessitate several grave site changes. Consequently, the Diocesan Committee suggested that a lengthy canopied walkway be constructed between the two buildings, and the vestry concurred. To stay within budget, the vestry discussed reducing the seating occupancy from 400 to 350, but that idea was dismissed. Ultimately, the vestry approved a budget of $4 million for the construction of the new Ministry Center and the renovation of the current parish house.[18] Vestry member Becky Williams reported that a draft from the architect proposed an "L" shaped structure, eliminating a portion of the canopied walkway and moving the building nearer to the present church building by sixty feet. Craig, Gaulden, and Davis Architects were hired for the designing of the Ministry Center.[19]

Many more details needed to be addressed: soil samples and a geotechnical survey for the architects (done by Wright Padgett Christopher), tree preservation, land surveys to the west of the church, cash flow projections, and possible wetlands in the area proposed for the Ministry Center. By September 2000 the vestry was told that pilings were not going to be required for the building, but the parking and road might have to be relocated. In November, the vestry was informed that an area of the building site had indeed been declared to be wetlands, and they had to consider alternatives.[20]

Becky Williams and her subcommittee led discussions and plans addressing the sound system, acoustics, stage, seating, flooring, audio/visual placement, and the commercial kitchen design.[21] Also, Pat Gould provided input regarding needs of the choir, and Randall Horres gave feedback for future dramatic performances in the Ministry Center.[22] Meanwhile Ben Horne oversaw renovations of the parish hall.

Eri Schultz, arborist for the City of Charleston, and Gren Winthrop from Historic Tree Preservation, designated trees that building plans would impact. Ultimately, the Building Committee was granted permission to use their discretion to remove four trees, if needed. Meanwhile, vestry members met with the Charleston County Board of Zoning Appeals regarding proposed development of Parrot Point.[23]

As of April 2004, the last remaining large construction job was that of finishing the colonnade. The cost was elevated due to concern of trees to be preserved. An arborist determined the required pilings. The colonnade was necessary to connect the main sanctuary to the Ministry Center, providing a safe, raised walkway that would be user-friendly for worshippers in wheelchairs. The covering would be advantageous in inclement weather.[24]

A report in the 2004 vestry minutes stated that the Ministry Center's approved budget increased to $4,237,250. According to several vestry reports, Art Field oversaw many of the final details of construction. The consecration for the Ministry Center was on July 31, 2004 with Bishops Salmon and Skilton as well as former rectors John Howard and Paul Zahl present.[25]

Meanwhile, the staff at Saint James continued to evolve. In the beginning of this decade, Marilyn Powell, ordained in 1985 as a vocational deacon, served primarily in outreach ministries. She was a chaplain at Bishop Gadsden Retirement Community as well as a deacon for Saint James, often assisting in worship services.[26]

In May of 2000, the vestry honored Assistant Rector Marc Boutan's request for a leave of absence from Easter until Pentecost as he sought God's calling on his life and his profession.[27] In August Rev. Boutan told the vestry about his meeting with Bishop Salmon and his decision to "work with his hands first" and possibly pursue a music ministry elsewhere.[28] In November of 2000 Rev. Jenkins requested permission of the vestry to develop a formal arrangement with Rev. Carl Green to be a teacher at Saint James on a part time basis.

It was also at the March 2000 meeting when the vestry felt it wise to appoint a member of the congregation rather than a vestry member to serve as Saint James' representative on Bishop Gadsden's Board. Dr. Bell met with Mr. Trawick at Bishop Gadsden to determine if the retirement home's bylaws would honor this change. In June of 2000 Jane Horne agreed to fill this position.[29] Over upcoming years Bobbie Galbraith, David Cupka, Ben English, George Lyle, and Jim Bennett all served as board members at Bishop Gadsden as well.[30] Vestry notes from February 2007 indicate that Dr. Barbara Edlund—RN, PhD, ANP-C, Associate Professor in the College of Nursing, MUSC—was chosen to serve as an *ex officio* member of the vestry on the Board of Bishop Gadsden. Dr. Edlund had clinical expertise in primary care of the older adult. She served in this capacity into the next decade.[31]

At the June 2000 vestry meeting, Rev. Finch reported that he had celebrated his 45th anniversary to the priesthood on St. Barnabas Day at Cursillo #118 at Camp St. Christopher.[32] In 2001 he and his wife Leona became residents of Bishop Gadsden.[33] For two years Rev. Finch served both as the pastoral associate of Saint James and as chaplain of Bishop Gadsden. Due to this demanding schedule, he resigned from Saint James December 31, 2003.[34] The new chapel at Bishop Gadsden was dedicated and consecrated on Holy Saturday, April 15, 2006. The chapel's 100-year-old stations of the cross, which came from a church in Paris, France, are dedicated in honor of Rev. Floyd and Leona Finch as is the chapel's vesting room. The first Sunday service was held in the chapel the next day, which was Easter.

In June 2001 Rev. Marshall Huey joined Saint James as assistant rector. Rev. Huey was a graduate of Duke University and Vanderbilt Law School. He was an attorney for fifteen years before entering seminary in 1998 at the University of the South in Sewanee, Tennessee.[35] He said that he kept a photograph in his office of the sun coming up over James Island, a photo taken on June 24, 2001, his first Sunday at Saint James. On January 5, 2002, Bishops Salmon, Skilton, and Haynsworth ordained him at Saint James to the priesthood. Rev. Huey used his skills as a lawyer to help the church navigate the ongoing, complex legal issues regarding the sale of Parrot Point, and he certainly used his skills as a priest to bring the ALPHA course to Saint James and to minister to those in vacation Bible school, Bible studies, small groups, and the young adults' Sunday Supper Club.[36]

In February of 2001 Louise Weld, Christian counselor for the Low Country Pastoral Counseling Center, expressed her desire to become a candidate for Holy Orders.[37] On October 15, 2001, her Discernment Committee unanimously endorsed her to the Diocese as an Aspirant for Holy Orders. In November 2002, after her graduation from Trinity School of Ministry, Rev. Jenkins extended to her a position on the Saint James staff to minister to the congregation through pastoral care, to plan and develop future ministries, and to teach adult Sunday school and ALPHA classes. On February 8, 2006, the congregation joined Rev. Louise Weld as she was ordained into the Deaconate after having completed her studies as a seminarian. Present were The Right Reverends Edward L. Salmon, Jr., William J. Skilton, and G. Edward Haynsworth.[38]

Saint James' former rector Rev. John Howard was serving at Trinity Wall Street Episcopal Church and Saint Paul's Chapel in New York City when the horrendous 9-11 attacks took place. The World Trade Center towers came crashing down after two planes, piloted by terrorists, hit the tall buildings. On September 11, 2001, the nation, along with the world, watched televised broadcasts in utter horror of the carnage that took over two thousand lives. Throughout the day parishioners received calls and emails that Saint James was hosting a prayer service that evening. Members of the congregation and community poured through the front doors of the church to regain composure, seek solace, find direction, and reaffirm their faith in God in the midst of this tragedy.

Throughout building, renovating, and experiencing staff changes, many programs thrived at Saint James, some of which were the tape ministry, LEMS (lay Eucharist ministers to take communion to shut-ins), Mothers' Morning Out, EYC (Episcopal Youth Council), Fifty Plus Group, and Parish Life. Committees, usually headed by vestry members, were also thriving. Saint James' youth band called "Saturday Night Jesus," was asked to play for the closing Eucharist at the Diocesan Convention.[39]

Worshippers of this decade were also fortunate to have Pat Gould as the director of music. Having been at Saint James for ten years by 2002, she had built a multigenerational choir as well as youth choirs known as the Carolers and Choristers. Helping to promote the praise services, she often incorporated the musical skills of Michael McIntyre, Dee Rhodes, Gay DuPre, Tom Fair, Kelley Ellsworth, Lynette Kelley, and Carol Thompson. The "Resurrection Choir" was made of vocalists to sing at funerals held at Saint James. She helped to expand the music library, incorporate guests (ex. Naval Academy Women's Glee Club), and enhance fellowship among members of the choir and congregation.[40]

Teaching was often intertwined with entertainment. Mark Barwick, part-time leader of Christian Education, coordinated vacation Bible school and taught confirmation and first communion classes. Saint James hosted the South Carolina "Tell-Around" in November of 2002, a night of biblical storytelling in commemoration of National Bible Week. Several able storytellers, including Saint James member Mike Miller, presented tales of inspiration and humor.[41]

The pizza lunches that Saint James had been successfully hosting at James Island High were also extended to Fort Johnson Middle School, with Michael McIntyre serving as a mentor for the leaders from Clearview Baptist and a couple of Presbyterian churches with representatives helping to lead the studies.[42] In the 2000 congregational report, Michael stated that the pizza ministry had grown from an average of forty students to an incredible 400 students each week where many unchurched teens heard about Jesus in detail for the first time.[43] By 2001 Saint James was budgeting $10,000 for this "pizza ministry." In early 2001, Michael went to Sydney, Australia for a month of continuing education for youth ministry.[44]

In March of 2004, the vestry unanimously voted to call Rev. Robert Horn as associate rector. At the time Horn was rector at Trinity Church in Pinopolis.[45] He and his wife Martha moved into the rectory on Majestic Oaks in Seaside Subdivision.[46]

Katherine Lundy gave a Kimball baby grand piano to Saint James. Lillie McGougan arranged for Bobby Cunningham, with Atlas Van Lines, to move it from Johns Island to Saint James at no charge.[47] This piano is located in the choir room of the Ministry Center.

In the fall of 2004, Saint James began "40 Days of Purpose," as small groups gathered weekly in homes and at church to study Rick Warren's book *Purpose Driven Life*. 19,000 churches had already completed the "40 Days of Purpose," and 10,000 were scheduled to study it that fall.[48] On November 7, the congregation concluded the study with a "Celebration Sunday" in which parishioners provided testimonies in the church services followed by lunch.[49]

In October 2005 the congregation began a study called "40 Days of Community." The first study had focused on the question, "What on earth am *I* here for," and this study focused on "What on earth are *we* here for?" Several other Bible studies were led by different priests and parishioners at this time as well.[50] The January 2006 *Epistle* listed thirteen small groups involved in community outreach, emphasizing acts of kindness and generosity, including the following: helping a handicapped church member with yardwork, "adopting" five older couples to assist, visiting the Farmington Community Home for mentally retarded adults, hosting a luncheon for teachers at Murray LaSaine Elementary, creating a program "Provide a Ride" for those needing transportation, giving a Christmas party at the Hermina Traeye Nursing Home on Johns Island, and riding in a Harley Davidson group as a fundraiser for children.[51]

Like other decades, this one contained great emphasis on prayer. The *Epistles* posted monthly articles about prayers being requested and being offered. Prayer teams were available on Sunday mornings at designated times during and after services. A telephone prayer chain was set up. Prayer time and intercessory prayer were available in the chapel. A list of those on active service in the military was included in the Sunday bulletins so parishioners could pray for them. Selected prayers from the *Book of Common Prayer* were reprinted in the *Epistle*. Personal testimonies were included about the healing power of prayers.[52] A poem about unspoken prayers was included in the September 2005 *Epistle*.[53] When a sergeant (not a member of Saint James) serving in Iraq wrote a letter to the congregation requesting prayer for soldiers serving in Bagdad, it was published in the August 2005 *Epistle*.[54] For a time, monthly evening prayer services were offered in the Ministry Center, especially for those requesting healing.[55] The cancer support group met monthly for years and prayed, offering thanksgiving for attendees who were cancer survivors and asking for healing for those suffering from the disease. In conjunction with prayers for cancer patients were "Pink Sundays," on which parishioners were asked to wear pink in memory or in honor of those whose lives had been touched by this disease. In 2008 another prayer group called "The Daniel's Den" was formed "to wrestle with the question of how we might be a faithful and public witness of a Biblically-based, Cross-centered, transforming faith in the foreign land of our denomination and the foreign land of the fallen world and culture in which we find ourselves."[56] According to the February 2009 *Epistle*, "soaking prayer" was offered during which participants sit in silence, listen to worship music, and focus on the Lord.

Robert and Martha Horn participated in another ministry, that of Victorious Ministry Through Christ (VMTC). Traveling to Sweden and England, they led a prayer ministry which "frees committed Christian people from the bondages which block them from experiencing God's healing power in their lives, and enables them to make a deeper commitment to Jesus." Participants might feel plagued by experiences that hinder their worship of God and who He calls them to be. Through counseling and prayer sessions, the troubled person can develop a healthier faith walk.[57] Some parishioners were trained in the ministry so that VMTC is a part of the prayer ministry offered at Saint James.

The *Epistles* of this decade often included some interesting entries. The monthly article "Meet Our Saint James Family" gave biographical information about members. Students who had won awards at school and parishioners who had had articles written about them in the newspaper were often also highlighted in the church periodical. Even Dennis the Menace cartoons pertaining to his worship and prayers were featured. The *Epistles* also listed Saint James' births, deaths, baptisms, weddings, transfers, and new members. Some *Epistles* included opportunities to attend functions at other churches, such as lectures by visiting speakers and teas for fundraisers. The women's chapter meetings and activities were added.

Minutes from vestry meetings throughout 2006-2007 address five main goals. The first was to increase lay ministry development through leadership training and team building. The second was to improve pastoral care, especially through Stephen Ministries. The third was to increase home group development, mainly through small groups. The fourth was to enhance outreach through the establishment of the Childhood Development Center. The final goal was to enhance the music program for adults and children.[58]

To welcome new members, the vestry created a "Come and See" invitation that focused on the Biblical model of Jesus inviting Philip, and then Philip inviting Nathanael, and so forth, all to "come see" and share the Good News. Parishioners were encouraged to consider who invited them to come see this One named Jesus and then start being intentional about inviting others to Saint James to "come and see" how the body of believers grow in love of Christ.[59]

The report presented at the annual congregational meeting in 2007 revealed a change in Saint James' perspective about the primary role of family in discipling the youth. Using Rob and Amy Rienow's *Visionary Parenting*, the church focused on Deuteronomy 6:5, which, in part, says, "These commands are to be upon your hearts. Impress them on your children." Rev. Jenkins stated, "The formation of one's faith…takes place best at the knee of a parent, grandparent and/or sitting with friends in a trusted Home Group."[60]

Thus, Saint James moved away from the traditional Sunday school model because statistics showed that it was ineffective in enabling the youth to articulate the Gospel. Alternatives for more effective discipleship included children's chapel during worship, youth groups, family nights, family vacation Bible school, and family conferences. Rev. Robert Horn focused on newcomer incorporation and home groups.[61] Youth director Michael McIntyre kept the preteens and adolescents actively engaged in programs, enabling them to develop better relationships among themselves, with their families, and with Christ. The January 2010 *Epistle* included an invitation to a parenting seminar led by Jeff Hoyle, with Focus on the Family, and Rev. Mark Holmen of Faith@HOME.[62]

Other initiatives were undertaken. Associate Pastor Louise Weld focused on healing relationships. She wrote, "More and more, the theme of reconciliation defines the shape of my pastoral care ministry at Saint James," and she emphasized the importance of healing wounded individuals and wounded relationships.[63] Mary Ellen Doran, in charge of Christian Education, also emphasized the importance of spiritual and emotional health in the family.[64]

Saint James has also trained parishioners to work through Stephen Ministry. One-on-one mission work is done through "Stephen Ministry," in which a trained parishioner comes alongside another person in the church who is in crisis (due to problems like illness, unemployment, divorce, or death of a loved one). Stephen ministers are taught how to listen, pray, and support their care-receivers in whatever ways are deemed best. For weeks and sometimes months, the Stephen minister and his/her assigned care-receiver meet regularly so that they can build a trusting, confidential relationship that fosters a renewal based on healing, hope, and Scripture.[65]

Throughout 2007 extensive plans were made to inaugurate Saint James Day School. Philip Clark, an attorney, set the school up as a business and helped write the by-laws. David

Cupka, Scooter Barnette, Keith Doran, and Joyce Daughtrey were committee members who worked to establish the foundation of the day school. Approximately $91,000, much of which was funded through a gift from Frances Frampton, was invested in improving the building's plumbing, electricity, doors, walkways, playground, fencing, computers, painting, fire alarms, floors, and furniture. Of course, the committee also had to plan for employment, classroom supplies, licensing, advertising, insurance, and employee training. The fire marshal had to approve the architectural plans for the renovations.[66] The Department of Social Services (DSS) inspected the school. Saint James Day School opened March 3, 2008[67] with an enrollment of twenty-three children.[68] In April of 2008 renovations had to be made to enlarge the infant area and move the toddlers to the infant room; three of the Board Members paid for the renovations for this change.[69]

Dr. David Egleston did a presentation for the vestry on the Automated External Defibrillator (AED), which cost $1,500. If placed in the front hallway of the Ministry Center, it would also be accessible to the church. The congregation was asked to make contributions to buy one in case of emergencies.[70]

Several staff positions turned over midway in this decade. In 2007 Richard Scott resigned as Saint James' music director,[71] and Ward Moore was hired as the new organist and choirmaster.[72] Sexton Leonard Taylor was no longer able to work due to surgery, medical leave, and disabilities.[73] Longtime parish coordinator Francis Fuchs accepted a job at St. Helena's Church in Beaufort.[74] In 2007 Rev. Robert Horn, associate pastor, resigned and later accepted a job as rector in Barnwell, South Carolina.[75] In July of 2008 Yvonne Jordan was hired as parish life coordinator to cater in the Ministry Center. In an effort to reduce staff costs, Berta Puckhaber, as parish coordinator, took on what had been the duties of a former bookkeeper, and Jessica Shelton, who worked at the front desk, also took on additional tasks.[76] Mary Ellen Doran resigned as full-time director of Christian Education and assumed the role as director of the Saint James Day School.[77] In May of 2009 she stepped down as Day School director but stayed on the board. Crystal Strickland was hired as director and continued to work in this capacity for many upcoming years. On October 20, 2009, Erin Cooley was hired as the new Praise Team leader.

In the summer of 2008, the vestry began plans to promote a program called "Simple Church," based on a book with that title, by authors Thom Rainer and Eric Geiger. Focusing on clarity, movement, alignment, and focus, the authors advocate a return to God's process for making disciples and an elimination of extraneous activities that distract from that main goal.[78] As of September 2008, the *Epistles* added Saint James' new mission statement: Love God, Love People, Build Community.[79]

By June of 2008 the vestry sought ways to improve the church's budget. Because of deficit operations budgets from 2004-2007 and another similar situation projected for 2008, nearly all investment reserves had been used to cover operation expenses, and membership growth and income were below expectations. One major proposal included plans to increase membership, encouraging each family to bring at least one new individual to Saint James, asking the choirs to perform in the community to bring awareness particularly to the youth and teen programs, and reaching out more to visitors. Another initiative was to make parishioners more cognizant of how important their pledges were. There was discussion about the use of Saint James facilities for fundraising, particularly the Ministry Center for wedding receptions, public and private school events, and meetings of organizations. Vestry members wanted to initiate fundraisers to cover unbudgeted expenses with the air conditioning, sprinkler systems, and roof and organ repairs. Additional proposals included the encouragement of self-funding of some of the church's programs and the use of volunteers instead of paid employees, when possible.[80]

Additional plans were made to ask the day school to pay $2,000 monthly rent and repay their loan of $45,000.[81] Discussion took place about whether to further reduce staff or their compensations, require mission expenditures to be self-funding, and possibly to refinance the Ministry Center. Costs were reduced with air conditioning, lighting, and insurance deductibles. A donor pledged $30,000 if parishioners matched that amount, and they did.[82]

On November 11, 2008 the vestry signed the letter approving Craig Stephan's candidacy for seminary. His ordination was later scheduled for December 19, 2009, at Saint James.[83]

In closing this reflection on the decade of Saint James' history from 2000-2010 are words taken from the April 21, 2002 Saint James congregational report, which includes some profound comments made by senior warden Ann L. King, words that pertain not only to this decade but also to the history recorded in this book. Two paragraphs especially stand out as developing the theme of this text:

> This place is holy ground. A place sanctified by bishops and ministers offering prayers and church buildings rising over 300 years ago on this same spot, an historically significant location for this community. When I look at this church, I think no other structure could have been more beautiful. It will become more so as needlepoint cushions, lovingly made by the women of this church, adorn it. As one architect commented, 'This is the most significant building on James Island.'...As beautiful as the Bishop Gadsden complex across the street is, it centers itself on the front of this building. But buildings, as our history tells us, are built, swept away by war and fire and wind and rebuilt using different plans. So certainly God is so much greater than any building we can build or imagine.

> Our graveyard, another historical location with old graves, some stones unreadable, others forgotten, families gone as well as new graves, freshly placed is a mark of our Christianity. If we go looking, we will find the per-

son we love gone on to Christ to live an eternal life. This graveyard is a place where we can walk and remember the person we love and miss. It is especially a place of hope. A reminder that we too will one day be with Christ, 'face to face and know Him fully as we are fully known' (I Cor. 12:12). This is a place well cared for by many: by June Dickerson's beautiful book, a record of every grave here; by the work of the cemetery committee, of new copings around graves and of change—a new building with a footprint on one side of the graveyard. It is one piece in a set of buildings that will one day surround the graveyard. But again, like the building, we are not a beautiful yard of old graves and huge oak trees. We are God's people, believers in a Savior we desperately need, a risen Lord who loves us beyond understanding; one who gives us the way the truth and the life.[84]

Ann died in 2019 and was buried in the cemetery about which she wrote these beautiful reflections. Her words portray this place of worship for all who have gone before, for all currently here, and all who are yet to come. This decade certainly left a footprint on the history of Saint James.

CHAPTER EIGHTEEN

Break from the National Episcopal Church

By 2012 people were asking Saint James parishioners questions like the following: Why did you take the word "Episcopal" out of your church's name? Why are you not a part of the National Episcopal Church anymore? What are you going to do if you lose your church property? Why are you spending all that money on court fees when you could be spending it on missions? The questions might be simply worded, but they can be answered only by complex theological and legal explanations. For decades, a schism became harder to resolve between The National Episcopal Church (TEC) and the parishes in the Diocese of South Carolina, spanning from Myrtle Beach to Hilton Head. Thus, the story of Saint James' splitting from TEC is intertwined with the story of the Diocese of South Carolina. (Note: The name "Diocese of South Carolina" is used in this chapter up until 2019 when the name was changed to "Anglican Diocese of South Carolina" for the churches that separated from TEC.)

The 212ᵗʰ Convention of the Diocese of South Carolina issued a proposed resolution January 4, 2002, which, in part, stated the following:

> Whereas, in the name of inclusivity, pluralism, and equal rights, the Episcopal Church in the United States…has for the last quarter century… progressively usurped for itself a position of judgment over, arbitration of, and departure from that "Faith delivered to the Saints,"…and
>
> Whereas, the departures from the biblical and traditional Faith include a denial of the unique Person and Lordship of Jesus Christ, and thus of the Triune nature of the Godhead; …the use of "expansive language" liturgies which compromise the nature of baptism and threaten the practice of com-

mon prayer in this Church [... human life at conception...marriage...sexual relationships...ordination...] the failure to discipline those who jeopardize... the Church by such actions...

Whereas, it is the duty of all faithful Christians, humbly acknowledging their own sin and failing, nevertheless to speak the truth in love...for the continuing reformation, revival and deepening unity of the Church...,

Resolved...that the Presiding Bishop of the Episcopal Church..., and its several dioceses, are placed on notice that the Diocese of South Carolina finds itself in a state of impaired relationship with the National Church; states its fervent objection to the deviations from Catholic Faith and Order...; considers such deviations null and void; and for the love of our brothers and sisters in the Faith will take ...action... to...[preserve] the doctrine, discipline, and worship of Christ as this Church has received them...[1]

Succinctly put, the schism came about because of TEC's "emphasis on political correctness and inclusiveness over sound Christian doctrine"[2] and because of "disputes over governance and theological matters, including the interpretation of basic Christian doctrine and what was perceived as the liberalization of church policies and practices."[3]

The Diocese of South Carolina voiced concerns about TEC's positions that many of the local churches, Saint James included, felt were not theologically sound. In an article entitled, "The Real Story behind Our Split with The Episcopal Church," Rev. Canon Jim Lewis of the Diocese of South Carolina explains, as follows:

The denomination [TEC] has been redefining itself since the 1970s effectively evolving into two churches under one roof—a traditional one that embraced historic Anglican doctrines and a modernist one. By the 1990s, the modernist faction was gaining dominance within the denomination. For example, TEC's then-Presiding Bishop, the Most Rev. Frank Griswold, proclaimed that "truth" is "pluriform." This meant the church recognized no single truth, no single theology, no single pathway to salvation. He effectively said that one person's truth is as good as another's.[4]

The Diocese of South Carolina was alarmed about Presiding Bishop Katharine Jefferts-Schori (head of TEC) for what they perceived to be "equivocation"—the use of ambiguous language to conceal the truth or to avoid committing oneself—of Christ's supremacy.[5] In a 2006 interview with *Time Magazine*, Bishop Jefferts-Schori stated that to believe that Jesus was "*the* way, *the* truth and *the* life; no one comes to the Father but through Him" was to put

God in an "awfully small box." Many took that statement to mean that she was denying Jesus' essential role in salvation.[6]

Same-sex marriages, openly gay clergy, and transgender issues were some of the other causes leading to the ultimate split from TEC.[7] The following is an explanation on the website of the (Anglican) Diocese of South Carolina:

> While [sexuality] is one issue about which we are in disagreement with TEC, it is not the central issue…We believe God has revealed in scripture a model for living that is in keeping with His created order, is subject to His blessing and has the greatest likelihood of experiencing that wholeness of life we crave. …TEC has chosen the path of least resistance, opting to bless what the culture wishes to bless…We will love and accept everyone who comes through our doors, whatever their sexual orientation…Redeemed by grace,…we are called to… a new life in Jesus Christ.[8]

Many within the Diocese of South Carolina believe that leaders of TEC, in their words and actions, live "over scripture." One TEC bishop stated, "The church wrote the bible. It can rewrite the bible." The South Carolina parishes withdrawing from TEC strive to live "under the authority of scripture."[9]

Problems became more evident as the Diocese of South Carolina proceeded to elect its new bishop. In 2006 Rev. Mark J. Lawrence, from Bakersfield, California, was elected by the annual convention of the Diocese of South Carolina to be its fourteenth bishop. However, in 2007, Presiding Bishop Jefferts-Schori declared that Lawrence's election was "null and void" because "the consent responses [supporting votes] from a number of standing committees of other Episcopal dioceses [within the United States] did not adhere to canonical requirements."[10] Nevertheless, the Diocese of South Carolina decided to re-certify the bishop-elect and in 2007 held another convention electing Rev. Lawrence as bishop. On January 26, 2008, Mark Lawrence was consecrated as the fourteenth Bishop of South Carolina, the service being held at the Cathedral Church of St. Luke and St. Paul in downtown Charleston.[11]

After the General Convention, on August 13, 2009, Bishop Lawrence addressed the clergy of the Diocese about "a multitude of false teachings" and "a common pattern in how the core doctrines of our faith are being systematically deconstructed."[12] He stated that he intended "to uphold orthodox Anglicanism."[13] The Diocese of South Carolina resented what they considered to be "overreach" on the part of TEC into local matters and grew even more concerned when TEC decided to discipline Lawrence by suspending him.[14]

TEC tried to take disciplinary actions in 2009 to put local clergy under TEC's control, but the Diocese of South Carolina said these actions were at odds with the Episcopal Church's constitution, which reserves clergy discipline exclusively to the diocese. Secondly, the Diocese of South Carolina said that TEC was trying to increase the power of the national presiding bishop, thus violating the constitutional protections of the diocese against external intrusion into its affairs. Consequently, the Diocese amended its constitution and canons in 2010 and 2011 by removing its accession to (compliance with) TECs canons.[15]

The schism also resulted in property disputes. In 2009 the South Carolina Supreme Court heard the case *All Saints Parish Waccamaw v. The Protestant Episcopal Church*, which resulted in the legal decision that individual churches owned their property, not the national church or the diocese. Nevertheless, further precautions were taken in 2011 when Bishop Lawrence conveyed to Saint James and other diocesan Episcopal churches quitclaim deeds, with the idea that one owns the property if he owns the deed.[16]

In 2011 anonymous members of the Diocese of South Carolina charged Bishop Lawrence with "abandonment." Abandonment is defined as a priest's open renunciation of the Church's doctrine, discipline, or worship by preaching or writing things contrary to the theology and tenets of the Church. However, the Disciplinary Board of Bishops concluded that allegations made against Bishop Lawrence did not constitute abandonment of the Episcopal Church.[17]

Saint James joined other local churches in the diocese at a special convention on November 17, 2012, at St. Philip's Church, downtown Charleston, where the Diocese of South Carolina declared itself disassociated from the national church. Attendees voted to remove all references to The Episcopal Church in the diocesan constitution and canons.[18] Every church of the diocese was given the opportunity to choose whether it would remain a member of the Diocese or return to TEC.[19] In 2013 eighty percent of the membership had aligned with the Diocese of South Carolina and Bishop Mark Lawrence.[20] Twenty percent remained affiliated with TEC.

In addition to the issue of ownership of church property was the ownership of the Diocese's name, marks, and other identities (referred to as "intellectual properties"). Up until 2012, TEC continued to use the Diocesan seal and name, but in January 2013 the circuit court blocked the use of the Diocese of South Carolina's identity by anyone outside the Diocese.[21]

In a three-week, non-jury trial in 2014, Circuit Court Judge Diane Goodstein ruled that the breakaway parishes could rightfully leave and take the Diocese of South Carolina's name and church properties with them. She said that in South Carolina so-called "neutral principles of law" override the church's constitution and canons.[22] "Neutral principles of law" include civil, corporate, contract and trust laws.[23] She went on to say that "For over 200 years the Diocese has governed itself…[that] with the freedom to associate goes its corollary, the freedom to disassociate."[24]

In June of 2015 an article (accessible through the timeline posted on the Anglican Diocese of South Carolina website) describes a settlement offer proposed by a local attorney advocating for TEC. The article labels the offer as "spurious" and states the following:

The parishes of the Diocese of South Carolina in the lawsuit against the Episcopal Church have unanimously rejected what the Episcopal Church called a "settlement offer" that would have required them to voluntarily give up the historical identity and property that a South Carolina Circuit Court judge has ruled is owned by the diocese.

The offer was made by a local attorney who represents the 20 percent of members who remained with TEC when most of the Diocese disaffiliated in 2012. It promised that TEC would end its multimillion dollar legal campaign to seize local church properties if the parishes agree to hand over the Diocese's identity, its other assets and the St. Christopher Camp and Conference Center, which is prime real estate that could be sold off by the cash-strapped denomination.

"This is not a legitimate offer of good faith negotiation and never was intended to be," said the Rev. Canon Jim Lewis, Assistant to Bishop Mark Lawrence.[25]

The Diocesan website states, "TEC has never, in the 90+ cases litigated nationwide, agreed to a settlement—even when it was requested. For these reasons...the proposal was unanimously rejected by all parties to the litigation for the Diocese of South Carolina."[26]

The legal dispute regarding church property ownership can be traced to what was called "The Dennis Canon," named for the church official who drafted the law. This canon says that parishes have full authority over their church property as long as they remain part of the National Episcopal Church and subject to its constitution and canons. The parishes are held in trust for the national church. The Diocese of South Carolina amended its constitution and canons in 1987 to include the "Dennis Canon." Each church was asked to adopt the Dennis Canon, but seven churches in the Diocese, for whatever reason, did not. Therefore, in 2017, the South Carolina Supreme Court identified those churches, for which no documentation of accession to the Dennis Canon could be found, as being "independent" from the national church. When they withdrew from the National Episcopal Church, they were permitted to have full ownership of their properties.[27]

In September 2017 the Diocese of South Carolina filed a petition on behalf of the remaining twenty-nine churches for a rehearing after the South Carolina Supreme Court reversed the 2014 rulings of Judge Goodstein, which had stated that the breakaway parishes had the right to leave and take their church properties. The Diocese argues that the Dennis Canon does not create a trust under South Carolina law. The word "trust" "does not unequivocally convey an intention to transfer ownership of property."[28] However, TEC argues that the parishes' accession to the Dennis Canon created the trust. The twenty-nine churches, having in good faith adopted the Dennis Canon through the Diocese of South Carolina, were informed by the National Episcopal Church in August of 2017 that TEC wanted their properties, estimated to be worth $500 million or more. This included the 314-acre Camp St. Christopher on Seabrook Island, much of which is valuable beachfront property.[29]

One Charleston newspaper article stated, "The Diocese of South Carolina spans the entire eastern half of the state, so the ruling will have profound implications on thousands of clergy and congregants, including those whose families have worshipped at several colonial churches for generations and now could face a decision over whether to stay or leave."[30] In this legal state of limbo, some clergy wondered if even the houses in which they lived would still be theirs when the appeals had run their course.[31] In June of 2013, TEC held "hostage" the pensions of more than eighty disassociated staff members, refusing to allow them to move their retirement savings.[32]

Rulings impacted twenty-nine parishes, including St. Philip's (probably the oldest congregation in the state), St. Michael's (the oldest surviving religious building in Charleston), Old St. Andrews (Saint James' "mother church"), and Saint James.[33] Legal outcomes pertain to churches in Charleston, Beaufort, Edisto, Summerville, Georgetown, Myrtle Beach, Florence and elsewhere in the coastal half of South Carolina.[34] Charleston newspaper reporters Jennifer Hawes and Adam Parker stated, "The key issues at stake in the case included whether the national church held parish properties in trust and whether the break-away group took proper actions under state nonprofit law to separate from the national body."[35]

The churches disassociating from TEC asked that they be allowed to worship as they feel is right and that the churches remaining with TEC be allowed to worship as they feel is right.[36] Although the National Episcopal Church invited the disassociated churches to rejoin TEC, the breakaway churches felt that trust had been broken and that compromise on Biblically-rooted doctrine was not feasible. Consequently, an article on the Diocesan website states, "It is a certainty that we will not return to the denomination that rejected our adherence to the faith once received even if we are forced from our spiritual homes and required to rebuild."[37]

One argument set forth by the Diocese of South Carolina is that the diocese is older than the National Episcopal Church. The early churches, dating back as far as 1680, were a part of the Church of England overseen by the bishop of London. The Episcopal Church was not convened until 1785. Thus, some of the historic churches now claim their identity with the Anglican church through their heritage, which predates TEC.[38] Many members of the Diocese of South Carolina feel that they are in legal and spiritual battle with a corporate business housed in New York rather with fellow believers of their state.

For decades parishioners have paid for, constructed, and maintained their own properties independent of finances from the National Episcopal Church.[39] Thus, another argument—do not those who paid for it also own it? TEC says that parishes hold all property "in trust;

it's all ultimately 'owned' by the national church."[40] The Rev. Jeffery Miller responded, "The national Episcopal Church has never contributed a dime to this congregation or its buildings [St. Philip's]. Indeed, over the years, money has flowed from St. Philip's to the Episcopal Church, not the other way around."[41]

By 2018, the Diocese had filed a claim for twenty-nine parishes under the state "Betterments Statute," which says that "if [property owners], in good faith, believing they own their property, [make] improvements, only to later have a court determine it belongs to another, they must be reimbursed for the value of those improvements."[42] Rev. Cannon Jim Lewis sent an email on August 28, 2019 entitled "South Carolina Circuit Court Rules in Favor of Diocese of South Carolina on Betterments Statute." In it Lewis reported that Judge Edgar W. Dickson ruled that he was denying TEC's and the National Episcopal Church in South Carolina's (TECSC) motion to dismiss the Betterments Statute claim filed by the Diocese of South Carolina.[43]

In that 2019 email Rev. Jim Lewis wrote,

> Many of the parishes in the Diocese of South Carolina can trace their unbroken history back to the colonial era of the state. During that entire time, there has never been any question of their unencumbered title to property or legal identity. All have proceeded throughout their history with the maintaining and improving of their properties in the good faith belief of their ownership of them…If Judge Dickson rules TEC/TECSC does have a trust interest in any parish property, then those parishes have claims against TEC/TECSC for the value of the improvements made in good faith to those properties since they were created.[44]

TEC states that a diocese is a geographic designation, governed by a bishop in which affiliated parishes operate. Therefore, TEC claims that a diocese made up of churches cannot leave the national church, but people can leave the local church.[45] However, the Diocese of South Carolina bases arguments on the First Amendment right to the "free exercise of religion."[46] Therefore, regarding the Diocese of South Carolina, Rev. Miller asks, "Does the right to voluntarily associate not imply the right to voluntarily disassociate and revoke prior commitments?"[47]

A Post and Courier article stated, "In fall 2015, the Supreme Court agreed to bypass the state appellate court to hear arguments in the dispute, which by then had spanned three years of court wrangling, millions of dollars in legal fees, a three-week trial, 1,300 exhibits and the unrequited settlement offer."[48] Retired Chief Justice Jean Toal said that even at the level of the state supreme court, the case has been difficult because of the "five different, strongly-held opinions" among justices.[49]

Adam Parker, Charleston newspaper reporter, stated that in 2017 two of the justices clearly decided in favor of the Diocese, two clearly on the side of TEC, and one, who was the "swing vote, determining that most of the breakaway parishes had in fact acceded to the Dennis Canon."[50] Edward Gilbreth of the *Post and Courier* stated in his article, "The essence of the legalities appears to have boiled down to canon law vs. civil law—and canon law won" in 2017.[51]

Andrew Knapp wrote in his *Post and Courier* article, "It was no secret that S.C. Supreme Court Justice Kay Hearn had belonged to an Episcopalian parish that split into two congregations. But when a legal dispute arising from the divisions statewide wound up in her courtroom, Hearn ultimately penned a ruling that favored the national church she and her husband had aligned with."[52] State judicial rules state that judges must recuse themselves if their impartiality might be reasonably in question. When lawyers representing the Diocese of South Carolina challenged Hearn's role after she had decided in favor of the national church, TEC lawyers said that the diocese lawyers should have voiced any objections before Hearn took the case.[53]

Indicative of how complex this court case became is the following sentence in a 2017 newspaper report, "The justices issued their 77-page divided opinion almost two years after hearing arguments in the case."[54] This article goes on to say, "At issue in the case is whether South Carolina civil law trumps a hierarchical national church's own canons, backed by the First Amendment's religious protections."[55] Parker paraphrases in his article, asking, "Does the First Amendment guarantee the right of religious organizations to decide their own destiny irrespective of prior affiliation or previous commitment, or does the First Amendment guarantee the right of a hierarchical church…to govern itself according to its own rules?"[56]

In 2017 *The Post and Courier* included a picture of Bishop Lawrence in a line of priests and bishops. The brief article states, as follows:

> Bishop Mark Lawrence of the Diocese of South Carolina leads a procession of clergy and bishops into service on June 27 at Wheaton College in Wheaton, Illinois. Archbishop Foley Beach of the Anglican Church in North America welcomed Lawrence and the Diocese into the church at the opening service of the ACNA's three-day Provincial Assembly. Earlier, the church's Provincial Council had unanimously approved the reception of the Diocese into the larger body. The Diocese comprises 22,000 members from 52 congregations across the Eastern part of South Carolina. More than 1,400 clergy, lay delegates and guests attended the assembly.[57]

Thus, a long-debated period of spiritual discernment and legal counsel had been brought to some closure. No longer being affiliated with TEC, most of the Diocese of South Carolina became affiliated with the Anglican Church in North America (ACNA) as well as with the Global Fellowship of Confessing Anglicans (GAFCON) and the Global South Primates.[58]

In 2017 in the *Post and Courier* Rt. Rev. Dr. C. Fitzsimons Allison wrote an article entitled "Seek Just Settlement in Church Dispute." He pointed out that TEC had been promoting the idea of reconciliation between the two quarreling factions, but that reconciliation, although an attractive word, creates false expectations by implying that coming back together requires one or both parties to repent for their positions. Instead, he advocates that each group allow the other to go its own way in peace to pursue their separate callings. He stated, "The resources of both groups would be preferably spent on the work of ministry to which each feels called."[59] Otherwise, he stated, the litigation will continue. After listing other parishes and Dioceses in other states embroiled in disputes with TEC, Allison cited a disturbing incident, as follows: "The people of Good Shepherd, Binghamton, N.Y, were denied the purchase of their former church, seeing it sold for one-third their offer to become a mosque instead. The pattern of behavior is clear. For TEC, 'reconciliation' has meant 'surrender, return the property and we'll forgive you so you can rejoin us'."[60]

Many ask about mediation and compromise between these two bodies of worshippers. Rev. Canon Lewis of the Diocese of South Carolina addressed that question in the following:

> TEC has filed more than 80 lawsuits seeking to seize the property of individual parishes and dioceses that left the denomination. TEC itself has admitted to spending more than $22 million on its legal action. These efforts have largely succeeded when TEC attempts to seize the property of individual parishes. Parishes across the country have been evicted from their churches.
>
> TEC's policy is simple and punitive: No one who leaves TEC may buy the seized church buildings. In several cases where TEC has succeeded in seizing a church, it has evicted the congregation and shuttered the building. In some cases, the church has been handed over to remnant groups that remained loyal to TEC. In other cases, the church [property] has been sold to another religious group.
>
> ...TEC wants to keep those millions of dollars in property–an attractive prize for a denomination that is losing members and closing churches.[61]

In February of 2018 the Diocese of South Carolina filed a Petition for Writ of Certiorari (a court process to seek judicial review of a decision of a lower court) with the United States Supreme Court[62] but was denied a hearing.[63] Throughout 2018 and 2019 Judge Edgar W. Dickson reviewed court records to determine what the state supreme court opinions mean.

In the summer of 2019 Judge Dickson ordered that mediation be attempted once again with the services of Mr. Tom Wills of the law firm Wills, Massalon, and Allen of Charleston, but it was unsuccessful.[64]

On September 20, 2019, in an article entitled "Federal Judge Enjoins Use of Diocese Names and Seal," District Court Judge Richard M. Gergel ruled in favor of TEC and its local diocese, TECSC, in a federal trademark case. Judge Gergel issued an injunction preventing the Diocese from using the following: "Diocese of South Carolina," "The Episcopal Diocese of South Carolina," "The Protestant Episcopal Church in the Diocese of South Carolina," and The Diocesan Seal. The Standing Committee's president, Rev. Marcus Kaiser of the Church of the Holy Comforter in Sumter, said that consequently his advisory board members voted unanimously to adopt the name "The Anglican Diocese of South Carolina."[65]

An article on the front page of *The Post and Courier* dated June 23, 2020, was entitled "Breakaway Diocese Can Keep Properties." Judge Dickson declared the Dennis Canon does not create a legally cognizable trust, nor does it transfer title to property.

Saint James' priests, vestry, staff, and congregation have sought God's direction in a painful, but what they perceive to be, morally right decision to preserve the core of their Christian doctrines and faith. Saint James has been a part of these legal actions and theological discernments since the discord with the National Episcopal Church began. Saint James' priests have attended numerous diocesan meetings and conferred with Bishop Lawrence. They have communicated regularly with parishioners, pored over legal and theological documents, participated in fasts and corporate prayer, hired attorneys, altered budgets to pay for legal fees, conducted vestry meetings into overtime, and brainstormed possible mediations and possible outcomes, all pertaining to this situation with TEC. In these uncertain times, parishioners have put on hold long-term planning and new construction on church campuses. Bishop Lawrence stated that the "years of litigation [have] taken [a] toll…in the very complicated ecclesiastical and judicial landscape," but "it has also been a refiner's fire."[66]

Organizations within Saint James changed names or affiliations throughout this process. The Episcopal Church Women (ECW) has become Women of the Anglican Diocese of South Carolina. The young people are no longer referred to as the Episcopal Youth Council (EYC). The Daughters of the King (DOK) at Saint James resigned their memberships and unanimously returned their crosses to the national order to become members of Daughters of the Holy Cross (DHC), the order of women affiliated with the Anglican Church.

The Anglican Diocese of South Carolina has had the legal representation of Attorney C. Alan Runyon, and the Saint James congregation has fortunately had the legal representation of its church member Attorney Mark Evans. Of course, many others have been involved in sharing their legal expertise, including former Diocesan Canon Wade Logan.

Friends have risen up to support the Anglican Diocese. In 2017, 110 "Palmetto Family" signers—religious leaders from various denominations, churches, and ministries from throughout South Carolina—signed a document, stating that they expected South Carolina courts to uphold the religious freedom of the congregants of the Anglican Diocese of South Carolina.[67] At the Global Anglicans Future Conference in Jerusalem (GAFCON) Bishop Lawrence represented the Anglican Diocese of South Carolina as a bishop of the Anglican Church in North America (ACNA), of which the diocese has been welcomed as a member.[68]

Saint James' priests have also remained sensitive to the heartache felt by many Saint James members separated from devout Christian friends and family who have remained in congregations affiliated with the National Episcopal Church. Above all, in spite of our differences, priests and parishioners have sought to live by God's commandment "Love one another as I have loved you." (John 13:34) Rev. Weld wrote about the break from the Episcopal Church: "The result for me has been a deep sadness to be separated from a church which has nurtured my spiritual life since before I was born. At the same time, I have a new sense of freedom as I pursue the calling I believe I have received from God to commend Jesus Christ to the world around me." [69] Rev. Jenkins stated, "Our opposition are not bad people. They are good people trying to do a good thing. We just disagree with the way they are trying to accomplish it. Pray for them as I hope they pray for us."[70]

In one of his many assurances sent to his congregation, Rev. Arthur Jenkins wrote to remind members of the Lord's promise of Peace: "Peace I leave with you, my peace I give to you. Not as the world gives do I give to you. Let not your hearts be troubled, neither let them be afraid." (John 14:27) Secondly, he reminded the congregation that the church is not the buildings, but the people. The church is the body of Christ, and Rev. Jenkins quoted, "And God placed all things under His feet and appointed Him to be head over everything for the church, which is His body, the fullness of Him who fills everything in every way." (Ephesians 1:22-23) In his own words, Rev. Jenkins said, "So rest in peace my brothers and sisters-in-Christ. Of course, I love our beautiful campus and history. But I have the greatest love for the beauty of you who are the church and who gather here to worship and find your lives in love and service of Jesus Christ our Savior."[71]

Saint James Choir from Early Days, many of whom are discussed in the book

FRONT ROW: *George Porcher, Clark Morrison, Rev. Edward Guerry, John Rivers*

SECOND ROW: *Bill Porcher, Polly Mikell Grimball, Jeannine Meggett, Miss Martha Rivers*

THIRD ROW: *Stiles Mikell, Mr. Porcher, Tady Snowden, Mary Rivers Wheeler, Mrs. Guerry*

Louise and Clark Morrison, two long-time active parishioners, on their wedding day October 10, 1959

Like many families at Saint James, several generations of the Morrison family have worshipped and served at the church.

Saint James' Fifth Church Building

With the leadership of W. G. Hinson, E. L. Rivers, and Rev. Cornish, construction began in 1898 on this wooden church of gothic design. It was consecrated in 1902. Gray Spanish moss hung from the huge surrounding oak trees. After the sixth church was constructed in 1959, this fifth church was de-consecrated and dismantled in 1964.

Saint James' Active Youth Group from the 1970s

Youth Leaders: Lynda Owen Cole and Lillie McGougan

Five pictured here entered the priesthood.

FIRST ROW: *Rev. Chris Huff, Kim Huff, Cheryl Vincent, Rev. Martha McGougan Horn, Nina Evans, Rev. Creighton Evans, Rev. Robert Horn*

SECOND ROW: *Rev. Suzy McCall, Karen Hendriksen*

THIRD ROW: *Debby Heuer, Sue Saunders, Cathy Lawson*

FOURTH ROW: *Astrid Hendriksen, Norsey Dawson*

FIFTH ROW: *Tim Evans, Lisa Evans, Edward Vincent*

SIXTH ROW: *Laura Hipp, Ingrid Hendriksen*

SEVENTH ROW: *Sarah Ash, Loyd Ash, Ann Bailey King, Bobby Grayson*

1983 Easter Egg hunt at Saint James: Pictured here are Joseph D. Ward, age two, and his sister Melissa A. Ward, age seven, with their mother Virginia

Painting Titled "St. James' Episcopal Church" by Jean Badger Lynn

Dated September 1989

Abstract Painting of Saint James by parishioner Dee Rhodes

Saint James' steeple is in the foreground with James Island, the marsh, the harbor, and the city of Charleston creatively portrayed in the background

Aerial View of Saint James' Campus

The parish hall is barely visible in the upper left corner, the church is indicated by the steeple, and the Ministry Center has the large gray roof. Across Camp Road (in the top of the picture) is Bishop Gadsden Retirement Community. The cemetery is seen between and below the church and the Ministry Center. The paved semicircle parking area leads back to the outdoor chapel on Ellis Creek.

Interior of the Ministry Center

The dedication and consecration of the Ministry Center was July 31, 2004, in the presence of The Right Reverends Salmon, Skilton, Howard, and Haynsworth. Rev. Arthur Jenkins was rector, and The Rev. J. Robert Horn was associate rector. The Rev. Dr. Paul Zahl preached the sermon. Many additional clergy were present.

Charleston artist Joan Loy painted this picture of Melissa Annette Ward standing in front of Saint James Church where she married Mark Durinsky on August 2, 1997. Rev. John Howard officiated at the wedding.

Aerial View of Saint James Church, depicting the huge oak trees that surround it.

Photo taken by Thomas L. Read
October 6, 1994

One of Saint James' Women's Cabin Retreats at "The Sanctuary"
Near Hendersonville, North Carolina, September 2017

FIRST ROW: *Carolyn Hlavac, Colleen Sallee*

SECOND ROW: *Carolyn Powless, Joyce Wichmann, Doreen Warner*

THIRD ROW: *Rev. Elizabeth Bumpas, Virginia Bartels, Rev. Louise Weld*

BACK ROW: *Melissa Durinsky, Jean Griggs, Jocelyn Hubbell, Amy Knox, Liz Paige*

Saint James Outdoor Chapel on Ellis Creek

(photo taken by parishioner Sonya Droze, 2013)

Saint James Church Altar Decorated at Christmas

Poinsettias are given in memory of and thanksgiving for loved ones.

Note the plaques hanging on the side walls, as discussed in the book.

(Photo provided by David Cupka)

Saint James Choir

Evensong for Persecuted Christians
April 2018

FIRST ROW: *The Rev. Jason Hamshaw (Rector, All Saints', Florence, SC), The Rev. Arthur Jenkins, Lucy Mulkeen, Kendall Welch, Jane Read, Jenny White, Tyler Bancroft, Chris Walchesky, The Rt. Rev. Mark J. Lawrence*

SECOND ROW: *Linda Smith, Joan Hilton, Lexi Fletcher, Diane Corbett, Raquel Clark*

THIRD ROW: *Jean Griggs, Rosalyn McDonald, Brooks Hawkins*

FOURTH ROW: *The Rev. Mark Cooke, Mary Staats, Berta Puckhaber*

BACK ROW: *Osia Brummett, Bruce McDonald, Jason Bendezu, Mack Swafford, Eli Major-Wright*

Saint James Christmas Eve Pageant 2019

For decades Saint James' children, teens, and adults have presented the story of Christ's birth. Youth directors Scott and Cyndee Cave have also included live animals—donkey, sheep, lambs—making the event all the more real and interesting.

Men's Hike: Pisgah National Forest, NC "Turkey Pen Gap" April 12-15, 2018

FIRST ROW: *Jay Millen, the coach, Rev. Mark Cooke*

SECOND ROW: *Roy Hamby, Charles Holliday, Mark Durinsky, Fred Whittle, Thomas Rehm*

THIRD ROW: *Dylan Marquis, Zander Read, Kurtz Smith, Jim Early, Brandon Hamby*

FOURTH ROW: *Bill Read, Jim Marshall, Paul Pennington, Tim Sallee*

Daughters of the Holy Cross Installation Service February 2020

FIRST ROW FROM LEFT TO RIGHT: *Virginia Bartels, Diane Corbett, Beverly Howell, Tina Thompson, Vivian Watts, Lillie McGougan, Janet Wilson, Marcia Porter, Shannon Sears, Jan Temple, Deborah Harley, Donna Lewis*

SECOND ROW: *Harriett Brummett, Sonya Droze, Amy Knox, Barbara McDonald, Betty Floyd, Carol Shue, Julie Lamson-Scribner, Maxine Swafford*

PICTURED IN THE BACK MIDDLE: *Rev. Arthur Jenkins, the chaplain*

One of several mission trips to Uganda led by Rev. Elizabeth Bumpas (second lady on the right). (2019)

Seminarians received Bibles that included a study portion written from the perspective of African culture.

Mission team members pictured here are Libby Paul, Mark Durinsky, Rosie Colson, and Donna Lewis (standing by Elizabeth).

Saint James' Boy Scout Troop

Philmont Scout Ranch at Philmont Base Camp, Cimarron, New Mexico.

The rock featured in the background is called "Tooth of Time."

July 2019.

FRONT ROW: Grant Cyrulik, Christopher Inabinet, Max Hartwig, Jonathan Marchant, Ranger Nick, Ranger Calen, Jackson Cyrulik, Ben Cox, Ed Hessert

BACK ROW: Andrew Pennington, David Klinger, Ulf Hartwig, John Jones, Paul Pennington, Hilton Blenis, Parker Cook, Joey Greenwood, Terrell Cook, Brody McMillan, Erik Cox, Derald McMaillan

CHAPTER NINETEEN

2011 to 2020—Perseverance, with God's Help

Past, present, future—this culminating chapter of consecutive events brings the reader to a point in which he can see the present through a lens that penetrates and magnifies Saint James' history, contemporary times, and perhaps the future. Parishioners have groaned and strained—and reveled and celebrated—throughout three centuries. Repeatedly this body of believers teetered on fragility, even near collapse, yet persevered. The unique leaders and followers of this latest decade have persevered, through persistence, as well.

To begin, in June of 2011 Rev. Arthur Jenkins was surprised with his congregation's celebration of his twentieth year of ordained ministry, most of which had been served at Saint James. In his letter of thanks to his parishioners, he wrote with humor, "I was a little concerned that 300+ people could know something I didn't know. It just shows you Who is in charge." As part of a well-earned respite, Rev. Jenkins rode his motorcycle over one thousand miles through North and South Carolina that summer.[1]

Throughout these three hundred years at Saint James, outstanding leaders have emerged to take on challenging issues of their day. In the May 2013 *Epistle*, Rev. Jenkins wrote a tribute to senior warden Bruce McDonald, Canadian Army retired, who was chosen to fulfill an unexpired vestry term and then was re-elected, serving five years as rector's warden. Bruce spearheaded the initiative for Saint James to use endowed funds to pay off the mortgage on the Ministry Center, enabling the church to balance the budget and become more ministry-minded. He also served on the Diocesan Council, the Ecclesiastical Court of the Diocese, and the Diocesan Communications Team regarding news articles about the Diocesan's challenges with the National Episcopal Church. He went on to be elected senior warden again and to become a valued choir member and lay reader, all the while praying for many parishioners when he visited them in hospitals.[2]

In this decade involving many legal, financial, and spiritual issues, the congregation selected two more capable vestrymen who became senior wardens—Tom Hilton and Fred Whittle. Employed at the Medical University of South Carolina in the finance division and the internal audit department, Tom utilized his financial knowledge to the benefit of Saint James. As senior warden, Tom was instrumental in leading what was called SOS-"Share Our Sacrifice" (sometimes referred to as "Save Our Sanctuary")—setting a goal of $100,000 to do extensive church repairs. The staff took the lead in modeling financial sacrifices for the sake of the church's budget, some volunteering to accept reduced salaries at reduced hours.[3] An update in the December 2014 *Epistle* stated that $98,491 had been collected by November 2014. Much of the routine maintenance of the campus had been put on hold over recent years due to other pressing expenses, such as legal fees. Some of these funds went to replace the air conditioning in the Ministry Center, address moisture problems and repairs in the church sanctuary, and paint the exterior of the church.[4] A visible change made within the sanctuary was the soft blue color of paint chosen for the ceiling.[5] Serving as both junior and senior warden, Tom spearheaded additional endeavors, including the hiring of priests, the development of a nontraditional worship service for families with young children, and ongoing fundraising to repair the church steeple. Using Rev. Jenkins' wording, Tom said that he does not *have* to—he *gets* to—serve at Saint James.[6]

After Fred Whittle attended a Christmas Eve service in the Ministry Center in 2014, he experienced a religious epiphany, became a regular worshipper at Saint James, and was confirmed in 2015. A native of New England, he had attended The Citadel where he was an accomplished leader as regimental commander. In the Marine Corps, he was an AV-8 Harrier "Jump Jet" pilot, flying thirty-six combat missions in the 1991 Persian Gulf War, and retired as a lieutenant colonel. He is vice president and chief operation officer at Jupiter Holdings. The Citadel awarded him an honorary Doctor of Commerce in May 2016.[7] In 2019 when Fred was scheduled to conclude his role as senior warden, the vestry asked that he continue in this capacity due to his understanding of many complex issues, especially with current legal and financial concerns.[8] Fred also is president of Saint James' Friday Morning Men's breakfast, is active in many civic organizations such as three exchange clubs, and has published numerous editorials on political, economic, ethical, and leadership subjects.[9]

In 2011 Mary Ellen Doran and Tammy Sease informed the vestry of a policy called "Safeguarding God's Children," a program the diocese promoted to protect children and teens in church. These two staff members had previously put into place strict policies on behalf of children in Saint James Day School and the nursery.[10] As a training offered on-line, "Safeguarding God's Children" was required of all those who worked with the youth at the church.[11] Within this same decade, "Me, Too" became a national movement and ultimately an initiative at Saint James. Those who had suffered from sexual abuse were encouraged to speak about their victimization and to seek professional counseling and spiritual healing, with Saint James' priests available to serve the victims.

As early as March 19, 2013, vestry minutes include discussions regarding parish safety from acts of violence. For example, when a parishioner asked for permission to carry a firearm to church as a safety measure, the vestry thanked him but declined his offer.[12] Guidelines for safeguarding worshippers were provided to the vestry, clergy, and ministry group leaders based on procedures promoted in a video entitled *Run, Hide, Fight*.[13] Vestryman Sonny Eppes attended a security conference about churches taking safety precautions and on October 13, 2015 gave a presentation and provided a safety booklet to the vestry. At the January 23, 2018 vestry meeting, members discussed hiring an off-duty policeman to be on campus, but that would have required thousands of more dollars to be added to an already strained church budget. When the vestry voted on whether to pay a security guard at services, the vestry did not have enough votes to carry through on this motion.[14] Because of escalating incidents throughout the state and nation of active shooters attacking worshippers, the vestry re-visited this serious topic six months later.[15] Vestryman Artie Horne reported to the vestry that he had talked with Sheriff Al Cannon and brainstormed additional safety precautions to take.[16]

On file in vestry papers is a copy of the letter that Rev. Jenkins and senior warden Bruce McDonald sent to the congregation of Mother Emanuel (Emanuel African Methodist Episcopal Church) in downtown Charleston following the June 17, 2015 evening Bible study, in which nine of their members had been gunned down by a young white male. Among those nine was senior pastor and state senator Clementa C. Pinckney, who served in that congregation that can trace its beginnings back to 1816 and worshipped in a sanctuary built in 1891. The letter (dated July 1, 2015) states, in part, "We of the fellowship of the Faith at Saint James Church, James Island, your brothers and sisters in Christ, mourn with you. We long to wrap your sorrow with our love and our compassion. We are wounded in our souls that such evil should be visited upon you. We grieve with you, but, thanks be to God, not as those who have no hope." The letter goes on to offer individual and corporate prayers as well as assistance. Included was a check for the church members to use to help their congregation "in moving forward in the faith."

In 2012-2013, all of Saint James, even those in small groups and Day School, studied *The Story*, with books for all age-levels—kindergartners, elementary-grade children, middle schoolers, teens, and adults.[17] *The Story* was a year-long study that involved "reading, marking, learning, and…digesting the Word of God, beginning at Creation and concluding with Revelation." [18] The purpose was "to see God's big story and to find our place in it…The Bible is how we know who God is, who we are, and where we are going."[19]

A brief but important segment was added to Sunday worship services in 2012. After the peace was shared, parishioners were given the opportunity to stand and share something for which they were recently thankful. Encouraged by Rev. Jenkins' words, "Let your thanksgivings overwhelm your complaints," the congregation has been brought closer as they have listened to one another's testimonies of how God intervened and blessed their lives and the lives of loved ones.[20]

Shirley Brown repeatedly led a ten-week course based on Mark Virkler's *How to Hear God's Voice*. It consisted of a ten-hour video, discussion, and exploration of Biblical keys to listening to God.[21]

Throughout the decades the church has selected a wide variety of books, videos, speakers, and programs to promote parenthood rooted in Christine doctrine. Rev. Jenkins used the phrase, "building faith by building families of faith." By 2013 a new tradition was established at baptism for fathers to pray a blessing over their newly baptized children before the congregation.[22] In 2013 parishioners also turned their focus onto the important roles of grandparents in mentoring their grandchildren to know and follow the Lord. Cavin Harper's *Not on our Watch: Courageous Grandparenting in a Turbulent World* was the basis of the family intergenerational ministry in workshops, book studies, and small groups.[23] Camp St. Christopher started offering summer camp for grandparents and grandchildren to attend together.

In March 2013 four historic island churches—St. John's, Our Savior, Christ/St. Paul's, and Saint James—planned "Holy Week Mission for the Island Churches." Dr. Peter Walker, professor from Trinity School for Ministry and author of *The Weekend that Changed the World*, served as a speaker. Parishioners traveled to each other's churches during Holy Week to hear a series of lectures. On Good Friday an evangelist evening event was held in the gym of St. Johns High School.[24]

In this decade Saint James parishioners reached out in love to one of their youngest and bravest church members—Conor McManus. His parents Rod and Miranda oversaw intense medical procedures for their son, beginning in infancy when he was diagnosed with neurofibromatosis type 1. A team of oncologists, neurologists, geneticists, and neurosurgeons in Charleston and the Children's Hospital in Philadelphia have been involved in extensive ongoing medical procedures, involving the removal of Conor's right eye, abstraction of tumors, and facial reconstruction. Sometimes undergoing several surgeries a year, Conor remains good-natured, hopeful, and proactive—exuding the personality of a typical energetic boy. In the fall of 2012 and early spring of 2012, the congregation honored Conor with an article entitled "Conor: Young in Years, Mature in Character,"[25] a musical concert and reception[26] and a fundraiser oyster roast[27] At this writing, Conor is a dynamic, accomplished young teen who has amazed his family, physicians, and parishioners.

In December 2012 Rev. Jenkins assembled a search committee to interview and ultimately recommend a new assistant priest.[28] In April of 2013, Saint James called Rev. Andrew

Williams and his wife, Rev. Jill Williams. Andrew had attended Hargrave Military Academy, Virginia Military Institute, and Virginia Theological Seminary. He, Jill, and their two little sons came to Saint James from the Diocese of Western Massachusetts, where Andrew had been a rector at Trinity Church of Ware, Massachusetts, and Jill had worked as the head of Christian Faith Formation for the diocese. Rev. Andrew Williams' first Sunday at Saint James was June 9, 2013.[29]

The congregation looked forward to this couple's bringing new perspectives, especially of young parents, to reach this generation of worshippers.[30] Much of Andrew's focus was on multigenerational ministry, with members worshipping together regardless of age, both in Sunday school and in vacation Bible school.[31] His ministry also focused on young families, resulting in an activity to give husbands and wives some quality time together—"parents' date night" while care was provided for the children at church.[32] He and Jill initiated the Flip-Flop interactive service for families with small children.

Repeatedly mentioned in Rev. Arthur Jenkin's and Rev. Louise Weld's reports in the annual congregational publications is the fact that their ministry was unique within the Diocese. Louise wrote, "Arthur and I have ventured into some new and important (and sometimes difficult) territory as we have worked together, male and female, to model a fuller picture of God's revelation for relationship and ministry. There is not another church in the diocese where this model of ministry is being practiced."[33] Arthur wrote about Louise, "She …plays a major role in the understanding of women's ministry and ordination…She is a symbol of the fullness of ministry that is to be shared by men and women…Louise and I, clerics male and female…represent a small part of how the Kingdom of God…works."[34]

In a letter to the congregation written on August 1, 2016, Rev. Jenkins asked parishioners to honor Rev. Louise Weld's ten years of ordained ministry by writing cards, letters, well wishes, and anecdotes of thankfulness for her ministry. In this letter to the congregation, Rev. Jenkins wrote, "From her pastoral care, to the Wednesday service, to her guidance and wisdom with women's ministries to a plethora of other ministries and services, we have all reaped blessing upon blessing from her ministry." This collection of messages was presented to her on September 11, 2016.

Women's ministry, through the orders of Daughters of the King (DOK) and Daughters of the Holy Cross (DHC), was evident by way of prayer boxes, banners, and public vows. In addition to the Saint James' banner consisting of the shield and sword was the Daughters of the King banner designed and created by Amy Knox in September 2013. Using blue and white, colors of the order, Amy selected an upholstery sateen fabric, and Erin Cooley painted the emblem of the order, a modified Greek fleury cross of silver, inscribed with the Greek words "Magnanimiter Crucem Sustine," meaning "With heart, mind and spirit, uphold and bear the cross."[35] In August 2014 prayer boxes were placed in the church and the Ministry Center where parishioners could leave written prayer requests confidentially for which

Daughters prayed.[36] In 2019 members of the Daughters of the King began the transition into becoming Daughters of the Holy Cross, more aligned with the Anglican Church, and took vows to begin their new chapter on February 9, 2020.[37] Amy Knox created a new banner for Ruth Chapter made of members who dedicate themselves to prayer, service, evangelism, and study.

To be good stewards of the church's finances and to make efforts to conserve the environment, Saint James stopped mailing copies of the *Epistle* in January 2014 and began sending this monthly means of communication electronically. A limited number of printed copies were still available to parishioners not having email. Weekly e-newsletters were emailed to members of the congregation.[38] The church web site remains an ongoing work-in-progress. With the expertise of Bill Read, another change made in this decade (2018) was for parishioners to give financially on-line, especially since fewer people currently write checks.[39] Just as technological advances have changed society, they have also benefitted the church and diocese.

Because of the ongoing financial deficit in this decade, parishioners often gave generously of their time and money to benefit the church campus. Keith Doren redesigned the church's front sign and completed indoor painting in the parish hall. Clark and Louise Morrison paid for the paving of additional handicapped parking in front of the colonnade.[40] Artie Horne repaired signs—located at Folly and Camp Roads as well as Camp Road and Riverland Drive—that provided directions for guests trying to find the church. Les Sease used his technological expertise to install software for the church's computer files.[41] Likewise, Art Field and Bill Read upgraded technology at Saint James for no fees.[42] Volunteers pruned azalea and rose bushes, and members of the Men's Breakfast volunteered to maintain the flower beds in front of the Ministry Center.[43] Clark and Jen DeCiantis and Jim Graf, master brick mason, completed additional construction and landscaping for the church's front sign.[44]

Other parishioners have served in non-paying capacities throughout this decade. This list includes Peggy Spell—altar guild; Dale White—flower guild; David White—treasurer; Dick Bartels—lay reader coordinator; Carolyn Candler and Barbara Evans—bazaar co-leaders; Sue Morrison—welcome team; Pat Bozard and Judy West—usher schedules; Kay Jenkins—welcome desk; Jane Read—choir soloist; Carolyn Powless—mission team; Martha Jerman—encouraging emails; Maxine Swafford—women's Bible studies teacher; Carlton "OC" Brummett—volunteer extraordinaire; John and Yvonne Waite as well as Shirley Brown, Scooter Barnette, Jack Cranwell—prayer intercessors—to name a few, only a few. Their services, and the services of so many others, are invaluable.

As in previous years, current parishioners have given in creative, generous ways to the church. In January 2017 another baby grand piano was donated by a parishioner to Saint James. Two front pews in the church were removed in order to make room for it, and flooring was installed where carpet had been in this section.[45] In 2018 parishioner Jackie Wright passed away and left her house and its contents to Saint James. Rev. Weld handled the legal and real estate proceedings, thus benefitting the church in many ways.[46]

Saint James joined the Diocese of South Carolina at the 222nd Convention in participating in the formation of the "Anglicans for Life Chapter." Rev. Jenkins and Rev. Williams specified that the Declaration of Life Statement was not a mere political stance against abortion but instead a sound theological belief in the sacredness of life. The statement is as follows: "We believe God, and not man, is the creator of human life. Therefore, from conception to natural death, we will protect and respect the sanctity of every human life. Furthermore, we recognize that the unjustified taking of life is sinful, but God gives absolution to those who ask for His forgiveness."[47]

In July 2014 Rev. Jenkins wrote an article in which he shared the news that both Mary Ellen Doren and Jeremy Shelton had become Postulants for Holy Orders—approved to attend seminary. The people of Saint James bid farewell to Mary Ellen, a member of the church staff for twelve years, to begin her coursework with Trinity School for Ministry. In her place Berta Puckhaber became the parish administrator. In the summer of 2015 Jeremy officially began his coursework in Ambridge, Pennsylvania. His move resulted in his wife's—Jessica Shelton—leaving her position as Saint James' publishing administrative assistant, a job that she had handled for seven years. Rev. Jenkins likened this parish transition to that of a family encouraging loved ones to grow.[48]

Deacon Ron Warfuel coordinated the Lay Eucharist Visitors (LEVs). Previously, this group of volunteers were called Lay Eucharist Ministers (LEMs). LEVs deliver communion in a variety of places—private homes, assisted living centers, nursing homes, or hospitals—on Sundays after worship. Using the Eucharistic service in the prayer book and praying with the recipients, the LEVs offer the bread and wine to those who are unable to go to church, helping them to stay more connected to the Body of Christ.[49]

Youth directors in this decade—including Brent Cooley, Phillip Waite, and Alisha Griggs—reached out to children as young as fourth grade, to teens, and to college students, both within and beyond Saint James. Fellowship through weekly scripture-focused activities engaged those in middle school, high school, and college in multiple ways to help them find their identity in Christ.[50] The youth directors' work often involved reaching the unchurched, the parents and families, the schools, and the community at large.[51] These youth leaders also incorporated many out-of-town retreats, service projects, and diocesan gatherings for young people, especially those hosted at Camp St. Christopher.

In May of 2013, after his fifteenth year as rector and pastor at Saint James, Rev. Jenkins began a long overdue sabbatical—a time of renewal, education, reflection, and ministry direction. He traveled to Jerusalem, Israel, and the Holy Land, taking two courses of study at St. George's College. While there, he took with him the list of members of Saint James to the Mount of Olives and prayed for each parishioner by name.[52] Several parishioners had contributed to a fund to support this opportunity.[53] Since this trip to the Holy Lands, Rev. Jenkins has returned several times, building an impressive collection of photographs and accounts of Biblical-based places, sharing them in Sunday school classes.[54]

"Activation Sundays" began in September 2015 with a focus on education and discipleship. Rev. Andrew Williams shared a report, stating that small group ministry would bring people together (ex. dinner groups, groups of similar ages, groups of same gender, all-inclusive groups). Small groups provide vital fellowship and pastoral care through deeper conversations and more powerful relationships. Rev. Williams said that "discipleship is about learning how to walk out [apply] our faith practically in community with other Christians." The first "Activation Day" focused on blessings—to be blessed and to be a blessing to others.[55]

Midway through this decade, Consultant Kurtz Smith proposed "Ministry Action Plans" (MAP) to be implemented over the next year or two. They addressed many topics, including leadership, communication, vestry, lay leader ministry, web site, worship services, discipleship, teachings, prayer training, ALPHA, Christian education, connections with other Anglican churches, visitor connections and assimilation, and missions (evangelism and outreach). Many of these recommendations are still being implemented at Saint James.[56]

In 2017 Cyndee and Scott Cave and their three daughters came to Saint James to lead the Children, Family, and Student Ministry.[57] With their leadership, the Flip Flops services, grew in attendance and participation. They also added "Pancakes and Prayers" from 10:00 to noon, for the younger children to gather after Flip Flops worship for breakfast and additional scripturally-based videos, story time, crafts, games, and a group prayer circle.[58] Employing the services of some Christian college students, the Caves added several more youth ministries, pre-teen and teen dances, and in-town and out-of-town events. They planned several family celebrations, such as the Mother's Day tea, Donuts for Dads on Father's Day, the Christmas Eve pageant which included live animals, and both Thanksgiving and Christmas lunches for the Day School students. The Mothers Morning Out Program grew to the point that additional rooms on the church campus were converted for child care.

Further changes occurred with Saint James' staff in this decade. In August of 2017 Reverends Andrew and Jill Williams left to seek other professions in which to serve.[59] In 2017 Rev. Elizabeth Bumpas joined the priests at Saint James as pastor, small life-groups coordinator, and bookkeeper. In December of 2017 Rev. Mark Cooke joined the staff, primarily to teach, preach, assist with the men's ministry, and provide pastoral care to the ill.[60] After being on staff at Saint James for almost two decades, Rev. Louise Weld transitioned from the role as associate pastor to assisting pastor, transferring some of her former duties to Rev. Mark Cooke. Replacing long-time parish administrator Berta Puckhaber, who retired in May of 2018,[61] and moved out-of-state to be closer to family, was Rhonda Myers.[62]

Over the years Saint James has had sextons who were valuable stewards of our worshipping community. In May of 2011 Dustin Chavis became the new custodian. Wearing many hats, Dustin did much of the care of the grounds, handled many of the repairs in the buildings, added his gifted voice to the choir, served as lay reader, and used his culinary skills in the kitchen to help prepare for huge meals.[63] In 2018 Saint James hired Karen Bartlett as the new sexton. Karen was invaluable at helping to organize for one event after another, whether it was for the Day School Programs, the bazaar, banquets, weddings, and more. Of course, many additional hardworking staff members have filled this sexton position, making the flow of services and ceremonies appear seamless, all the while cleaning three large buildings on the church campus.

Continued into this decade were the Connection Sundays, paid for, prepared by, and hosted by the vestry. In preparation, each vestry person called and/or emailed an assigned list of parishioners to invite them to the parish lunch and to get updated information for the church directory. During the meal, throughout the Ministry Center, were displays and brochures about various ministries. Booklets entitled *Saint James Ministries* with pictures, information, and contacts for leaders were distributed. Also called "Celebration Sunday" other years, events such as these highlighted vestry members' leadership, provided fellowship, and promoted participation within the congregation.[64]

As Saint James prepared for its 300th anniversary celebrations at the conclusion of this decade, the congregation honored other churches that reached this milestone earlier. The vestry sent a letter to St. Helena's in Beaufort to honor its 300th year of ministry in January of 2012. Over the decades Saint James and Saint Helena have shared priests, parish coordinators, music directors, youth ministers, and parishioners, giving them much in common as two historical parishes of the Low Country of South Carolina.[65]

By 2018 Saint James began plans to celebrate their own upcoming 300th anniversary. In the congregational report of May 2018, Rev. Jenkins wrote, "Our Parish Church was formed from Old St. Andrews in 1720. The Reverend Mr. Guy, then rector of St. Andrews, would row down the Ashley River to hold Anglican Services on James Island. From that beginning God formed a ministry that would be part of the life and faith of James Island for centuries."[66] Rev. Weld wrote, "When you think about the long and rich, and often difficult, presence of the Anglican Christians on James Island who worship at Saint James, you think with awe about people and families who have been steadfastly available to God and who have been used by God to guard the Gospel and to carry it out to James Island and the world."[67]

In 2017, acclaimed Low Country artist Jim Booth agreed to do a painting of Saint James in honor of the church's 300th anniversary in 2020.[68] Mr. Booth has personal and spiritual ties to Saint James, having participated in its services as a youth and seen his parents actively involved as parishioners. Initially, in 2018, he took photos of the front of the 1959 sanctuary and met with Rev. Jenkins to discuss his plans for the painting, deciding not to include adjacent structures—the Ministry Center and the parish hall. He also contemplated how much to reveal of the steeple hidden behind the large moss-laden oak limbs extending out in front of the spire. In the midst of his plans for this painting, Mr. Booth closed his thriving art gallery on Maybank Highway, James Island, and then completed what he said might be his final work of art for sale to the public. When he revealed his painting for the first time to Rev. Jenkins and a small gathering of vestrymen and church leaders, the group gasped. They found the painting to be breath-takingly beautiful, especially with a heavenly light beaming down on the church. *Sea Island Glory* was the name chosen for the painting. The history of this sanctuary is intertwined with its geography, a barrier island on the South Carolina coast—thus, the "sea island" part of the name. The "glory" refers to the glory of God and His presence in this church. Mr. Booth generously gave Saint James the rights to the painting and the profits from its sales. He was also magnanimous in giving Saint James permission to put his work on the cover of this book, the church's three hundred years of history. The painting was featured in the Winter 2020 *Jubilate Deo* issue.[69]

Many events for 2020 were planned for this 300-year anniversary. On January 25, vestryman and chef Art Field prepared a dinner in the Ministry Center for over two hundred people attending "Saint James History Weekend." On that Saturday evening, Doug Bostick, author of twenty-six books, most of which are about the Low Country's history, spoke and shared stories and slides about this area that he knows firsthand, being a James Island resident. Jim Booth was honored for his painting of Saint James. Virginia Bartels was invited to read the foreword from *History of Saint James Church: Worshipping in the Presence of the Past 1720-2020*.[70]

On Sunday, January 26, 2020, the history weekend continued with parishioner Bonum Wilson providing the congregation with anecdotes—humorous, informative, inspirational—about worshipping at Saint James for decades.[71]

On February 14, 2020, Chef Robert Dickson hosted an elaborate dinner to raise funds to send the choir to England to perform in recognition of the church's 300th anniversary. Robert had owned a Charleston restaurant well-known for its multi-course dinners and the "singing chef." Reminiscent of that fine restaurant before its being sold at Robert's retirement, Robert and his wife Pam, and a host of volunteers from the parish, re-created "Robert's" while guests enjoyed fine dining, Chris Walchesky's piano playing, and Robert's singing Broadway numbers. Several more events, including combined worship services and guest speakers, a homecoming and preaching mission were planned for throughout this year of tri-centennial celebrations, but the choir's trip and other events were canceled due to the pandemic.[72]

An important group within the Saint James Church is the Boy Scouts, Troop 44, which celebrates its 50th anniversary as Saint James celebrates its 300th. Charles Wilson was the troop's first member to earn the rank of Eagle scout on November 7, 1945. To date, Troop 44 has produced seventy-six Eagle scouts, an impressive number for a troop that went defunct for a while in the 1960s and was reestablished in 1970. Their service to Saint James has been substantial.[73]

Effective leaders plan for the future, whether it seems certain or unpredictable. In the latter part of this decade the vestry gave much consideration to what they referred to as a "contingency plan" in case the congregation was required by The Episcopal Church to leave the property and buildings of Saint James. Planning for financial and legal consequences, relocation, communication, recordkeeping, inventory, transition—all this and more was based on this plan's two opening statements of "People are more important than possessions" and "Insure continued Gospel focus/priority." On December 1, 2017 the vestry generated four pages of possible proposals, all reflecting Biblical, prayerful discernment to meet the parish's emotional and spiritual needs. Thus, alternative places of worship were proposed, such as other church campuses, commercial spaces, schools, gymnasiums, hospitals, and a county park. The vestry also gave thought to varying worship times, such as moving "church" to Saturday or Sunday evenings, if need be.[74]

Saint James first used the new Anglican *Book of Common Prayer* (copyright 2019) on September 29, 2019. Rt. Rev'd Mark J. Lawrence was present to lead the presentation, exhortation, and examination of candidates to be confirmed, followed by prayer and his laying hands on them. In his sermon Bishop Lawrence pointed out one significant change in the *BCP* regarding confirmation. The Anglican confirmation, in part, reads as follows:

> The Anglican Church requires a public and personal profession of the Faith from every adult believer in Jesus Christ. Confirmation or Reception by a Bishop is its liturgical expression. Confirmation is clearly grounded in Scripture: The Apostles prayed for, and laid their hands on those who had already been baptized (2 Timothy 1: 6-7; Acts 8:14-17; 19:6) In Confirmation, through the Bishop's laying on of hands and prayer for daily increase in the Holy Spirit, God strengthens the believer for Christian life in the service of Christ and his kingdom. Grace is God's gift, and we pray that he will pour out his Holy Spirit... (p. 174)

The 2019 *Book of Common Prayer* is a comprehensive publication of liturgy and services for Anglican churches tracing their lineage back to the Church of England. The Anglican 2019 BCP is closer to the tradition of the 1662 BCP and is approved by the Global Anglican Future Conference (GAFCON).[75]

Another important group at Saint James is the Day School. Accounts throughout this written history have shown the ups and downs, the openings and closings of this program. Starting and sustaining a school is costly. The current school, conceptualized in 2007, has been supported by several generous donors, some remaining anonymous. Frances Frampton initially donated almost $100,000 to Saint James, and Rev. Jenkins proposed that the church start a day care program named "Frampton School." However, Mrs. Frampton declined the honor, hence the name Saint James Day School. Long-time board members for the school include Scooter Barnette, David Cupka, and Joyce Daughtery. Over the years, more donations to add to that of Mrs. Frampton have included gifts as memorials and gifts of grateful parents who had their children in the school.[76]

At one time, when the school was in danger of closing due to severe financial struggles, an anonymous donor gave $10,000 in order for the doors to remain open. Scooter Barnette stated that three other donors, in later years, have given sizable gifts ($5,000 to $30,000) to help the school. In 2020, in its eleventh year of operation, the Day School has given just under $300,000 to Faith Assistance, a scholarship and staff assistance and family assistance program.[77]

Day School Director Crystal Strickland hired staff and chose a curriculum to provide emotional, social, physical, and intellectual growth for children from infancy to four-year-olds, working according to the mission statement "Nurturing the Next Generation with Christ's Love." More recently the Mothers Morning Out Program, under the directorship of Cyndee Cave, has expanded to offer additional services to young families needing high-quality, part-time child care in the James Island community.[78]

Chris Walchesky became the new music director at Saint James in 2017. In addition to many musical offerings, the choir went to Florence, South Carolina, to perform in a service of evensong to raise support for Christians persecuted for their faith. Chris has coordinated the Advent/Lent Wednesday Recital Series.[79] As part of the 300th anniversary celebrations, the choir planned to travel to Carlisle Cathedral in the United Kingdom to perform July 13-19, 2020.[80] A well-attended oyster roast hosted at Lee and Charleigh Glover's home was another choir fundraiser; unfortunately, the trip abroad was cancelled due to the coronavirus.

On March 15-16, 2019 Saint James hosted the 228th Convention of the Diocese of South Carolina. Featured on the front of the Eucharist's program was a picture of the outdoor chapel with its cross near the creek that backs up to Saint James' property. The cover also included Saint James' mission statement: "Love God. Love People. Build Community." Rev. Dave Runyon, author of *The Art of Neighboring*, preached the sermon and conducted workshops, which focused on various aspects of loving one's neighbors. Bishop Mark Lawrence, Bishop of the Anglican Diocese of South Carolina, shared his vision for the coming year as participants celebrate 228 years together as a Diocese. Four hundred delegates, clergy, and guests attended, representing 22,000 baptized members across the eastern and coastal regions of South Carolina.[81]

A common theme emerging from this three-hundred-year history is that the community impacts the church, and the church impacts the community. In late February of 2020, the world watched as the highly contagious disease COVID-19, caused by the coronavirus, initially spread in China, North Korea, and Italy, then throughout much of Europe and the United States, and into the Charleston area. Saint James began with cautious steps such as not shaking hands during the peace, placing hand sanitizer throughout the buildings, and giving specific instructions about taking communion. However, as Americans infected with the virus reached into the thousands, with many hospitalized in intensive care units and placed on ventilators, and the numbers of deaths increased, instructions from the Trump Administration and the Centers for Disease Control and Prevention ultimately led to the closings of day care centers, schools, colleges, beaches, gyms, many businesses, and "in person" church meetings. Scheduled weddings were postponed, and funerals went to small "family only" gatherings, with memorial services to be held at a later date, or services live-streamed by the funeral home for guests who could not attend. Rapidly, Anglicans through-out the diocese saw the cancelations of the Diocesan Convention to be held in Bluffton, the Lenten services, Camp St. Christopher programs, and many more. National borders were closed, international travel came to a halt, the stock market did a swan dive, restaurants were closed except for take-out orders, a state of national emergency was declared, and many found themselves out of work. People were encouraged to stay at home, practicing "social distancing" and even self-quarantine.

As millions of lives seemed to "hang in the balance" as this pandemic reached into every aspect of daily life, the people of Saint James and other churches took a proactive stance. On March 17, 2020, Bishop Lawrence issued a letter via email entitled "Faithfulness in an Age of Pandemic" in which he cited several historical trials fraught with plagues, wars, and hardships—all dealt with through faith. He promoted silence, solitude, journaling, reading Scripture, enhancing family time, participating in live-streamed church services, and sacrificing for the common good. Also, on March 17, 2020, the congregation received an email entitled "A Message from Arthur" in which Rev. Jenkins supported Bishop Lawrence's leadership through this crisis and explained online and computer meetings for Saint James' small groups, Bible studies, and worship services. Even though many parishioners faced extreme financial hardship brought about by this illness, those who could were encouraged to continue with their tithes and offerings. Just as households were struggling to meet their budgets, so were many of the churches. Rev. Elizabeth Bumpas sent an email to encourage life groups to choose alternative methods to stay supportive and united. She also offered a service to pick up groceries and pharmacy items for the ill and elderly. Rev. Mark Cooke continued to post emails of scripture and prayers. Rev. Louise Weld offered counseling to parishioners via ZOOM, FaceTime, and telephone. On March 22, 2020, Rev. Jenkins and Rev. Weld conducted Saint James' first live-streamed Sunday service. Throughout this unprecedented pandemic, Christians at Saint James and elsewhere turned to Ephesians 4:6-7: "Do not be anxious about anything, but in everything, by prayer and supplication with thanksgiving, let your requests be made known to God

And the peace of God, which surpasses all understanding, will guard your hearts and your minds in Christ Jesus."

Yet another common theme emerging in this three-hundred-year history is revealed in vestry minutes that span decades—centuries, in the case of Saint James—address the ongoing, reoccurring topics dealing with the facilities—painting, roofing, furnishings, organs, insurance, repairs, heating and air conditioning. Grounds maintenance has continued regarding fences, trees, boundaries, roads, landscaping, cemetery. When the vestry could not pay for services, they often put their own heads and hands together to do the work themselves, alongside members of the congregation. Again and again the minutes are concerned with hiring priests and staff, adhering to a balanced budget, increasing membership, and seeking ways to ignite faith. Trainings, programs, and services have been steadily offered to meet spiritual needs. Committees have abounded to handle the issues that provide structure to a church and for its people. Over and over the priests have kept the vestry members focused on God's Word and God's Work. Solutions have not necessarily been found from one meeting to the next, or from one season to the next, or even from one year to the next. However, the coming together of priests and parishioners time and again, handling these seemingly tedious details, has sustained Saint James. Discussing, debating, and delegating duties have perpetuated the perpetual worship—the church and its mission.

Neglect in one form or another has left too many sacred places of worship abandoned. All one needs to do is ride out into the countryside and see small, boarded-up churches where weeds overtook lawns and cemeteries years ago. All one needs to do is stroll downtown and see large, inner city churches bound in chains and pad locks, closed to members and visitors alike. Across the nation, too many churches—restructured into museums, concert halls, and other means of businesses—attest to this fact. According to Dave Olson's study published in the *Journal for the Scientific Study of Religion*, 3,700 American churches close their doors every year.[82] By God's grace, Saint James is neither neglected nor obsolete.

The persistent oversight of Saint James' sanctified structures and the worship within have provided safe havens where parishioners learned to walk by faith and not by sight. Saint James has been blessed with a long list of dedicated Christians who answered the call to serve as vestrymen, committee members, volunteers, tithers, worshippers, and prayer warriors.

As a chapter in life ends, so a chapter of a three-hundred story ends. Yet, endings can lead to beginnings. Beginnings can bring renewal. The tides, the seasons, the ages have come and gone on Camp Road where six sanctuaries have stood, and the tides, seasons, and ages will come and go yet again and again. Somehow Saint James has managed to balance stability with change throughout time. This persistence was assisted with divine guidance, as evidenced through the story of this once chapel-of-ease that has been transformed into a three-building church campus. The chronological narration ends with this chapter, but the chapters that follow tell more of the story, as indicated by the titles of the chapters.

CHAPTER TWENTY

Female Priests with Spiritual Roots at Saint James

For years members of the Episcopal Church Women (ECW)—later changed to Diocesan Women's Ministry (DWM)—exhibited leadership, contributed financially, and supported the congregation's societal and spiritual efforts. Yet the priesthood remained closed to them. Then in 1970, the South Carolina Diocesan Convention voted to allow women to serve on vestries.[1] By the 1980s women were entering the priesthood, evoking both disapproval and approval.[2] At Saint James, gender barriers were further broken by girls becoming acolytes and by women serving as lay readers, chalice bearers, vestry members, and diocesan convention representatives. Some women even considered and entered the priesthood.

In vestry retreat minutes of January 17, 1987, "The Rector [Rev. Morris J. Lent, Jr.] expressed a desire to appoint Mrs. Daniel W. (Anna "Kitty") Ellis [to be] a Lay Eucharistic Cup Bearer. After discussion a motion was passed unanimously" for her to serve. When Rev. Morey Lent attended the 69th General Convention in Detroit, he reported on the diverse group of almost 900 members making up the House of Deputies. In the September 1988 *Jubilate Deo*, he stated, "One area in which there was no confusion is the quality of women… we are boldly in support of full participation of women in this church at all levels."[3] Following are the stories of several Saint James women and their varied paths to ordination.

REV. JENNIE CLARKSON OLBRYCH

Jennie Clarkson Olbrych, with her husband, came to Saint James in 1980, seeking a church to join. She attended her first worship service at Saint James when the congregation had become divided, and several parishioners had transferred membership to be with Rev. Richard Dority when he left. In fact, the first Sunday Ms. Olbrych attended Saint James was the Sunday before Rev. Morey Lent arrived. He had just resigned from his position as assistant rector at St. Michael's downtown to accept the call to Saint James. The rift among the congregation had left many worshippers with mixed emotions, including confusion, depression, and bitterness.

In spite of this discord, Rev. Lent's presence was reassuring and uplifting, and Mrs. Olbrych felt as if God were saying to her, "This is where I want you." She began to feel a spiritual call when two devoted women at Saint James—Kitty Ellis and Mary Townsend—inspired her with their church leadership. She also received encouragement from members of her ECW chapter, the assistant rector Rev. Greg Prior, summer seminarian Cindy Taylor, and fellow parishioner Mrs. Miriam Keeler, then in her eighties. Perhaps most importantly, Mrs. Olbrych felt that Rev. Lent believed that she had both the potential and the passion to serve as a priest. Mrs. Olbrych started taking on more leadership roles in the church.[4]

Although aware of the barriers to women being ordained, Jennie Olbrych felt that God was calling her to enter the priesthood. Meanwhile, she studied accounting and became involved in establishing Bishop Gadsden, the Episcopal retirement home across the street from Saint James. The nagging at her heart continued; after all, she was the great-granddaughter of one of Saint James' former priests, Rev. Andrew Cornish, who had served at Saint James from 1898 until 1907 and supervised Sheltering Arms. She was the granddaughter of Rev. Henry de Saussure Bull, former rector of Prince George Winyah Episcopal Church of Georgetown, South Carolina. Then one of the older male members at Saint James, Mr. Henry McManus, encouraged her by saying, "Jennie, don't miss your call."[5]

She wrestled with the decision until her husband John said, "Jennie, it's time to decide. Either let it go or do something with it." She went to Folly Beach's end and was looking out on Morris Island where years ago the orphanage entitled "Sheltering Arms" was located when His still, small voice said to her, "Be my priest," and a peace came over her.[6] In November of 1984 the vestry interviewed Mrs. Olbyrch and voted to sign her application, indicating support of her seeking ordination. Initially, she did not receive permission from the diocese to proceed with these plans. However, August 18, 1986 vestry notes state that she was approved as a candidate for admission to seminary.

After receiving a Masters of Divinity from Virginia Theological Seminary, she was ordained as a deacon June 23, 1988 and ordained as a priest the following year. She earned her Doctor of Ministry from Princeton Theological Seminary in 2012.[7]

Serving as assistant to the interim dean, The Rev. Canon John C. Ball, at the Cathedral of St. Luke and St. Paul in downtown Charleston, Jennie was the first woman on the altar there except members of the altar guild. An article in the March 1989 *Jubilate Deo* stated, "Jennie is, at present, the only ordained woman serving in the Diocese of South Carolina."[8] In years to come, Rev. Olybrych accepted the call to become assistant rector at St. Paul's in Summerville and then as the canon for interim ministry, working especially with congregations in transition, conflict, or trauma. She realized that just as families can be healthy or dysfunctional in how they interact, so can church parishes. She went on to serve as the rector at St. Peter and St. John (now Good Shepherd). The mother of five adopted children, Rev. Olbrych stayed home with her children for a year (2005-2006). From 2006 to 2018 she served as vicar of the historic St. James Santee Parish Episcopal Church in McClellanville as well as associate chaplain in the Lower School at Porter-Gaud (2008-2016).[9] In May of 2018 Rev. Olbrych retired from active parish ministry, concluding thirty years of ordained ministry.[10]

REV. SUZY MCCALL

Suzy McCall worshipped at Holy Apostles in Barnwell, South Carolina, became a part of the 1970s college group at Saint James while attending the College of Charleston, and taught high school English for seven years.[11] She first traveled to Honduras in 1990 as part of a church planting team. As Ms. McCall and her youth group in Tegucigalpa worked to rebuild the area after Hurricane Mitch devastated Honduras in 1998, she dreamt of a new ministry, to be called LAMB Institute, to train Hondurans for missionary work. She made that happen and established a three-year curriculum of study, beginning with six students in Flor del Campo, an extremely poor barrio in Honduras's capital.

In 2000 she purchased a small house for the school, and then she said that God gave her another dream of a school that LAMB would build. By 2002 the Carlson Ministry, Discovery Service Projects (DSP), built a school and Ms. McCall began taking in babies who needed safety and love. In 2004 a daycare was built for abused and neglected children. Today the school serves poverty-stricken students from kindergarten through eighth grade. In 2006 LAMB bought land in San Buenaventura and now houses over seventy previously abused and neglected children.[12]

LAMB assists others as well. A microcredit program provides small loans to fledgling business owners, who in turn, pay back the loans designed to help them get out of poverty. Thus, a little seed money enables a mother to begin a self-supporting business such as sewing clothes, making jewelry, or baking goods to sell. After Alonzo, a LAMB scholarship student, was murdered for his cell phone, a scholarship was established in his name to offer youth alternatives to gang life. By 2010 LAMB opened a safehouse to rescue girls from human sex trafficking.[13]

Over the years, Ms. McCall adopted seven children, was ordained, and now serves in an advisory position to the numerous staffs spearheading the various LAMB programs. For several years Saint James and other area churches have hosted an annual mission banquet to raise thousands of dollars for LAMB's humanitarian endeavors.

Rev. McCall wrote the novel *Tania de la Cantera* (ISBN 9781480191464). Her dedication states "anyone in need is our neighbor, and...sometimes a smoked turkey is more welcome than an eloquent sermon."[14] Susan Clarkson Keller, then Board Chair of LAMB Institute, wrote that the book comes from "Suzy's lifetime desire to express the devastating plight of a child born into poverty, the limited choices of women who live in these crippling situations and the opportunity all of us have as Christians to make the difference in their lives."[15] About Rev. McCall, Keller wrote,

> There is an unparalleled determination in this one single woman...With the fire of justice alongside mercy..., she will stand up to evil and fight for those lost in body, soul, or spirit... She is known by hundreds of children in the poor barrio of Flor del Camoo in Teguc, as "Mami Suzy!"[16]

REV. LOUISE WELD

With a Masters of Fine Arts and license as a family therapist, Louise Weld came to Saint James seeking a church to join and to serve as substitute organist. Rev. Arthur Jenkins, who had left Saint James as an associate priest a few years earlier for a church in Massachusetts, had recently returned to Saint James as rector. Rev. Jenkins asked Louise to join the church staff, teaching adult Sunday school and providing counseling and pastoral care.[17]

When Louise began to feel the call to priesthood, her initial reaction was "No way!" However, when the feeling continued, she talked to Rev. Jenkins and her children. All encouraged her. It became clear that her entire life had been leading her to this new role.[18]

When Ms. Weld first sought diocesan approval to go to seminary and seek ordination, she was denied approval just as Rev. Olbrych had also experienced. However, as a therapist, she knew the importance of perseverance. She returned to her church work for another year and was finally approved to begin seminary courses at Trinity School for Ministry in Pennsylvania. There she earned a Masters in Divinity. She felt especially supported by Rev. Robert Horn and his wife Martha, another female parishioner eventually sponsored by Saint James to work towards ordination.[19]

Rev. Weld tells the story of attending a prayer camp with Rev. Jenkins where there were some ladies "crazy for the Lord," as she put it. During the fervent praying, one of the women took Louise's hand and Rev. Jenkins' hand, and placing them together, declared, "You are called to work together." When Louise finished seminary, Saint James called her to return to the staff as an assistant pastor.[20]

Rev. Weld also talks candidly about how God can use one's woundedness to lead others to Him. She draws on her personal experiences and shares them in what is most important to her in her ministry: preaching the Gospel; caring for people in all stages of life; and teaching, training, and modeling pastoral care.

Like Rev. Olbrych, Rev. Louise Weld has often found herself to be the only woman among mostly male clergy. However, even those who doubted that a woman should be a priest have seen she (as well as other male priests) has not let those so called "political feelings" stand in the way of their friendships and their camaraderie as pastors. Louise is cognizant of the modeling that male and female clergy can exhibit as they work together in relational leadership on behalf of the church.[21]

REV. MARTHA MCGOUGAN HORN

Martha McGougan Horn had her own journey to priesthood as well. Her Christian roots were well nourished at Saint James. Married to Robert Horn, also from Saint James, she traveled with him to seminary where their son and daughter were born. Their family made their way to various parishes in South Carolina, Georgia, Louisiana, and Alabama before they returned to Saint James when her husband accepted a call to be assistant rector there. Having been an x-ray technician for years, Mrs. Horn first sensed that God was calling her to the priesthood when she and her husband were in Alabama, where parishioners responded so well to her Bible teaching.[22]

Ironically, Martha initially believed that women should not fulfill the role of a priest, that females should instead fulfill other important roles in the church. As the founder of 100 Fold Life Ministry, she had traveled to teach the Gospel nationally and internationally, including England, New Zealand, and Australia. When she set the goal to become a deacon, Bishop Charles Duvall, former rector at Saint James and the bishop in Florida and Alabama, strongly supported her becoming a priest. When Bishop Salmon of Charleston learned of her intent to become a deacon, he asked her, "Why not a priest?"[23]

Ultimately, Mrs. Horn enrolled at Trinity School of Ministry, where she earned her Master of Divinity degree and was then ordained a deacon at Saint James. Rev. Jenkins and Rev. Weld remained her champions as she went through a series of setbacks to ordination to priesthood, and she carried forth serving as a chaplain with Bishop Bill Skilton for Province IV Daughters of the King, a trainer for Stephen Ministry, a member of the Coastal Crisis Chaplaincy, a chaplain for the Diocesan Women's Ministry, a member of the spiritual team for Cursillo Ministry, and a deacon at Holy Trinity Episcopal Church in Ridgeland with her husband Robert.[24]

She was the deacon-in-charge of the Episcopal church in Hampton until most of the Diocese of South Carolina left the National Episcopal Church. Ultimately, she was ordained October 3, 2015, becoming Rev. Martha Horn, at St. Luke's Church, Hilton Head Island, where she was already working as assistant rector.[25]

In December of 2012 she began yet another ordeal—striving to overcome cancer. In and out of hospitals, feeling weak and then regaining enough strength to deliver her next sermon or lead her next conference, moving residences, and emotionally supporting her husband Robert, who was also going through cancer—such experiences summarize these challenging years. She passed away from cancer December, 28, 2015, at the age of sixty-three.[26]

Martha's husband said, "Her primary gift was in discipling people—in order that they recognize the gifts God had given them—and helping them to develop those gifts."[27] Her mother Lillie McGougan stated, "God gave her a gift to preach and teach. Even when in the throes of cancer, by the power of the Holy Spirit, Martha was able to rise up and give life-changing messages. She praised God that she could use it for His glory."[28]

About one thousand people attended her funeral in December 2016. (Services were held simultaneously in Holy Apostles, Barnwell; St. Lukes, Hilton Head; and Saint James, James Island.) Saint James Church could not seat all who came to honor her life, so cameras and speakers were also set up in the adjacent Ministry Center. After the service, throngs of priests in their white cassocks and red stoles collectively walked across the green grounds of Saint James' cemetery to bury one of their own.

Her burial plot is next to that of her beloved son, Joseph Robert Horn V, lost when he was eighteen. Mother and son are in the same cemetery as Joseph's grandfather, The Rev. Canon Joseph Robert Horn III (1921-1971) and grandmother Jean Hayden Horn (1926-1998). Young Joseph had wondered if God might be calling him to be a priest. His tombstone reads, "Joseph R. Horn V / FEB. 11, 1981 / AUG. 30, 1999 / He was our Boy Joy and his sister's best friend / He lived and died in Jesus."[29]

REV. ELIZABETH F. BUMPAS

Elizabeth F. Bumpas took a circuitous route to ordination, a route that spanned the country and ultimately the world. From 1993 to 1996 she worked at the Crisis Ministries Homeless Shelter in Charleston. Then from 1996 to 2001 she became both bookkeeper and Director of Christian Education at the Church of the Holy Cross on Sullivan's Island. After a ministry internship at St. Thomas' Church in Sheffield, England, she earned a Master of Divinity at Fuller Theological Seminary in Pasadena, California. In 2005 she went to work for Christian Assembly Church in Los Angeles, California, to supervise Life Group Leaders and provide pastoral care for young female adults. She returned to Church of the Holy Cross on Sullivan's Island in 2006 as the Director of Adult Education. She said that she sensed a call to the priesthood while there but chose to ignore it.[30]

For almost five years Elizabeth worked at Saint Christopher Camp and Conference Center where she initiated and led silent meditative retreats called "Be Still." She also handled accounts and conferences as well as coordinated tasks for both employees and volunteers.[31] While there, she gave deep thought to The Parable of the Talents and knew even more so that she was being called to the priesthood. She realized she could not imagine anything else with her life that would matter more.[32]

Throughout this myriad of local, national, and international experiences, Ms. Bumpas continued to feel a "nagging" from the Lord about pursuing priesthood. Knowing that both Rev. Arthur Jenkins and Rev. Louise Weld championed women answering the call to ordination, she began attending Saint James. However, just as Rev. Olbrych and Rev. Weld experienced initial rejection before the diocesan board examining their desires to become priests, Ms. Bumpas was denied. Nevertheless, she felt that the Lord had given her a body of believers and priests at Saint James, who were willing to support her. Although still hurt and angry, she heard God's compassionate voice, "Trust what is coming. Okay? This process is not easy."[33]

Elizabeth then accepted a call as missionary to Gulu, Uganda, where she served as an assistant to the Bishop of International Relations and was bursar and lecturer at Archbishop Janani Luwum Theological College. She was the team leader for the Jesus Film Ministry, which has brought hundreds of thousands to Christ all over the world. She also worked with the women's Development Center to enable women to support themselves and their families.[34]

Still, Elizabeth yearned to be ordained. The Bishop of Northern Uganda Johnson Gakumba recognized her call to the priesthood and said that he would ordain her. Then with the blessings of Bishop Mark Lawrence and the Standing Committee of the Diocese of South Carolina, Ms. Bumpas became Rev. Bumpas. Her ordination took place in Uganda in May 2016, and Rev. Weld, along with two other faithful Charleston-area women, flew to Uganda to attend the ceremony. To Rev. Bumpas it had been a long journey from her first being called in 2000 until she became a priest in 2016.[35] She returned to Charleston and became an associate rector as well as bookkeeper at Saint James, specializing in establishing small-group ministries, leading Bible studies, and taking groups back to Uganda on short-term mission trips.[36]

REV. MARY ELLEN DORAN

Mary Ellen Doran has a fascinating route to becoming a priest as well. She had a successful career as a businesswoman working with stock brokerage. Although reared in a devout Catholic family, she became inactive in her worship for a while, even thinking that Sundays were meant for shopping while her husband took their daughters to church. Her older daughter's positive experiences in church started to draw Mary Ellen back to regular worship,[37] and she eventually became the director of children's ministry at Holy Trinity Church in Charleston. She enrolled at Charleston Southern University, earning a BA in Religion/Christian Leadership in 2003.[38]

Then Mary Ellen moved to Saint James as the parish administrator and director of Christian Education at Saint James. More and more she delved into ministry work and finally answered the call to ordination, initially seeking to become a deacon. Just before she had completed that process, she felt that the Lord was saying, "Not deacon, Mary Ellen, *priest.*" Although dubious of this calling, she thought, "If it is of God, no one can stop it."[39]

In 2009 her father died, and Mary Ellen then learned from her aunt that her father had wanted to become a Catholic priest. Instead, he had married and reared his family. While seeking discernment at Camp Saint Christopher about whether to be a deacon or priest, she thought about Abraham answering God's call. It was as if she heard the message, "You are going to fulfill your father's call, Mary Ellen, but it is your call, too." Thus, began her arduous process of seeking the support of the diocese, starting with going to Trinity School for Ministry. Her mother died in 2016, and Rev. Doran chose May 30, 2017, her mother's birthday, for her ordination to transitional deacon.[40]

Rev. Doran speaks highly of her mentors, including Rev. Louise Weld and Rev. Martha Horn. After Martha's death shortly following Doran's ordination, Martha's family gave her vestments to Rev. Doran, who said, "I feel honored when I put on the robes, surplices, and stoles that had belonged to my friend." Rev. Doran wants to mentor other women going through the process to be ordained.[41]

An "ontological shift" can occur after ordination when a priest knows he or she is changed by that special call on his or her life.[42] On November 30, 2017, Mary Ellen Doran experienced that shift when she was ordained at Church of Our Savior, Johns Island, where she accepted the position of associate pastor. In the summer of 2018, she became rector of both St. David's Church in Cheraw and St. Paul's Church in Bennettsville.[43]

REV. EMILY ANDERSON LUKANICH

In the 1980s and 1990s, Emily Anderson was one of Saint James' most active youths. Daughter of Jonathan and Janet Anderson and the oldest of three children, she and her sister Kathryn were baptized, according to the Sunday bulletin, at Saint James on May 22, 1983. Parishioners of all ages shaped her. Recalling significant people with whom she worshipped decades earlier, she stated,

> I was raised, mentored, and befriended by many adults at Saint James.
> Willie McLeod, Fred Wichmann, Elise Badger, Katherine and Vic Burrell,
> Ann and Phil King, Virginia Bartels, Barbara McKeithan, Ann and Tom
> Read, Robert Hall, Pat and Gene Gould, and Martha and Walter Ameika

are among a few of the adults who ...taught me through their actions ... that God's presence in the world was not limited to Sunday morning.[44]

Many of these church members have since died, but their positive influence lives on in this priest. Rev. Lukanich said that "God is found in the relationships of people who worship there." She cited Reverends Paul Zahl, Jennie Olbrych, Floyd Finch and Arthur Jenkins as Saint James priests who taught her that ministry is "about helping the people to see how God moves in our community."[45]

Emily went to the University of Illinois at Urbana-Champaign, graduating with a BA in French literature. She became a curate at St. Mary's Catholic Church in Blacksburg, Virginia, and an education specialist in Lynchburg City Schools. In her mid-twenties, she felt a calling to the priesthood. After she married Christopher Lukanich, also a teacher, she had two sons and earned her Master in Divinity at Virginia Theological Seminary in 2014. She became assistant rector in Vail Valley, Colorado, at the Episcopal Church of the Transfiguration.[46]

Although Rev. Emily Anderson Lukanich was not sponsored by Saint James through her theological studies and ordination, her experiences there played a positive role in her seeking this leadership role in ministry, and church members still consider her "one of their own."

In John MacArthur's book *Twelve Extraordinary Women: How God Shaped Women of the Bible and What He Wants to Do with You,* the author portrays the Biblical stories of Eve, Sarah, Rahab, Ruth, Hannah, Mary, Anna, Mary Magdalene, Lydia, Martha and Mary, and the Samaritan woman.[47] Each has a story of how she was called from a seemingly common walk in life to a higher purpose. Likewise, each of these "ordinary" women of Saint James has her own story of accepting the calling of wearing "the cloth": Jennie, Suzy, Louise, Martha, Elizabeth, Mary Ellen, Emily.

CHAPTER TWENTY-ONE

Male Priests with Spiritual Roots at Saint James

It is hard to determine all the men who have worshipped at Saint James, who had the seeds of faith fall on fertile soil, and who then moved forward to ordination and priesthood. Rev. Stiles Mellichamp's ministry was rooted here in the mid-1800s[1] as were the ministries of John Rivers in 1956[2] and Edmond Campbell in 1965.[3] Robert Horn, Creighton Evans, Mark Cooke, and Chris Huff—all part of the 1970s Saint James college group called The Disciples—were ordained. More followed, including Craig Stephans and Jeremy Shelton. Their stories reveal how each took a unique path to the pulpit.

REV. JOSEPH ROBERT HORN IV

Rev. Joseph Robert Horn IV, known as Robert, became a part of the vibrant college program at Saint James in the 1970s. His father and two uncles were also priests. As a young man, Robert lost his father in 1971 and emotionally and spiritually spiraled down to the point of wondering if God existed. However, Lynda Owen Cole, Saint James' youth director at the time, stayed in contact with Robert, calling him weekly, visiting him, and telling him, "God has His hand on you. He is going to have you. Call me when He does." Robert remained angry with God over his father's sudden death from a heart attack.[4]

Enrolled at the College of Charleston, sporting long hair often tied back in a ponytail, and smoking pot and drinking alcohol, Robert remained resistant to this "call" that Ms. Cole insisted he was going to experience. Having witnessed the challenges his father and uncles faced in their careers as ministers, he knew firsthand that the profession was not an easy one.[5]

Robert tells the story about planning to hitchhike home in the rain one day. Walking down St. Philips Street in downtown Charleston, he spotted two young men walking toward him. He rolled his eyes and uttered to himself, "Oh, no...looks like two evangelists to me." The two did engage Robert in a conversation in which they shared the Gospel with him. Backed up against a gate as these two men talked with him, Robert fell to his knees right there on St. Philips Street and asked the Lord to come into his heart. Ironically, Robert never saw these two young "evangelists" again. When he arrived home, he called the youth leader Lynda Cole to tell her about this conversion experience and became more active in the Saint James college program, which he said was as close to what a Christian unit of believers could aspire to be. These members often met at the College of Charleston library to pray together. To this day the former Disciples remain friends.[6]

Robert had begun college as an English literature major with the ultimate goal of becoming a lawyer. However, one day after his morning classes, he went home, took a nap, and had a dream in which God told him He had a different direction planned for him. Since Robert was the son of a priest, many people had assumed that one day he would be a priest, too, but he had resisted that path. After this dream, he knew that he would answer God's call. When he became engaged to Martha McGougan, also in the Saint James college group, she said to him, "I will go anywhere God tells us to go as long as we can retire in Charleston." Thus began Robert's steps towards ordination. While enrolled at Virginia Seminary, his son and daughter were born, and Robert earned $20 a week painting and helping a retired disabled professor. Rev. Horn was ordained to the diaconate [deacon] June 24, 1981, at Saint James.[7]

Once ordained, Robert began an interesting and diverse journey, completing a three-year ministry at St. Mathias in Summerton and serving as assistant rector in Savannah's historic Christ Church. He moved to Lafayette, Louisiana, where his congregation bought a school to convert into a sanctuary and sent out nine of their members to be ordained.[8]

Transferring to Foley, Alabama, Robert doubled the size of his congregation and eventually helped to plant a new church in nearby Lillian, Alabama. While there, his wife discovered her gift of teaching and started to believe that God was calling her to work in ministry. Robert went on to serve in Pinopolis and then back to his home church, Saint James. He became the priest in-charge at Church of the Holy Apostles in Barnwell, where there was mutual admiration and appreciation between the congregation and their priest.[9] After an extended illness, Rev. Horn died in 2020.

REV. CHRISTOPHER MERCER HUFF

Rev. Chris Huff and his wife-to-be Kim were born and reared on James Island. He said,

I was raised in First Scots Presbyterian Church downtown, and at age twelve, I publicly acknowledged my faith in the Lord... I had already sensed a call as a young boy to the ordained ministry. My involvement at Saint James as a teen steered me more to the sacramental side of spirituality. I was confirmed at the age of sixteen by Bishop Grey Temple... Since Richard Dority was my priest during these formative years, my spirituality took on a charismatic leaning. During and after seminary, however, my spirituality became more rounded to include classical Anglican evangelical and even Anglo-Catholic expressions.[10]

While at the College of Charleston completing his B.A. degree in history,[11] Chris had started taking on more leadership roles at Saint James. He said that serving as a member of the search committee that hired Rev. Morey Lent helped prepare him for the "business side" of ministry—collaborating with the vestry and hiring personnel. After being married, he found singing in the choir with his father-in-law, mother-in-law, wife, and "the old crowd" to be enriching.[12]

Before entering seminary, Chris worked as a bank manager in Charleston and as a printing sales representative in Atlanta. After graduating from Trinity Episcopal School for Ministry in Ambridge, Pennsylvania with a Master in Divinity, he became rector of St. Paul's Episcopal Church in Bennettsville, South Carolina, where the congregational attendance doubled (1988-1993). For the next five years he was rector of St. Peter's Episcopal Church, now Good Shepherd, in Charleston. Then Rev. Huff founded West Shore Episcopal Church in Charleston designed to embrace the unchurched, seekers, and non-Episcopalians into the Episcopal Church. He was there from 1998 to 2008.

For a couple years he took a sabbatical, operated a retail clock shop on James Island, and served part time as an assisting supply priest at Saint James. In 2010 Rev. Huff accepted a call to be assistant rector at St. George's Episcopal Church in Summerville and since 2016 has been the rector there.[13]

Chris stated, "My personal spirituality [draws] strength...from the Benedictine disciplines of stability, humility, obedience (listening), work and prayer." His pastoral emphasis is on relationships and trust based on a shared love of Jesus.[14]

Reflecting on his experiences at Saint James, Rev. Huff said,

There was one negative experience at Saint James that taught me something deeply important. It was the very traumatic congregational split that ended in Richard Dority's resignation and the exodus of a large portion of the congregation with him to another church...My family was injured by it, as were many of my friends...The lesson learned...was this: regardless of theological differences, dogmatic disagreements or plain old passion brought on by a sense of who's right and who's wrong, nothing is worth tearing apart the Body of Christ. Doctrine can always be corrected, but schism has a more permanent and devastating effect.[15]

Rev. Huff went on to say, "I was confirmed at Saint James, and I was married there...One of my children...and one of my grandchildren [were] baptized there. My father is buried there and my sister...[and] my father-in-law...My mother [was] buried there as will my wife and I."[16]

REV. MARK DEAN COOKE

Mark Cooke grew up in the West Ashley area of Charleston. Attending a Baptist church with his family, he had a conversion experience and was baptized at the age of eight. He attended the College of Charleston from 1974-1978, where he earned a bachelor of arts degree in history.[17]

After being ordained by Ashley River Baptist Church in 1979, Mark and his wife Jane went to Fort Worth, Texas, where he served as an associate pastor at Tabernacle Baptist Church. After graduating in 1981 with a Masters of Divinity at Southwestern Baptist Theological Seminary, he became associate pastor for youth, college, and singles in the 2,000-member congregation of Northside Baptist Church in West Columbia, South Carolina.[18]

Subsequently, as pastor of the Isle of Palms Baptist Church for ten years, much of Mark's initial focus was on spiritual healing and unifying. He conducted services at the local resort of Wild Dunes, led his church in Hurricane Hugo recovery, and served as adjunct professor of the Old Testament for Charleston Southern University. During this time, he also completed his Doctor of Ministry studies (all but the dissertation) at the Reformed Theological Seminary in Jackson, Mississippi. From 1992 to 1998, he served as senior pastor at Westport Baptist Church and then Grace Covenant Fellowship, both in Denver, North Carolina.[19]

From 1998 until 2001 Rev. Cook worked with Christian Associates International in Lisbon, Portugal and Barcelona, Spain—in English-speaking international churches. During his sabbatical, he decided to return to the United States for the education of their two sons and three daughters.[20]

Having moved back to the Charleston area, Mark was hired by Doulos Disciples Ministries, his home parish being St. Andrew's Anglican in Mount Plesant. He worked on behalf of mission trips, pulpit supply, and community-wide healing services. He was also chaplain of the Charleston Port and Seafarers Society, a ministry to American and international seafarers (merchant marines). He was an interim pastor of a Presbyterian church and did cross-denominational ministry.[21]

From 2003 to 2005, Rev. Cooke served as senior pastor at James Island Christian Church where he led the congregation through a recovery process based on Biblical principles of reconciliation and conflict resolution. He was headmaster of the church's school and baptized forty-six members in two years.[22]

Throughout his ministry in Texas, North Carolina, South Carolina, Portugal, and Spain, Rev. Cooke had used the *Book of Common Prayer* in his personal devotionals and used an adapted version of Rite II in many of his churches. Meanwhile, when the opportunities arose, he visited local Episcopal and Anglican churches for communion services.[23] In 2007 he was ordained a deacon into the Episcopal church by Bishop Ed Salmon at St. Andrew's. On February 2, 2008, he was ordained a priest by Bishop Mark Lawrence at The Cathedral Church of St. Luke and St. Paul in downtown Charleston. There he served as pastoral assistant to the dean and was a conference speaker for missions.[24]

Rev. Cooke accepted the position of rector at Grace Anglican Church in New Bern, North Carolina—yet another congregation that needed Christian leadership through a restart, lawsuit, and recovery—and partnered churches in multiple, community ministries. In 2012 he returned to Charleston, as a church planter and in itinerant ministry, both locally and globally. Since 2001 he has averaged one to two overseas mission trips annually.[25]

Rev. Cooke joined the pastoral team at Saint James where the college group in the 1970s had invited him to join them in their worship. Little did any of them know the impact that that worship would have on Mark's life-long ministry.[26] He said, "Jane and I are thrilled that God has brought us back full circle to the place where our journey with the Holy Spirit, the Sacraments, and the Anglican world all began." [27]

REV. VERNON CREIGHTON EVANS, JR.

In an autobiographical passage on the website of All Souls Anglican Church where Rev. Evans last served, he wrote,

> I was born and raised in Charleston, SC, and I am one of those so-called "cradle Episcopalians," meaning I was raised in the Episcopal Church… I grew up only a few doors away from the Rectory and knew my early priests closely and they had an important influence on me…At an early age I could think of nothing better than to serve God and God's people.[28]

As a student at the College of Charleston in the 1970s, Creighton also participated in the college group at Saint James, while earning a B.S. in psychology. He and his wife Nina had two children. He worked in Charleston County's Department of Social Services and other businesses for sixteen years. Then at age thirty-eight, he went to seminary,[29] earning a Master of Divinity from Trinity School for Ministry, and was ordained into priesthood in 1995.[30] Creighton served first at St. Matthias in Summerton and secondly at the Church of the Epiphany in Eutawville, both in South Carolina. In 1998 he became the vicar at All Souls in North Ft. Myers, Florida.[31] After that Rev. Evans served as an interim rector in both Florida and South Carolina.[32]

Beginning in 2013 he was rector for a multicultural congregation at All Souls Church, Chatan Okinawa, Japan, under Bishop Uehara. In the early 1950s, two American missionary priests, both World War II veterans, along with Americans stationed or working on Okinawa, founded this church while Okinawa was still a United States possession after the war. Because over 236,000 lives had been lost in the Battle of Okinawa in 1945, the church was named "All Souls" in memory of those of every nation who had died there. The congregation was unique in that many of the residents were afflicted with Hansen's disease (leprosy).

In 1972, when Okinawa was transferred back to Japanese ownership, the Episcopal Church transferred the leadership at All Souls to Nippon Sei Ko Kai (the Japanese Anglican Church). All Souls is the only English-speaking congregation of the Diocese of Okinawa, which now consists of twelve churches. Japanese-speaking parishioners have access to *The Book of Common Prayer* in Japanese.[33]

Serving in a culture very different from his own, Creighton told his Okinawan congregation "God has called me to bless you so that you can go out and bless others in His name."[34] After a year-long illness, Rev. Evans died in May of 2018 while still residing in Japan.[35] As one of the priests who emerged from Saint James' 1970s college group, Creighton Evans traced his spiritual roots to the Episcopal church on James Island and left a legacy to believers on the other side of the world.

REV. CRAIG STEPHANS

Craig and Missy Stephans' first contact with Saint James occurred in 1998 when they went to the youths' dog-washing fund raiser on the church's front lawn. In the fall of 2002, when in between churches, they again visited Saint James. Sitting in the back of the church with their baby daughter, they hoped that she would not disturb the service. They immediately felt at home with the genuine welcome they received from Rev. Jenkins after the service. Eventually Arthur Jenkins, Robert Horn, and Louise Weld assisted him through the discernment process, seminary, and ordination. Craig said,

> If not for Arthur's persistence in listening to and obeying the Holy Spirit, I would not have pursued ordination due to my own resistance to the idea of stopping everything and heading off to seminary. By the time Arthur talked to me about discernment and seminary, I had come to know him and the people of St. James as folks who listened to God, prayed often and were in tune with the Holy Spirit.[36]

Craig had been reared in Oklahoma and attended a Catholic church. After high school graduation, he was enrolled at The Citadel "due to God's providence and my own ignorance of the school," Craig joked. At the military college, he attended Catholic mass and The Navigators, a discipleship group. As a Citadel cadet, he joined the Full Gospel Businessmen's Fellowship International and went to the Summerall Chapel on the campus daily to pray. He continued to grow spiritually when working with a Christian sports summer camp called Kamp Kankuk near Branson, Missouri, and participated in a sports mission trip through Europe. Also, while at the Citadel, Craig developed a lifelong habit of "prayer walking"—walking and praying in the presence of outdoors and nature. After ministers prayed over Craig in tongues, he, too, learned to do so.[37]

He met his future wife Missy, a student at the College of Charleston, who had had little experience in the Christian faith and was eager to learn. They were married two weeks after his graduation from The Citadel. Craig graduated with a B.A. in English in 1991 and a Masters in Education in Counseling in 1994.[38]

Initially he worked for a home for abused children and then in sales and marketing jobs, public relations, and a small business. While completing a Masters in Divinity degree at Trinity School of Ministry, he became keenly aware of how the Christian community must intentionally intermix with those outside the church. Developing close relationships with students from Africa and South America, he began to see himself as part of the global body of Christ and the need to take responsibility for his brothers and sisters in Christ around the world. He was ordained to the diaconate at Saint James December 19, 2009, and ordained to the priesthood April 12, 2010, at the Church of the Redeemer in Camden, North Carolina.[39]

Craig has become increasingly aware of spiritual warfare and the benefits of prayer. In his autobiography, he wrote, "Being a pastor seems to be a vocation in which a person can never become competent; rather, one can only become more trusting that God will fill the gap between what needs to be done and what one can do."

He went on to say,

> [God] leads me through open doors to minister outside the walls of the church. In addition to ministering at the church this week, I will minister at a Teen Challenge program, Pregnancy Resource Center, Christian school, public elementary school, public high school, Relay for Life banquet, home for mentally disabled adults, parishioner's home, coffee shop and restaurant.[40]

Craig's closing remarks in his spiritual autobiography reveal his humility, humor, gratitude, and ties to Saint James:

Three areas of ministry that were especially meaningful to me while at St. James were the men's breakfasts, the Victorious Ministry through Christ International, and the monthly Holy Spirit Ministry events. I wonder if any men's breakfast chef has set off the fire alarm and welcomed the James Island firemen into the kitchen since I last cooked breakfast there…that's one way to get people to church. At Church of the Redeemer, we have a Men's Prayer Group and monthly Healing Service that are both influenced by my experiences at St. James.

St. James certainly helped set the course and trajectory for my ministry. The emphases on Spirit-filled ministry, Scripture, fellowship and community/global outreach have been the theme of my priesthood.

Our family [has] been incredibly blessed by the love and care from St. James. Madeline and Jack were both baptized at St. James. I was ordained a deacon at St. James by Bishop Lawrence with Arthur preaching. There are so many warm memories of St. James and our family of faith there that I feel as if I could write my own book![41]

REV. JEREMY ALAN SHELTON

Reared in Louisville, Kentucky, Jeremy Shelton eventually came to Charleston in 2004. His career background was in operations management. In an interview, he said,

I was not a Christian before coming to Charleston and Saint James in 2005. I remember the first time I worshipped in the church sanctuary. During the Eucharist, I had a profound and deep acknowledgment that something was happening. I wasn't sure what it was, but I knew something important was taking place on the altar…I couldn't partake because I wasn't baptized, but I was intrigued. It was in the Ministry Center that God spoke to me and welcomed me, *literally by name*, into a life and relationship with Him.

Jeremy came to a life with Christ after two visits to Saint James at the encouragement of his wife Jessica, who worked at the church. He was baptized at Saint James in 2006.[42]

Jeremy went on to say, "My own personal discernment, along with the discernment from and with people at Saint James, and the mentorship from Arthur Jenkins, are all aspects of the role Saint James has had in my relationship with Jesus and my calling to the priesthood."[43]

With his wife and three sons (Will, Ben, and Hayes), he attended Trinity School for Ministry and graduated in 2018. He was ordained to the transitional diaconate at Saint James on June 6, 2018, with the Rt. Rev. Mark Lawrence presiding. Jeremy accepted a call to serve as curate (a clergyman who assists a vicar or rector) at St. John's Parish Church on Johns Island and was ordained there into the priesthood December 1, 2018.[44]

He is especially interested in family discipleship, men's ministry, and missions. He said, "I am thankful for the long and twisting road that has led me to St. John's Parish Church. I pray that my ministry will be a light to the Sea Islands for many years to come."[45]

Men in the Old and New Testaments—shepherds, tax collectors, doctors, fishermen, slaves, soldiers, lawyers, kings—answered the call to spread God's word. Likewise, these present-day college students, businessmen, and social workers allowed God to "interrupt" their lives to be His Voice. Originally Presbyterian, Catholic, Baptist, "cradle Episcopalian," and one not yet claiming a faith—they drew spiritual nourishment at Saint James and joined the Episcopal and Anglican priesthoods to enrich others spiritually. They have obeyed their Father as He sent them forth all over the United States—and to Portugal, Spain, and Japan—and "to the ends of the earth." Truly these faithful men of the collar and cloth took up His yoke and followed Him.

Chapter Twenty-two

Profiles of Some Parishioners

For three hundred years those who have occupied the pews at Saint James have made their contributions to society, as various newspaper reports have indicated. This chapter consists of "clippings" to profile some of the church's parishioners. Their portrayals vary, from those of children dressed for holidays, to those who have exceptional skills, to those in leadership roles in education, business, church, politics, and more. Some of these articles show a mere glimpse into a singular event, and others portray decades of service. Acts 17:26, paraphrased, states that God determines the times set for each man and the exact places where he would live. The stories of these parishioners are part of a more important story— that of God, Whose story is revealed in the history of His individual people.

Hinson Lebby Mikell, Jr.

In 1957 Saint James' new organist was Hinson Lebby Mikell, Jr., who was not quite fifteen years old (a high school rising junior) and who had no formal training to play the organ. He had studied piano with Saint James' former organist Eugene H. Koester, but Mikell taught himself what he knew about the organ over a period of about a year and a half. As a football player and high jumper on the track team for the James Island High Rams, he sometimes had little time to practice the organ, but eventually he studied under organist Vernon W. Weston, who said, "His talent is exceptional," and the caption under the newspaper picture of him labeled him as "organist extraordinary." He started playing for vacation Bible school, church services, and events at Camp St. Christopher.[1] An article published about Mikell in

1960 identified him as the organist for both St. James and St. John's Episcopal Churches. He was the organist for the performance "The Elijah Oratorio" by Mendelssohn, performed April 5, 1960, at the Dock Street Theater.[2] After playing the organ for three years and before leaving for Elon College in North Carolina, he gave a recital open to the public during which he performed with several church soloists and played numbers by Handel, Bach, Roberts, Franck, Arne, and Mendelssohn.[3]

LEHMAN AND AMANDA DOSCHER

The News and Courier of December 11, 1970, highlighted the artistic craftsmanship of a Saint James family—Lehman and Amanda Doscher and their son Robert Scott. The reporter Gale Young wrote the following:

> The Doschers…spend hours and hours making elaborate Christmas decorations—Styrofoam models of churches and houses, draped angels and pinecone wreaths. And never have they sold a single decoration for personal profit. Their works have been given to friends and relatives and to their church, St. James Episcopal…Notable among [Mr. Doscher's] creations are miniature models of historic Charleston churches. He has made models of St. Michael's, St. Philip's, the Episcopal Cathedral, Citadel Square Baptist and First Baptist. The historic church models are now on display in a village scene set up in a shop window in the old post office building in Mount Pleasant.

They built a workshop at their James Island residence so friends could use their equipment and get instruction on how to make their own.[4]

ANNA SWINTON WELCH "KITTY" ELLIS

In a section entitled "Profiles in Leadership" of the May 1982 *Jubilate Deo*, an article entitled "Kitty Ellis, St. James, James Island" honors one of the many outstanding female members in the congregation. Kitty's husband, Dr. Dan Ellis, was the church historian quoted often throughout this text. Following are excerpts from the article:

> Mrs. Daniel (Kitty) Ellis…has held virtually every lay position in the Diocese…
>> Both Kitty and Dan Ellis are lifelong residents of James Island—Kitty… from Wappoo Plantation and Dan from his family plantation at Folly Road, where the Ellises now live.

Kitty has been a leader in both parish and diocesan life, and…has accumulated an impressive number of 'firsts.' At St. James, where she has been choir member, choir director, chairman of the altar guild, and headed the ECW, she was also [the] first woman elected to the vestry, first woman to be senior warden—and very likely the first woman in the diocese asked to be an honorary pallbearer.

In the Diocese, she not only headed the ECW but was the first woman elected to the Diocesan Council. She has served as Chairman of the Department of Camps and Conferences and the Finance Committee, and has been a member of the Department of Missions and Church Extension. She is now on the Stewardship Committee. She was a delegate to the Woman's Triennial at the 1970 General Convention in Houston…

She believes that we need to be far more involved in the Diocese and its programs… Her major plea is for more volunteers, spending more time for their Church.[5]

W. Gresham Meggett

Yet another notable longtime worshipper at Saint James was W. Gresham Meggett. His life is testimony of how one takes his faith into his community. The *News and Courier* published a feature article July 12, 1987, highlighting many of his accomplishments, as demonstrated in the following excerpts:

A Charlestonian and resident of James Island for most of his life, Meggett, 84, has given more than his fair share…

He was chairman of the James Island school board for 24 years. In that time, he assisted in the construction of 10 schools.

In the 1930s, he helped build a four-room school building, Sol Legare School, for black elementary children…

When he was senior warden at St. James Episcopal Church, he asked the vestry to sell the county 15 acres to build a new high school. This became the first James Island High School. Before, children on James Island had to go to the city to school.

…He helped build yet another school…made into a complete vocational high school…W. Gresham Meggett Educational Occupation Center.

Meggett was also instrumental in the building of the old Fort Johnson High School, which is the present James Island [Charter] High School…

He helped reorganize the James Island Yacht Club and served as commodore and skipper of the *Cygnet*, which was the club racing boat in the 1930s.

Meggett also helped organize the James Island Exchange Club in the 1940s. He was the original treasurer and was soon elected president...

He was chairman of the Democratic Party for six years, but joined the Republican Party when Ronald Reagan ran for president...

Meggett was recognized nationally. An American flag was dedicated to him in the Rotunda of the U.S. Capitol for his service to the Republicans.

Reagan sent Meggett a Medal of Merit from the Republican Presidential Task Force as well as a personal letter of thanks.

Meggett's personal life is as rich as his involvement with his community. He got married in 1928 to Lila Seabrook Oswald. "I couldn't have found a sweeter girl. I'm still as happy as the day I got married."

... "We go to church every Sunday and say our prayers together at night. Then I kiss her goodnight and say, I'll see you in the morning, God willing...."

Their land...used to be part of a cotton planation. "Our house [was] a cotton gin house."...Meggett rebuilt it with his own hands and that is where they have lived since 1929.[6]

Meggett also served as president of the Agricultural Society of James Island, chairman of the Parks and Playground Commission of James Island, and member of the Charleston Chamber of Commerce Highways and Bridges Committee.[7]

Ms. Hazel Carte

The February 1987 issue of *Jubilate Deo* highlighted a Saint James parishioner Hazel Carte, who was a secretary and receptionist from 1974 until 1987 for the Diocese's King Street headquarters. She was said to have an "encyclopedic knowledge of parishes and parishioners." She told the story of being confirmed by a bishop when she was eighteen in a hospital where her appendix had just been removed. She also shared the story about making arrangements for a convention in Walterboro, but a fire in the motor court required her to find emergency overnight housing for attendees. Ms. Carte was a long-time communicant of Holy Communion, but she was a resident of James Island, became a part-time receptionist-clerk at Bishop Gadsden Retirement Community, and attended Saint James.[8]

REP. ARTHUR RAVENEL, JR,.AND MARY ALLEN RAVENEL

In the "Tempo" section of the Charleston newspaper, David MacDougall wrote a Mother's Day article in which Saint James parishioner Mary Allen Ravenel, mother of 1st District Rep. Arthur Ravenel, Jr., was interviewed, along with her son. Congressman Ravenel said that he was the oldest of four children, growing up in the Depression. His father was a truck driver who had to quit to work with the W.P.A. He said, "My mother was a great strength through all those times." She said, "I'm very proud of [Arthur] because he keeps doing what he believes in."[9]

CHILDREN ATTENDING SAINT JAMES

Some newspaper clippings portray the church's children. Former Saint James member and reporter Ellen Anderson wrote a Halloween article picturing four three-year-olds at Saint James—David Ash, John Linton, Jamie Sosnowski, and Katie Porcher—with their childlike responses to questions about their costumes and trick-or-treating.[10] In another article entitled "Easter Best," Mrs. Anderson featured a picture of Saint James church with members Debbie Brinson and her two daughters Sarabeth and Lauren wearing matching pastel dresses.[11] A February 1987 article featured two-year-old twin sisters Sarah and Elizabeth with their mother Sharon A. Hills wearing Laura Ashley-designed dresses.[12] The newspaper section "This Week in West Ashley" featured a picture with the caption "A Child Is Born" and told about 46 children ages two through six from Christ Kindergarten and Preschool at Saint James. Directed by Carol Shue, Mary was played by Cadence Morillo and Joseph by Rossi Wooten, along with angels and other nativity figures.[13] Yet another article featured the Saint James children at their annual May Day Program, with director Carol Shue and assistant director Sharon Eason.[14]

VERNON AND MARY WESTON

Another article entitled "After 48 Years, Couple Still Making Music Together" documents the marriage, music careers, and community service of Mary and Vernon Weston, long-time residents of Riverland Terrace. Mrs. Weston was a music teacher at Ashley Hall School. Mr. Weston was a former organist at Saint James, lecturer in fine arts at the College of Charleston and The Citadel, and director of the Charleston Choral Society and the Charleston Opera Company. The reporter portrayed the couple's humor, active lifestyle, appreciation of the Low Country, and grace as they got up in years.[15]

Dr. Herman and Ruth Nimitz

Having majored in agricultural chemistry, Dr. Nimitz became a specialist in animal and fowl nutrition and marketed the first all-mash starter for feeding chickens. This interest expanded to include human nutrition, so he went into internal medicine at an older age than most in medical school. Clemson awarded him a Distinguished Service Award. His wife Ruth was an avid volunteer for the local soup kitchen and the Charleston Symphony and was known for her superb recipes. The newspaper article about them emphasizes how active they remained in their retirement years, with traveling worldwide, volunteering at Saint James, and staying connected to family and friends.[16]

Mrs. Charles (Phyllis) Rooke

Another reporter for *The News and Courier*, Skip Johnson, wrote an inspirational article entitled "Phyllis Rooke's Tragedy Turned into Success." Phyllis' husband, Charles S. Rooke, was the owner of Rooke Homes, a construction company, when he was diagnosed with an inoperable brain tumor. Parishioners' hearts ached as they watched Charles' health steadily decline, and yet he made heroic efforts to continue to worship at Saint James with his wife and sons. His death impending, Charles encouraged—insisted—that his wife fulfill her personal goal to start her own interior decorating business entitled "Window Shopping Interiors," and with the help of family members, she did.[17]

Frank Antalek

In the April 2, 1989 *Post and Courier*, Janice Shumake wrote an article entitled "Circus Still Lives in Senior Citizen," honoring parishioner Frank Antalek. Born into a circus family in Hungary, he began performing at the age of five as an acrobat and trapeze artist. Quitting the circus when he was a teen, he was the first member of his family in many generations to leave this livelihood. He became a German citizen, and, as a Roman Catholic living in a Jewish community, he was horrified when he saw German soldiers murder a retired Jewish rabbi in the town square. Arriving in the United States, he obtained American citizenship, joined the army, and was in the first wave of Allied Forces landing on Normandy Beach in World War II. In the Korean War, he served in the air force as an interpreter, rifleman, and explosives expert. Retired from the military, while working in a textile mill in Greenville, he suffered from an accident, which seriously injured his arms. Eventually, he moved to Charleston and became a barber and hair stylist. At age sixty-six Frank Antalek became what he called "a church clown," fondly known as Poppy, and his wife joined him as Rosie the clown. He entertained children at Saint James as a juggler and paid frequent visits to the

Medical University's Children's Ward, Red Cross events, nursing homes, church functions, local schools, and the James Island Senior Citizens Center.[18]

Eugene Platt

On October 8, 1992, *The Post and Courier* reporter Deidre C. Mays wrote an article entitled "Book's Proceeds Going to Homeless Charities." Eugene Platt, a local poet, published his first novel *Bubba Missy and Me*, dedicated it to Rev. Arthur Jenkins, and donated all the first-edition proceeds to the Star Gospel Mission and Charleston Interfaith Crisis Ministry. Bubba is the name of the Episcopal priest in the book.[19] Platt served as James Island Public Service Commissioner for many years.

William "Willie" Ellis McLeod

On January 19, 1990, one of Saint James' long-time members, William E. McLeod, died at the age of 104. He was known affectionately as "Mr. Willie," a nickname that farm workers used to distinguish him from his father, William W. McLeod.[20] His grandfather, William Wallace McLeod, an Edisto Island planter, had bought the James Island property—McLeod Plantation—which had been labeled "a pickpocket place" because everyone who had farmed the land lost money until a drainage problem was corrected.[21] McLeod's grandfather built the planation house in 1854, but during the Civil War, the house was occupied first by the Confederate and secondly by the Union forces as headquarters and a hospital. After the war, the Freedman's Bureau was located there.[22]

Born February 4, 1885, in this plantation house, "Mr. Willie" was among the last of the sea island cotton planters. At one time the estate consisted of about 1,400 acres used mostly for growing cotton, but the last cotton crop in 1918 was destroyed by boll weevils. In the 1940s he farmed potatoes and cucumbers and kept dairy cows. McLeod, in interviews, often talked about how the roads had changed on the island—many from dirt to oyster-shell layers to asphalt. He also talked about the onset of automobiles and how they frightened horses. In the 1950s when the current bridge was to be built over Wappoo Creek, the new Folly Road was scheduled to cut across the McLeod property, destroying some of the ancient oaks and old slave cabins, but McLeod was able to get changes made in the proposed route, with the help of the Charleston County legislative delegation, to keep his estate intact.[23]

William McLeod served on the Saint James vestry for decades, sometimes "when a Sunday congregation of 18-20 persons was considered a good size." When Saint James hosted a party to honor his one-hundredth birthday, Mr. Willie teased assistant rector Greg Prior, who had written an article about him, telling Rev. Prior, "I have been everything from assistant janitor to assistant rector."[24] The text of this history book documents many more roles Mr. Willie fulfilled at Saint James. Reared at First Scots Presbyterian Church in Charleston and attending the Episcopal Porter Military Academy, he alternately worshipped at both the Episcopal and Presbyterian James Island churches,[25] as written about in *Sea Island Yankee* by Clyde Bresee. Mr. Willie was also instrumental in helping the Lutheran and Methodist congregations as they built their churches on James Island. In another article entitled "Centenarians Meet Each Year with Grace," the journalist asked, "To what do you attribute your long life?" Mr. Willie responded "Moderation in everything."[26]

In his will Mr. McLeod left money to Bishop Gadsden Episcopal Retirement Community, Porter-Gaud School, the College of Charleston, The Citadel, Saint James, his former priests, some fellow parishioners, and several more individuals and organizations. One of his sisters Wilhelmina W. McLeod died in 1952, leaving her third of the plantation to First Scots Presbyterian Church, Saint James, and the Thornwell Orphanage. His sister Rose M. Barnwell died in 1982, leaving her portion to a number of charitable causes including a local hospital, seminary, churches (including Saint James), an animal rights organization, and retirement homes.

Currently, McLeod Plantation, managed by Charleston County Parks, is open for tours. Capturing the history, the park's website states the following:

> Tour guides present themed tours that include but are not limited to, sea island cultivation and processing, Gullah/Geechee culture, and organized and individual resistance to slavery and its legacy...All daily tours focus on the transition to freedom for generations of African-American people who lived at the site during and after slavery.[27]

ROBERT A. BARBER

Several newspaper articles have addressed undertakings of former parishioner Robert A. Barber, Jr. After receiving a Master of Divinity from Duke University in 1976, he served as a minister before entering law school at the South Texas College of Law. While serving in a Charleston law practice, Barber was elected to the Charleston County School Board in 1984 and was chairman from 1986-1988. He was elected to serve in the South Carolina House of Representatives from 1989-1994. He has volunteered with organizations as a conservationist, health care advisor, and advocate for the elderly.[28] Perhaps most parishioners know him as the owner of Bowen's Island Seafood Restaurant, founded by his grandparents in the 1940s, and even featured in national television food shows. A combination Low Country history book and cook book called *Bowen's Island* includes anecdotes, pictures, and details of this area known and loved by many Saint James parishioners. Barber has helped Saint James host several fund raisers, especially with oyster roasts.[29]

Rev. Arthur Jenkins, Wyman Frampton, Ken Childress, O.P. White, George "Tank" Barnette, Sandy Brockington

On January 21, 2001, *The News and Courier* published an article entitled "Faith with a Healing Touch: Believers Share Their Stories," which focused collectively on several Saint James parishioners and Rev. Jenkins. Each story shows how prayer brought about miraculous healing. For example, in spite of Wyman Frampton's visits to a cardiologist and gastroenterologist, medication changes, and even surgery, he continued to suffer from excessive weight loss and debilitating weakness. He stated that he got on his knees and prayed at the communion rail at Saint James; in fact, Rev. Jenkins had to hold on to him so that he did not fall. Frampton felt that he was cured overnight, telling his wife the next morning that he had not felt that well in years. Another example concerned Ken Childress, who had complications from surgery, was rushed to intensive care with kidney and liver failure, and was on a ventilator for two weeks. In fact, he was told later that he had "died twice." Throughout a month he recalled people coming into his hospital room to pray for him, and eventually he was healed. Childress said, "Doctors were fighting as hard as they possibly could along with divine help." George "Tank" Barnette, former submariner and registered nurse, was diagnosed with melanoma, which required surgery and medication that had unbearable side effects. Not being able to tolerate the treatments, he decided to quit injections and rely solely on prayer, entrusting the outcome, whatever it would be, to God. Consequently, he was blessed with a physical and spiritual healing. Sandra Brockington had a heart valve replaced, which at the time was predicted to last an estimated five years, but it had lasted twenty-five years at the time this article was published. She felt that she avoided painful surgery due to sustained prayer and Rev. Jenkins' placing his hands on her, praying for healing. Summarizing these miracles, O. P. White, retired from the Air Force and a member of Saint James, stated that a half-dozen people were supernaturally healed within a few months.[30]

Frances "Frank" Walpole Clement, Jr.

On May 29, 2018, another well-known parishioner, Frances "Frank" Walpole Clement, Jr., died at the age of ninety-five. Born in 1922, he was the oldest living member of Saint James at the time of his death. As a U.S. merchant marine, he served aboard merchant ships in World War II, and, as a civilian, he held leadership roles in various companies and organizations as an insurance agent. For many years he sailed the James Island Yacht Club's Sea Island One Design, *Cygnet II*, served as Commodore five times, and was named Commodore Emeritus of the James Island Yacht Club in 2006. Interested in local history, he was a member of both The Sons of Confederate Veterans and the Society of First Families of South Carolina 1670-1700. He was a member and past president of The Exchange Club of James Island. Enjoying the company of church and community members, he and his wife Suzanne were charter members of the James Island Dance Club, which started on James Island in the 1940s when couples, mostly from Saint James and James Island Presbyterian Churches, gathered monthly to share meals, music, and dancing. The Dance Club, which started when funds were scarce but socialization was important, has been sustained for generations. In his latter years, Mr. Clement was a resident of the Bishop Gadsden Retirement Home. He remained an active member of Saint James throughout his life and is buried in Saint James' Cemetery.[31]

People from all walks of life—whether their jobs were part-time or life-long, blue collar or white collar, local or international—have worshipped at Saint James. What they drew from their church became intertwined with society. Likewise, their skills from avocations and vocations became blessings at Saint James. These few "profiles of parishioners" portray sketches of some outstanding members of the congregation within the broader community. Thousands more have "profiles" that are just as interesting. Saint James has been filled by worshippers who heeded Colossians 3: 23-24: "Whatever you do, work at it with all your heart, as working for the Lord, not for men, since you know that you will receive an inheritance from the Lord as a reward. It is the Lord Christ you are serving."

CHAPTER TWENTY-THREE
Saint James Missions

Taking seriously God's command in Acts 1:8 to "be my witnesses…to the ends of the earth," the people of Saint James have become more and more involved in missions over the years. Mission work has taken on many forms locally, nationally, and internationally: food, clothing, shelter, and services; prayer and evangelism; independently and collectively.

Women's church records from the 1940s and 1950s mention having prayer partners in the Philippines, shipping quilt scraps and children's clothing to an orphanage in Virginia, mailing Christmas boxes to the Seamen's Church Institute in New York, donating safety pins to a mission in Puerto Rico, and corresponding with St. Mark Mission (school and orphanage) in Nenana, Alaska, sending such things as soap, crayons, books, and letters of encouragement. Following on the heels of the Depression and intermixed with the personal sacrifices brought about by World War II, some of these seemingly simple contributions were monumental as Saint James' women reached out in the name of Christian fellowship and evangelism to other parts of the nation and the world.

These women also kept their mission work close to home. For example, they collaborated with James Island Baptist Church in Riverland Terrace, working in honor of the World Day of Prayer Service. Annually, from fields about to be plowed under, they gleaned tomatoes either to freeze or to can. Hundreds of jars for the local soup kitchen made chili, spaghetti sauce, red rice, and vegetable soup.[1]

Vestry minutes over the last fifty years abound with details pertaining to the support of missions. In 1976 organist and vestryman Seth Cutter was accepted to Wycliff Bible Translators to prepare to be a missionary[2] The vestry continued to send financial contributions in the latter 1970s and early 1980s to Dr. Dean Samuelson, who was traveling to Zaire as a medical missionary.[3] A Missions Committee was founded in March of 1982 with Dr. David Egleston, chairman, Dr. Wayne King, Mildred Joseph, Wallace Vale, and Lorene Johnson to determine how to allocate funds for missions. In July of 1983, $1500 was given to Chuck and Beth Boardman for their work in Uganda. $1,000 was designated for local missions—Soup Kitchen, My Sister's House (for abused women and their children), and the Good Samaritan Mission.[4] In March of 1985 money was given to Flight of Mercy for Chad, Africa.

In 1983 "Love Loaves" (also referred to as Lenten offering boxes) generated $1,035, with 40% going to World Vision International, 30% to the Presiding Bishop's Fund for World Relief, and 30% to the Ronald McDonald House where families stay when children undergo extended medical treatments at nearby hospitals.[5]

Saint James records are filled with details of individual members being called to do mission work. Having lived in a Spanish-speaking country as a child, parishioner Mary Bailey King had the personal and educational background to become a middle and high school Spanish teacher. Using her bi-lingual skills over several decades, she repeatedly traveled as a missionary and interpreter to other countries, including Argentina, Honduras, and the Dominican Republic.[6] In 1994 the parish made financial contributions to Rev. Suzy McCall serving in Honduras as well as to Paul Beliasov in Bangladesh.[7] In 1995 and 1996, Sue Crawford, a Sunday school teacher and head of the Foreign Missions Committee, led mission trips to Honduras.[8]

Other parishioners have also gone to faraway regions of the world on behalf of missions. George Martindale made several trips to Russia with Josh McDowell Ministries as a member of Carelift.[9] Dr. David Egleston and his wife Francie (a nurse) made two medical mission trips to Haiti and to Bangladesh through the World Health Mission. Dr. Egleston and his son Dubose went on a mission trip to the Ivory Coast of Africa.[10] Dr. Egleston and his daughter Anne went on a medial mission trip to Haiti, and Francie went to Haiti the following year.[11]

In March of 1997 Rev. Howard shared with the vestry that Saint James had been listed in a recent issue of *Living Church* as one of the seventeen most mission-minded Episcopal churches. Financial support of $10,000 was given to the North American Missionary Society [NAMS] in both 1996 and 1997 for establishing churches, thus making Saint James an "Antioch Parish."[12]

Rev. Geoffrey and Helen Ochana received financial aid to help support their mission work in Kenya.[13] In July 1998 the Ochanas were serving in Nairobi when Rev. Ochana asked about the vehicle for which Saint James had expended $12,500 in June 1997, but the vehicle had not been delivered to him. Although the office of Mobile Outreach Ministries (MOM) in Minneapolis was contacted repeatedly for information or for a refund, the vehicle was never delivered to the Ochanas, and the predicament was revisited time and again at vestry meetings.[14] In June of 2000, an Order of Judgement was filed against Mobile Outreach Ministries.[15] Vestry records do not include a resolution to this situation.

In a letter to the congregation June 3, 2001, Rev. Jenkins stated that Saint James had "laid the foundation for mission trips to Honduras, Dominican Republic, Tampa, Orlando, Russia, Cuba and Roatan." Saint James included in their 2002 budget $9,100 for various local and international missions for the following: hosting the Diocesan World Missions Day at Saint James, supporting the ministry of Rev. Suzy McCall in Honduras, working with St. John's and San Juan Missions as "Jesus Carpenters" volunteers at Sea Island Habitat for Humanity, and collecting and shipping clothing to Central America. Members in the congregation also worked with PLUTO (People's Lives United to Others) and helped to remodel an old school building on Grimball Road to be used as a community center for James Island. The outreach team initiated a Families Adopting Families program at Christmas.[16] Randell Horres[17] and George and Tina Martindale were a part of RAMCARE, an outreach mission in Cuba.[18] Emily Yarnell went to Ireland to participate in a teen evangelism mission.[19] In 2005 Saint James responded to the Southern Asia tsunami relief through Water Missions International by donating $10,000[20] and participating in Charleston's "Walk for Water" on behalf of Water Missions International.[21]

Additional parishioners have traveled in pairs and as families to various mission sites. As a part of Medical Ministry International (MMI), Dick and Virginia Bartels went to San Pedro Sula, Honduras in 2006 on a medical mission trip with Dr. James A. Brown, a surgeon, and his wife Carolyn, a nurse, to work in a government-supported hospital.[22] Peter Rothermel, his wife Jackie, and their son and daughter did mission work in the war-torn city of Gulu in northern Uganda, Africa,[23] and Breezy Rothermel went on a mission trip to Fiji in 2015. Vestry notes from June 3, 2017 state that Jack Henley went to Mozambique with a team of seven people for over two weeks.

For many years in the last two decades, Saint James parishioners have served on mission trips to the Dominican Republic. Peggy Spell, a retired nurse, has made numerous trips, working with the children of the Albergue Day Care Center and the Church of Cristo Salvador.[24] In 2008 Mary King, working as an interpreter, joined Peggy and a team of doctors and dentists from the Diocese of South Carolina. They distributed medicines and provided dental care to almost 800 people.[25]

Several Saint James parishioners have traveled to Honduras to work with Rev. Suzy McCall with LAMB Institute. Church records are filled with articles in the *Epistles* about those who have traveled to help this ministry. Amy Badger's article includes the details that many others have experienced. She described the dirt floors, garbage-filled streets, clothes washed in polluted rivers, and houses constructed of scrap materials. She created images of many of the children—dirty, unattended, partially clad, hungry, homeless, abandoned. Later she shared anecdotes about dinners of plantains and beans and rice—all served to her with generosity and grace, smiles, kind words, optimism, appreciation, and Christian faith—all extended in spite of what most Americans would consider to be intolerable economic oppression.[26]

On their 2008 mission trip to Honduras, parishioners took over fifty child-size "wooden hands," each pierced with a hole and marked by a drop of red paint to represent Christ's blood. As the children pressed their hands to the wooden ones held by the Saint James mission team members, the parishioners said, "manos de Cristo"—hands of Christ. These wooden hands made by Bruce and Cathy Yarnell were given to the children at LAMB Institute. Mission team members, who noticed that several toddlers were barefooted, traced their feet on paper and purchased size-appropriate shoes for them.[27] Sales of Honduran coffees helped to fund mission trips.[28]

Additional examples of missions come under the label "Backyard Missions," which include local outreach and ministry. "John 8:36 Prison Ministry," led by Rev. Carl Green and his wife Gill, has ministered to inmates in South Carolina Department of Corrections prisons, especially in Allendale. They also have provided counseling, Bible study, marriage classes, and Sunday morning worship services to military members imprisoned in the navy brig in North Charleston. Working tirelessly throughout many years, they helped to change the hearts and lives of many to whom they witnessed.[29]

Another close-by annual mission—Operation Inasmuch—is based on Matthew 25:40: "Inasmuch as you have done it unto the least of these, my brothers, you have done it unto me." Their slogan is "Mobilizing Believers in Their Community." On May 16, 2009 and on April 24, 2010, parishioners divided themselves into small groups to lend helping hands to those close to Saint James—volunteering to clean off and edge sidewalks along Camp Road, painting and repairing houses belonging to residents who did not have the means to do the work themselves, and hosting a neighborhood picnic. On Saturday, April 20, 2011, seventy people from five James Island churches, including Saint James, took on eleven diverse projects for the needy around the island. Some parishioners provided materials and labor for roof and plumbing projects while others picked up litter along the roads, did yard work, delivered food, and offered prayer. The day's work culminated in a picnic at the Ferguson Road Picnic Shelter.[30]

Saint James has also participated, along with other island churches, in the "Convoy of Hope," an annual interdenominational outreach program to bring community members together for food, fun activities, and gift boxes. The spiritual impetus of convoyofhope.org is "I have come so that people may live, and that they may enjoy life to the full."[31] On December 10, 2011, James Island was one of four sites in the Charleston area to involve churches, businesses, and other organizations to provide such things as haircuts, job placement, medical services, and live entertainment to impoverished residents.[32]

Food donations have often been the focal point for missions. In 2006, 2007, and 2008, parishioners built what they called a "Food Wall." Placing canned and dry food items in several stacks and rows, donors watched the contributions mount up in the Ministry Center. Then near Thanksgiving the food offerings were blessed and distributed to families in need.[33]

James Island Outreach began in the fall of 1989 when James Island churches united to help local citizens whose residences had been devastated by Hurricane Hugo. When the ministry of rebuilding concluded, the program shifted its focus to providing for basic human needs, especially food. Originally housed for several years at Bethany United Methodist Church on Maybank Highway, it relocated to 1872 Camp Road on property belonging to Saint James. The consecration of the new James Island Outreach site was held on June 30, 2018 after volunteers and Lowe's Home Improvement store renovated two trailers donated by James Island Christian Church. Saint James parishioner Cal Worthington spearheaded the efforts to bring about this more centrally located and expanded facility for James Island and Folly Beach residents in need of groceries as well as assistance with shelter, utility bills, medicines, and earning one's GED, the equivalent of a high school diploma. Twenty-seven island churches contribute as donors and volunteers; the Low Country Food Bank, local grocery stores, and businesses contribute likewise. To guarantee a variety of staples, each church is assigned certain food items to keep stocked at the outreach center. For example, Saint James Anglican is known as the "cereal church."[34] This outreach program is known as "islanders helping islanders."[35]

James Island Outreach identifies beforehand local residents in need of a turkey for holidays such as Thanksgiving and Christmas. Coming together on a Saturday morning, the men of Saint James deep-fry about sixty turkeys, distributing them to families as they arrive to get them.[36]

"Missions" have been done with boxes and bags. For example, "birthday boxes" were shipped to LAMB Institute in Honduras so that each child would receive a gift in the upcoming year. Saint James participated in "Treats for Troops," to honor Veterans Day; boxes included knitted caps, snacks, and reading materials.[37] The Samaritan's Purse boxes, created by the Franklin Graham ministry called "Operation Christmas Child," were filled annually with small age-and-gender-appropriate gifts flown to various locations internationally.[38] According to the October 2019 *Epistle*, care packages—boxes with prayers and goodies—were mailed to Saint James college students. In 2008 Angel Food Ministries included $65 worth of food made available to donors at the cost of $30. Varied monthly menus consisted of fresh, frozen and packaged foods—boxed to feed a family of four.[39] Welcome gift bags were filled with discount coupons, seed packets, olive wood crosses, candles, etc. and a current issue of the *Epistle* for parishioners to give to new neighbors to welcome them to the community.[40] With suggestions from Rev. Andrew Williams in the September 2015 *Epistle*, parishioners filled the back packs of students, who were in need of school supplies, to give to them in August. All of these boxes and bags indicated givers reaching out in Christian love.

The youth have been involved in many missions. In the summer of 2006 Saint James' middle schoolers, along with young people from Christ Saint Paul's, stayed together at a Methodist church while volunteering in the Greenville, South Carolina area. Also in 2006 high school students joined teens from five other Episcopal churches in the South Carolina Diocese to assist people in Asheville, North Carolina.[41]

For over a decade Saint James has sent dozens of parishioners, funds, and supplies to Save R Kids, a Christian home in Guyana (the only English-speaking country in South America) for children who are homeless and helpless due to poverty, abuse, abandonment, physical and mental deficiencies, and being orphaned. This mission was promoted by Mary Joan Oxemann and Paul Mitchell. For years Rev. Arthur Jenkins and parishioners worked at Save R Kids, making repairs on the residential home, building a house for the gardener, providing Bible lessons in a predominantly Muslim community for hundreds of children as well as those at Save R Kids, and sending funds for the children's uniforms, shoes, school supplies, and other needs. In 2005 nine parishioners went to build a bathroom for the children and a guest room for visiting missionaries, all while conducting a vacation Bible school for the community.[42] Some of the visiting teams consisted of as many as sixteen people, teenagers and adults.

In November 2006, fifteen months after the category 4 Hurricane Katrina struck with 145 mph winds, ten parishioners went to work with Trinity Christian Community near the French Quarter of New Orleans. Since the levees of Lake Pontchartrain were broken, eighty percent of the city had been under water for three weeks due to flooding from the 2005 hurricane. The mission team reported, "From what we saw there, the storm could have happened only weeks ago," indicating that damage was still widespread and that restoration was still desperately needed. Saint James volunteers took on a daily task of removing ruined sheetrock and rotten wood, cleaning away mold, and preparing houses for repairs.[43]

Saint James was the sending agency for Rev. Elizabeth Bumpas, a missionary in Uganda for three years, serving Bishop Gakumba Johnson in the Diocese of Northern Uganda. Elizabeth was the priest-in-charge of the English service at Christ Church, Gulu; taught classes at the Janani Luwum Theological College to train men and women for ordained ministry; and assisted with fundraising at the Women's Development Center, where women developed marketable skills to provide for their families. In remote villages she was also the team leader for the Jesus Film Ministry, which portrayed the Gospel of Luke. Sometimes crowds as large as 500 would gather to see the video (dubbed in the Acholi language) and consequently commit their lives to Christ. She returns regularly to visit and has taken parishioners from Saint James and St. Johns with her. On one of her several return trips, October 2019, she was accompanied by Libby Paul, Mark Durinsky, Donna Lewis, and Rosie Colson. They distributed to seminarian students Bibles written in English but with a study portion written by Africans from the perspective of African culture. They also visited Sudanese refugees of Adjumani, Uganda.[44]

"The Bridge Church Ministry," coordinated at Saint James by Doreen Warner, involves parishioners preparing meals and going to downtown Charleston under the Ravenel Bridge (at the intersection of Meeting and Huger Streets) and North Charleston (in a high-crime area at the corner of Rivers and Cosgrove Avenues) where they not only serve the hungry and homeless a delicious meal but also provide a worship service. Working with other churches who do likewise, Saint James' volunteers—led by Mission Committee chairperson Mark Von Allmen, his wife Robin, and Charles Holliday—participate in this "backyard mission."[45]

Local missions have reached out to the Hispanic communities. In the summer of 2011 Robin Von Allmen wrote an article for the *Epistle* in which she portrayed the dire working conditions of migrant workers on Edisto Island and in Hollywood, both south of Charleston. Separated from their relatives in their homelands, unable to communicate locally because of language barriers, and oppressed by poverty and little formal education, these farmhands feel trapped in a dismal lifestyle. Robin invited parishioners to contribute to and join her husband Mark and her in their visits.[46] Over the years Saint James also conducted services, provided meals, and engaged the migrant workers and Hispanic immigrants in weekly Sunday afternoon gatherings on Johns Island, often doing so with Saint James parishioner Amy Case and Rev. David Dubay, rector of Holy Trinity Windermere. In December 2019 Carolyn and Steedley Candler, Rev. Mark Cooke, and Virginia Bartels accompanied Rev. Dubay to La Mision de San Juan, an Hispanic camp on Johns Island, to distribute thirty new men's jackets, hygiene bags assembled by parishioners, and a large homemade breakfast.

Many students attending Murray Lasaine Elementary School, James Island, received assistance through the church's local mission endeavors in a program called "Jubilee." In the Ministry Center for two-week periods in the summers, volunteers, led by Joyce Wichmann, tutored children and provided healthy snacks. The focus was on reading readiness for kindergarteners and reading skills for older pupils. Throughout the school year, church volunteers often mentored and tutored children on a one-to-one basis on the Murray Lasaine school campus.[47] For several years at Christmas, the women of Saint James purchased different items such as blankets, children's books, and T-shirts with the school's name. Each age-appropriate gift was wrapped and labeled with a child's name for Santa (aka Rev. Arthur Jenkins) to distribute—often with the help of "Elf Boy" (a very tall Deacon Ron Warfuel). On the final day before the Christmas holiday, the children and teachers stood outside the school building waiting for "Santa," donned in his full red suit plus a helmet, to arrive on his noisy Harley Davidson motorcycle, much to the delight of the teachers and the squeals and laughter of the students.

Realizing the effectiveness of supporting indigenous missionaries knowledgeable of their own country's culture and language, Saint James members have sought to be more supportive of this kind of outreach. Throughout several years the church has co-partnered with Frontline Missions, a Christian organization established to train and equip missionaries in hard-to-reach areas of the world. For example, Saint James has helped to support an indigenous missionary named Shu Shu, who goes deep into the jungles of Brazil to share the Gospel with those who have often never heard about God.[48] Saint James has helped to sponsor an indigenous missionary named Bidhya Rai in the Darjeeling region of Bengal. Working with women who are often depressed and abused, Bidhya provides teaching, training, and faith-based hope to those who are often hearing about Jesus for the first time.[49]

Parishioner Jack Henley established two homes as residences for men in need of conversion experiences and a safe, supportive environment to turn their lives around. Benjamin's Way homes, located in Charleston and Augusta, Georgia, are for healing and discipleship for men in need of redirection and rehabilitation. These houses are hybrids of a long-term recovery community, a half-way home, and a school of ministry for drug addicts and alcoholics seeking sobriety and God's calling on their lives. Through the "Twelve Steps" of Alcoholics Anonymous and the Holy Scriptures, the men develop a new sense of purpose and a new self-identity.[50]

Fresh Start is yet another mission that Saint James has supported. This program works to stop the recidivism in prisons by providing teachings on redemption, reconciliation, and re-entry to society for those who have been incarcerated. Participants complete a 20-week course called "Men in Transition," focusing on developing character traits critical for successful employment and family life.[51]

Many Saint James parishioners have participated in the Kairos Prison Ministry. "Kairos" is a Greek word, found in the New Testament, which means "God's Special Time."[52] The mission of this program is as follows:

> Kairos Prison Ministry International [shares] the transforming love and forgiveness of Jesus Christ to impact the hearts and lives of incarcerated men, women, and youth, as well as their families, to become loving and productive citizens of their communities.[53]

After participating in a training program and preparation, a team enters a prison for four days of lessons, discussions, activities, testimonies, prayers, and meals with a selected group of participants from the prison to promote forgiveness and fellowship. This spiritual experience has reduced the number of problems occurring within prisons as well as the number of crimes committed outside prison after the incarcerated have been released to return to society.[54] Both Bonum Wilson, Jr. and Bill McDaniel served several years in the men's Kairos Program at the Kirkland Prison in Columbia, and Bonum also served at Lieber Prison in Ridgeville, South Carolina.[55] For several years Rev. Louise Weld has served as clergy participating in women's Kairos ministries. Parishioner Maureen McDaniel worked on the Kairos women's team for three years, and Mary Lane Weckenman has taken on many leadership roles at Camille Griffin Graham Correctional Institution for Women in Columbia, South Carolina.[56] Several women from Saint James have participated in this mission work. The people of Saint James have baked thousands of cookies to be distributed to all prisoners, not just those participating in Kairos, as a part of this ministry. These homemade sweets, a significant rarity to the recipients, symbolize generosity and love.[57]

For over ten years the Mission Committee and parish volunteers hosted a "Heart for World Missions" (sometimes called "World Missions Dinner") banquet near Valentine's Day. The evening consisted of a wine reception, silent auction or sale of donated items, live music, a slide presentation of Saint James' ministry in various countries, and a delicious meal prepared by Saint James' The Upper Room Catering or other volunteers. Speakers included, among others, Rev. Alan Winter, founder of Frontline Missions; Rev. Suzy McCall, founder of LAMB Institute in Honduras; and Dr. and Mrs. James Brown, medical missionaries with PAACS (Pan-African Academy of Christian Surgeons) in Cameroon. The earnings and donations from the missions banquet were divided among various missions locally and worldwide.[58]

Talented crafters at Saint James have used their craftsman skills to earn mission funds. Pat Majors fashioned a wide variety of quilted items as well as wine cork wreaths and trivets, donating her time and the entire earnings for missions. Likewise, Sonya Droze made hundreds of crafts from oyster shells and sand dollars to create candle holders, wreaths, and tree ornaments, also donating earnings to missions and charities.

In the summer of 2019 Rev. Elizabeth Bumpas spearheaded the distribution of a brochure entitled "Christmas in July: Missions Catalog," for which Missions Committee members paid printing and postage costs. Parishioners read about each of the eleven missions which Saint James helped to support at the time and made donations—over $11,500—to the causes to which they felt called to contribute, helping people in crisis and spreading the Gospel across the globe. An additional anonymous contribution of $29,000 was also given to missions in response to this catalogue.[59]

Dr. Jim Brown and his wife Carolyn have spoken at the Saint James' men's breakfast, Sunday services, and the mission banquet. Although not members of Saint James, they have received funds from the church, on behalf of PAACS, to train African doctors to become surgeons to practice in areas where there might be one surgeon to a million people.[60] As a visiting medical missionary at Saint James, Dr. Brown gave a sermon in which he addressed missions:

> The needs of the world are infinite…It is easy to think that we cannot make
> a difference and retreat into our private lives….It is very easy to insulate

ourselves from the suffering of others by focusing on our own needs, or seeking diversions…but even good things can so easily become distractions and idols that blind us from the harvest around us…The harvest is plentiful but the laborers are few…What we do with our lives, every day, in every situation, in every interaction with another person, matters forever, in one way or another…Pray that the Lord of the harvest will send laborers into His field. You cannot pray that prayer in faith without realizing that He may actually be sending you. You may be the answer to your own prayers…Let your heart be broken with the things that break His heart. Recognize that wherever you are, you are standing in a field ripe for harvest, prepared by the Lord Himself. Pray for laborers, fully aware that He is sending you in one way or another.

Saint James parishioners have gone to those "fields" to labor in such places as orphanages, hospitals, prisons, schools—to reach out to the homeless, the hungry, the heartbroken. Venturing into both familiar and foreign neighborhoods, the congregation heard the often-quoted questions in Scripture, "Whom shall I send, and who will go for us?" Throughout the church's existence, the people of Saint James have responded, "Here I am. Send me." Send us. (Isaiah 6:8)

CHAPTER TWENTY-FOUR

Make a Joyful Noise

Throughout the existence of Saint James Church, the congregations have created community through social gatherings based on the era, geography, resources, and interests. Some of these events occurred briefly and sporadically, and others have been sustained for years. Camaraderie among believers is promoted time and again in Scripture: "Encourage one another…build each other up." (1Thessalonians 5:11) "Spur one another on toward love and good deeds." (Hebrews 10:24) "Two are better than one because they have a good return for their work." (Ecclesiastes 4:1) "If we walk in the light…we have fellowship with one another." (1 John 1:7) This "joyful noise making" has permeated Bible-based messages and strengthened the bonding of brothers and sisters in Christian fellowship through three centuries.

Just as many of the Biblical stories revolve around food, so do many of the events at Saint James. The "Cross of Nails" came about after World War II when much of Europe had been divided due to racial, national, religious, and political differences; however, as the diverse population of Europe started entering one another's homes to share meals, reconciliation occurred, bringing about a healing and spirituality across the continent. Likewise, diverse members of Saint James, with the leadership of Bobbie Galbraith, were brought closer through "Cross of Nails" dinner parties rotated among the members at each other's houses. Whether the parishioner was single or married, lived in a modest apartment or one of the grandest homes on the island, the small groups gathered monthly for six months to share a simple meal. No agenda was planned, thus creating space for personal conversations to evolve.[1]

Saint James is known for its picnics. For years the congregation traveled to Camp Saint Christopher on Seabrook Island, worshipped together in a beach chapel, and then went to the pavilion and formed lines to fill their plates with the members' specialties cooked for the event. Afterwards they flocked to the beach to swim, fish, crab, play volleyball, build sandcastles, and bask in the sun. James Island County Park has been yet another location for the congregation's picnics. Many of these casual meals, featuring fried chicken, barbeques, and pot luck lunches, have been held after Sunday services on the church grounds, followed by games and contests.

A typical Southern meal often hosted by Saint James over the years has been the oyster roast indigenous to the Low Country. The oysters are harvested along tidal banks at low tide during the colder months, washed, and then usually cooked in a large bucket lowered into a pot of hot water (the pot heated by a propane tank). Once the shells open about one-fourth of an inch, the oyster clusters are poured on top of an outdoor table where parishioners gather, wearing their thick gloves to prevent oyster cuts and using oyster knives to pry the shells open. The steamed oysters are often dipped into butter and lemon or cocktail sauce and sometimes eaten on saltine crackers. Since some people do not like oysters, these gatherings usually include chili and hot dogs as well. The oyster shells are frequently recycled back into nature or used in clever crafts.

In the 1980s the women also periodically hosted Sunday Share-a-Meals to promote fellowship and "Feed the Hungry" luncheons, regularly offering okra or chicken soup, to earn money for the bishop's Fund for World Relief.[2] Church records include announcements about Wednesday and Friday night suppers with entertainment, family bingo nights with refreshments, barbecues, ladies' luncheons featuring a fashion show, harbor cruise serving finger foods, and periodic bake sales. In the latter 1990s Saint James regularly hosted Friday night suppers.[3]

When the bishop visits Saint James for confirmations, the parish looks forward to the festive reception that follows the service. Annually the vestry has provided a brunch paid for, prepared by, and served by its members.[4] Welcoming and ordaining new priests, bidding priests farewell when they accept another calling, thanking the congregation for their financial pledges—all these events are marked with gatherings of food.

The "pounding" is a Southern tradition sometimes still honored today when a new priest arrives at Saint James. This practice is rooted in the custom of parishioners providing the new rector and his family with a "pound of this and a pound of that"—butter, flour, sugar, etc. Of course, today's modern "pounding" can consist of any type of nonperishable food to stock the cupboards of a minister moving to the area to join Saint James' staff.

The Shrove Tuesday pancake suppers have promised a variety of delicious foods. Prepared by the men of Saint James, a variety of gourmet pancakes, syrups, meats, and fruits draw large crowds.[5] Gunnar Johnson was known for his Swedish desserts. Art Field is known for his homemade donuts. Many of Saint James' superb cooks have contributed their specialties to these suppers to mark the beginning of Lent on Wednesday.

Food is a ministry of its own. The congregations' members have individually and collectively provided food for the ill, the elderly, the shut-ins, and the poor. They have prepared and served the hungry and homeless in the downtown Soup Kitchen and "Bridge Ministries." Following the burial services of loved ones in Saint James' church cemetery are often church receptions in the Ministry Center for friends and family to console the bereaved and celebrate the life of the departed.

Beginning in the 1990s and extending over a decade, youth director Michael McIntyre established what was called "The St. James Association," which was recognized as an official club at James Island High School. Joining Michael was another youth director, David Dubay, now rector at Holy Trinity. Meeting every other week, they played their guitars, sang praise music, and offered a brief biblical message as they served pizza to dozens of students. Eventually they extended this same lunch service at the middle schools as well and involved some other pastors from James Island. Some of the teachers also attended the lunches. To accommodate these school lunches, Saint James budgeted thousands of dollars annually to pay for the pizzas.[6]

Chaired by Pat Majors, the "Beverage and Bagel" Ministry for years has provided coffee, tea, lemonade, bagels (provided as a weekly gift by a local baker), and other treats every Sunday morning so that worshippers can socialize before and after services.[7] Many summers the congregation has gathered under the church's trees to chat and share "lemonade under the oaks."

In 1979 the women compiled favorite recipes into *Saint James Sampler,*[8] and in 1994 the women published *The Second Tasting of Our St. James' Sampler II Cook Book.*[9] Each includes a fascinating synopsis of Saint James' history. Intended for fundraisers, these books have also become records of parishioners' names, family culinary traditions, and Low Country cuisine.

Annual bazaars include a bakery station featuring homemade candy, brownies, cookies, pies, cakes, pastries, and sometimes quiches and tomato pies. Also available are home canned goods such as pear relish, green tomatoes, pickled okra, varied jams and preserves, and other great foods indigenous to the area.[10] Signature dishes served for lunch include homemade vegetable soup and shrimp and grits. Other food-themed fund-raisers have included wine and cheese parties with a silent auction, and a wine and cheese art sale to raise money for youth mission trips.[11]

In addition to food-centered fellowship activities are puppet shows, skits, and short plays for worshipers to congregate and be entertained. In the 1980s Biblical lessons were presented through drama, with members of the congregation acting out parts to convey a lesson.[12] These performances were parts of Sunday school lessons, sermons, and evening gatherings. "Poppy," the parish clown, was known to show up at intergenerational events.[13] The character "Aunt Agatha" evoked humor as skits were performed. The ancient art of role plays has brought performers and audiences of all ages together in their fun and worship.

At times the Ministry Center has been converted into a movie theater as parishioners gathered to see a film with a message of faith. For example, in April of 2010, members watched *Faith like Potatoes*, based on a true story that chronicles the spiritual journey of a South African farmer struggling to rebuild his life, discover his purpose, and experience transformational faith.[14] March 12, 2012, they watched *Courageous* about four brave policemen learning to rear their children in a God-honoring way.[15]

Fellowship has often been centered around seasonal holidays. Throughout decades at Christmas, children have donned clothing to represent Mary, Joseph, wise men, shepherds, angels, and even the stable animals, such as donkeys, sheep, and lambs. The Day School programs and Christmas Eve services bring this Bethlehem scene in a stable to life.[16] The Nativity scene captures the spirit of the season as proud parents capture images with their cameras to last lifetimes. Six pictures of the 2019 pageant were featured in the January 2020 *Carolina Compass* newspaper.

In 1985 Saint James published a thirty-one page booklet entitled *Angels We Have Heard on High* to enrich the families' honoring Advent at home. It included a passage on the Advent season, invitations to a variety of Christmas parties for parishioners of all ages, details about the children's Christmas pageant, announcements regarding the nativity scene recreated on the church's lawn, instructions for children's religious crafts, Christmas poetry and songs, and even recipes to prepare for the month.

Christmases provide special opportunities for fellowship. Children have relished the hayrides, caroling, parties, ornament decorating, and drives through the Charleston County Park to see the extraordinary display of lights, depicting both secular and Biblical scenes. Boys and girls "pick an angel" from angel Christmas trees and shop for appropriate gifts for their selected children.[17] Families pack shoe boxes as part of the Samaritan's Purse, gifts shipped to youth around the world. The choirs provide special musical programs about the Christ Child.

Easter-related services have also brought joy to all ages in the congregation. On Palm Sunday "Rector" the donkey—a live donkey—was brought to the front lawn of Saint James to be a part of the scene taken from the Gospel of Matthew portraying Christ's triumphant entry into Jerusalem riding on a donkey.[18] Renewing this front-lawn church event from past years, family minister Cyndee Cave has included not only a live donkey, but also a sheep and lamb on Palm Sunday.[19]

Maundy Thursday has taken on various forms of celebration. On March 31, 1988, Rev. Clark W. P. Lowenfield led a Maundy Thursday service during which there was a ceremony of the washing of the feet. Other Maundy Thursday events have included a Seder meal consisting of foods, drinks. and traditions of the Biblical times.

The conclusion of the Maundy Thursday is the stripping of the altar, always a somber process as everything on the altar and lecterns is taken away, except the cross, which is draped in black in preparation for Good Friday. Parishioners gather in the sanctuary to watch this step-by-step removal of altar furnishings to prepare for the reality of the crucifixion. Usually three services are offered on Good Friday, sometimes followed by a procession through fourteen stations of the cross, portraying Christ's last day and crucifixion.[20] This precedes the joy that comes with Easter services celebrating the empty tomb and the risen Christ. On Saturdays prior to Easter as well as on Easter Sundays, little children, with baskets in hand, scamper around the church grounds picking up their prizes in egg hunts.[21]

The youth—future leaders of the church—have held a special place in Saint James' fellowship. Many have served as acolytes and crucifers while in grades four through twelve, assisting the clergy at Sunday services as well as at weddings, funerals and other special services. Sometimes wearing a cassock and surplice—sometimes not—they enjoy participating in the processions beginning and concluding services, leading with the cross and carrying lit candles to the altar. They have also served as lay readers and as prayer ministers.[22]

Christian education programs have varied over the years, sometimes providing age-based classes and other times sponsoring more intergenerational and family-based Sunday school services. Many of the youth participate in Saint Christopher summer camp programs, sometimes receiving scholarships from the women of the church (ECW/DWM). In the 1980s vacation Bible school was called "Summer Celebration."[23] Throughout the years "a joyful noise" has come about at vacation Bible school, whether it was held summer mornings or summer evenings, whether it was child-focused with adult teachers or family-focused for children and parents to get involved in activities together. Saint James' teens have also participated in a number of retreats with different names—"Happening," "Jesus Weekend," "Epic"—meeting with other teens from the Diocese at Camp St. Christopher on a weekend.[24]

In February 2000 the vestry approved of a sign that read "Saturday Night Jesus" to display out front and promote the services held on Saturday evening in the Parish Hall for teens and college students. Young people were drawn to the gatherings, enjoying age-related messages and praise music.

In 2014, with the leadership of Reverends Andrew and Jill Williams, Saint James added yet another Sunday service named "Flip Flops and Faith," designed to meet the needs of families with young children who might not normally attend worship. Consisting of mostly young families, worshippers can come dressed casually, and the children are involved with their mothers and fathers in interactive sermons. The boys and girls are invited to participate in hands-on activities, mini-videos, and whole-group question and answer sessions, as well as preparation of the table and serving communion, making their worship active and engaging.[25] This service has grown in numbers over the years and, at this writing, is thriving with the leadership of youth leaders Scott and Cyndee Cave.[26]

In the back of the parish hall is the Saint James Day School where children are provided on weekdays with a safe haven while their parents work. There they are introduced to healthy social and academic skills during their most impressionable years. Mothers Morning Out has grown and spilled over into the Ministry Center.[27] Whether in their classrooms or on the playground, these outreach programs have been vital to young parents throughout the community. There are indeed "joyful noises" coming from these little ones at play!

Scouting has been a major part of Saint James for decades. The Boy Scouts—Troop 44—meet at Saint James and have camped at Camp Ho Non Wah on Wadmalaw Island as well as Parrot Point, Francis Marion National Forest, Rocks Pond, Table Rock, Myrtle Beach, Lake Marion, Beaufort, Folly Beach, the Tea Farm on US 17 S, and many more places.[28] In the summer of 2019, Scoutmaster and vestryman Paul Pennington, along with other scout leaders, took a large group of scouts to Philmont Scout Ranch in New Mexico. For several days their physical endurance was tested as they climbed the 12,441-foot summit of Baldy Mountain and grew in their appreciation of the 140,000 acres of this rugged western area.[29] These scouts also know how to turn work into play when cleaning the church grounds, hosting fundraiser meals, and celebrating award ceremonies that have included those of many Eagle Scouts throughout the years. Although not a member of Troop 44, Tradd Horne painted the teen center of Saint James' parish hall when completing his project for Eagle,[30] and Andrew Pennington of Troop 44 built a brick walkway for James Island Outreach.[31] Equally active is the Cub Scout Pack 44. The Girl Scouts (Troop 477 and part of Service Unit 8), along with Brownies, have been involved in their annual cookie sales, summer camps, badge earnings, and other worthy endeavors.[32]

To celebrate St. Francis Day is the annual Blessing of the Animals, which takes place at the outdoor Creek Chapel on a Sunday afternoon. Parishioners bring their dogs, cats, and other animals for priests to place their hands upon their pets, asking God to bless these loving and loved members of families.[33]

Sunday birthday celebrations were also held in the past. All parishioners having a birthday within a month were called to the altar to receive a blessing. The priests would pray for wisdom, grace, and trust in God's goodness as each person marked the beginning of another year.

Music, included throughout this book, has been yet another part of the joy found at Saint James. Groups have varied according to the choir director and the congregation. Junior choirs have included St. James' Carolers (ages four and five) and Young Episcopal Choristers (first through eighth grades).[34] In addition to the traditional choir and praise band, the Young Episcopal Choristers and the Carolers have seized opportunities to sing during church services. At the Flip Flops services, music is led by an intergenerational band. In the Ministry Center at the conclusion of contemporary services, the children run to the area in front of the praise band and take up rhythm band instruments, knowing that in their beating and dancing and twirling, they, too, are part of the concluding song. Piano, organ, harp, guitars, drums, flutes, violins, trumpets, and more—all contribute to the joyful noise. For a few years the church hosted the Saint James Community Orchestra, under the leadership of Ward Moore, made up of talented musicians from Saint James and the community. They practiced and performed regularly.[35] Choir director and organist Chris Walchesky added Advent and Lent mid-week music services as well as Evensong, sometimes including traditional historic pieces and other church and school choirs.[36]

Just as the children and teens have had their groups for social activities, so have the adults. In the 1980s a group called "The Mixed Nuts" met once every month or two simply to have fun, play games, eat casual meals, meet in members' homes, go on hayrides, participate in square dancing, and enjoy good Christian fun and fellowship, forming friendships. At one time the ECW offered an exercise class.[37] The Fifties Plus group (sometimes called 50 & Better) met periodically for years for a covered dish supper followed by an informative speaker or an entertaining performance of sorts.[38]

Throughout the years many parishioners have participated in conferences at Kanuga Conference Center, set in a mountainous area near Hendersonville and Asheville, North Carolina. Many women have participated in a weekend mountain retreat at the Bartels' cabin called "The Sanctuary" in the outskirts of Hendersonville.[39] Rev. Louise Weld wrote in her associate pastor's report in the 2016 Annual Congregational Meeting of Saint James, "I've just returned from our spring Women's Retreat at the Bartels' cabin in North Carolina. My heart is full from the blessings of women aged 25-75 growing together as we share our lives in the Lord."[40] These retreats—fun, relaxing, and spiritually renewing—have even been known to include zip-lining. Over the years Tom and Anne Read and their grown children opened their family beach home in North Carolina for overnight church retreats, and Bonum and Janet Wilson have invited small groups and women's church organizations to meet in their home on Folly Beach.[41] The gift of hospitality flourishes at Saint James.

Since 1977 Saint James has benefitted from the experiences of many who have attended *Cursillo,* which is Spanish for "short course in Christianity." Led by both priests and lay team members, participants from throughout the Diocese meet at Camp St. Christopher for an enriching, intense focus on the Christian faith. One of the highlights of the weekend is the participants' receiving a bag of letters and cards, individually addressed, from former Cursillo members and church members—all to share a sense of well-being in the fellowship of one another and with Christ. The purposes of Cursillo are to help participants understand their individual callings to be Christian leaders and to bring others to Christ.[42]

The *Saint James Parish Profile of 1998* states, "Despite the fact that the earliest records found concerning the Episcopal Church Women of St. James' Church date back only to 1907, the women of St. James' Church certainly were as hard working and giving to their congregation in the two centuries prior to that date as they have been since 1907."[43] Throughout the decades the women of the church, once known as the ECW (Episcopal Church Women) and later known as the DWM (Diocesan Women's Ministry), have hosted an annual bazaar. Collecting donations (many contributed in recent years by John G. Brown's business Carolopolis Antiques), the women assign bargain prices to eclectic items and display them by categories. Making crafts, rooting plants, baking delicacies, creating silent auctions, and serving lunch—these women conduct an outreach on behalf of the congregation and community to earn money for charities, missions, youth scholarships, and church maintenance projects. Throughout the months beforehand, intense work is invested in this yearly endeavor to raise funds, forge friendships, and generate camaraderie.[44]

Other significant women's groups were the three church chapters, St. Anne's, St. Catherine's, and St. Martha's, who held small-group Bible studies and supported charitable causes as they met sometimes weekly and sometimes monthly. In 1985 members of these chapters and ECW hosted a luncheon and fashion show in which women modeled clothing by Ashby's for a fundraiser.[45]

The men of Saint James have also had their special groups, some of which have been athletic in nature. In the 1980s Saint James sponsored an adult softball team, often coached by Midge Jenkins, called St. James' Archangels, part of the James Island YMCA church league. Team members ranged from age 18 to 65. In fact, vestry minutes from August 20, 1984 indicate that Saint James' softball team won the trophy for being the "best" in the YMCA church league. The church also had a golf team and coed volleyball team. The "Parish Profile: St. James' Episcopal Church" stated, "Our teams have been successful, but success can only be measured by the Christian fellowship and moral strength that is developed through physical activity."[46] Beginning about 2016, men have taken annually a three-day mountain weekend to hike, pray, bond as brothers-in-Christ, and enjoy the outdoors throughout North and South Carolina.[47]

The men's gatherings often center on food, fellowship, and worship. For years the men of Saint James met on Thursdays at Athens Greek Restaurant for lunch and Bible study.[48] More recently about thirty men meet early on Friday mornings in the Ministry Center to share breakfast, hear an informative speaker, pray, and volunteer for church-related services.[49] In years past, many of the men at Saint James participated in Promise Keepers, in which they shared fellowship, Bible study, prayer, and even a trip to Washington, D.C. in 1997 to join over one million men who had gathered to pray for the United States.[50] Periodically, they gather at Saint James to share a steak dinner, which approximately eighty men of all ages attend.[51]

Many of the fun activities have been incorporated with other church parishes on the island. One has been Sea Island Habitat for Humanity. Although the volunteers know the muscle and sweat involved in building houses, they also know how worthy their work is in providing a home to a family who might otherwise be homeless. In January of 2012 the church staff, vestry, priests, and members of small groups volunteered their time, money, and materials to construct five homes on the island.[52]

Two annual James Island events also provide support for James Island Outreach. "A Taste of James Island" hosts a fun gathering and cooking contest of community residents, church chefs, and restaurants to raise money and food supplies. Saint James chef Art Field has won several awards.[53]

"Community Thanksgiving Services" are hosted annually by several of the larger island churches where worshippers gather in late November for an interdenominational service led by multiple clergy and varied choirs performing gospel, spirituals, jazz, rock, folk music, bell ringing, traditional hymns, and contemporary praise songs. A rousing sermon is given by an island preacher designated from one of the local churches. Congregations, either predominantly white or black, host the event for hundreds of islanders, and Saint James has housed this inspirational community worship service several times. Saint James' parishioners, clergy, and choir participate annually. Worshippers bring nonperishable food items, and attendees and congregations contribute money for Outreach endeavors.[54]

At times when church budgets have been stretched, the congregation of Saint James has taken on maintenance assignments instead of hiring a company to do the jobs. For example, Saturday mornings men and women, young and old, took on the tedious work of prepping and painting all the black railings in front of the parish hall, church, and Ministry Center.[55] Other Saturday mornings groups have weeded flower beds, trimmed trees, edged walks, cut back bushes, raked leaves, pruned azaleas, cleaned up the outdoor chapel area, and done a wide assortment of tasks to beautify our grounds and buildings.[56]

Bible studies abound. The Rector's Bible study on Wednesday mornings is followed by a communion service and prayer. Tuesday and Thursday Bible studies have also helped address the spiritual needs of parishioners. Small groups (sometimes called life groups) have selected their own study materials and held their gatherings in each other's homes. The Friday Morning Women's Bible study has thrived over the years. Sometimes using a book and sometimes using the combination of a book and a video, the women have studied the Bible in breadth and depth.[57] Other Bible studies have included "Precept Bible Study,"[58] "ACTS 2:42,"[59] "Men's Thursday Luncheon Bible Study," and more. Church members have participated in studies on college campuses, in other churches, and in their neighborhoods, just as Saint James has welcomed non-members into their Bible study groups.

Again and again the congregation has been involved in studies and trainings to deal with the difficult passages of life. The ALPHA series (consisting of dinners, videos, and discussions) have empowered parishioners to reach out to the unchurched, the nonbelievers, the troubled.[60] Courses in how to cope with divorce have also been provided. The "Cancer Support Group," led by Jane Horne, met regularly on behalf of those battling cancer, cancer survivors recuperating, and caregivers needing support.[61] Through fellowship and the Word, the burdens become more bearable.

Some of the most significant bonding among Saint James parishioners has occurred on trips to the Holy Land. For several years Rev. Jenkins has led not only people from Saint James but also members of other parishes. Walking where Jesus walked, connecting geographical places to Biblical events, admiring monuments built to honor long-ago religious leaders, examining relics in museums, and tying art and culture to scripture have taken the fellow travelers back to Israel again and again, all marking holy passages with a renewed and personal significance.[62]

In recent years parishioners have been invited to submit an entry to a Lenten meditation booklet. Their submissions can be personal anecdotes, testimonies, poems, diary reflections, memoirs, quoted Scripture—anything that promotes faith as the congregation prepares their hearts for Lent. Members of the congregation—Erin Cooley, Faith Durinsky, and Virginia Read—have done the artwork. Having the opportunity year after year to read others' creative, insightful passages brings the worshippers closer to one another. Even after church members die, their stories live on in these Lenten publications.[63]

Floral arrangements have also played a large part in fellowship among parishioners. Each Easter members can order lilies, and each Christmas they can order poinsettias in thanksgiving for or in memory of others. Arranged on the altars according to the seasons, dozens of these potted plants display the white in spring and the red in winter, adorning the front of the church and the Ministry Center. Included in the programs are alphabetized lists of those who gave the flowers, making readers more cognizant of those dear to their fellow worshippers.[64]

Parishioner Scooter Barnett has spearheaded annual Sunday gatherings such as "Saint James Day Celebration July 25, 1999," "Ministry Fair August 29, 1999," and "Connection Sunday" hosted in September 2018 and 2019. Although different names were attributed to these congregational gatherings, they had this in common: to heighten the awareness of Saint James' members of how they can come together in small groups, committees, projects, and events for many purposes, one being to reach out to others locally and elsewhere to spread the Gospel and offer assistance, as needed, through local and international missions.

To close this chapter that mentions only some of the activities that have evoked so much fulfillment at Saint James is this excerpt from Rev. Floyd William Finch, Jr., assistant to Rev. John Howard and Rev. Arthur Jenkins. Father Finch wrote:

> Love, Learn, Laugh, and Labor for God in the love of Jesus Christ. These 'Four L's... I... recommend them to every brother and sister of the St. James' Church family...Give your heart to Jesus Christ, and 'Rejoice in the Lord always; again, I will say, Rejoice'.[65]

CHAPTER TWENTY-FIVE

Saint James' Angel

A frequently asked theological question is "Do churches have angels?" In Revelation 2:1 John the Apostle begins, "To the angel of the church in Ephesus…:" Revelation 2:8 begins "To the angel of the church in Smyrna… And the list continues: to the angel of the church in Pergamum…Thyatira…Sardis…Philadelphia…Laodicea. Can one assume that churches have angels, depending on how one interprets the word "angel"? Does God assign angels to be with an assembly of His people? A "church angel" is a possibility.[1]

When asked to give his answer to this question, Rev. Jenkins said, "Years ago, when I was studying the Letters to the Seven Churches in the Book of Revelation, it came to me by the Holy Spirit that, 'Yes, we, too, have an angel.' Saint James has an Angel assigned to us by God. Since that day, early every Sunday morning as I pray for our worship, our Sabbath, I give thanks for the Angel of Saint James and ask God to give our Angel fresh messages for us. I also pray that we may have the heart and faith to listen."

Some of Saint James' worshippers can give testimony regarding their church's angel(s). One parishioner witnessed the image of a large angel with outstretched wings above Saint James during a storm. Jack Cranwell talks about Saint James' angels, using the plural form of "angel." He confidently states that for years he has sensed the presence of angels within the church and the Ministry Center. He has also witnessed spiritual beings on the church grounds, especially during burials in the cemetery. He declares that their semblance is big and strong and often comes bearing a sword to protect the premises.

Shirley Brown shared a fleeting but profound experience that she had one day as she drove into the church parking lot. She saw two angels, one over the church and the other over the Ministry Center. She saw their large forms enter through the doors, almost "stooping" to fit their long white robes with their gold sashes through the portals. Although she was not able to glimpse a visage on either one, she saw their long hair and each holding a double-edged sword. This hand-held weapon can symbolize authority (Isaiah 49:2), warfare (Matthew 10:34), protection (Ephesians 6:17), the Word of God (Hebrew 4:12), or truth (Hosea 6:5).[2] Ms. Brown called them "wakey-wakey" angels, an appellation to identify the holy beings who are here to wake us up spiritually. As a member of several prayer teams, she has seen visions of angels hover, as bodies of light, over people. In her intercessory prayers, she often invokes angels to come to minister to those in need.

In Dr. David Jeremiah's book entitled *Angels: Who They Are and How They Help…What the Bible Reveals*, he states, "Angels are mentioned 108 times in the Old Testament and 165 times in the New Testament,"[3] protecting, guiding, encouraging, delivering, enlightening, and empowering us.[4] He cautions that they are not meant to replace God in our lives, be reshaped to meet our own fancy, or receive worship.[5]

Psalm 34:7 states, "The angel of the Lord encamps around those who fear Him, and He delivers them." Psalm 91:11 states, "For He will command His angels concerning you to guard you in all your ways." Hebrews 1:14 asks, "Are not all angels ministering spirits sent to serve those who will inherit salvation?" Many of Saint James' parishioners believe that one or more angels "encamp" on the church campus to deliver, guard, and minister to the people, becoming a part of the three centuries of history.

REFLECTIONS OF REV. LOUISE WELD

In the newcomers' classes held at Saint James from time to time, people are asked what brought them to Saint James. Often they answer, "We were driving down Camp Road and saw the church, and we felt like something was drawing us here."

That "something," of course, may appear to be the lovely campus: the sun slanting through the white columns of the church, the graceful colonnade to the Ministry Center, the canopy of live oaks in the wide graveyard, and the steeple in the middle of it all, pointing to heaven. But in fact, the "something" is God himself, Who, since He called Abraham, has been forming and shaping a people for Himself and for His good purposes, which are, of course, to reconcile the world to Himself. The same God Who delivered the Israelites from bondage in Egypt, Who appointed prophets to encourage the people in exile in Babylon, the same God Who sent the followers of Jesus into all the world, in the 1600s sent missionaries from the Society for the Propagation of the Gospel in Foreign Parts from England to the Lowcountry of the Carolinas. And God Himself, who for 300 years has had His graceful hand on Saint James, drawing people to this kingdom community by various means, mostly through relationships, friend to friend, parents to children. And mostly TO relationships. Once they come, they find Saint James to be a people to whom personal relationships matter, with whom they experience the love of Christ.

I think of my own introduction to Saint James 20+ years ago, when I came to be an occasional substitute organist for my good friend Rev. Paul Zahl, and sensed immediately that this was a special place. I felt the presence of the Lord in the welcoming parishioners. When the time came that I needed to find a church of my own in which to settle, I slipped into the back pew of the church one Sunday and knew myself to have come home.

During the rectorship of Arthur Jenkins, it came to be recognized by many that Saint James had a special calling as a spiritual hospital, and often attracted and always welcomed broken people, including pastors from other churches. In the power of the Holy Spirit, the people of Saint James have loved them, prayed for them, and patched them up. Some stayed and became agents of grace and healing themselves; some, after a season, went on to share God's grace with others. I stayed, with no idea that God might have plans for me that were way beyond my occupying the back pew for worship on Sundays. That's one of the lovely things about Saint James. No matter the condition in which you arrive, no matter your misgivings about your gifts or your usefulness to the kingdom, God has a transforming plan for you to be a part of what He is up to, a plan for you to come to know the depth of His power and love, and a plan to use you as part of what He wants to accomplish on James Island and in the world. Love God, love people, build community.

As an unlikely candidate sent to seminary by Saint James, ordained at Saint James by Bishop Salmon, and then called to serve here, I often tell people that the only reason I dare to get into the pulpit to preach God's word, or to help a family in crisis, or to show up at a clergy meeting where I am the only woman in sight, is because this is a praying church who prays for their pastors. The people of Saint James expect the Holy Spirit to show up (especially where the priests may be lacking!) and to do for us what we cannot do for ourselves. The people of Saint James believe they, too, are called to share the Gospel and have done so with grace and eloquence year after year in every walk of life. I believe it is the faithful and persevering prayers of generation upon generation that make this history so rich a witness to God's love for His world.

One of the unique ways God has used Saint James in the greater body of Christ during the last few decades is as a church known to support women for ordained ministry. (See Chapter 20.) It seems that God has often said to our congregation and those we touch, "Look at Me. I am more than you think. I want to stretch you and to bless you. I want you to know all there is to know about Me." And so, for fifteen years, it is no small thing, the opportunity Arthur Jenkins has provided for a male and female priest to work together to model male/female leadership in the church. It has been a unique witness in our diocese-the mutual respect and collaboration as we have led our congregation to worship, to wrestle with hard issues personal and cultural, to offer counsel with both male and female perspectives, to disagree and reconcile, as we have committed to the hard work of relationship that is God's most useful way of conforming each of us to the image of Christ.

As you read the history of Saint James you cannot help think of the truth of Ecclesiastes-*for every season, for everything a season… a time to be born, and a time to die, a time to plant and a time to pluck up what has been planted… a time to kill and a time to heal…a time to break down and a time to build up.* Season after season, some of plenty and some of want, some of dissension and some of renewal (and many seasons in which both dissension and renewal go on at the same time), the priests and leaders and the congregation have initiated and persevered- embraced the difficult questions of the day, always seeking God's will, sometimes disagreeing with what they think they are hearing from God, but nevertheless, continuing to pray until they find unity.

Again and again, you also see the truth of Romans 8: 28: "And we know that in all things God works for the good of those who love Him, who have been called according to His purpose."

As you read the story of Saint James, you see the same concerns, season after season, guiding the decisions of the first Anglican families on James Island, and then later, vestries and priests and church leaders:

+ How do we establish a faithful presence of worshippers on James Island? First in our homes, whenever the preacher could make his way down the roads and over the creeks to James Island. Then we build the first of our churches, and the second, and the third… And we join with the Presbyterians. Why not?

+ How do we contribute to the growth and development of the island? What an interesting history of the acres of land Saint James acquired over the years and then sold or gave away—to Bishop Gadsden, to the community to be used for churches and schools, to build our Ministry Center, which would be both a worship center and a resource space for the island. Always the leaders with a view for what they could contribute to the welfare of the island.

+ How do we maintain the faith as delivered to the saints? We call priests who will maintain Biblical integrity, encourage Bible study and prayer. Both the pastors who have ministered here and those who have been raised up and sent forth from here testify that the Word of God is alive and powerful at Saint James.

+ How do we care for our people in such a way that they experience and display the love of Christ? By excellence in all forms of worship. By the focus always on personal relationship, first with God, and then with each other, in our families, through life groups, prayer groups, choirs and praise teams, ministry groups.

+ How do we encourage our young people to follow Jesus Christ as their Lord and Savior? We offer them opportunities at church and at home (and at school, with pizza, if necessary) and on mission trips and ski trips to learn

God's word and experience the Holy Spirit. And when, as has happened so often at Saint James, their faith bursts into flame, we bless them, listen to and learn from them.

+ How do we deal with loss and setbacks, criticisms, and disappointments (church buildings burning up or blowing away in a hurricane, people dying or leaving the church in anger, our theological dispute with the national church, our own personal struggles)? We keep our focus on Scripture, which contains everything necessary for teaching, reproof, correction, training in righteousness (2 Timothy 3: 16). And we encourage each other's faith with our presence, with prayer, and with casseroles when needed.

+ How do we reach out to our neighbors on James Island and around the world, with the good news of the saving grace of Jesus Christ? Through our Day School. By raising money. By supporting missionaries. By being missionaries ourselves. By joining other churches to form James Island Outreach.

Generation unto generation. Love God. Love people. Build community.

300 years ago James Island was rural. Until the 1940s Camp Road was a dusty, sandy connection between Folly Road and Riverland Drive. James Island farmers delivered milk and produce to the Charleston peninsula every morning by boat. Getting to church could be affected by the tides and the weather and the condition of your horse and buggy. People lived on what they caught, or killed, or grew: fish, shellfish, beef, pork, corn, cherries, apples, wild turkeys and deer. I love the problems considered by the vestry as late as 1948: not only how to get Camp Road paved, but how to keep the neighbors' hogs and cows off the church grounds.

These days the traffic from vacationers headed down Folly Road to the beach and others NOT going to church, are more likely to make you late for worship than a dirt road possibly with a cow in the middle of it. Today the old plantations are crowded neighborhoods with the names of plantations; the cotton, indigo, tomato fields are apartment complexes and shopping centers. All of which makes James Island a field ripe for the harvest of souls that Jesus spoke about.

After I read a draft of Virginia Bartels' wonderful account of Saint James, I wondered to myself -Why isn't Saint James three times the size it is? All the programs, all the ministries, all the extraordinary leaders and hardworking gifted parishioners…the wonderful worship, both traditional and contemporary, the generosity to those in need, the care for each other, the loyalty to tradition and also openness to change, the frequent, miraculous signs of divine guidance and intervention. My conclusion is that we are the people God wants us to be. He has shaped, sized, and positioned and equipped us uniquely for the work He has prepared for us as a church on James Island, now with so much development, so many new residents, many of whom have never heard the Gospel.

He still brings people down Camp Road who have no idea they are about to be drawn to the kingdom community that is Saint James. He also calls us to go out and invite them, our neighbors, our fellow workers, whomever He puts in our path. The history of God at Saint James is the history of His reconciling love for those created in His image, and gathered together for His good purposes. May the Gospel message be true in us, that we are known as His people by our love for each other and for His world. To God be the glory!

AUTHOR'S CLOSING THOUGHTS

Much of Saint James' story pertains to the vestrymen and vestrywomen who were elected and entrusted to build and maintain its six houses of worship that have sustained and enhanced the spiritual bonds with their Heavenly Father. A vestryman of one of Charleston's inner city churches—St. Michaels—stated in 1883 what he called a fundamental principle—"the Church is a perpetual institution… its property therefore belongs to all its future members as well as the present." I would like to add that a congregation's church belongs to its previous worshippers as well. That churchman in 1883 went on to say, "the living members…are bound to keep it in sound condition, and transmit it entire, and unencumbered to their successors."[1] Thus, the subtitle of my book stands: *Worshipping in the Presence of the Past*, and an even longer subtitle would also include *Worshipping in the Present for the Sake of the Future*.

A person often reflects on his life in his latter years and becomes cognizant of some changes he would make for the better if he had his life to live again. Likewise, generations of worshippers may reflect on the life of their church and realize that some eras might have been more pleasing in the eyes of God if His sons and daughters had made different decisions. So often man operates as best he can in circumstances based on what he knows and has at the time. Readers probably experienced a range of reactions to various topics and times of Saint James, from wincing at a few incidents to wondering in awe at many others.

I began this history of Saint James Church with the year 1720. Actually, it began much earlier than this. Its roots are in Genesis 1:1—"In the beginning God created the heavens and the earth." With a mere utterance, "God translate[d] divine sound into matter and being, thereby bringing the cosmos, the earth, and the earth's inhabitants, great and small, into temporal existence."[2] God selected prophets and poets and people from all walks of life to record His Word in the Old Testament. In the New Testament the most important Voice is that of His Son, our Lord and Savior, Who provided mankind, including those at Saint James for more than three centuries, with spiritual illumination—God's Light and Word incarnate. Using metaphors, lyrics, narratives, parables, and maxims, this sandal-footed Messiah imparted wisdom to save us from our sins in our temporal lives and to purify our souls for yet glorious, eternal lives with His Father, Who is our Father, too.

Aramaic, Hebrew, Greek, Syriac, Armenian, Coptic, Ethopic, Latin, German, English—all these languages across the centuries have been a part of the history that has made its way into the hymnals, prayer books, and Bibles placed in the pews of the six church buildings at the present site of Saint James.[3] History tells us that scholarly saints like John Wyclif and William Tyndal were deemed heretics and executed because of their efforts to bring this Word to the common man, such as those who ultimately have worshipped at Saint James.[4]

A humble man who walked the shores of Galilee over two thousand years ago is the one and same omniscient, omnipotent, omnipresent One on the shores that surround James Island, on the acreage of Saint James Church, on all the land masses of the earth. The Words of this charismatic Jewish rabbi—whether they were read, chanted, or preached—have been the focus for over three hundred years as the fishermen, farmers, and families of Saint James faced the altar—whichever one it was at the time—to absorb His messages into their beings, into their souls.

"Life marks a land," according to Southern historian Nell Graydon.[5] Feet have trod, ears have listened, eyes have seen, hands have built, mouths have prayed, where worshippers have marked this plot of land consecrated for the fellowship and salvation of God's people of Saint James. Their lives have been marking this soil for three centuries. Scripture records the history of God's people of ancient times. With no intention to elevate any other writing to the level of God's Word, we must still record the history of the human race in modern times.

Baptisms, Eucharists, confirmations, weddings, funerals, Christmases, Thanksgivings, and Easters have also marked life's seasons, magnified our human conditions, and honored our Maker. This history of Saint James affirms Romans 8: 37-39: "In all these things we are more than conquerors through Him Who loved us...Neither death nor life, nor angels, nor rulers, nor things present nor things to come, nor powers, nor height nor depth, not anything else in all creation, will be able to separate us from the love of God in Christ Jesus our Lord." This history of Saint James affirms that neither wars nor poverty nor politics nor disease nor disasters nor death—nor things past, present or future—can separate the worshippers of Saint James Church from their Master. For three centuries Saint James has been a symbol of what is eternal. Throughout the ages the congregation has sung, "Surely the presence of the Lord is in this place; you can feel His Mighty power and His grace." Take off your sandals, you visitors and worshippers at Saint James; you are standing on holy ground.

ACKNOWLEDGEMENTS

Clark and Louise Morrison, long-time church members, generously provided me with not only multi-generational records via church bulletins, records, pictures, legal documents, and newspaper articles but also stories and oral histories regarding Saint James. The family of Matt and Mary Townsend provided decades of church and diocesan records. The media specialists in Charleston's library on Calhoun Street assisted me as I researched Saint James in the South Carolina History Room

Other parishioners were very helpful with sharing documents: John and Kathy Mikell, Joel and Mary Porcher, Lillie McGougan, Gene Miller, Judy West, Steve and Debbie Morillo, Gresham and Carole Meggett, and Bonum Wilson, Jr. and his wife Janet. Mary Staats, daughter of Dr. Dan and Kitty Ellis, graciously gave me permission to quote much of her father's research regarding the church's history up to 1979, a history that was later extended by his wife Kitty in 1992. Berta Puckhaber and Rhonda Myers, parish coordinators, helped me find a wealth of preserved church records.

I am grateful to all who granted me interviews in person, on the phone, and through letters and emails: Beau Booker, Dr. James A. Brown, Shirley Brown, Rev. Elizabeth Bumpas, Lynda Owen Cole, Rev. Mark Cooke, Jack Cranwell, David Cupka, Rev. Mary Ellen Doran, Rev. Floyd Finch, Rev. Robert Horn, Rev. Chris Huff, Rev. Arthur Jenkins, Rev. Suzy McCall, Lillie McGougan, Clark and Louise Morrison, Rev. Jennie Olbrych, Rev. Craig Stephans, and Rev. Louise Weld.

For over two years I pondered the idea of writing about Saint James and then began reading other church histories. Initially, I asked Rev. Louise Weld to co-author the book with me. Instead, she has been my prayer warrior, sat in on interviews, and even invited two Boy Scouts to a meeting in her office to hear some of my stories as they worked on merit badges. To her credit, she helped me eliminate extraneous information, reorganize content for clarity, and edited multiple drafts. I was further inspired when Rev. Arthur

Jenkins telephoned to ask if I would write this book in celebration of our church's 300th anniversary.

I am extraordinarily grateful to Charleston's renowned artist Jim Booth, who used his artistic gifts to paint the picture—*Sea Island Glory*—of our beloved church Saint James and to allow me to use this masterpiece on the cover of this book.

I have called on the expertise of several editors. Many people whom I interviewed graciously read and edited portions pertaining to them. I wanted their stories to be accurate.

David Cupka, specializing in rare Low Country historical publications and owner of Palmetto Books, read multiple drafts, providing valuable feedback, especially regarding historical and church details.

Clark Morrison and John Mikell, who have worshipped at Saint James for decades, provided authentic, detailed feedback about the specifics of the church and the island.

Fred Whittle—a scholarly vestry member, avid reader, and gifted writer—assisted me especially with logic, accuracy, and diction.

Attorney Mark Evans helped with legal content regarding the litigation between The National Episcopal Church and the Anglican Diocese of South Carolina.

William (Will) Felts, a fellow faculty member in the James Island High English Department, used his skills as a journalism teacher to assist me with detailed editing of syntax, structure, logic, clarity, and organization.

Rev. Arthur Jenkins and Rev. Louise Weld provided valuable input regarding church details and theological insight in addition to their writing their own reflections on the history of our beloved church.

I appreciate my family. After hearing me say over and over again that I *wanted* to write this book, my daughter Melissa Ward Durinsky said, "Mama, just write the book!" My son Joseph D. Ward and his wife Mary Kate have championed me in all my undertakings as I wrote and rewrote draft after draft. My sister Julie G. Moon and my brothers Dr. James A. Brown and John Gregory Brown have encouraged me to see this project to its end. My husband Lt. Col. Richard "Dick" Bartels has sustained me with prayer and praise throughout each stage, especially when I felt both inadequate and overwhelmed with the task. My son-in-law Mark J. Durinsky has been my "technological guru," helping me with computer issues and saving multiple drafts for me.

Several sisters-in-Christ attending Saint James' women's retreats at our cabin "The Sanctuary" laid their hands on me and called upon the Holy Spirit to direct this book—a book intended to glorify God's work that He has done through His people. Members of the Friday Morning Women's Bible Study, Daughters of the Holy Cross Ruth Chapter, Saint James' prayer team, Saint James' vestry, as well as members of the James Island High 1967 graduating class have all lifted me in prayer as I struggled to do justice to a place and a people I hold dear to my heart.

FOOTNOTES

FOOTNOTES FOR CHAPTER ONE

¹ "An Unfinished History of St. James' Episcopal Church: James Island, South Carolina. The Story of a Pioneer Church on a Carolina Sea Island." Revised and edited by St. James' Historical Project. Charleston, SC. November 29, 1987, p. 1.

² Williams, George W. *St. Michael's: Charleston, 1751-1951, with Supplements, 1951-2001.* Columbia: College of Charleston Library, 2001, p. 1.

³ "An Unfinished History of St. James' Episcopal Church," p. 1.

⁴ Ibid.

⁵ Ibid, pp. 2-3.

⁶ Ibid, p. 4.

⁷ Ibid.

⁸ Ibid, pp. 4-5.

⁹ *St. James Sampler II* (with introduction entitled "History of St. James Church" by Dr. Daniel W. Ellis, Mrs. Kitty Ellis, and Mr. Stanley Cross). Charleston: Quin Press, no date listed (circa 1994), p. iii.

¹⁰ Ibid, p. xii.

¹¹ Porwoll, Paul. *Against All Odds: History of Saint Andrew's Parish Church, Charleston, 1706-2013.* Bloomington, IN: WestBow Press, 2014, pp. 9-10.

¹² Ibid, p. 13.

¹³ "An Unfinished History of St. James' Episcopal Church," pp. 5-6.

¹⁴ Stringer-Robinson, Gretchen. "The Sacrifices of the Slaves of James Island Have Not Been Forgotten." *Bugle James Island.* February 8, 2017, p. 1.

¹⁵ Anderson, Dorothy Middleton and Margaret Middleton Rivers Eastman. *St. Philip's Church of Charleston: An Early History of the Oldest Parish in South Carolina.* Charleston, SC: The History Press, 2014, p. 9.

¹⁶ Ibid.

[17] Porwoll, p. 10.

[18] Ibid, pp. 12-14.

[19] Ibid, pp. 12-13.

[20] Payne, Barbara R. editor. *Amazing Grace: The Parish Church of St. Helena Beaufort, South Carolina.* Beaufort: Lydia Inglett Ltd. Publishing, 2012, p. 28.

[21] Porwoll, p. 13.

[22] Ibid, p. 4.

[23] Bostick, Douglas W. *A Brief History of James Island: Jewel of the Sea Islands.* Charleston: History Press, 2008. p. 11.

[24] *James Island and Johns Island Historical Survey.* Project carried out for South Carolina Department of Archives and History. City of Charleston and Charleston County. Summer 1989, p. 6. http://www.jamesislandsc.us/Data/sites/1/media/james-island-and-johns-island-historical-survey.pdf.

[25] "An Unfinished History of St. James' Episcopal Church," p. 4.

[26] Bostick, p. 9.

[27] Porwoll, p. 7.

[28] Ibid, p. 11.

[29] Ibid, p. 9.

[30] Bonstelle, Carolyn Ackerly and Geordie Buxton. *Images of America: James Island.* Charleston: Arcadia Publishing, 2008, preface.

[31] "Parish Profile: St. James' Episcopal Church." Charleston, SC. 1998, p. 19.

[32] Ibid, p. 20.

[33] An Unfinished History of St. James' Episcopal Church," pp. 8-9.

[34] Bostick, p. 15.

[35] *St. James Sampler II,* p. xii.

[36] Bostick, p. 9.

[37] Ibid, p. 21.

[38] Porwoll, p. 9.

[39] Bostick, pp. 36-37.

[40] Ibid, pp. 28-29.

[41] Anderson, p. 10.

[42] Rivers, Captain E. L. "A History of St. James' Episcopal Church, James Island." 1894. Revised and completed by Daniel W. Ellis, 1930. Published by the Vestry in connection with the Bi-Centennial Service of St. James' Church, held November 9, 1930, p 1.

[43] Way, Rev. William. *The History of Grace Church, Charleston, South Carolina: The First Hundred Years.* Durham, NC: Seeman Printery, 1948, p. ix.

FOOTNOTES FOR CHAPTER TWO

1. *St. James Sampler II* (with introduction entitled "History of St. James Church" by Dr. Daniel W. Ellis, Mrs. Kitty Ellis, and Mr. Stanley Cross). Charleston: Quin Press, no date listed (circa 1994), p iii.

2. Ibid, p. xii.

3. Williams, George W. *St. Michael's: Charleston, 1751-1951, with Supplements, 1951-2001.* Columbia: College of Charleston Library, 2001, p. 315.

4. Porwoll, Paul. *Against All Odds: History of Saint Andrew's Parish Church, Charleston, 1706-2013.* Bloomington, IN: WestBow Press, 2014, pp, 45-46.

5. Anderson, Dorothy Middleton and Margaret Middleton Rivers Eastman. *St. Philip's Church of Charleston: An Early History of the Oldest Parish in South Carolina.* Charleston, SC: The History Press, 2014, p. 41.

6. Porwoll, p. 29.

7. Ibid, p. 30.

8. Anderson, p. 49

9. Payne, Barbara R. editor. *Amazing Grace: The Parish Church of St. Helena Beaufort, South Carolina.* Beaufort: Lydia Inglett Ltd. Publishing, 2012. p. 20.

10. "An Unfinished History of St. James' Episcopal Church: James Island, South Carolina. The Story of a Pioneer Church on a Carolina Sea Island." Revised and edited by St. James' Historical Project. Charleston, SC. November 29, 1987, p. 5.

11. Porwoll, p. 68.

12. *St. James Sampler II*, p. iv.

13. Porwoll, p. 71.

14. Ibid, p. 72.

15. Ibid, pp. 45-47.

16. Ibid, p. 49.

17. Ibid, p. 52.

18. Ibid, p. 73.

19. Ibid, p. 53.

20. Hinson, William G. "Transcribed from Manuscript Attributed to Wm. G. Hinson—Sketch of James Island, South Carolina. Based on Topographic Inquiries March 9-12, 1895. Cornell University, Ithaca, NY. June 12, 1895. Filed 19 March 1975, p. 6.

21. *St. James Sampler II*, p. xii.

22. Video Scenarios—St. James' Episcopal Church, James Island, Charleston County, South Carolina. 11/23/1987-88. p. 8.

23. An Unfinished History of St. James' Episcopal Church, p. 2.

24. Porwoll, p. 68.

25. *St. James Sampler II*, p. xii.

[26] Dalcho, Frederick, M.D. *An Historical Account of the Protestant Episcopal Church in South Carolina 1670-1820.* Charleston: E. Thayer (at his theological bookstore—Broadstreet), 1820, p. 342.

[27] Haynie, Connie Walpole. *Images of America: Johns Island.* Charleston: Arcadia Publishing, 2007, p. 15.

[28] Porwoll, p. 69.

[29] Anderson, p. 34.

[30] *St. James Sampler II*, p. iv.

[31] Porwoll, p. 68.

[32] Ibid, p. 70.

[33] Anderson, p. 80.

[34] Porwoll, p. 70.

[35] Anderson, p. 80.

[36] Porwoll, p. 71.

[37] Anderson, p. 81.

[38] Porwoll, p. 45.

[39] Ibid, p. 72.

[40] Ibid, p. 73.

[41] *St. James Sampler II*, p. ix.

FOOTNOTES FOR CHAPTER THREE

[1] Anderson, Dorothy Middleton and Margaret Middleton Rivers Eastman. *St. Philip's Church of Charleston: An Early History of the Oldest Parish in South Carolina.* Charleston, SC: The History Press, 2014, p. 85.

[2] Anderson, p. 82.

[3] *St. James Sampler II* (with introduction entitled "History of St. James Church" by Dr. Daniel W. Ellis, Mrs. Kitty Ellis, and Mr. Stanley Cross). Charleston: Quin Press, no date listed (circa 1994), p. iv.

[4] Ibid.

[5] Payne, Barbara R. editor. *Amazing Grace: The Parish Church of St. Helena Beaufort, South Carolina.* Beaufort: Lydia Inglett Ltd. Publishing, 2012, p. 33.

[6] Porwoll, Paul. *Against All Odds: History of Saint Andrew's Parish Church, Charleston, 1706-2013.* Bloomington, IN: WestBow Press, 2014, p. 354.

[7] Ibid, p. 74.

[8] Ibid, p. 75.

[9] Ibid, p. 76.

[10] Ibid, p. 77.

[11] Ibid, p. 78.

[12] Ibid.

[13] Dalcho, Frederick, M.D. *An Historical Account of the Protestant Episcopal Church in South Carolina 1670-1820.* Charleston: E. Thayer (at his theological bookstore—Broadstreet), 1820, p. 341.

[14] Porwoll, pp. 79-81.

[15] Ibid, p. 80.

[16] Ibid, pp. 80-81.

[17] Dickerson, June. "Cemetery: Saint James Episcopal Church James Island, S.C." November 26, 2001. (no page—timeline in front of booklet).

[18] Ibid, p. 13.

[19] Ibid, p. 22.

[20] Video Scenarios—St. James' Episcopal Church, James Island, Charleston County, South Carolina. 11/23/1987-88, scene 3.

[21] *St. James Sampler II*, p. ix.

FOOTNOTES FOR CHAPTER FOUR

[1] "An Unfinished History of St. James' Episcopal Church: James Island, South Carolina. The Story of a Pioneer Church on a Carolina Sea Island." Revised and edited by St. James' Historical Project. Charleston, SC. November 29, 1987, p.8.

[2] *St. James Sampler II* (with introduction entitled "History of St. James Church" by Dr. Daniel W. Ellis, Mrs. Kitty Ellis, and Mr. Stanley Cross). Charleston: Quin Press, no date listed (circa 1994), p. ix.

[3] Porwoll, Paul. *Against All Odds: History of Saint Andrew's Parish Church, Charleston, 1706-2013.* Bloomington, IN: WestBow Press, 2014, p. 93.

[4] Ibid, pp. 93-94.

[5] Ibid, p. 94.

[6] *St. James Sampler II*, p. ix.

[7] "Saint James Church. Love God. Love People. Build Community" website. https://saint-james.org/our-history 2019.

[8] *St. James Sampler II*, p. ix.

[9] Dalcho, Frederick, M.D. *An Historical Account of the Protestant Episcopal Church in South Carolina 1670-1820.* Charleston: E. Thayer (at his theological bookstore—Broad Street), 1820, p. 343.

[10] *St. James Sampler II*, p. xii.

[11] Porwoll, p. 94.

[12] Williams, George W. *St. Michael's: Charleston, 1751-1951, with Supplements, 1951-2001.* Columbia: College of Charleston Library, 2001, pp. 38-39.

[13] *St. James Sampler II*, p. xii.

[14] Way, Rev. William. *The History of Grace Church, Charleston, South Carolina: The First Hundred Years.* Durham, NC: Seeman Printery, 1948, pp. ix-x.

[15] "An Unfinished History of St. James' Episcopal Church," p. 11.

[16] Ibid.

[17] McLeod, W. E. "An Outline of the History of James Island, S.C." Program in Honor of James Islanders Serving in the Armed Forces. Published by the Exchange Club of James Island, June 1944, no page number.

[18] Bostick, Douglas W. *A Brief History of James Island: Jewel of the Sea Islands.* Charleston: History Press, 2008, p. 44.

[19] Porwoll, p. 98.

[20] Anderson, Dorothy Middleton and Margaret Middleton Rivers Eastman. *St. Philip's Church of Charleston: An Early History of the Oldest Parish in South Carolina.* Charleston, SC: The History Press, 2014, pp. 98-99.

[21] *St. James Sampler II*, p. xii.

[22] Anderson, p. 101.

[23] *James Island and Johns Island Historical Survey.* Project Carried out for South Carolina Department of Archives and History. City of Charleston and Charleston County. Summer 1989. http://www.jamesislandsc.us/Data/sites/1/media/james-island-and-johns-island-historical-survey.pdf, p. 18.

[24] Payne, Barbara R. editor. *Amazing Grace: The Parish Church of St. Helena Beaufort, South Carolina.* Beaufort: Lydia Inglett Ltd. Publishing, 2012, p. 57.

[25] *St. James Sampler II*, p. iv.

[26] Ibid, p. ix.

[27] Porwoll, p. 101.

[28] Ibid, p. 102.

[29] Ibid, p. 105.

[30] Ibid, p. 99.

[31] Ibid, p. 103.

[32] Payne, p. 58.

[33] Anderson, p. 103.

[34] Porwoll, p. 101.

[35] Ibid, p. 106.

[36] *St. James Sampler II*, pp. iv-v.

FOOTNOTES FOR CHAPTER FIVE

[1] Bresee, Clyde. *How Grand a Flame: A Chronicle of a Plantation Family 1813-1947.* Chapel Hill: Algonquin Books, 1992, p. 14.

2   Ibid, p. 28.

3   Bostick, Douglas. W. *A Brief History of James Island: Jewel of the Sea Islands*. Charleston: History Press, 2008, p. 52.

4   "Historical Sketch of St. James' Parish, James Island, South Carolina" (no further publishing information given; contents reveal publication 1969 or later), p. 1.

5   Bostick, p. 52.

6   Hinson, William G. "Transcribed from Manuscript Attributed to Wm. G. Hinson—Sketch of James Island, South Carolina. Based on Topographic Inquiries March 9-12, 1895. Cornell University, Ithaca, NY. June 12, 1895. Filed 19 March 1975, p. 3.

7   Bostick, p. 52.

8   Video Scenarios—St. James' Episcopal Church, James Island, Charleston County, South Carolina. 11/23/1987-88, p. 8.

9   Bonstelle, Carolyn Ackerly and Geordie Buxton. *Images of America: James Island*. Charleston: Arcadia Publishing, 2008, p.70.

10 Porwoll, Paul. *Against All Odds: History of Saint Andrew's Parish Church, Charleston, 1706-2013*. Bloomington, IN: WestBow Press, 2014, p. 113.

11 *St. James Sampler II* (with introduction entitled "History of St. James Church" by Dr. Daniel W. Ellis, Mrs. Kitty Ellis, and Mr. Stanley Cross). Charleston: Quin Press, no date listed (circa 1994), p. x.

12 "St. James Church James Island." No author or publishing information available. (document consisting of seven double-spaced typed pages included in church's historical records at the parish)

13 Hinson, p. 8.

14 "An Unfinished History of St. James' Episcopal Church: James Island, South Carolina. The Story of a Pioneer Church on a Carolina Sea Island." Revised and edited by St. James' Historical Project. Charleston, SC. November 29, 1987, p. 12.

15 *St. James Sampler II*, p. xii.

16 Stackhouse, Mrs. M.S. "St. James Church James Island, S.C. 1947." Typed four-page history mailed from Mrs. M.S. Stackhouse of Dillon, S.C. to Mr. William McLeod February 1953, p. 3.

17 *St. James Sampler II*, p. x.

18 Porwoll, pp. 111-112.

19 Ibid, pp. 110-11.

20 Ibid, p. 112.

21 Ibid, p. 114.

22 "Historical Sketch of St. James' Parish," p. 1.

23 Porwoll, pp. 113-114.

24 Ibid, p. 114.

25 Ibid, p. 115.

26 Williams, George W. *St. Michael's: Charleston, 1751-1951, with Supplements, 1951-2001.* Columbia: College of Charleston Library, 2001, pp. 316, 318.

27 Porwoll, p. 115.

28 Ibid, p. 117.

29 *St. James Sampler II*, p. x.

30 Williams, p. 316.

31 *St. James Sampler II*, p. x.

32 "Cemetery: Saint James Episcopal Church James Island, S.C." published by the Cemetery Committee of Saint James. April 24, 2005, p. 8.

33 *St. James Sampler II*, p. xiii.

34 "Historical Sketch of St. James' Parish," pp. 1-2.

35 *St. James Sampler II*, p. x.

36 Ibid.

37 *St. James Sampler II*, p. xiii.

38 Bostick, p. 49.

39 Historical Sketch of St. James' Parish," p. 2.

40 Payne, Barbara R. editor. *Amazing Grace: The Parish Church of St. Helena Beaufort, South Carolina.* Beaufort: Lydia Inglett Ltd. Publishing, 2012, p. 84.

41 Bostick, p. 92.

42 Porwoll, p. 121.

43 Ibid.

44 Ibid, p. 122.

45 Anderson, Dorothy Middleton and Margaret Middleton Rivers Eastman. *St. Philip's Church of Charleston: An Early History of the Oldest Parish in South Carolina.* Charleston, SC: The History Press, 2014, p. 141.

46 Thomas, Albert Sidney. *Historical Account of the Protestant Episcopal Church in South Carolina 1820-1957: Being a Continuation of Dalcho's Account 1670-1820.* Charleston: The R.L. Bryan Company, 1957, p. 335.

47 *St. James Sampler II*, p. v.

48 Ibid, p. xiii.

49 Stackhouse, p. 2.

50 *St. James Sampler II*, p. x.

51 Bostick, p. 49.

52 *St. James Sampler II*, p. x.

53 Bostick, p. 49.

54 Hinson, pp. 8-9.

55 "Saint James Church. Love God. Love People. Build Community" website. https://saint-james.org. 2019.

⁵⁶ Bostick, p. 49.

⁵⁷ Ibid, p. 50.

⁵⁸ "Cemetery: Saint James Episcopal," p. 22.

⁵⁹ Ibid, p. 21.

FOOTNOTES FOR CHAPTER SIX

¹ "An Unfinished History of St. James' Episcopal Church: James Island, South Carolina. The Story of a Pioneer Church on a Carolina Sea Island." Revised and edited by St. James' Historical Project. Charleston, SC. November 29, 1987, p. 11.

² Porwoll, Paul. *Against All Odds: History of Saint Andrew's Parish Church, Charleston, 1706-2013.* Bloomington, IN: WestBow Press, 2014, p. 149.

³ Ibid, pp. 149-150.

⁴ Bostick, Douglas. W. *A Brief History of James Island: Jewel of the Sea Islands.* Charleston: History Press, 2008, p. 57.

⁵ Ibid, p. 57.

⁶ Ibid.

⁷ Jarrell, Frank P. "Bresee's Latest Goes Back to Past." *Post and Courier.* No date available, p. D1.

⁸ Hayes, Jim. *James and Related Sea Islands.* Charleston: Walker, Evans, and Cogswell, 1978, p. 122.

⁹ "Saint James Church. Love God. Love People. Build Community" website. https://saint-james.org. 2019.

¹⁰ "Cemetery: Saint James Episcopal Church James Island, S.C." published by the Cemetery Committee of Saint James. April 24, 2005, p. 12.

¹¹ "Saint James Church. website. https://saint-james.org. 2019.

¹² "Historical Sketch of St. James' Parish, James Island, South Carolina" (no further publishing information given; contents reveal publication 1969 or later), p. 2.

¹³ Bostick, pp. 57-58, 67.

¹⁴ Ibid, pp 57, 81.

¹⁵ *St. James Sampler II* (with introduction entitled "History of St. James Church" by Dr. Daniel W. Ellis, Mrs. Kitty Ellis, and Mr. Stanley Cross). Charleston: Quin Press, no date listed (circa 1994), p. xiii.

¹⁶ Ibid, p. v.

¹⁷ Hayes, p. 85.

¹⁸ Williams, George W. *St. Michael's: Charleston, 1751-1951, with Supplements, 1951-2001.* Columbia: College of Charleston Library, 2001, p. 97.

¹⁹ Anderson, Dorothy Middleton and Margaret Middleton Rivers Eastman. *St. Philip's Church of Charleston: An Early History of the Oldest Parish in South Carolina.* Charleston, SC: The History Press, 2014, p. 144.

[20] Ibid, p. 145.

[21] Bostick, p. 82.

[22] Bresee, Clyde. *How Grand a Flame: A Chronicle of a Plantation Family 1813-1947*. Chapel Hill: Algonquin Books, 1992, p. 108.

[23] Hinson, William G. "Transcribed from Manuscript Attributed to Wm. G. Hinson—Sketch of James Island, South Carolina. Based on Topographic Inquiries March 9-12, 1895. Cornell University, Ithaca, NY. June 12, 1895. Filed 19 March 1975, p. 9.

[24] Ibid, pp. 9-11.

[25] Bostick, p. 74.

[26] Ibid, p. 76.

[27] Ibid, p. 82.

[28] Payne, Barbara R. editor. *Amazing Grace: The Parish Church of St. Helena Beaufort, South Carolina*. Beaufort: Lydia Inglett Ltd. Publishing, 2012, p. 114.

[29] Way, Rev. William. *The History of Grace Church, Charleston, South Carolina: The First Hundred Years*. Durham, NC: Seeman Printery, 1948, p. 51.

FOOTNOTES FOR CHAPTER SEVEN

[1] Payne, Barbara R. editor. *Amazing Grace: The Parish Church of St. Helena Beaufort, South Carolina*. Beaufort: Lydia Inglett Ltd. Publishing, 2012, p. 123.

[2] Ibid, p. 125.

[3] Williams, George W. *St. Michael's: Charleston, 1751-1951, with Supplements, 1951-2001*. Columbia: College of Charleston Library, 2001, p. 101.

[4] Porwoll, Paul. *Against All Odds: History of Saint Andrew's Parish Church, Charleston, 1706-2013*. Bloomington, IN: WestBow Press, 2014, p. 183.

[5] Video Scenarios—St. James' Episcopal Church, James Island, Charleston County, South Carolina. 11/23/1987-88, p. 7.

[6] Rivers, Captain E. L. "A History of St. James' Episcopal Church, James Island." 1894. Revised and completed by Daniel W. Ellis, 1930. Published by the Vestry in connection with the Bi-Centennial Service of St. James' Church, held November 9, 1930, p. 2.

[7] Bostick, Douglas. W. *A Brief History of James Island: Jewel of the Sea Islands*. Charleston: History Press, 2008, p. 19.

[8] Ibid, p. 89.

[9] *James Island and Johns Island Historical Survey*. Project carried out for South Carolina Department of Archives and History. City of Charleston and Charleston County. Summer 1989. http://www.jamesislandsc.us/Data/sites/1/media/james-island-and-johns-island-historical-survey.pdf, p. 28.

[10] Hinson, William G. "Transcribed from Manuscript Attributed to Wm. G. Hinson—Sketch of James Is-

land, South Carolina." Based on Topographic Inquiries March 9-12, 1895. Cornell University, Ithaca, NY. June 12, 1895. Filed 19 March 1975, p. 4.

[11] Porwoll, p. 161.

[12] Payne, p. 84.

[13] Hinson, p. 8.

[14] Porwoll, p. 162.

[15] Ibid, p. 163.

[16] Ibid, p. 175.

[17] *St. James Sampler II* (with introduction entitled "History of St. James Church" by Dr. Daniel W. Ellis, Mrs. Kitty Ellis, and Mr. Stanley Cross). Charleston: Quin Press, no date listed (circa 1994), p. v.

[18] Payne, p. 128.

[19] Bresee, Clyde. *How Grand a Flame: A Chronicle of a Plantation Family 1813-1947*. Chapel Hill: Algonquin Books, 1992, p. 182.

[20] Ibid, p. 201.

[21] Graydon, Nell S. *Tales of Edisto*. Orangeburg, SC: Sandlapper Publishing Co., Inc., 1955. Seventh printing, January 1983, p. 151.

[22] "Cemetery: Saint James Episcopal Church James Island, S.C." published by the Cemetery Committee of Saint James. April 24, 2005, p. 6.

[23] *St. James Sampler II,* p. v.

[24] Williams, p. 160.

[25] Porwoll, p. 177.

[26] *James Island and Johns Island Historical Survey*, p. 28.

[27] Bostick, p. 101.

[28] Anderson, Dorothy Middleton and Margaret Middleton Rivers Eastman. *St. Philip's Church of Charleston: An Early History of the Oldest Parish in South Carolina*. Charleston, SC: The History Press, 2014, p. 146.

[29] Bostick, pp. 89, 101.

[30] *James Island and Johns Island Historical Survey*, p. 28.

[31] Hayes, Jim. *James and Related Sea Islands*. Charleston: Walker, Evans, and Cogswell, 1978, p. 84.

[32] Bostick, p. 47.

[33] *James Island and Johns Island Historical Survey*, p. 18.

[34] "Cemetery: Saint James Episcopal," p. 32.

[35] *James Island and Johns Island Historical Survey*, p. 28.

[36] Hayes, p. 88.

[37] Bostick, p. 50.

[38] Hinson, pp. 2, 6.

[39] *St. James Sampler II,* p. xiii.

[40] Ibid, p. v.

[41] Ibid, p. xiii.

[42] "St. James Church James Island." No author or publishing information available. (document consisting of seven double-spaced typed pages included in church's historical records at the parish).

[43] *St. James Sampler II*, p. x.

[44] "An Unfinished History of St. James' Episcopal Church: James Island, South Carolina. The Story of a Pioneer Church on a Carolina Sea Island." Revised and edited by St. James' Historical Project. Charleston, SC. November 29, 1987, p. 13.

[45] "St. James Church James Island."

[46] *St. James Sampler II*, p. x.

[47] Thomas, Albert Sidney. *Historical Account of the Protestant Episcopal Church in South Carolina 1820-1957: Being a Continuation of Dalcho's Account 1670-1820.* Charleston: The R.L. Bryan Company, 1957, p. 335.

[48] *St. James Sampler II*, p. x.

[49] Rivers and Ellis, pp. 2-3.

[50] "An Unfinished History of St. James' Episcopal Church," p. 14.

[51] Thomas, p. 336.

[52] "Saint James Church. Love God. Love People. Build Community." website. https://saint-james.org. 2019.

[53] Olbrych, Rev. Jennie. E-mail. July 19, 2017.

[54] Hayes, pp. 2, 86.

[55] Mikell, John. Personal interview. July 2018.

[56] "Bishop's Journal." Article among Saint James' historical papers. "May 1903" written at the top of the copy. No other publishing information available.

[57] Hayes, p. 126.

[58] "Cemetery: Saint James Episcopal," p. 16.

[59] Ibid, p. 6a.

[60] Thomas, p. 336.

[61] Hayden, Frances. "St. James Church to be Included in Garden Tour." *The News and Courier*. October 4, 1953, p. C6.

[62] *St. James Sampler II*, p. v.

[63] Hayden, p. C6.

[64] Ibid.

[65] Ibid.

[66] *St. James Sampler II*, p. vi.

[67] "Certificate of Incorporation." Granted to Saint James by the State of South Carolina. May 14, 1903.

[68] Hayden, p. C6.

[69] *St. James Sampler II*, p. xi.

[70] *St. James Sampler II*, p. xiii.

[71] Rivers and Ellis, p. 3.

[72] *St. James Sampler II*, p. xi.

[73] Haynie, Connie Walpole. *Images of America: Johns Island.* Charleston: Arcadia Publishing, 2007, p. 15.

[74] "Historical Sketch of St. James' Parish, James Island, South Carolina" (no further publishing information given; contents reveal publication 1969 or later), p. 3.

[75] Ibid.

[76] St. James Episc. Church, James Island, SCHS 50-94 RNC.

[77] Rivers and Ellis, p. 3.

[78] Olbrych, Rev. Jennie. E-mail. July 19. 2017.

[79] "Cemetery: Saint James Episcopal," p. 5.

[80] Olbrych, Rev. Jennie. E-mail. July 19. 2017.

[81] "Cemetery: Saint James Episcopal," p. 5.

[82] Hayden, p. C6.

[83] "Cemetery: Saint James Episcopal," no page (listed near front of booklet)

FOOTNOTES FOR CHAPTER EIGHT

[1] Bresee, Clyde. *Sea Island Yankee.* Chapel Hill: Algonquin Books of Chapel Hill, 1986.

[2] Ibid, pp. 25-26.

[3] Ibid, p. 62.

[4] Ibid, pp. 64-66.

[5] Ibid, p. 66.

[6] Ibid, p.67.

[7] Ibid, pp. 68-70.

[8] Ibid, p. 175.

[9] Ibid, p. 176.

[10] Ibid.

[11] Ibid, p. 177.

[12] Ibid, pp.187-188.

[13] Ibid, jacket cover.

[14] Ibid.

FOOTNOTES FOR CHAPTER NINE

1 Bostick, Douglas. W. *A Brief History of James Island: Jewel of the Sea Islands*. Charleston: History Press, 2008, p. 123.

2 Ibid, p. 124.

3 Hayes, Jim. *James and Related Sea Islands*. Charleston: Walker, Evans, and Cogswell, 1978, p. 87.

4 Bostick, p. 102.

5 Ibid, p. 121.

6 Ibid, p. 117.

7 Ibid, p. 118.

8 *St. James Sampler II* (with introduction entitled "History of St. James Church" by Dr. Daniel W. Ellis, Mrs. Kitty Ellis, and Mr. Stanley Cross). Charleston: Quin Press, no date listed (circa 1994), p. xi.

9 Stackhouse, Mrs. M.S. "St. James Church James Island, S.C. 1947." Typed four-page history mailed from Mrs. M.S. Stackhouse of Dillon, S.C. to Mr. William McLeod February 1953, p. 4.

10 "An Unfinished History of St. James' Episcopal Church: James Island, South Carolina. The Story of a Pioneer Church on a Carolina Sea Island." Revised and edited by St. James' Historical Project. Charleston, SC. November 29, 1987, p.15.

11 Payne, Barbara R. editor. *Amazing Grace: The Parish Church of St. Helena Beaufort, South Carolina*. Beaufort: Lydia Inglett Ltd. Publishing, 2012, p. 149.

12 Morrison, Clark, John Mikell, and Joel Porcher. Personal interview. July 2018.

13 "An Unfinished History of St. James' Episcopal Church," p. 2.

14 Maher, John Edward. *An Old Timer's Memories of Charleston, South Carolina*. Summerville, SC: Words Unlimited, 1992, pp. 115-120.

15 Saint James vestry minutes, March 1937.

16 "An Unfinished History of St. James' Episcopal Church," p. 15.

17 Rivers, Captain E. L. "A History of St. James' Episcopal Church, James Island." 1894. Revised and completed by Daniel W. Ellis, 1930. Published by the Vestry in connection with the Bi-Centennial Service of St. James' Church, held November 9, 1930, p.3.

FOOTNOTES FOR CHAPTER TEN

1 "Cemetery: Saint James Episcopal Church James Island, S.C." published by the Cemetery Committee of Saint James. April 24, 2005, p. 32.

2 Saint James vestry minutes, April 2, 1945.

3 "An Unfinished History of St. James' Episcopal Church: James Island, South Carolina. The Story of a Pioneer Church on a Carolina Sea Island." Revised and edited by St. James' Historical Project. Charleston, SC. November 29, 1987, p. 15.

4 Porwoll, Paul. *Against All Odds: History of Saint Andrew's Parish Church, Charleston, 1706-2013*. Bloom-

ington, IN: WestBow Press, 2014, p. 207.

5   Saint James vestry minutes, April 1946.

6   "Historical Sketch of St. James' Parish, James Island, South Carolina" (no further publishing information given; contents reveal publication 1969 or later), p. 3.

7   Saint James vestry minutes, April 24, 1943.

8   "Cemetery: Saint James Episcopal Church" (no page—in front of booklet).

9   Payne, Barbara R. editor. *Amazing Grace: The Parish Church of St. Helena Beaufort, South Carolina.* Beaufort: Lydia Inglett Ltd. Publishing, 2012, p. 160.

10 Saint James vestry minutes, April 2, 1945.

11 Stackhouse, Mrs. M.S. "St. James Church James Island, S.C. 1947." Typed four-page history mailed from Mrs. M.S. Stackhouse of Dillon, S.C. to Mr. William McLeod February 1953, p. 4.

12 Saint James vestry minutes, January 19, 1947.

13 *St. James Sampler II* (with introduction entitled "History of St. James Church" by Dr. Daniel W. Ellis, Mrs. Kitty Ellis, and Mr. Stanley Cross). Charleston: Quin Press, no date listed (circa 1994), p. xiii.

14 Ibid, p. xi.

15 "The Rev. Canon E.B. Guerry Dies." *The Post and Courier.* October 20, 1992, p. B 2.

16 Saint James vestry minutes, May 9, 1946.

17 Saint James vestry minutes, January 9, 1952.

18 *St. James Sampler II*, p. vi.

19 Hayden, Frances. "St. James Church to be Included in Garden Tour." *The News and Courier.* October 4, 1953, p. C6.

20 Stackhouse, p. 4.

21 "An Unfinished History of St. James' Episcopal Church," p. 15.

22 "Cemetery: Saint James Episcopal Church" (no page—timeline in front of booklet).

23 "St. James Church Parish House Will Be Dedicated Today." *The News and Courier.* October 30, 1949. No page number available.

24 Stackhouse, p. 4.

25 St. James Church Parish House Will Be Dedicated Today."

26 *St. James Sampler II*, p. vi.

FOOTNOTES FOR CHAPTER ELEVEN

1   "Saint James Church. Love God. Love People. Build Community." website. https://saint-james.org. 2019.

2   "The Rev. Canon E.B. Guerry Dies." *The Post and Courier.* October 20, 1992, p. B 2.

3   Hayden, Frances. "St. James Church to be Included in Garden Tour." *The News and Courier.* October 4,

1953. p. C6.

4   Simmons, William H. "Junior Warden's Final Report." *Saint James Congregational Report.* January 15, 1989, p. 12.

5   Payne, Barbara R. editor. *Amazing Grace: The Parish Church of St. Helena Beaufort, South Carolina.* Beaufort: Lydia Inglett Ltd. Publishing, 2012, pp. 166-167.

6   Saint James vestry minutes, November 8, 1954.

7   Saint James vestry minutes, June 30, 1955.

8   "An Unfinished History of St. James' Episcopal Church: James Island, South Carolina. The Story of a Pioneer Church on a Carolina Sea Island." Revised and edited by St. James' Historical Project. Charleston, SC. November 29, 1987, p. 15.

9   Saint James vestry minutes, January 25, 1959.

10 *St. James Sampler II* (with introduction entitled "History of St. James Church" by Dr. Daniel W. Ellis, Mrs. Kitty Ellis, and Mr. Stanley Cross). Charleston: Quin Press, no date listed (circa 1994), p. vi.

11 Saint James vestry minutes, September 11, 1957.

12 Saint James vestry minutes, February 2, 1959.

13 Saint James vestry minutes, January 8, 1958.

14 Saint James vestry minutes, September 4, 1958.

15 Saint James vestry minutes, March 2, 1959.

16 Saint James vestry minutes, November 22, 1959.

17 Williams, George W. *St. Michael's: Charleston, 1751-1951, with Supplements, 1951-2001.* Columbia: College of Charleston Library, 2001, p. 128.

18 Campbell, Marjorie. "Cornerstone Laying Set for St. James Church." *The News and Courier.* May 10, 1959, p. C4.

19 Ibid.

20 "Laying of Cornerstone: Remarks by the Rector—The Rev. Edward B. Guerry." St. James Episcopal Church. May 10, 1959.

21 "The Order for Laying the Cornerstone of St. James Church, James Island, Diocese of South Carolina." Saint James Church Program. May 10, 1959.

22 "New St. James Church Opens Its Doors Today." *The News and Courier.* August 28, 1960, p. C4.

23 Saint James vestry minutes, July 24, 1960.

24 *St. James Sampler II,* p. xi.

FOOTNOTES FOR CHAPTER TWELVE

1   *St. James Sampler II* (with introduction entitled "History of St. James Church" by Dr. Daniel W. Ellis, Mrs. Kitty Ellis, and Mr. Stanley Cross). Charleston: Quin Press, no date listed (circa 1994), p. vi.

[2] Saint James vestry minutes, May 10, 1960.

[3] "New St. James Church Opens Its Doors Today." *The News and Courier.* August 28, 1960, p. C4.

[4] "Sixth Church of St. James' Consecrated." *The Diocese: Official Publication of the Diocese of South Carolina.* Autumn, 1964, p. 10.

[5] Ibid.

[6] Ibid.

[7] Ibid.

[8] *St. James Sampler II,* pp. vi-vii.

[9] Ibid, p. vii.

[10] Saint James vestry minutes, March 24, 1961.

[11] Saint James vestry minutes, December 4, 1961.

[12] Saint James vestry minutes, January 14, 1962.

[13] Saint James vestry minutes, March 5, 1962.

[14] Saint James vestry minutes, May 20, 1962.

[15] Saint James vestry minutes, March 5, 1962.

[16] Saint James vestry minutes, November 5, 1962.

[17] Saint James vestry minutes, August 15, 1960.

[18] Saint James vestry minutes, October 31, 1963.

[19] "Sixth Church of St. James' Consecrated," p. 10.

[20] Saint James vestry minutes, August 3, 1964.

[21] Saint James vestry minutes, June 27, 1965.

[22] "The Rt. Rev. Charles F. Duvall, *Report of the Committee for the Election of the 13th Bishop of the Diocese of South Carolina.*" Published by the Diocese of South Carolina. August 1, 1989, p. 4.

[23] "Cemetery: Saint James Episcopal Church James Island, S.C." published by the Cemetery Committee of Saint James. April 24, 2005, pp. 27, 36.

[24] Saint James vestry minutes, December 1, 1969.

[25] Saint James vestry minutes, May 6, 1968.

[26] "Saint James Church. Love God. Love People. Build Community" website. https://saint-james.org. 2019.

[27] "Groundbreaking—New Classrooms; St. James', James Island; May 5, 1968" ceremony program.

[28] Saint James vestry minutes, May 6, 1968.

[29] Payne, Barbara R. editor. *Amazing Grace: The Parish Church of St. Helena Beaufort, South Carolina.* Beaufort: Lydia Inglett Ltd. Publishing, 2012, pp. 166-167.

[30] Porwoll, Paul. *Against All Odds: History of Saint Andrew's Parish Church, Charleston, 1706-2013.* Bloomington, IN: WestBow Press, 2014, p. 233.

[31] Ibid, p. 242.

[32] Ibid, p. 265.

[33] Ibid, p. 248.

[34] Ibid, p. 249.

[35] Payne, pp. 175-176.

[36] "St. James' Episcopal Church James Island, SC Parish Profile." Written by St. James' vestry, Charleston, SC. 1998, p. 3.

[37] "Bishop Duvall to Speak on Protestant Hour." *Jubilate Deo*. October 1987, p. 7.

[38] "Historical Sketch of St. James' Parish, James Island, South Carolina," p. 4.

FOOTNOTES FOR CHAPTER THIRTEEN

[1] *St. James Sampler II* (with introduction entitled "History of St. James Church" by Dr. Daniel W. Ellis, Mrs. Kitty Ellis, and Mr. Stanley Cross). Charleston: Quin Press, no date listed (circa 1994), p. vii.

[2] McDowell, Elsa F. "New Church Making Progress." *The News and Courier*. July 5, 1987, p. D5.

[3] "Saint James Church. Love God. Love People. Build Community." website. https://saint-james.org. 2019.

[4] Saint James vestry minutes, November 3, 1971.

[5] Saint James vestry minutes, December 7, 1970.

[6] Saint James congregational meeting, January 24, 1971.

[7] Saint James vestry minutes, April 5, 1971.

[8] Saint James vestry minutes, May 3 and 27, 1971.

[9] Saint James vestry minutes, June 4, 1972.

[10] Saint James vestry minutes, April 16, 1973.

[11] Saint James vestry minutes, August 4, 1971.

[12] Saint James vestry minutes, October 24, 1971.

[13] Saint James vestry minutes, December 7, 1971.

[14] Saint James vestry minutes, March 1, 1972.

[15] Saint James vestry minutes, February 19, 1973.

[16] Saint James vestry minutes, February 18, 1974.

[17] Saint James vestry minutes, February 1, 1971.

[18] Saint James vestry minutes, March 1, 1971.

[19] Saint James vestry minutes, April 5, 1971.

[20] Saint James vestry minutes, September 1, 1971.

[21] Saint James vestry minutes, March 3, 1972.

[22] Saint James vestry minutes, May 20, 1974.

[23] Saint James vestry minutes, April 5, 1972.

[24] Ibid.

[25] Saint James vestry minutes, April 14, 1975.

[26] Saint James vestry minutes, September 6, 1972.

[27] Saint James vestry minutes, February 18, 1974.

[28] Saint James vestry minutes, July 5, 1972.

[29] Saint James vestry minutes, October 5, 1972.

[30] Saint James vestry minutes, June 18, 1973.

[31] Saint James vestry minutes, March 10, 1975.

[32] Saint James vestry minutes, August 4, 1971.

[33] Saint James vestry minutes, January 5, 1972.

[34] Ibid.

[35] Saint James vestry minutes, July 7, 1971.

[36] Saint James vestry minutes, August 4, 1971.

[37] Saint James vestry minutes, November 3, 1971.

[38] Saint James vestry minutes, February 2, 1971.

[39] Saint James vestry minutes, July 5, 1972.

[40] Saint James vestry minutes, April 16, 1973.

[41] Saint James vestry minutes, July 15, 1974.

[42] Saint James vestry minutes, February 19, 1973.

[43] Saint James vestry minutes, July 15, 1974.

[44] Saint James vestry minutes, August 19, 1974.

[45] Saint James vestry minutes, June 9, 1975.

[46] Saint James vestry minutes, September 8, 1975.

[47] Saint James vestry minutes, July 1, 1972.

[48] Saint James vestry minutes, March 15, 1976.

[49] Saint James vestry minutes, June 21, 1976.

[50] Saint James vestry minutes, October 13, 1979.

[51] Saint James vestry minutes, April 17, 1978.

[52] Saint James vestry minutes, June 19, 1978.

[53] Saint James vestry minutes, July 17, 1978.

[54] Saint James vestry minutes, April 16, 1979.

[55] Saint James vestry minutes, October 16, 1978.

[56] Saint James vestry minutes, November 19 and December 9, 1979.

[57] Saint James vestry minutes, December 17, 1979.

Footnotes for Chapter Fourteen

[1] Cole, Lynda Owen. Letter. January 23, 2019.

[2] "Cemetery: Saint James Episcopal Church James Island, S.C." published by the Cemetery Committee of Saint James. April 24, 2005, p. 27.

[3] McGougan, Lillie. Personal interview. July 31, 2017.

[4] Ibid.

[5] Saint James vestry minutes, June 21, 1976.

[6] Saint James vestry minutes, July 19, 1976.

[7] Cole.

[8] McGougan.

[9] Saint James vestry minutes, December 21, 1981.

[10] Horn, The Rev. J. Robert. Personal interview. August 10, 2017.

[11] Saint James vestry minutes, September 20, 1976.

[12] McGougan.

[13] McCall, Suzy. Email. June 18, 2018.

[14] Cooke, The Rev. Mark Dean. Resume and email. May 11, 2018.

[15] Weld, Rev. Louise, editor. *Saint James Lenten Booklet 2019*, featuring 500-word entries by church's priests and parishioners.

[16] Cooke.

[17] Huff, The Very Rev. Christopher Mercer. Resume. 2017.

[18] McGougan.

[19] McGougan.

Footnotes for Chapter Fifteen

[1] McDowell, Elsa F. "Pastor Has Found His Niche in Life." *The News and Courier.* May 12, 1985, no page number available.

[2] Ibid.

[3] Ibid.

[4] Saint James vestry minutes, November 17, 1980.

[5] Saint James vestry minutes, December 1, 1980.

[6] Saint James vestry minutes, July 16, 1984.

[7] Saint James vestry minutes, September 21, 1981.

[8] Saint James vestry minutes, April 15, 1985.

[9] Saint James vestry minutes, July 15, 1985.

[10] Saint James vestry minutes, February 21, 1983.

[11] Burrell, Vic. "Senior Warden's Report 1983." *Saint James Congregational Report 1984.* p. 1.

[12] Reed, Anne. "Chapel Altar Guild 1983." *Saint James Congregational Report 1984.* p. 11.

[13] Burrell, p. 1.

[14] "Priors Moving to Hilton Head." *Jubilate Deo.* March 1993, p. 3.

[15] Saint James vestry minutes, April 18, 1983.

[16] Saint James vestry minutes, December 19, 1983.

[17] Saint James vestry minutes, January 16, 1984.

[18] Watkins, Susan. "Christian Education Report." *Saint James Congregational Report 1987.* p. 12.

[19] Saint James vestry minutes, January 16, 1984.

[20] Ash, Sr., Lloyd M. "Scouting at Saint James." *Saint James Congregational Report 1984.* pp. 9-10.

[21] Olbrych, Jennie. "Adult Christian Education Commission." *Saint James Congregational Report 1985.* p. 17.

[22] "Priors…" p.3.

[23] "Rev. Dr. J. Gregory Prior, Recent Vicars and Rectors." www.standrews/lc.org, July 1, 2019.

[24] Saint James vestry minutes, November 18, 1985.

[25] Shue, Carol. "Christ Kindergarten." *Saint James Congregational Report 1985.* pp. 15-16.

[26] Albinger, Brenda. "Organist/Choir Director Report." *Saint James Congregational Report 1984.* pp.7-8.

[27] Albinger, Brenda. "Organist/Choir Director Report." *Saint James Congregational Report 1987.* p. 15.

[28] Egleston, David D. "Outreach and Evangelism Commission." *Saint James Congregational Report 1984.* pp. 11-12.

[29] Johnson, Lorene, "Outreach and Evangelism Commission." *Saint James Congregational Report 1985.* p. 12.

[30] Rhodes, Dee. "Outreach Commission." *Saint James Congregational Report 1987.* p. 9.

[31] Gibson, Kimberly. "Pastoral Care Commission." *Saint James Congregational Report 1985.* p. 14.

[32] McManus, Henry B. "Evangelism Commission." *Saint James Congregational Report 1987.* p. 11.

[33] Gibson, Royal (Chip). "Saint James' Church Stewardship Committee Report." *Saint James Congregational Report 1987.* p. 19.

[34] Saint James vestry minutes, February 1986 and September 1986.

[35] "Bishop Gadsden: An Episcopal Retirement Community." *Jubilate Deo.* February 1987, p. D.

[36] Saint James vestry minutes, August 13, 1983.

[37] Saint James vestry minutes, July 16, 1984.

[38] Saint James vestry minutes, September 15, 1986.

[39] "Diocesan Leadership: The Rt. Rev'd Clark W.P. Lowenfield." Diocesan of Western Gulf Coast webpage. http://www.dwgc.org, July 1, 2019.

[40] "Bishop Gadsden: An Episcopal Retirement Community," p. C.

[41] Saint James vestry minutes, July 21, 1986.

[42] Saint James vestry minutes, January 8, 1989.

[43] Saint James vestry minutes, June 19, 1989.

[44] "Historiographer Named." *Jubilate Deo*. March 1989, p. A.

[45] "Tributes to Canon Guerry." *Jubilate Deo*. December 1991, p. 3.

[46] Hampton, Harriott. "Trip to Holy Land Is a Gift of Love." (source of article unknown)

[47] "Tributes to Canon Guerry."

[48] The Rev. Canon E.B. Guerry Dies." *The Post and Courier*. October 20, 1992, p. B2.

[49] Saint James vestry minutes, January 17, 1987.

[50] "An Unfinished History of St. James' Episcopal Church: James Island, South Carolina. The Story of a Pioneer Church on a Carolina Sea Island." Revised and edited by St. James' Historical Project. Charleston, SC. November 29, 1987, pp. 16-17.

[51] Saint James' December 6, 1987 church bulletin.

[52] Saint James vestry minutes, June 15, 1987.

[53] "St. James to Host Convention." *Jubilate Deo*. February 1987, p. A.

[54] Ibid, p. B.

[55] McDowell, Elsa F. "Lent Becomes Chaplain of Porter-Gaud School." *The News and Courier*. July 5, 1987, p. D5.

[56] "Diocesan Leadership: The Rt. Rev'd Clark WP Lowenfield."

[57] "The Dill Sanctuary—Charleston, S.C." http://www.charlestonmuseum.org/about-factsheet) March 14, 2019.

[58] Stringer-Robinson, Gretchen. "The Sacrifices of the Slaves of James Island Have Not Been Forgotten." *Bugle James Island*. February 8, 2017.

[59] "Cemetery: Saint James Episcopal Church James Island, S.C." published by the Cemetery Committee of Saint James. April 24, 2005, pp. 6 and 6a.

[60] "Zahl Called to St. James." *Jubilate Deo*. September 1988, p. 3.

[61] Zahl, Paul F.M. *Who Will Deliver Us? The Present Power of the Death of Christ*. New York: The Seabury Press, 1983.

[62] Johnson, Skip. "Minister Communicates through Music." *The News and Courier*. June 25, 1989, p. D10.

[63] Saint James vestry minutes, March 13, 1987, April 20, 1987, May 18, 1988.

[64] Source Case No. 88-CP-10-2003 in the Court of Common Pleas, State of South Carolina, County of Charleston. St. James Church, James Island, SC an Eleemosynard South Carolina corporation, Honor-

able Louis E. Condon, Master of equity for the County of Charleston. September 22, 1988.

[65] "Prominent Musician Joins Staff at St. James." *Jubilate Deo*. March 1989, p. 3.

[66] McDowell, Elsa F. "Churches Attract Serious Musicians." *The News and Courier*. February 5, 1989, p. D5.

[67] Payne, Barbara R. editor. *Amazing Grace: The Parish Church of St. Helena Beaufort, South Carolina*. Beaufort: Lydia Inglett Ltd. Publishing, 2012, pp. 187-188.

[68] Ibid, p. 188.

[69] "Limehouse to be Hartsville Rector." *Jubilate Deo*. May 1991, p. 6.

[70] Bonstelle, Carolyn Ackerly and Geordie Buxton. *Images of America: James Island*. Charleston, SC: Arcadia Publishing, 2008, pp. 123, 126.

[71] Morrison, Clark and Louise. Personal interview. July 17, 2017.

[72] Saint James vestry minutes, October 23, 1989.

[73] Saint James vestry minutes, October 23, 1989.

[74] "Cemetery: Saint James Episcopal Church James Island, S.C." timeline in front of booklet but no page number.

[75] Saint James vestry minutes, September 27, 1989

[76] Schatz, Helen. "ECW Kitchen Report." *Saint James Congregational Report 1990*. p. 17.

[77] "The Day after Hugo…Destruction Everywhere." *Jubilate Deo*. November/December 1989, p. 10.

[78] Saint James vestry minutes, September 27, 1989.

[79] Townsend, Matthew. "Junior Warden's Report." *Saint James Congregational Report 1991*. pp. 18-20.

[80] Bresee, Clyde. *How Grand a Flame: A Chronicle of a Plantation Family 1813-1947*. Chapel Hill: Algonquin Books, 1992, pp. 218-219.

FOOTNOTES FOR CHAPTER SIXTEEN

[1] Zahl, Rev. Paul. "The Rector's Report on the State of the Parish." *Saint James Congregational Report*. January 21, 1990, p. 7.

[2] Ibid, p. 8.

[3] Limehouse, Rev. Frank. "Assistant Rector's Report." *Saint James Congregational Report*. January 21, 1990, p. 9.

[4] Watkins, Susan. "Christian Education Report." *Saint James Congregational Report*. January 21, 1990, p. 9.

[5] King, Ann L. "Christian Education Report." *Saint James Congregational Report*. January 13, 1991, p. 17.

[6] Carter, William. "Senior Warden's Report." *Saint James Congregational Report*. January 13, 1991, p. 16.

[7] Saint James vestry minutes, April 1990.

[8] Saint James vestry minutes, May 1990.

[9] Saint James vestry minutes, April 1990.

[10] "St. James to Host Choir Festival." *Jubilate Deo.* May 1990, p. 1.

[11] Zahl, Rev. Paul. "Rector's Report." *Saint James Congregational Report.* January 12, 1992, p. 6.

[12] Saint James vestry minutes, August 1990.

[13] Saint James vestry minutes, August 26, 1990.

[14] Saint James vestry minutes, September 1990.

[15] Saint James vestry minutes, August 21, 1995.

[16] Saint James vestry minutes, April 29, 1991.

[17] Saint James vestry minutes, August 19, 1991.

[18] Saint James vestry minutes, June 4, 2001.

[19] Saint James vestry minutes, October 15, 1990.

[20] Saint James *Epistle*, September 1990.

[21] Saint James vestry minutes, November 19, 1990 and June 17, 1991.

[22] Saint James vestry minutes, August 13, 1990.

[23] Saint James vestry minutes, August 19, 1991.

[24] Saint James vestry minutes, November 18, 1991.

[25] Limehouse, Rev. Frank. "Associate Rector's Annual Message." *Saint James Congregational Report.* January 13, 1991, p. 12.

[26] Saint James vestry minutes, January 26, 1991.

[27] Saint James vestry minutes, January 6, 1992.

[28] Saint James vestry minutes, November 16, 1992.

[29] Saint James vestry minutes, November 15, 1993.

[30] Zahl, Rev. Paul. "Rector's Annual Message." *Saint James Congregational Report.* January 13, 1991, p. 10.

[31] Payne, Barbara R. editor. *Amazing Grace: The Parish Church of St. Helena Beaufort, South Carolina.* Beaufort: Lydia Inglett Ltd. Publishing, 2012, p. 189.

[32] Ibid, p. 208.

[33] *Jubilate Deo*, May 1991.

[34] *Jubilate Deo*, January 1993.

[35] Saint James vestry minutes, May 20, 1991.

[36] "Saint James Church. Love God. Love People. Build Community." website. https://saint-james.org. 2019.

[37] Jenkins, Rev. Arthur. "Assistant Rector's Annual Report." *Saint James Congregational Report.* January 10, 1993, pp. 6-7.

[38] Ibid, p. 6.

[39] DuPre, James H. "Senior Warden's Report." *Saint James Congregational Report.* January 8, 1995, p. 5.

[40] "St. James' Welcomes New Rector." *Jubilate Deo.* December 1992/January 1993, p. 3.

[41] Howard, Rev. John. "Rector's Report." *Saint James Congregational Report*. January 10, 1993, pp. 4-5.

[42] Taylor, Ashby and Anne Read. "Christian Giving Report." *Saint James Congregational Report*. January 10, 1993, p. 5.

[43] Porcher, Mary C. "Memorials and Gifts Committee." *Saint James Congregational Report*. January 10, 1993, p. 6.

[44] Jenkins, Rev. Arthur. "Assistant Rector's Annual Report." *Saint James Congregational Report*. January 10, 1993, pp. 6-7.

[45] Saint James vestry minutes, May 17, 1993.

[46] Saint James vestry minutes, January 22, 1994.

[47] Jenkins, Rev. Arthur. Email. February 6, 2019.

[48] Saint James vestry minutes, March 21, 1994.

[49] Saint James vestry minutes, August 21, 1995.

[50] Saint James vestry minutes, January 22, 1994.

[51] Saint James vestry minutes, March 20, 1995.

[52] Saint James vestry minutes, June 16, 1997.

[53] Saint James vestry minutes, January 22, 1994.

[54] Saint James vestry minutes, August 15, 1994.

[55] Saint James vestry minutes, April 19, 1999.

[56] Mikell, John. Personal interview. March 3, 2019.

[57] Saint James vestry minutes, August 23, 1999.

[58] Payne, p. 213.

[59] Miller, Rev. Jeffrey. "Assistant to the Rector's Report." *Saint James Congregational Report*. January 14, 1996, p. 4.

[60] Saint James vestry minutes, May 16, 1994.

[61] Saint James vestry minutes, February 20, 1995.

[62] Saint James vestry minutes, November 21, 1994.

[63] Saint James vestry minutes, August 1, 1994 and March 20, 1995.

[64] Saint James vestry minutes, August 21, 1995.

[65] Saint James vestry minutes, July 21, 1997.

[66] Saint James vestry minutes, December 18, 1995.

[67] Cupka, David. "Senior Warden's Report." *Saint James Congregational Report*. January 12, 1997, p. 1.

[68] Payne, p. 198.

[69] Ibid, p. 209.

[70] Ibid, pp. 224-225.

[71] Phillips, Mark. "The Search Committee Report." *2015 Annual Report St. Philips Church*. p. 8.

[72] Saint James vestry minutes, September 16, 1996.

[73] McIntyre, Michael. "Youth Minister's Annual Report." *Saint James Congregational Report.* January 11, 1998, p. 10.

[74] Saint James vestry minutes, May 15, 1995.

[75] Saint James vestry minutes, February 1, 1997.

[76] Cupka, p. 2.

[77] Saint James vestry minutes, November 11, 1999.

[78] Saint James vestry minutes, February 21, 2000.

[79] Saint James vestry minutes, February 17, 1997 and March 17, 1997.

[80] Saint James vestry minutes, March 17, 1997.

[81] Saint James vestry minutes, September 1995.

[82] Saint James vestry minutes, December 19, 1994.

[83] Saint James vestry minutes, March 1996.

[84] Saint James vestry minutes, June 16, 1997.

[85] Saint James vestry minutes, March 1999.

[86] "Cemetery: Saint James Episcopal Church James Island, S.C." published by the Cemetery Committee of Saint James. April 24, 2005.

[87] Saint James vestry minutes, April 15, 1996.

[88] Saint James vestry minutes, March 18, 1996.

[89] Finch, Jr., Rev. Floyd W. Vita. 2017.

[90] Saint James vestry minutes, September 22, 1997.

[91] Saint James vestry minutes, September 28, 1998.

[92] Finch, Rev. Floyd. "Pastoral Associate's Report 1999." *Saint James Congregational Report.* January 17, 1999, p. 11.

[93] "Howard, The Right Reverend Samuel Johnson." Bishop of Florida.: http://www.diocesefl.org/about-us/the-diocese/bishop-of-florida. 2/3/2018.

[94] Saint James vestry minutes, January 1998.

[95] Saint James vestry minutes, February 1998.

[96] "Parish Profile: St. James' Episcopal Church." Charleston, SC. 1998, p. 1.

[97] Ibid.

[98] Saint James vestry minutes, January 16, 1998.

[99] "Cemetery" (timeline).

[100] Saint James vestry minutes, June 21, 1999.

[101] Saint James vestry minutes, July 17, 1999.

[102] Saint James vestry minutes, August 2, 1999.

[103]Saint James vestry minutes, July 19, 1999.

[104]Saint James vestry minutes, August 23, 1999.

[105]Saint James vestry minutes, February 5, 2001.

[106]"Parish Profile," p. 16.

FOOTNOTES FOR CHAPTER SEVENTEEN

[1] Saint James vestry minutes, January 17, 2000.

[2] Saint James vestry minutes, March 20, 2000.

[3] Jenkins, Rev. Arthur. "When They Had Prayed." *Saint James Congregational Report*. April 21, 2002, p. 6.

[4] Saint James vestry minutes, March 19, 2001.

[5] Saint James vestry minutes, April 2, 2001.

[6] King, Ann. "Report of the Senior Warden." *Saint James Congregational Report*. April 21, 2002, p. 4.

[7] Stroud, Mike. "Battery Haskell." *The Historical Marker Database*. June 16, 2016, p. 2. https://www.hmdb.org/marker.asp?marker=39708.

[8] Saint James vestry minutes, December 17, 2001.

[9] *Historic Sites of James Island*. Compiled by the James Island History Commission of the Town of James Island. www.jamesislandsc.us. 2019, p. 13.

[10] Ibid, p. 12.

[11] Saint James vestry minutes, December 17, 2001.

[12] King, p. 5.

[13] Saint James vestry minutes, September 17, 2001.

[14] King, p. 4.

[15] Saint James vestry minutes, September 18, 2000.

[16] Jenkins, Rev. Arthur. "When They Had Prayed." p. 7.

[17] Jenkins, Rev. Arthur. "Divinity Working through Humanity." *Saint James Congregational Report*. January 23, 2000, p. 7.

[18] Saint James vestry minutes, March 20, 2000.

[19] Saint James vestry minutes, May 15, 2000.

[20] Saint James vestry minutes, November 6, 2000.

[21] Saint James vestry minutes, June 19, 2000.

[22] Saint James vestry minutes, September 18, 2000.

[23] Saint James vestry minutes, December 4, 2000.

[24] Saint James vestry minutes, April 20, 2004.

[25] Saint James vestry minutes, February 3, 2004.

[26] Powell, Marilyn, "From the Deacon." *Saint James Congregational Report.* April 21, 2002, p. 6.

[27] Saint James vestry minutes, May 1, 2000.

[28] Saint James vestry minutes, August 7, 2000.

[29] Saint James vestry minutes, June 19, 2000.

[30] Trawick, C. William "Bill." Letter from Bishop Gadsden Director to Rev. Jenkins. February 19, 2007.

[31] Saint James vestry minutes, November 19, 2019.

[32] Saint James vestry minutes, June 19, 2000.

[33] Saint James vestry minutes, December 4, 2000.

[34] Saint James vestry minutes, December 16, 2003.

[35] Porwoll, Paul. *Against All Odds: History of Saint Andrew's Parish Church, Charleston, 1706-2013.* Bloomington, IN: WestBow Press, 2014, pp.308-309.

[36] Huey, Marshall. "Assistant Rector's Report." *Saint James Congregational Report.* April 21, 2002, pp. 8-9.

[37] Saint James vestry minutes, February 5, 2001.

[38] Saint James *Epistle.* March 2006, p. 1.

[39] Saint James vestry minutes, March 5, 2001.

[40] Gould, Pat. "Report from the Director of Music." *Saint James Congregational Report.* April 21, 2002, pp. 13-14.

[41] Barwick Mark. "Report on Christian Education." *Saint James Congregational Report.* April 21, 2002, p. 15.

[42] Saint James vestry minutes, August 7, 2000.

[43] McIntyre, Michael. "Youth Ministry." *Saint James Congregational Report.* January 23, 2000, pp. 13-15.

[44] McIntyre, Michael. "Youth Ministry Annual Report." *Saint James Congregational Report.* April 21, 2002, pp. 11-12.

[45] Saint James vestry minutes, March 30, 2004.

[46] Saint James vestry minutes, April 20, 2004.

[47] Ibid.

[48] Saint James *Epistle,* October 2004, p. 1.

[49] Saint James *Epistle,* November 2004, p. 1.

[50] Saint James *Epistle,* October 2005, p. 1.

[51] Saint James *Epistle,* January 2006, p. 4.

[52] Saint James Epistle, April 2005, p. 2.

[53] Saint James *Epistle,* September 2005. p. 2.

[54] Saint James *Epistle,* August 2005, p. 2.

[55] Saint James *Epistle,* June 2006, p. 2.

[56] Saint James *Epistle,* September 2008, p. 6.

[57] Saint James *Epistle*, October 2004, p. 3.

[58] Saint James vestry minutes, November 21, 2006.

[59] Jenkins, Rev. Arthur. "Come and See." *Saint James Congregational Report*. May 6, 2007, p. 2.

[60] Ibid.

[61] Horn, Rev. Robert. "Associate Pastor Horn." *Saint James Congregational Report*. May 6, 2007, p. 4.

[62] Saint James *Epistle,* January 2010, p. 5.

[63] Weld, Rev. Louise. "Associate Pastor Weld." *Saint James Congregational Report*. May 6, 2007, p. 6.

[64] Doran, Mary Ellen. "Christian Education." *Saint James Congregational Report*. May 6, 2007, p. 9.

[65] Saint James *Epistle*, June 2011, p. 3.

[66] Saint James vestry minutes, July 17, 2007.

[67] Saint James vestry minutes, August 7, 2007.

[68] Saint James vestry minutes, March 4, 2008.

[69] Saint James vestry minutes, April 1, 2008.

[70] Saint James vestry minutes, April 15, 2008.

[71] Ibid.

[72] Saint James vestry minutes, February 13, 2007.

[73] Saint James vestry minutes, June 5, 2007.

[74] Saint James vestry minutes, October 6, 2007.

[75] Ibid.

[76] Saint James vestry minutes, July 1 2008.

[77] Saint James vestry minutes, August 16, 2008.

[78] Saint James *Epistle*, August 2008, p. 2.

[79] Saint James *Epistle*, September 2008, p. 1.

[80] Saint James vestry minutes, June 10, 2008.

[81] Saint James vestry minutes, June 17, 2008.

[82] Saint James vestry minutes, September 13, 2008.

[83] Saint James vestry minutes, November 17, 2009.

[84] King, p. 4.

FOOTNOTES FOR CHAPTER EIGHTEEN

[1] Allen, Patrick, et. Al. "Diocese of South Carolina: 212th Convention—Proposed Resolution." January 4, 2002.

[2] Parker, Adam and Jennifer Berry Hawes. "Episcopal Church Enters New Chapter in Schism." *The Post and Courier*. August 6, 2017, p. G6.

3 Parker, Adam. "Diocese Wants South Carolina Supreme Court to Rehear Case." *Post and Courier*. September 4, 2017, p. A5.

4 Lewis, The Rev. Canon Jim. "The Real Story behind Our Split with the Episcopal Church." *Charleston Mercury*. October 2, 2013, p. 1.

5 Parker, Adam. "Getting up to Speed with the Episcopal-Anglican Legal Battle. *Post and Courier*. October 1, 2017. p. G8.

6 Lewis, "The Real Story…", p. 2.

7 Parker, "Diocese Wants…," p. A5.

8 "Frequently Asked Questions." "News and Events: Legal News." Diocese of South Carolina website. https://www.dioceseofsc.org. August 6, 2019. p. 8.

9 Ibid, p. 3.

10 Payne, Barbara R. editor. *Amazing Grace: The Parish Church of St. Helena Beaufort, South Carolina*. Beaufort: Lydia Inglett Ltd. Publishing, 2012, p. 222.

11 Ibid.

12 Ibid, p. 235.

13 Parker, "Getting Up to Speed…," p.G-8.

14 Ibid.

15 Payne, p. 235.

16 Porwoll, Paul. *Against All Odds: History of Saint Andrew's Parish Church, Charleston, 1706-2013*. Bloomington, IN: WestBow Press, 2014, p. 318.

17 Payne, pp. 235-236.

18 Porwoll, p. 320.

19 "Litigation Facts." "News and Events: Legal News." Diocese of South Carolina website. https://www.dioceseofsc.org. August 6, 2019, p.2.

20 Porwoll, p. 321.

21 "Timeline." "News and Events: Legal News." Diocese of South Carolina website. https://www.dioceseofsc.org. August 6, 2019, p.4.

22 Hawes, Jennifer Berry and Adam Parker, "S.C. Supreme Court Ruling a Win for Episcopal Church." *Post and Courier*. August 3, 2017. p. A4.

23 Ibid.

24 Gilbreth, Edward M. "Vexing Times for Many S.C. Episcopalians." *Post and Courier*. August 17, 2017, p. A3.

25 "Churches in Diocese of South Carolina Rejects Episcopal Church's 'Spurious' Offer to Settle," *The Anglican Diocese of South Carolina News*, June 15, 2015. (posted on the website of The Anglican Diocese of South Carolina and accessible on the 'Timeline.')

26 "Frequently Asked Questions…," p. 7.

27 Hawes and Parker, "S.C. Supreme Court Ruling…" p. A4.

[28] Gilbreth, Edward M. "Strong Judicial Disagreements Fuel Episcopal Controversy." *Post and Courier.* November 2, 2017, p. A3.

[29] Hawes and Parker, "S.C. Supreme Court Ruling..." pp. A1 and A4.

[30] Ibid, p. A4.

[31] Gilbreth, "Vexing Times…," p. A3.

[32] "Timeline," p. 4.

[33] Hawes and Parker, "S.C. Supreme Court Ruling..." pp. A1 and A4.

[34] Parker and Hawes, "Episcopal Church Enters…" p. G1.

[35] Hawes and Parker, "S.C. Supreme Court Ruling..." p. A4.

[36] "Litigation Facts," p. 2.

[37] Ibid, p. 1.

[38] Parker, "Getting Up to Speed," p. G1.

[39] Gilbreth, "Vexing Times…," p. A3.

[40] Parker, "Getting Up to Speed," p. G1.

[41] Miller, Rev. Jeffrey. "Opinion: SC Supreme Court Ruling Against Diocese of South Carolina Threatens Religious Freedom." http://www.islandpacket.com/opinion/op-ed/article173705026. September 16, 2017, p. 2.

[42] "Litigation Facts," pp. 1-2.

[43] Lewis, The Rev. Canon Jim. "South Carolina Circuit Court Rules in Favor of Diocese of South Carolina on Betterments Statute." Email to vestry at Saint James. August 28, 2019.

[44] Ibid.

[45] Parker, "Getting Up to Speed," p. G8.

[46] Miller, p. 1.

[47] Miller, p. 3.

[48] Hawes and Parker, "S.C. Supreme Court Ruling..." p. A4.

[49] Ibid.

[50] Parker, "Diocese Wants…" p. A5.

[51] Gilbreth, "Vexing Times…," p. A3.

[52] Knapp, Andrew. "Justice's Episcopal Ties in Question." *Post and Courier.* October 15, 2017, pp. A1.

[53] Ibid, p. A8.

[54] Hawes and Parker, "S.C. Supreme Court Ruling..." p. A4.

[55] Ibid.

[56] Parker, "Getting Up to Speed," p. G8.

[57] "Anglican Church Receives Diocese of S.C." *The Post and Courier.* July 2, 2017, p. G6.

[58] "Frequently Asked Questions," p. 8.

59 Allison, C. Fitzsimons. "Seek Just Settlement in Church Dispute." *Post and Courier*. October 29, 2017, p. C3.

60 Ibid.

61 Lewis, "The Real Story...", pp. 3-4.

62 Lewis, The Rev. Canon Jim. "Petition filed with the United States Supreme Court." Email to members of the Diocese of South Carolina. February, 12, 2018.

63 Jenkins, Rev. Arthur. "Writ of Certiorari." Email sent to Saint James' congregation June 12, 2018.

64 Lewis, The Rev. Canon Jim. "The Mediation Process" email to rectors and vicars of the Diocese of South Carolina. August 6, 2019.

65 "Federal Judge Enjoins Use of Diocese Names and Seal." News from the Anglican Diocese of South Carolina. (email from Joy Hunter), September 20, 2019.

66 Lawrence, Bishop Mark. "A Letter from Bishop Lawrence: Post Denial from SCOTUS." Email sent by Rev. Canon Jim Lewis to Saint James vestry. June 14, 2018.

67 "Faith Signers." https://www.palmettofamily.org/diocese-supporters. 9/19/2017.

68 Lawrence, email, June 14, 2018.

69 Weld, Rev. Louise. "Associate Pastor's Report." *Saint James Congregational Report*. May 5, 2013, p. 4.

70 Jenkins, Rev. Arthur. "Rector's Annual Report." *Saint James Congregational Report*. May 17, 2015, p. 3.

71 Jenkins, Rev. Arthur. "South Carolina Supreme Court Decision." Email sent to Saint James' congregation. August 2, 2017.

FOOTNOTES FOR CHAPTER NINETEEN

1 Saint James *Epistle*, July 2011, p. 3.

2 Saint James *Epistle*, May 2013, p. 2.

3 Jenkins, Rev. Arthur. "Rector's Annual Report." *Saint James Congregational Report*. May 5, 2013, p. 1.

4 Saint James *Epistle*, December 2014, p. 4.

5 Saint James vestry minutes, September 13, 2014.

6 Hilton, Tom. Email. December 15, 2019.

7 Whittle, Fred. Email. December 4, 2019.

8 Saint James vestry minutes, June 8, 2019.

9 Whittle.

10 Saint James vestry minutes, February 17, 2011.

11 Saint James vestry minutes, March 15, 2011.

12 Saint James vestry minutes, May 11, 2013.

13 Saint James vestry minutes, September 13, 2014.

[14] Saint James vestry minutes, February 20, 2018.

[15] Saint James vestry minutes, August 20, 2019.

[16] Saint James vestry minutes, September 9, 2019.

[17] Saint James *Epistle*, July 2012, p. 3.

[18] Saint James *Epistle* June 2012, p. 3.

[19] Saint James *Epistle*, August 2012, p. 1.

[20] Jenkins, Rev. Arthur. "Rector's Annual Report." *Saint James Congregational Report*. May 6, 2012, p. 1.

[21] Brown, Shirley. "How to Hear God's Voice." *Saint James Congregational Report*. May 5, 2013, p. 13.

[22] Jenkins. May 5, 2013, p. 2.

[23] Saint James *Epistle*, February 2013, p. 3.

[24] Saint James *Epistle*, March 2013 p. 2.

[25] Saint James *Epistle*, October 2012, pp. 6-7.

[26] Saint James *Epistle,* March 2013, p. 3.

[27] Saint James *Epistle*, March 2014, p. 5.

[28] Saint James vestry minutes, December 21, 2012.

[29] Saint James *Epistle*, April 2013, p. 2.

[30] Jenkins. May 5, 2013, p. 1.

[31] Williams, Rev. Jill. "Family Discipleship." *Saint James Congregational Report*. May 18, 2014, p. 11.

[32] Saint James vestry minutes, April 21, 2015.

[33] Weld, Rev. Louise. "Associate Pastor's Report." *Saint James Congregational Report*. May 5, 2013, p. 4.

[34] Jenkins. May 5, 2013, p. 2.

[35] Saint James *Epistle,* December 2013, p. 7.

[36] Saint James *Epistle*, August 2014, p. 2.

[37] Saint James vestry minutes, February 18, 2020.

[38] Saint James *Epistle,* September 2013, p. 10.

[39] Saint James vestry minutes, November 20, 2018.

[40] Saint James vestry minutes, December 18, 2012.

[41] Saint James vestry minutes, February 19, 2013.

[42] Saint James vestry minutes, August 19, 2014.

[43] Saint James vestry minutes, July 16, 2013.

[44] Saint James vestry minutes, December 17, 2019.

[45] Saint James vestry minutes, January 17, 2017.

[46] Saint James vestry minutes, August 20, 2019.

[47] Saint James *Epistle*, February 2014, p. 1.

[48] Saint James *Epistle*, July 2014, p. 2.

[49] Warfuel, Deacon Ron. "Lay Eucharistic Visitors." *Saint James Congregational Report*. May 18, 2014, p. 12.

[50] Waite, Phillip. "Youth Ministry Report—High School." *Saint James Congregational Report*. May 17, 2015, p.16.

[51] Griggs, Alisha. "Youth Ministry Report—Middle School." *Saint James Congregational Report*. May 17, 2015, pp. 17-18.

[52] Jenkins. May 5, 2013, p. 3.

[53] Saint James *Epistle,* May 2013 p. 2.

[54] Saint James *Epistle*, March 2014, p. 6.

[55] Saint James vestry minutes, July 21, 2015.

[56] Saint James vestry minutes, September 19, 2016.

[57] Saint James vestry minutes, August 3, 2017.

[58] Jenkins, Rev. Arthur. "Rector's Annual Report." *Saint James Congregational Report*. May 6, 2018, p. 2.

[59] Saint James vestry minutes, August 2, 2017.

[60] Cooke, Rev. Mark. "Pastor's Report." *Saint James Congregational Report*. May 19, 2019, p. 4.

[61] Saint James vestry minutes, April 17, 2018.

[62] Jenkins, Rev. Arthur. "Rector's Annual Report." *Saint James Congregational Report*. May 19, 2019, p. 1.

[63] Chavis, Dustin. "Sexton." *Saint James Congregational Report*. May 6, 2012, p. 18.

[64] Saint James vestry minutes, September 17, 2019.

[65] Saint James vestry minutes, November 22, 2011.

[66] Jenkins. May 6, 2018, p. 2.

[67] Weld, Rev. Louise. "Associate Pastor's Report." *Saint James Congregational Report*. May 6, 2018, p. 5.

[68] Saint James vestry minutes, July 18, 2017.

[69] Bartels, Virginia. "*Sea Island Glory*: Jim Booth Painting of Saint James to Celebrate 300th Anniversary," *Jubilate Deo*, Winter 2020, p. 15.

[70] "Saint James Anglican Church 300th Anniversary Dinner." Evening program for Saint James Tricentennial Celebration: History Weekend—January 25, 2020.

[71] Saint James church bulletin, January 26, 2020.

[72] "Robert's of Charleston" dinner menu and program, Saint James Church, February 14, 2020.

[73] Pennington, Paul. Email. November 25, 2019.

[74] Saint James vestry minutes, January 23, 2018.

[75] Steele, Joshua. "The ACNA's 2019 Book of Common Prayer (BCP): A Rookie Anglican Guide" https://anglicanpastor.com/the-acnas-2019-book-of-common-prayer-bcp-a-rookie-anglican-guide/ 2019.

[76] Barnette, Scooter. Email. November 25, 2019.

[77] Ibid.

78 Dayschool@saint-james.org, November 25, 2019.

79 Walchesky, Chris. "Music Ministry Report." *Saint James Congregational Report.* May 6, 2018, p. 14.

80 Saint James vestry minutes, August 20, 2019.

81 "Diocese to Hold 2019 Annual Convention March 15-16." *The Anglican Diocese of South Carolina: Making Biblical Anglicans for a Global Age.* https://adosc.org/author-dave-runyon-to-speak-at-228th-annal-convention/

82 Denison, Mark. "Why Churches Close." www.churchmadebetter.com/why-churches-close/ December 14, 2015. p. 1.

FOOTNOTES FOR CHAPTER TWENTY

1 Payne, Barbara R. editor. *Amazing Grace: The Parish Church of St. Helena Beaufort, South Carolina.* Beaufort: Lydia Inglett Ltd. Publishing, 2012, p. 170.

2 Porwoll, Paul. *Against All Odds: History of Saint Andrew's Parish Church, Charleston, 1706-2013.* Bloomington, IN: WestBow Press, 2014, p. 243.

3 "Reports from Detroit: From Morey Lent." *Jubilate Deo.* September 1988, p. 7.

4 Olbrych, Rev. Jennie. Personal interview. July 19, 2017.

5 Ibid.

6 Ibid.

7 Olbrych, Rev. Jennie. Resume. July 2017.

8 "ECW Annual Meeting Agenda." *Jubilate Deo,* March 1989, p. 1.

9 Olbrych. Personal interview. July 19, 2017.

10 Olbrych, Rev. Jennie. E-mail. July 19, 2017.

11 "Suzy McCall Plans Mission to Latin America." *Jubilate Deo.* May 1990, p. 7.

12 "Lamb Institute: History Timeline." Lambinstitute.org. August 12, 2017.

13 Ibid.

14 McCall, Suzy. *Tania de la Cantera.* CreateSpace Independent Publishing Platform, November 15, 2012.

15 Ibid, p. 4.

16 Ibid, pp. 2-3.

17 Weld, Rev. Louise. Resume. 2017.

18 Weld, Rev. Louise. Personal interview. July19, 2017.

19 Ibid.

20 Ibid.

21 Ibid.

22 McGougan, Lillie. Personal interview. July 31, 2017.

[23] Horn, Rev. J. Robert. Personal interview. August 10, 2017.

[24] McGougan, Lillie. Personal interview. July 31, 2017.

[25] Horn, Rev. J. Robert. Personal interview. August 10, 2017.

[26] Ibid.

[27] Ibid.

[28] Ibid.

[29] "Cemetery: Saint James Episcopal Church James Island, S.C." published by the Cemetery Committee of Saint James. April 24, 2005, pp. 27 and 36.

[30] Bumpas, Rev. Elizabeth. Resume. July 2017.

[31] Ibid.

[32] Bumpas, Rev. Elizabeth. Personal interview. July 26. 2017.

[33] Ibid.

[34] Bumpas, Rev. Elizabeth. Resume. July 2017.

[35] Bumpas, Rev. Elizabeth. Personal interview. July 26. 2017.

[36] Bumpas, Rev. Elizabeth. Resume. July 2017.

[37] Doran, Rev. Mary Ellen. Personal interview. July 26, 2017.

[38] Doran, Rev. Mary Ellen. Resume. July 26, 2017.

[39] Doran, Rev. Mary Ellen. Interview. July 26, 2017.

[40] Ibid.

[41] Ibid.

[42] Ibid.

[43] Doran, Rev. Mary Ellen. Interview. July 26, 2017.

[44] Lukanich, Rev. Emily Anderson. Email. July 25, 2018.

[45] Ibid.

[46] "Lukanich, Rev. Emily Anderson: Assistant Rector—Clergy—Episcopal Church of the Transfiguration of Vail." http://episcopalvail.com/who-we-are/our-leadership. January 9, 2018.

[47] MacArthur, John. *Twelve Extraordinary Women: How God Shaped Women of the Bible and What He Wants to Do with You.* Nashville: Thomas Nelson, Inc., 2005.

FOOTNOTES FOR CHAPTER TWENTY-ONE

[1] *St. James Sampler II* (with introduction entitled "History of St. James Church" by Dr. Daniel W. Ellis, Mrs. Kitty Ellis, and Mr. Stanley Cross). Charleston: Quin Press, no date listed (circa 1994), p. xiii.

[2] Ibid, p. vi.

[3] Ibid, p. vii.

[4] Horn, Rev. J. Robert. Personal interview. August 10, 2017.

[5] Ibid.

[6] Ibid.

[7] Ibid.

[8] Ibid.

[9] Ibid.

[10] Huff, Rev. Christopher Mercer. Email. August 30, 2017.

[11] Huff, Rev. Christopher Mercer. Resume. 2017.

[12] Huff. Email. August 30, 2017.

[13] Huff. Resume. 2017.

[14] Ibid.

[15] Huff. Email. August 30, 2017.

[16] Ibid.

[17] Cooke, Rev. Mark Dean. Resume. May 11, 2018.

[18] Ibid.

[19] Ibid.

[20] Ibid.

[21] Ibid.

[22] Ibid.

[23] Cooke, Rev. Mark Dean. Email. May 11, 2018.

[24] Cooke, resume, 2018.

[25] Ibid.

[26] Ibid.

[27] Cooke, email, 2018.

[28] "All Souls Anglican Church Okinawa—Staff: Our Priest. Fr. Creighton Evans." www.allsoulsokinawa.com. June 16. 2018.

[29] Ibid.

[30] "Evans, Jr., Vernon Creighton: Obituary." *The Post and Courier.* July 8, 2018, p. C4.

[31] "Evans, Jr., The Rev. Vernon Creighton 1953-2018." Diocese of Southwest Florida. May 2018.

[32] "Evans, Jr. The Rev. Creighton June 17, 1953-May 17, 2018." Diocese of South Carolina. jhunter@dioceseofsc.org, May 2018.

[33] www.allsoulsokinawa.com. June 16. 2018.

[34] Ibid.

[35] "Evans, Jr., Vernon Creighton: Obituary.

[36] Stephans, Rev. Craig. "Habits that Sustain Ministry: Craig Stephans' Spiritual Autobiography." Summer 2016. Email. September 12, 2018.

[37] Ibid.

[38] Ibid.

[39] Ibid.

[40] Ibid.

[41] Ibid.

[42] Shelton, Rev.Jeremy. Email. June 27, 2018.

[43] Ibid.

[44] Shelton, Rev. Jeremy: "The Ordination of Jeremy Alan Shelton to the Sacred Order of Priests." December 1, 2018.

[45] Rev. Shelton. Email. June 27, 2018.

FOOTNOTES FOR CHAPTER TWENTY-TWO

[1] Snowden, Octavia. "Teenage Organist Gives Best Effort to Every Undertaking." *The News and Courier.* August 24, 1958, p. C2.

[2] "Choral Society to Present Oratorio by Mendelssohn: Hinson Mikell of James Island, at the Organ," March 1960 (newspaper article with no publishing information included)

[3] "St. James Organist Sets Recital." (newspaper article with no publishing information included)

[4] Young, Gale. "Family Decoration Project Spreads Christmas Spirit." *The News and Courier.* December 11, 1970, p. C1.

[5] "Kitty Ellis, St. James, James Island." Profiles in Leadership. *Jubilate Deo*, May 1982, p. C.

[6] Baxley, Colette. "James Island Senior Has No Regrets." *The News and Courier*, July 12, 1987, p. E2.

[7] "Meggett, Sr., Mr. W. Gresham (1903-1990)" (article has no additional publication information)

[8] "Hazel Carte to Retire February 28." *Jubilate Deo*, February 1987, p. 1.

[9] MacDougall, David W. "To Mother, with Love." *The News and Courier.* Tempo Section. May 10, 1987, p. E1.

[10] Anderson, Ellen. "Halloween." *The News and Courier.* October 30, 1987. (Page unknown)

[11] Anderson, Ellen. "Easter Best." *The New and Courier.* (Date and page unknown)

[12] Hood, Victoria. "Laura Ashley Blooms in Every Season." *The News and Courier.* February 26, 1987, p. C1.

[13] "A Child Is Born," *This Week in West Ashley*, December 23, 1993, p. 6.

[14] "Smiling Faces" (article about Christ Kindergarten celebrating its thirteenth annual May Day Program—no publication information available)

[15] Anderson, Ellen. "After 48 Years, Couple Still Making Music Together." *The News and Courier.* April 12,

1972, p. E2.

16 Legare, Anne. "Retired Couple Take on Life with Enthusiasm." Article may be from *The News and Courier*, but no additional publication information available except pp. C1 and C4.

17 Johnson, Skip. "Phyllis Rooke's Tragedy Turned into Success." *The News and Courier*. March 26, 1985. Pages 2 and 14.

18 Shumake, Janice. "Circus Still Lives in Senior Citizen." *The Post and Courier*. April 2, 1989, p. E3.

19 Mays, Deidre C. "Book's Proceeds Going to Homeless Charities." *The Post and Courier.* October 8, 1992, p. 10.

20 Prior, Greg. "Mr. Willie McLeod to be Honored on 100th Birthday." (no additional publishing information available)

21 Waring, Thomas R. "Planter Last Survivor." *The News and Courier*. October 25, 1981, p. E2.

22 "Noted Sea Island Cotton Farmer William E. McLeod, 104, Dies." January 21, 1990. (no additional publishing information available)

23 Ibid.

24 Prior.

25 Waring, Thomas R. "St. James Episcopal Church to Mark Mr. Willie's 100th." *The News and Courier*. February 3, 1985, p. F1.

26 MacDougall, David W. "Centenarians Meet Each Year with Grace." *The Evening Post*. Living Section. September 18, 1987, p. B4.

27 McLeod Plantation" https://www.ccprc.com/2085/Interpretive-tours. February 13, 2019.

28 "Robert A. Barber, Jr." https://en.wikipedia.org/w/index.php?title=Robert_A._Jr.&oldid=802732371.

29 *Bowens Island*. Charleston, SC: Evening Post Books, 2016.

30 Munday, Dave. "Faith with a Healing Touch: Believers Share Their Stories." Religion. *The Post and Courier*. January 21, 2001, p. G7.

31 "Clement, Jr., Francis 'Frank' Walpole Obituary." *The Post and Courier*. June 1, 2018, p. B4.

FOOTNOTES FOR CHAPTER TWENTY-THREE

1   Schatz, Helen C. "ECW Kitchen Report." *Saint James Congregational Report*. 1990, p. 17.

2   Saint James vestry minutes, August 1976.

3   Saint James vestry minutes, February 1978.

4   Saint James vestry minutes, September 19, 1983.

5   Saint James vestry minutes, April 1983.

6   Saint James vestry minutes, October 17, 1988.

7   Saint James vestry minutes, July 19, 1994.

8   Saint James vestry minutes, March 18, 1996.

[9] Crawford, Darren and Sue Crawford, "Mission Report." *Saint James Congregational Report.* January 11, 1998, p. 23.

[10] Saint James vestry minutes, May 17, 1993.

[11] Saint James vestry minutes, September 1995.

[12] Saint James vestry minutes, October 29, 1997.

[13] Saint James vestry minutes, March 17, 1997.

[14] Saint James vestry minutes, February 21, 2000.

[15] Saint James vestry minutes, June 19, 2000.

[16] Vestry report on missions, December 2002.

[17] King, Mary. "World Missions." *Saint James Congregational Report.* April 21, 2002, p. 19.

[18] King, Mary. "World Missions." *Saint James Congregational Report.* May 18, 2003, p. 13.

[19] Ibid.

[20] Saint James *Epistle,* January 2006, p. 2.

[21] Saint James *Epistle,* February 2013, p. 4.

[22] Medical Ministry International emails and pamphlets dated January-May, 2006 and mailed to Dick and Virginia Bartels.

[23] Saint James *Epistle,* June 2012, p. 6.

[24] Saint James *Epistle,* April 2006, p. 3.

[25] Saint James *Epistle* July 2008, p. 4.

[26] Saint James *Epistle,* August 2005, p. 1.

[27] Saint James *Epistle,* May 2008 p. 6.

[28] Saint James *Epistle,* December 2008, p. 5.

[29] Green, Rev. Carl. "John 8:36 Prison Ministry." *Saint James Congregational Report.* May 12, 2015, p. 12.

[30] Saint James *Epistle,* June 2011, p. 5.

[31] Saint James *Epistle,* November 2011, p. 4.

[32] Ibid, p. 9.

[33] Saint James *Epistle,* November 2008, p. 4.

[34] James Island Outreach, www.jioutreach.org, September 25, 2019.

[35] Saint James *Epistle,* November 2011, p. 8.

[36] Saint James vestry minutes, November 19, 2019.

[37] Saint James *Epistle,* November 2008, p. 1.

[38] Saint James *Epistle,* November 2004, p. 2.

[39] Saint James *Epistle,* December 2008, p. 4.

[40] Saint James *Epistle,* March 2006, p. 4.

[41] Saint James *Epistle,* May 2006 p. 4.

⁴² Saint James *Epistle,* January 2006, p. 2.

⁴³ Saint James *Epistle*, January 2007, p. 2.

⁴⁴ Bumpas, Rev. Elizabeth. Email. October 31, 2019.

⁴⁵ "Bridge Church to the Homeless." *Saint James Ministries.* 2019-2020, p. 26.

⁴⁶ Saint James *Epistle,* July 2001, p. 5.

⁴⁷ Saint James *Epistle,* April 2008 p 3.

⁴⁸ "Christmas in July: Missions Catalog 2019." Published by Saint James Mission Committee.

⁴⁹ Ibid.

⁵⁰ Ibid.

⁵¹ Ibid.

⁵² *Kairos Prison Ministry International, Inc.: Program Manual.* Winter Park, Florida. 2011 Edition, p. I-2.

⁵³ Ibid, p. I-1.

⁵⁴ Ibid, p. II-1.

⁵⁵ Wilson, Jr. Bonum. Email. September 24, 2019.

⁵⁶ "Kairos." *Saint James Ministries.* 2019-2020, p. 26.

⁵⁷ Saint James *Epistle,* April 2012, p. 9.

⁵⁸ Saint James *Epistle,* February 2014, p. 5.

⁵⁹ Bumpas, Rev. Elizabeth. Email. November 1, 2019.

⁶⁰ Saint James *Epistle,* January 2013, p. 9.

FOOTNOTES FOR CHAPTER TWENTY-FOUR

1 Saint James vestry minutes, September 15, 1986.

2 Schatz, Helen. "ECW Kitchen Committee Report." *Saint James Congregational Report.* 1987 p. 16.

3 Saint James vestry minutes, April 21, 1997.

4 Saint James *Epistle,* October 2014, p. 1.

5 Saint James *Epistle,* February 2013, p. 1.

6 Saint James vestry minutes, April 21, 1997.

7 Majors, Pat. "Beverage and Bagel Ministry." *Saint James Congregational Report.* May 19, 2019, p. 7.

8 *Saint James Sampler*, Compiled by the women of Saint James Episcopal Church, James Island, South Carolina. Shawnee Mission, Kansas: Circulation Service, 1979.

9 *St. James Sampler II* (with introduction entitled "History of St. James Church" by Dr. Daniel W. Ellis, Mrs. Kitty Ellis, and Mr. Stanley Cross). Charleston: Quin Press, no date listed (circa 1994).

10 Saint James *Epistle,* September 15, 2015, p. 4.

[11] Saint James *Epistle*, June 2014, p. 5.

[12] *St. James Episcopal Church Directory 1988*, p. 4.

[13] Watkins, Susan. "Christian Education Coordinator." *Saint James Congregational Report*. 1985. p. 8.

[14] Saint James *Epistle*, April 2010 p. 1.

[15] Saint James *Epistle,* March 2012, p. 1.

[16] Saint James Epistle, December 2011, p. 3.

[17] Saint James *Epistle*, December 2011, p. 5.

[18] *St. James Episcopal Church Directory 1988*, p. 4.

[19] "Saint James Church Program," 4:00 Family Christmas Eve Pageant, Ministry Center, December 24, 2019.

[20] Saint James *Epistle*, March 2014, p. 6.

[21] Saint James *Epistle,* April 2012, p. 3.

[22] McKee, Becky. "Acolyte Report." *Saint James Congregational Report*. May 1, 2016, p. 8.

[23] Watkins, Susan. "Christian Education Coordinator's Report." *Saint James Congregational Report*. January 22, 1984, p. 2.

[24] Saint James *Epistle,* February 2008, p. 4.

[25] Saint James *Epistle*, August 2014, p. 5.

[26] Saint James vestry minutes, August 20, 2019.

[27] Saint James *Epistle*, October 2019, p. 12.

[28] Ash, Sr., Lloyd M. "BSA Troop 44." *Saint James Congregational Report*. January 15, 1989. p. 31.

[29] Pennington, Paul. Email. November 25, 2019.

[30] Horne, Artie. Email. December 27, 2019.

[31] Saint James vestry minutes, December 17, 2019.

[32] "Parish Profile: St. James Episcopal Church." 1998, p. 14.

[33] Saint James *Epistle*, October 2014, p. 3.

[34] "Parish Profile: St. James' Episcopal Church." 1987, p. 29.

[35] Saint James *Epistle*, July 2011, p. 3.

[36] Saint James *Epistle*, October 2019, p. 9.

[37] Saint James Church bulletin. August 9, 1981.

[38] James *Epistle,* May 2012, p. 6.

[39] Bartels, Virginia. "Women's Cabin Retreat." *Saint James Congregational Report*. May 16, 2018, p. 16.

[40] Weld, Rev. Louise. "Associate Pastor's Report." *Saint James Congregational Report*. May 1, 2016, p. 4.

[41] Saint James *Epistle*, April 2005, p. 1.

[42] Saint James *Epistle,* July 2012, p. 9.

[43] "Parish Profile: St. James Episcopal Church." 1998, p. 10.

44 Saint James *Epistle*, September 2012, p. 5.

45 Saint James Church's Sunday bulletin. February 3, 1985.

46 "Parish Profile: St. James' Episcopal Church." 1987, p. 17.

47 "Men's Ministries and Events: Saint James Men's Hikes." *Saint James Connections.* 2017, p. 22.

48 DuPre, Jimmy. "Men's Thursday Luncheon Bible Study." *Saint James Congregational Report.* January 11, 1998, p. 24.

49 "Men's Ministries and Events: Friday Men's Breakfast." *Saint James Connections.* 2017, p. 22.

50 Kitchens, Bill. "Report from Promise Keepers." *Saint James Congregational Report.* January 11, 1998, p. 26.

51 Saint James vestry minutes, September 17, 2019.

52 Saint James *Epistle,* December 2011, p. 7.

53 Saint James *Epistle,* April 2013, p. 3.

54 Saint James *Epistle*, November 11, 2011, p. 3.

55 Saint James *Epistle,* April 2012, p. 4.

56 Saint James *Epistle,* July 2012, p. 4.

57 "Life Groups @ Saint James." *Saint James Ministries.* 2018. p 12.

58 McGougan, Lillie. "Precepts Bible Study." *Saint James Congregational Report.* April 21, 2002, p. 22.

59 Egleston, Francie. "Report of the ACTS 2:42 Bible Study Group." *Saint James Congregational Report.* January 17, 1999.

60 Saint James *Epistle*, September 2011, p. 4.

61 Saint James Epistle, December 2013, p. 10.

62 Saint James vestry minutes, October 15, 2019.

63 Saint James *Epistle*, January 2011, p. 3.

64 Saint James *Epistle*, April 2011, p. 3.

65 Finch, Rev. Floyd. "Report of the Pastoral Associate." *Saint James Congregational Report.* January 17, 1999, p. 9.

FOOTNOTES FOR CHAPTER TWENTY-FIVE

1 Huston, David A. "The Angels of the Seven Churches." http://www.gloriouschurch.com/html/angels-of-the-seven-churches.asp 2/3/2018, pp. 6-7.

2 Cooke, Rev. Mark. Notes for Sunday school lesson on Revelations 2:12-17, March 10, 2019.

3 Jeremiah, Dr. David. *Angels: Who They Are and How They Help…What the Bible Reveals. (Study Guide.)* San Diego: Turning Point for God, 2013, p. 11.

4 Ibid, pp. 12-13.

5 Ibid, pp. 13-14.

Footnotes for "Author's Closing Notes"

1   Williams, George W. *St. Michael's: Charleston, 1751-1951, with Supplements, 1951-2001.* Columbia: College of Charleston Library, 2001, p. 106.

2   Barnstone, Willis (translator). *The Poems of Jesus Christ.* New York: W.W. Norton and Company, 2012, p. 142.

3   Ibid, p. xix.

4   Ibid, pp. xxi-xxii.

5   Graydon, Nell S. *Tales of Edisto.* Orangeburg, SC: Sandlapper Publishing Co., Inc., 1955. Seventh printing, January 1983, p. 166.

BIBLIOGRAPHY

Albinger, Brenda. "Organist/Choir Director Report." *Saint James Congregational Report 1984.* pp.7-8.

Albinger, Brenda. "Organist/Choir Director Report." *Saint James Congregational Report 1987.* p. 15.

Allen, Patrick, et. al. "Diocese of South Carolina: 212th Convention—Proposed Resolution." January 4, 2002.

Allison, C. Fitzsimons. "Seek Just Settlement in Church Dispute." *Post and Courier.* October 29, 2017, p. C3.

"All Souls Anglican Church Okinawa—Staff: Our Priest. Fr. Creighton Evans." www.allsoulsokinawa.com. June 16. 2018.

Anderson, Dorothy Middleton and Margaret Middleton Rivers Eastman. *St. Philip's Church of Charleston: An Early History of the Oldest Parish in South Carolina.* Charleston, SC: The History Press, 2014.

Anderson, Ellen. "After 48 Years, Couple Still Making Music Together." *The News and Courier.* April 12, 1972, p. E2.

Anderson, Ellen. "Easter Best." *The News and Courier.* (date and page unknown).

Anderson, Ellen. "Halloween." *The News and Courier.* October 30, 1987. Page unknown.

"Angels We Have Heard on High: Advent 1985." Booklet published by Saint James Church.

"Anglican Church Receives Diocese of S.C." *The Post and Courier.* July 2, 2017, p. G6.

Ash, Sr., Lloyd M. "BSA Troop 44." *Saint James Congregational Report.* January 15, 1989, p. 31.

Ash, Sr., Lloyd M. "Scouting at Saint James." *Saint James Congregational Report 1984.* pp. 9-10.

Baldwin, William P. *Bowen's Island.* Charleston: Evening Post Books, 2016.

"Barber, Jr. Robert A." https://en.wikipedia.org/w/index.php?title=Robert_A._Barber_Jr.&oldid=802732371

Barnette, Scooter. Email. November 25, 2019.

Barnstone, Willis (translator). *The Poems of Jesus Christ.* New York: W.W. Norton and Company, 2012.

Bartelme, Tony. "Plantation's Future Lies in McLeod Family Wills." *Post and Courier.* May 17, 1990. (no page given)

Bartels, Virginia. "*Sea Island Glory*: Jim Booth Painting of Saint James to Celebrate 300th Anniversary," *Jubilate Deo*. Winter 2020, p. 15.

Bartels, Virginia. "Women's Cabin Retreat." *Saint James Congregational Report*. May 16, 2018, p. 16.

Barwick, Mark. "Report on Christian Education." *Saint James Congregational Report*. April 21, 2002, p. 15.

Baxley, Colette. "James Island Senior Has No Regrets." *The News and Courier*. July 12, 1987, p. E2.

"Bishop Duvall to Speak on Protestant Hour," *Jubilate Deo*. 1987, p. 7.

"Bishop Gadsden: An Episcopal Retirement Community." *Jubilate Deo*. February 1987, pp. C-F.

"Bishop's Journal." Article among Saint James' historical papers. "May 1903" written at the top of the copy. No other publishing information available.

Bonstelle, Carolyn Ackerly and Geordie Buxton. *Images of America: James Island*. Charleston: Arcadia Publishing, 2008.

Bostick, Douglas W. *A Brief History of James Island: Jewel of the Sea Islands*. Charleston: History Press, 2008.

Bowen's Island. Charleston, SC: Evening Post Books, 2016.

Bresee, Clyde. *How Grand a Flame: A Chronicle of a Plantation Family 1813-1947*. Chapel Hill: Algonquin Books, 1992.

Bresee, Clyde. *Sea Island Yankee*. Chapel Hill: Algonquin Books of Chapel Hill, 1986.

"Bridge Church to the Homeless." *Saint James Ministries*. 2019-2020, p. 26.

Brown, Dr. James Allen Brown. Sermon on missions delivered at Saint James on May 10 (year not recorded).

Brown, Shirley. "How to Hear God's Voice." *Saint James Congregational Report*. May 5, 2013, p. 13.

Bumpas, Rev. Elizabeth. Email. November 1, 2019.

Bumpas, Rev. Elizabeth. Email. October 31, 2019.

Bumpas, Rev. Elizabeth. Personal interview. July 26. 2017.

Bumpas, Rev. Elizabeth. Resume. July 2017.

Burrell, Vic. "Senior Warden's Report 1983." *Saint James Congregational Report 1984*. p. 1.

Campbell, Marjorie. "Cornerstone Laying Set for St. James Church." *The News and Courier*. May 10, 1959, p. C4.

Carter, William. "Senior Warden's Report." *Saint James' Congregational Report*. January 13, 1991, p. 16.

"Cemetery: Saint James Episcopal Church James Island, S.C." published by the Cemetery Committee of Saint James. April 24, 2005.

"Certificate of Incorporation." Granted to Saint James by the State of South Carolina. May 14, 1903.

Chavis, Dustin. "Sexton." *Saint James Congregational Report*. May 6, 2012, p. 18.

"A Child Is Born." *This Week in West Ashley*. December 23, 1993, p. 6.

"Choral Society to Present Oratorio by Mendelssohn: Hinson Mikell of James Island, at the Organ," March 1960 (newspaper article with no publishing information included)

"Christian Education Report." *Saint James Congregational Report 1987*. p. 12.

"Christmas in July: Missions Catalog 2019." Published by Saint James Mission Committee.

"Christmas Pageants of the Lowcountry: St. James Church." *Carolina Compass*. January 2020, p. 9.

"Churches in Diocese of South Carolina Rejects Episcopal Church's 'Spurious' Offer to Settle." *The Anglican Diocese of South Carolina News*, June 15, 2015. (posted on the website of The Anglican Diocese of South Carolina and accessible on the 'Timeline.')

"Clement, Jr., Francis 'Frank' Walpole—Obituary." *Post and Courier*. June 1, 2018, p. B4.

Cole, Lynda Owen. Letter. January 23, 2019.

"Contract Signed for New Church." *The News and Courier*, December 28, 1958, p. C4.

Cooke, Rev. Mark Dean. Email to Virginia Bartels. May 11, 2018.

Cooke, Rev. Mark. Notes for Sunday school lesson on Revelations 2:12-17, March 10, 2019.

Cooke, Rev. Mark. "Pastor's Report." *Saint James Congregational Report*, May 19, 2019, p. 4.

Cooke, Rev. Mark Dean. Resume and email sent to Virginia Bartels. May 11, 2018.

Crawford, Darren and Sue Crawford. "Mission Report," *Saint James Congregational Report*. January 11, 1998, p. 23.

Cupka, David. "Senior Warden's Report." *Saint James Congregational Report*. January 12, 1997, p. 1.

Dalcho, Frederick, M.D. *An Historical Account of the Protestant Episcopal Church in South Carolina 1670-1820*. Charleston: E. Thayer (at his theological bookstore—Broadstreet), 1820.

"The Day after Hugo…Destruction Everywhere." *Jubilate Deo*. November/December 1989, p. 10.

Dayschool@saint-james.org, November 25, 2019.

Denison, Mark. "Why Churches Close." p. 1. www.churchmadebetter.com/why-churches-close/ December 14, 2015.

Dickerson, June. "Cemetery: Saint James Episcopal Church James Island, S.C." November 26, 2001. (no page—timeline in front of booklet).

"The Dill Sanctuary—Charleston, S.C." http://www.charlestonmuseum.org/about-factsheet) March 14, 2019.

"Diocesan Leadership: The Rt. Rev'd Clark W.P. Lowenfield." Diocesan of Western Gulf Coast webpage. http://www.dwgc.org, July 1, 2019.

"Diocese to Hold 2019 Annual Convention March 15-16." *The Anglican Diocese of South Carolina: Making Biblical Anglicans for a Global Age*. https//adosc.org/author-dave-runyon-to-speak-at-228th-annal-convention/"

"Diocese of South Carolina website." http://www.dioceseofsc.org.

Doran, Mary Ellen. "Christian Education." *Saint James Congregational Report*. May 6, 2007, p. 9.

Doran, Rev. Mary Ellen. Personal interview. July 26, 2017.

Doran, Rev. Mary Ellen. Resume. July 26, 2017.

"Do You Know Your Charleston? St. James Church." *The News and Courier*. February 16, 1931, p. 10.

DuPre, Jimmy. "Men's Thursday Luncheon Bible Study." *Saint James Congregational Report*. January 11, 1998, p. 24.

DuPre, James H. "Senior Warden's Report." *Saint James Congregational Report*. January 8, 1995, p. 5.

"Duvall, The Rt. Rev. Charles F." "Report of the Committee for the Election of the 13th Bishop of the Diocese of South Carolina." August 1, 1989, pp. 4-5.

Easterby, J. H. "Introduction." Way, Rev. William. *The History of Grace Church: Charleston, South Carolina: The First Hundred Years*. Durham, NC: Seeman Printery, 1948.

"ECW Annual Meeting Agenda." *Jubilate Deo*, March 1989, p. 1.

Egleston, David D. "Outreach and Evangelism Commission." *Saint James Congregational Report 1984*. pp. 11-12.

Egleston, Francie. "Report of the ACTS 2:42 Bible Study Group." *Saint James Congregational Report*. January 17, 1999.

"Epistle to Saint James'." James Island: Saint James Church. September 1990.

"Evans, Jr. The Rev. Creighton June 17, 1953-May 17, 2018." Diocese of South Carolina. jhunter@diocese-ofsc.org, May 2018.

"Evans, Jr., The Rev. Vernon Creighton 1953-2018." Diocese of Southwest Florida. May 2018.

"Evans, Jr., Vernon Creighton: Obituary." *The Post and Courier*. July 8, 2018, p. C4.

"Faith Signers." https://www.palmettofamily.org/diocese-supporters. 9/19/2017.

"Federal Judge Enjoins Use of Diocese Names and Seal." News from the Anglican Diocese of South Carolina. (email from Joy Hunter), September 20, 2019.

Fennell, Edward C. "Bygone Days of James Island Recalled." *News and Courier*. (no date or page given)

Finch, Rev. Floyd. "Pastoral Associate's Report 1999." *Saint James Congregational Report*. January 17, 1999, p. 11.

Finch, Jr., Rev. Floyd. Personal interview. September 1, 2017.

Finch, Rev. Floyd. "Report of the Pastoral Associate." *Saint James Congregational Report*. January 17, 1999, p. 9.

Finch, Jr., Rev. Floyd W. Vita. 2017.

"Floyd Finch Retires; Accepts New Job." *Jubilate Deo*. June 1993, p. 3.

Frazier, Eugene, Sr. *A History of James Island: Slave Descendants & Plantation Owners*. Charleston: History Press, 2010.

"Frequently Asked Questions." "News and Events: Legal News." Diocese of South Carolina website. https://www.dioceseofsc.org. August 6, 2019.

"Funeral of Dr. Whaley: Services in Trinity Church on Edisto Island for Rector." *The News and Courier*. September 6, 1915.

Gibson, Kimberly. "Pastoral Care Commission. *Saint James Congregational Report 1985*. p. 14.

Gibson, Royal (Chip). "Saint James' Church Stewardship Committee Report." *Saint James Congregational Report 1987*. p. 19.

Gilbreth, Edward M. "Strong Judicial Disagreements Fuel Episcopal Controversy." *Post and Courier*. November 2, 2017, p. A3.

Gilbreth, Edward M. "Vexing Times for Many S.C. Episcopalians." *Post and Courier.* August 17, 2017, p. A3.

Gould, Pat. "Report from the Director of Music." *Saint James Congregational Report.* April 21, 2002, pp. 13-14.

Graydon, Nell S. *Tales of Edisto.* Orangeburg, SC: Sandlapper Publishing Co., Inc., 1955. Seventh printing, January 1983.

Green, Rev. Carl. "John 8:36 Prison Ministry." *Saint James Congregational Report.* May 12, 2015, p. 12.

Griggs, Alisha. "Youth Ministry Report—Middle School." *Saint James Congregational Report.* May 17, 2015, pp. 17-18.

"Groundbreaking—New Classrooms; St. James', James Island; May 5, 1968" ceremony program.

Hampton, Harriott. "Trip to Holy Land Is a Gift of Love." (source of article unknown)

Hawes, Jennifer Berry and Adam Parker. "S.C. Supreme Court Ruling a Win for Episcopal Church." *Post and Courier.* August 3, 2017. pp. A1 and A4.

Hayden, Frances. "St. James Church to be Included in Garden Tour." *The News and Courier.* October 4, 1953, p. C6.

Hayes, Jim. *James and Related Sea Islands.* Charleston: Walker, Evans, and Cogswell, 1978.

Haynie, Connie Walpole. *Images of America: Johns Island.* Charleston: Arcadia Publishing, 2007.

"Hazel Carte to Retire February 28." *Jubilate Deo.* February 1987, p. 1.

Hilton, Tom. Email. December 15, 2019.

Hinson, William G. "Transcribed from Manuscript Attributed to Wm. G. Hinson—Sketch of James Island, South Carolina." Based on Topographic Inquiries March 9-12, 1895. Cornell University, Ithaca, NY. June 12, 1895. Filed 19 March 1975.

Historic Sites of James Island. Compiled by the James Island History Commission of the Town of James Island. 2019. www.jamesislandsc.us.

"Historical Sketch of St. James' Parish, James Island, South Carolina." (no further publishing information given; contents reveal publication 1969 or later)

"Historiographer Named." *Jubilate Deo.* March 1989, p. A.

"History of 240 Year Old St. James Episcopal Church." *James Island Journal.* April 30, 1970. (first page of article not given, continued on page 8).

Hood, Victoria. "Laura Ashley Blooms in Every Season." *The News and Courier.* February 26, 1987, p. C1.

Horn, Rev. Robert. "Associate Pastor Horn." *Saint James Congregational Report.* May 6, 2007, p. 4.

Horn, Rev. J. Robert. Personal interview. August 10, 2017.

Horne, Artie. Email. December 27, 2019.

Howard, Rev. John. "Rector's Report." *Saint James Congregational Report.* January 10, 1993, pp. 4-5.

"Howard, The Right Reverend Samuel Johnson." Bishop of Florida.: http://www.diocesefl.org/about-us/the-diocese/bishop-of-florida. February 3, 2018.

Huey, Rev. Marshall. "Assistant Rector's Report." *Saint James Congregational Report*. April 21, 2002, pp. 8-9.

"Huff Named Rector of St. Peter's." *Jubilate Deo*, June 1993, p. 3.

Huff, Rev. Christopher Mercer. Email. August 30, 2017.

Huff, Rev. Christopher Mercer. Resume. 2017.

Huston, David A. "The Angels of the Seven Churches." http://www.gloriouschurch.com/html/angels-of-the-seven-churches.asp 2/3/2018.

"James Island Church: First Built Prior to 1730 as Shown in Early Records." Do You Know Your Charleston? *The News and Courier*. February 16, 1931, p. 10.

"James Island Church Will Mark 200th Anniversary: Services to Be Held Today, With Sermon by Bishop Thomas and Rev. Wallace Martin, Rector, Officiating; History Is Told." *The News and Courier*. November 9, 1930. P. A12.

James Island and Johns Island Historical Survey. Project carried out for South Carolina Department of Archives and History. City of Charleston and Charleston County. Summer 1989. http://www.jamesislandsc.us/Data/sites/1/media/james-island-and-johns-island-historical-survey.pdf.

James Island Outreach website. www.jioutreach.org. September 25, 2019.

Jarrell, Frank P. "Bresee's Latest Goes Back to Past." *Post and Courier*. No date available, p. D1.

Jenkins, Rev. Arthur. "Assistant Rector's Annual Report." *Saint James Congregational Report*. January 10, 1993, pp. 6-7.

Jenkins, Rev. Arthur. "Come and See." *Saint James Congregational Report*. May 6, 2007, p. 2.

Jenkins, Rev. Arthur. "Divinity Working through Humanity." *Saint James Congregational Report*. January 23, 2000, p. 7.

Jenkins, Rev. Arthur. Email. February 6, 2019.

Jenkins, Rev. Arthur. "Rector's Annual Report." *Saint James Congregational Report*. May 6, 2012, p. 1.

Jenkins, Rev. Arthur. "Rector's Annual Report." *Saint James Congregational Report*. May 5, 2013, p. 1.

Jenkins, Rev. Arthur. "Rector's Annual Report." *Saint James Congregational Report*. May 17, 2015, p. 3.

Jenkins, Rev. Arthur. "Rector's Annual Report." *Saint James Congregational Report*. May 6, 2018, p. 2.

Jenkins, Rev. Arthur. "Rector's Annual Report." *Saint James Congregational Report*. May 19, 2019, p. 1.

Jenkins, Rev. Arthur. "South Carolina Supreme Court Decision." Email sent to Saint James' congregation. August 2, 2017.

Jenkins, Rev. Arthur. "When They Had Prayed." *Saint James Congregational Report*. April 21, 2002. p. 6.

Jenkins, Rev. Arthur. "Who Do You Say I Am?" *Saint James Congregational Report*. May 4, 2008, p. 3.

Jenkins, Rev. Arthur. "Writ of Certiorari." Email sent to Saint James' congregation June 12, 2018.

Jeremiah, Dr. David. *Angels: Who They Are and How They Help…What the Bible Reveals. (Study Guide.)* San Diego: Turning Point for God, 2013.

Johnson, Lorene, "Outreach and Evangelism Commission." *Saint James Congregational Report 1985.* p. 12.

Johnson, Skip. "Minister Communicates through Music." *The News and Courier.* June 25, 1989, p. D10.

Johnson, Skip. "Phyllis Rooke's Tragedy Turned into Success." *The News and Courier.* March 26, 1985, pp. 2 and 14.

Jubilate Deo. Printed by The Episcopal Dioceses of South Carolina. Cited by articles and dates in text.

Kairos Prison Ministry International, Inc.: Program Manual. Winter Park, Florida. 2011 Edition.

"Kairos." *Saint James Ministries.* 2019-2020, p. 26.

King, Ann L. "Christian Education Report." *Saint James' Congregational Report.* January 13, 1991, p. 17.

King, Ann. "Report of the Senior Warden." *Saint James Congregational Report.* April 21, 2002, p. 4.

King, Mary. "World Missions." *Saint James Congregational Report.* April 21, 2002, p. 19.

King, Mary. "World Missions." *Saint James Congregational Report.* May 18, 2003, p. 13.

Kitchens, Bill. "Report from Promise Keepers." *Saint James Congregational Report.* January 11, 1998, p. 26.

"Kitty Ellis, St. James, James Island." Profiles in Leadership. *Jubilate Deo.* May 1982, p. C.

Knapp, Andrew. "Churches Eye Pivotal Moment in State's Episcopal Dispute." *Post and Courier.* June 5, 2018, p. A3.

Knapp, Andrew. "Diocese of South Carolina Hopes Its US Supreme Court Case Sees Daylight." *Post and Courier.* November 26, 2017, p. G1.

Knapp, Andrew. "Justice's Episcopal Ties in Question." *Post and Courier.* October 15, 2017, pp. A1 and A8.

"Lamb Institute: History Timeline." Lambinstitute.org. August 12, 2017.

"Last Will and Testament of William E. McLeod." Dated June 20, 1985.

Lawrence, Bishop Mark. "A Letter from Bishop Lawrence Post Denial from SCOTUS." Email sent by Rev. Canon Jim Lewis to Saint James vestry. June 14, 2018.

"Laying of Cornerstone: Remarks by the Rector—The Rev. Edward B. Guerry." St. James Episcopal Church. May 10, 1959.

Legare, Anne. "Retired Couple Take on Life with Enthusiasm." Article may be from *The News and Courier,* but no additional publication information available except pp. C1 and C4.

Legerton, Clifford L. *Historic Churches of Charleston, SC: A Collection of Photographs and Histories of Old Charleston Churches.* Charleston: Legerton and Company, 1966.

Lent, The Rev. Morris J. , Jr. "Why I Teach." *Porter-Gaud News.* August 1989, p. 12.

Lewis, The Rev. Canon Jim. "The Mediation Process" email to rectors and vicars of the Diocese of South Carolina. August 6, 2019.

Lewis, The Rev. Canon Jim. "Petition filed with the United States Supreme Court." Email to members of the Diocese of South Carolina. February, 12, 2018.

Lewis, The Rev. Canon Jim. "The Real Story behind Our Split with the Episcopal Church." *Charleston Mercury.* October 2, 2013, pp. 1-4.

Lewis, The Rev. Canon Jim. "South Carolina Circuit Court Rules in Favor of Diocese of South Carolina on Betterments Statute." Email to vestry at Saint James. August 28, 2019.

"Life Groups @ Saint James." *Saint James Ministries*. 2018. p 12.

"Limehouse to be Hartsville Rector." *Jubilate Deo*. May 1991, p. 6.

Limehouse, Rev. Frank. "Associate Rector's Annual Message." *Saint James Congregational Report*. January 13, 1991, p. 12.

Limehouse, Rev. Frank. "Assistant Rector's Report." *Saint James Congregational Report*. January 21, 1990, p. 9.

Limehouse, Rev. Frank. "Letter to the congregation of St. James' Episcopal Church." Charleston, SC. March 6, 1991.

"Litigation Facts." "News and Events: Legal News." Diocese of South Carolina website. https://www.dioceseofsc.org. August 6, 2019.

"Lukanich, Rev. Emily Anderson: Assistant Rector—Clergy—Episcopal Church of the Transfiguration of Vail." http://episcopalvail.com/who-we-are/our-leadership. 1/9/2018.

Lukanich, Rev. Emily Anderson. Email. July 25, 2018.

MacArthur, John. *Twelve Extraordinary Women: How God Shaped Women of the Bible and What He Wants to Do with You*. Nashville: Thomas Nelson, Inc., 2005.

MacDougall, David W. "Centenarians Meet Each Year with Grace." *The Evening Post*. Living Section. September 18, 1987, p. B4.

MacDougall, David W. "To Mother, with Love." *The News and Courier*. Tempo Section. May 10, 1987, p. E1.

Maher, John Edward. *An Old Timer's Memories of Charleston, South Carolina*. Summerville, SC: Words Unlimited, 1992.

Majors, Pat. "Beverage and Bagel Ministry." *Saint James Congregational Report*. May 19, 2019, p. 7.

Mays, Deirdre C. "Book's Proceeds Going to Homeless Charities." *The Post and Courier*. October 8, 1992, p. 10.

McCall, Suzy. Email. June 18, 2018.

McCall, Suzy. *Tania de la Cantera*. CreateSpace Independent Publishing Platform, November 15, 2012.

McCormick, Rev. J. Haden. "Message from the Rector." Anderson, Dorothy Middleton and Margaret Middleton Rivers Eastman. *St. Philip's Church of Charleston: An Early History of the Oldest Parish in South Carolina*. Charleston, SC: The History Press, 2014.

McDowell, Elsa F. "Churches Attract Serious Musicians." *The News and Courier*. February 5, 1989, p. D5.

McDowell, Elsa F. "Lent Becomes Chaplain of Porter-Gaud School." *The News and Courier*. July 5, 1987, p. D5.

McDowell, Elsa F. "New Church Making Progress." *The News and Courier*. July 5, 1987, p. D5.

McDowell, Elsa F. "Pastor Has Found His Niche in Life." *The News and Courier*. May 12, 1985, no page number available.

McGougan, Lillie. Personal interview. July 31, 2017.

McGougan, Lillie. "Precepts Bible Study." *Saint James Congregational Report*. April 21, 2002, p. 22.

McIntyre, Michael. "Youth Minister's Annual Report." *Saint James Congregational Report.* January 11, 1998, p. 10.

McIntyre, Michael. "Youth Ministry." *Saint James Congregational Report.* January 23, 2000, pp. 13-15.

McIntyre, Michael. "Youth Ministry Annual Report." *Saint James Congregational Report.* April 21, 2002, pp. 11-12.

McKee, Becky. "Acolyte Report." *Saint James Congregational Report.* May 1, 2016, p. 8.

"McLeod Plantation." httpps: / /www.ccprc.com/2085/ Interpretive-tours. February 13, 2019.

McLeod, W. E. "An Outline of the History of James Island, S.C." Program in Honor of James Islanders Serving in the Armed Forces. Published by the Exchange Club of James Island, June 1944.

McManus, Henry B. "Evangelism Commission." *Saint James Congregational Report 1987.* p. 11.

Medical Ministry International emails and pamphlets dated January-May, 2006 and mailed to Dick and Virginia Bartels.

"Meggett, Sr., Mr. W. Gresham (1903-1990)" (article has no additional publication information)

"Men's Ministries and Events: Friday Men's Breakfast." *Saint James Connections.* 2017, p. 22.

"Men's Ministries and Events: Saint James Men's Hikes." *Saint James Connections.* 2017, p. 22.

Mikell, John. Personal Interview. July 2018.

Mikell, John. Personal Interview. March 3, 2019.

Miller, Rev. Jeffrey. "Assistant to the Rector's Report." *Saint James Congregational Report.* January 14, 1996, p. 4.

Miller, Rev. Jeffrey. "Opinion: SC Supreme Court Ruling Against Diocese of South Carolina Threatens Religious Freedom." http:/ /www.islandpacket.com/opinion/op-ed/article173705026. September 16, 2017, pp. 1-6.

"Missionaries, Curates, Ministers-in Charge, and Rectors of St. James Episcopal Church on James Island, Charleston County, South Carolina." (list spanning from 1707 to 1960) publishing information unavailable. Resource obtained from John and Kathy Mikell, 2018.

Morrison, Clark, John Mikell, and Joel Porcher. Personal interview. July 2018.

Morrison, Clark and Louise. Personal interview. July 17, 2017.

"Mr. Watson Accepts Call to St. James." *The News and Courier.* October 26, 1960, no page.

Munday, Dave. "Faith with a Healing Touch: Believers Share Their Stories." "Religion." *The Post and Courier.* January 21, 2001, p. G7.

"New St. James Church Opens Its Doors Today." *The News and Courier.* August 28, 1960, p. C4.

"Noted Sea Island Cotton Farmer William E. McLeod, 104, Dies." January 21, 1990.

Olbrych, Jennie. "Adult Christian Education Commission." *Saint James Congregational Report 1985.* p. 17.

Olbrych, Rev. Jennie. E-mail. July 19, 2017.

Olbrych, Rev. Jennie. Personal interview. July 19, 2017.

Olbrych, Rev. Jennie. Resume. July 2017.

"The One Hundred and Seventy-Fifth Annual Convention of the Diocese of South Carolina Agenda for Convention." May 4 and 5, 1965.

"The Order for Laying the Cornerstone of St. James Church, James Island, Diocese of South Carolina." Saint James Church Program. May 10, 1959.

"The Ordination of Arthur Mack Jenkins to the Priesthood." Saint James' Episcopal Church. June 6, 1992.

"The Ordination of Frank F. Limehouse, III to the Priesthood." Saint James' Episcopal Church. June 17, 1990.

Parker, Adam. "Diocese Wants South Carolina Supreme Court to Rehear Case." *Post and Courier*. September 4, 2017, p. A5.

Parker, Adam. "Episcopal and Anglican Groups Agree to Mediation." *Post and Courier*. September 10, 2017, p. G6.

Parker, Adam. "Episcopal Case in S.C. Won't Get a Rehearing." *Post and Courier*. November 20, 2017, pp. A1 and A4.

Parker, Adam. "Getting up to Speed with the Episcopal-Anglican Legal Battle." *Post and Courier*. October 1, 2017. pp. G1 and G8.

Parker, Adam and Jennifer Berry Hawes. "Episcopal Church Enters New Chapter in Schism." *The Post and Courier*. August 6, 2017, pp. G1 and G6.

"Parish Profile: St. James' Episcopal Church." Charleston, SC. 1987.

Payne, Barbara R. editor. *Amazing Grace: The Parish Church of St. Helena Beaufort, South Carolina*. Beaufort: Lydia Inglett Ltd. Publishing, 2012.

Pennington, Paul. Email. November 25, 2019.

Phillips, Mark. "The Search Committee Report." *2015 Annual Report St. Philips Church*. p. 8.

Porcher, Mary C. "Memorials and Gifts Committee." *Saint James Congregational Report*. January 10, 1993. p. 6.

Porwoll, Paul. *Against All Odds: History of Saint Andrew's Parish Church, Charleston, 1706-2013*. Bloomington, IN: WestBow Press, 2014.

Powell, Marilyn, "From the Deacon." *Saint James Congregational Report*. April 21, 2002, p. 6.

Prior, Greg. "Mr. Willie' McLeod to be Honored on 100th Birthday." (no additional publishing information available)

"Priors Moving to Hilton Head." *Jubilate Deo*. March 1993, p. 3.

"Prominent Musician Joins Staff at St. James." *Jubilate Deo*. March 1989, p. 3.

Rainer, Thom S. and Eric Geiger. *Simple Church*. Nashville: B & H Publishing Group, 2006.

Reed, Anne. "Chapel Altar Guild 1983." *Saint James Congregational Report 1984*. p. 11.

"Reports from Detroit: From Morey Lent." *Jubilate Deo*. September 1988, p. 7.

"The Rev. Canon E.B. Guerry Dies." *The Post and Courier*. October 20, 1992, p. B2.

"Rev. Dr. J. Gregory Prior, Recent Vicars and Rectors." www.standrews/lc.org, July 1, 2019.

"The Reverend Emily Anderson Lukanich." emily@episcopalvail.com. 1/9/2018.

Rhodes, Dee. "Outreach Commission." *Saint James Congregational Report 1987*. p. 9.

Rienow, Rob and Amy. *Visionary Parenting: Capture a God-Size Vision for Your Family.* Nashville: Randall House, 2009.

Rivers, Captain E. L. "A History of St. James' Episcopal Church, James Island." 1894. Revised and completed by Daniel W. Ellis, 1930. Published by the Vestry in connection with the Bi-Centennial Service of St. James' Church, held November 9, 1930.

Rivers, Miss Martha L. "An Historical Sketch of St. James Church." On microfiche in the Charleston County Library, Calhoun Street. Slides 457-463. 1947.

"Robert A. Barber, Jr." https://en.wikipedia.org/w/index.php?title=Robert_A._Barber_Jr.&oldid=802732371

"Robert's of Charleston" dinner menu and program, Saint James Church, February 14, 2020.

"The Rt. Rev. Charles F. Duvall, *Report of the Committee for the Election of the 13th Bishop of the Diocese of South Carolina,*" published by the Diocese of South Carolina, August 1, 1989, p. 4.

"Saint James Anglican Church 300th Anniversary Dinner." Evening program for Saint James Tricentennial Celebration: History Weekend—January 25, 2020.

"Saint James Church. Love God. Love People. Build Community." website. https://saint-james.org. 2019.

"Saint James Church Program," 4:00 Family Christmas Eve Pageant, Ministry Center, December 24, 2019.

"Saint James Day School." dayschool@saint-james.org. November 25, 2019.

Saint James Sampler, Compiled by the women of Saint James Episcopal Church, James Island, South Carolina. Shawnee Mission, Kansas: Circulation Service, 1979.

Saint James vestry minutes (dates included in text and footnotes).

Salmon, Jr. The Right Rev. Edward L. "Letter of Invitation to Mr. Matthew Townsend." Charleston, SC. May 28, 1990.

Schatz, Helen. "ECW Kitchen Committee Report." *Saint James Congregational Report.* 1987 p. 16.

Schatz, Helen. "ECW Kitchen Report." *Saint James Congregational Report.* 1990, p. 17.

"Search Process Employed by St. James Church to Select a Minister to Replace The Reverend Morris J. Lent who Resigned Effective 1 August 1987." Printed by search committee appointed by the vestry. 1988.

Shelton, Rev. Jeremy. Email. June 27, 2018.

Shelton, Rev. Jeremy: "The Ordination of Jeremy Alan Shelton to the Sacred Order of Priests." December 1, 2018.

Shue, Carol. "Christ Kindergarten." *Saint James Congregational Report 1985*. pp. 15-16.

Shumake, Janice. "Circus Still Lives in Senior Citizen." *Post and Courier.* April 2, 1989, p. E3.

Simmons, William H. "Junior Warden's Final Report." *Saint James Congregational Report.* January 15, 1989, p. 12.

"Sixth Church of St. James' Consecrated." *The Diocese: Official Publication of the Diocese of South Carolina.* Autumn, 1964, p. 10.

"Smiling Faces" (article about Christ Kindergarten celebrating its thirteenth annual May Day Program— no publication information available).

Snowden, Octavia. "Teenage Organist Gives Best Effort to Every Undertaking." *The News and Courier.* August 24, 1958, p. C2.

Source Case No. 88-CP-10-2003 in the Court of Common Pleas, State of South Carolina, County of Charleston. St. James Church, James Island, SC an Eleemosynard South Carolina corporation, Honorable Louis E. Condon, Master of equity for the County of Charleston. September 22,1988.

Stackhouse, Mrs. M.S. "St. James Church James Island, S.C. 1947." Typed four-page history mailed from Mrs. M.S. Stackhouse of Dillon, S.C. to Mr. William McLeod February 1953.

Steele, Joshua. "The ACNA's 2019 Book of Common Prayer (BCP): A Rookie Anglican Guide" https://anglicanpastor.com/the-acnas-2019-book-of-common-prayer-bcp-a-rookie-anglican-guide/ 2019.

"St. James Church James Island." No author or publishing information available. (document consisting of seven double-spaced typed pages included in church's historical records at the parish)

"St. James Church, James Island, South Carolina. First Service in the New Church." Saint James church bulletin, August 28, 1960.

"St. James Church Parish House Will Be Dedicated Today." *The News and Courier.* October 30, 1949. No page number available.

"St. James' Episcopal Church" and "Saint James Anglican Church" bulletins, as cited within text by dates.

St. James Episcopal Church Directory 1988.

"St. James Episcopal Church James Island, S.C. Parish Profile." written by St. James' vestry. Charleston: June 1998.

St. James' (Saint James) *Epistles,* as cited within text by dates.

"St. James Organist Sets Recital." (newspaper article with no publishing information included)

"St. James to Host Choir Festival." *Jubilate Deo.* May 1990, p. 1.

"St. James to Host Convention." *Jubilate Deo.* February 1987, p. A

"St. James Protestant Episcopal Church on the Move." *The Post and Courier.* January 8, 1959. (no page available).

St. James Sampler II (with introduction entitled "History of St. James Church" by Dr. Daniel W. Ellis, Mrs. Kitty Ellis, and Mr. Stanley Cross). Charleston: Quin Press, no date listed (circa 1994).

"St. James' Welcomes New Rector." *Jubilate Deo.* December 1992/January 1993, p. 3.

Stephans, Rev. Craig. "Habits that Sustain Ministry: Craig Stephans' Spiritual Autobiography." Summer 2016. Attached to email sent to Virginia Bartels 2017 and September 12, 2018.

Stringer-Robinson, Gretchen. "The Sacrifices of the Slaves of James Island Have Not Been Forgotten." *Bugle James Island.* February 8, 2017.

Stroud, Mike. "Battery Haskell." *The Historical Marker Database.* https://www.hmdb.org/marker.asp?marker=39708. June 16, 2016. p. 2.

"Suzy McCall Plans Mission to Latin America." *Jubilate Deo.* May 1990, p. 7.

Taylor, Ashby and Anne Read. "Christian Giving Report." *Saint James Congregational Report.* January 10, 1993, p. 5.

Thomas, Albert Sidney. *Historical Account of the Protestant Episcopal Church in South Carolina 1820-1957: Being a Continuation of Dalcho's Account 1670-1820.* Charleston: The R.L. Bryan Company, 1957.

"Timeline." "News and Events: Legal News." Diocese of South Carolina website. https://www.diocese-ofsc.org. August 6, 2019.

Townsend, Matthew. "Junior Warden's Report." *Saint James Congregational Report 1991.* pp. 18-20.

Trawick, C. William "Bill." Letter from Bishop Gadsden Director to Rev. Jenkins. February 19, 2007.

"Tributes to Canon Guerry." *Jubilate Deo.* December 1991, p. 3.

"An Unfinished History of St. James' Episcopal Church: James Island, South Carolina. The Story of a Pioneer Church on a Carolina Sea Island." Revised and edited by St. James' Historical Project. Charleston, SC. November 29, 1987.

Video Scenarios—St. James' Episcopal Church, James Island, Charleston County, South Carolina. 11/23/1987-88.

Waite, Phillip. "Youth Ministry Report—High School." *Saint James Congregational Report.* May 17, 2015, p.16.

Walchesky, Chris. "Music Ministry Report." *Saint James Congregational Report.* May 6, 2018, p. 14.

Walker, Jr. William L. editor, *Porter-Gaud News.* August 1989.

Warfuel, Deacon Ron. "Lay Eucharistic Visitors." *Saint James Congregational Report.* May 18, 2014, p. 12.

Waring, Thomas R. "Planter Last Survivor." *The News and Courier.* October 25, 1981, p. E2.

Waring, Thomas R. "St. James Episcopal Church to Mark Mr. Willie's 100th." *The News and Courier.* February 3, 1985, p. F1.

Warren, Rev. Rick. *Better Together: What on Earth Are We Here For? 40 Days of Community.* Lake Forest, CA: Purpose Driven Publishing, 2004.

Warren, Rev. Rick. *The Purpose Driven Life.* Grand Rapids: Zondervan, 2002.

Watkins, Susan. "Christian Education Coordinator." *Saint James Congregational Report,* 1985. p. 8.

Watkins, Susan. "Christian Education Coordinator's Report," *Saint James Congregational Report,* January 22, 1984, p. 2.

Watkins, Susan. "Christian Education Coordinator's Report," *Saint James Congregational Report,* January 21, 1990, p. 9.

Watkins, Susan. "Christian Education Report." *Saint James Congregational Report,* 1987, p. 12.

Way, Rev. William. *The History of Grace Church, Charleston, South Carolina: The First Hundred Years.* Durham, NC: Seeman Printery, 1948.

"Welcome to St. James Episcopal Church." Brochure published in the early 1990s.

Weld, Rev. Louise. "Associate Pastor's Report." *Saint James Congregational Report,* May 5, 2013, p. 4.

Weld, Rev. Louise. "Associate Pastor's Report." *Saint James Congregational Report.* May 1, 2016, p. 4.

Weld, Rev. Louise. "Associate Pastor's Report." *Saint James Congregational Report,* May 6, 2018, p. 5.

Weld, Rev. Louise. "Associate Pastor Weld." *Saint James Congregational Report,* May 6, 2007, p. 6.

Weld, Rev. Louise, editor. *Saint James Lenten Booklet 2019,* featuring 500-word entries by church's priests and parishioners.

Weld, Rev. Louise. Personal interview. July 19, 2017.

Weld, Rev. Louise. Resume. 2017.

Whittle, Fred. Email. December 4, 2019.

Williams, George W. *St. Michael's: Charleston, 1751-1951, with Supplements, 1951-2001.* Columbia: College of Charleston Library, 2001.

Williams, Rev. Jill. "Family Discipleship." *Saint James Congregational Report.* May 18, 2014, p. 11.

Wilson, Bonum, Jr. Email. September 24, 2019.

Young, Gale. "Family Decoration Project Spreads Christmas Spirit." *The News and Courier.* December 11, 1970, p. C1.

"Zahl Called to St. James." *Jubilate Deo.* September 1988, p. 3.

Zahl, Rev. Paul. "Rector's Annual Message." *Saint James Congregational Report.* January 13, 1991, p. 10.

Zahl, Rev. Paul. "The Rector's Report on the State of the Parish." *Saint James Congregational Report.* January 21, 1990, p. 7.

Zahl, Rev. Paul. "Rector's Report." *Saint James' Congregational Report.* January 12, 1992, p. 6.

Zahl, Rev. Paul F.M. *Who Will Deliver Us? The Present Power of the Death of Christ.* New York: The Seabury Press, 1983.

Zahl, Rev. Paul F.M. "A Word from the Rector." Zahl's letter to the Saint James congregation. September 11, 1988.

APPENDIX A

Ministers of Saint James Church

Rev. William Guy	1719-1750	Also priest at St. Andrews; Preached at Saint James every fourth Sunday; Died in service
Rev. Charles Martyn	1752-1770	Also priest at St. Andrews; Preached at Saint James every fourth Sunday; Retired
Rev. Thomas Panting	1770-1771	Also headmaster of the Free School in Charleston; Preached at Saint James occasionally; Died in service
Rev. John Christopher Ernest Schwab	1771-1773	Died in service
	1773-1787	Services interrupted by Revolutionary War
Rev. Thomas Mills	1787-1816	Also priest at St. Andrews; Retired; moved upstate

Rev. Cranmore Wallace	1837-1839	Also principal of the South Carolina Society's Academy in Charleston; Resigned
Rev. Josiah Obear	1839-1842	Temporary Rector
Rev. Stiles Mellichamp	1842-1851	Also teacher; Transferred
Rev. Stiles Mellichamp	1853-1863	Services, for the most part, discontinued in 1862 due to war
Rev. W.O. Prentiss	1867-1869	Preached about once a month; some services in James Island Presbyterian Church
Rev. Stiles Mellichamp	1870-1872	Saint James listed as "suspended mission" in 1872; Died in service
Rev. S.E. Prentiss	1887-1888	Preached occasionally
Rev. John L. Egbert	January-March 1896	Held services twice a month at the James Island Presbyterian Church
Rev. Andrew Ernest Cornish	April-1896-April 1897	Held services twice a month at the James Island Presbyterian Church
Rev. Albert E. Cornish • Assistant Rector John Henry Brown	1898-1906	Also conducted mission farm and school "Sheltering Arms." Transferred
Rev. H. C. Mazyck	1907-1913	Also rector of St. Johns of Johns Island; minister in charge of Saint James
Rev. Percival Hanahan Whaley	1913-1915	Also rector of St. Johns of Johns Island; Died in service
Rev. Albert E. Cornish	1917-1920	Also in charge of Harriott Pinckney Home for Seamen; Died in service
Rev. Wallace Martin	1921-1944	Also in charge of Harriott Pinckney Home for Seamen; Died in service
Retired Bishop Albert Sidney Thomas	1945-1946	Locum tenens (one who temporarily fulfills duties)
Rev. Edward Brailsford Guerry	1946-1960	Also rector at St. Johns; resigned to become full-time rector at St. Johns on Johns Island

Rev. Robert Watson, Jr.	1960-1962	First full-time minister since 1862; resigned to enroll at Duke University to seek higher degree
Rev. Charles F. Duvall	1962-1970	Transferred to accept call to Church of the Advent in Spartanburg
Rev. Richard Dority • Assistant Rectors Robert L. Oliveros Fielder Israel Chip Nix	1970-1979	Transferred to accept call at St. John's Episcopal in Charleston
Rev. Sidney S. Holt	1979	Locum tenens
Rev. Morris J. Lent • Assistant Rectors Rev. Greg Prior Rev. Clark W. P. Lowenfield	1979-1987	Transferred to take chaplain's position at Porter Gaud School
• Rev. Clark W. P. Lowenfield • Mr. Knud Larsen	August 1987 to July 1988 July 1, 1988 to Sept. 4, 1988	Interim priests
Rev. Paul F. M. Zahl • Associate/counselor Rev. Frederick S. Sosnowski • Assistant Rectors Rev. Frank F. Limehouse III Rev. Arthur M. Jenkins	1988-1992	Resigned to work on doctoral studies at the University of Tubingen, Germany, in the area of Justification by Faith
Rev. Samuel Johnson Howard • Assistant Rectors Rev. Arthur M. Jenkins Rev. Jeffrey Scott Miller Rev. Jack F. Nietert Rev. Floyd William Finch, Jr.	1993-1997	Transferred to become vicar of Trinity Church on Wall Street in New York City

Rev. Arthur M. Jenkins   1998 to present
- • Assistant Rectors
  Rev. Floyd William Finch, Jr.
  Rev. Marc Bouton
  Rev. Marshall Huey
  Rev. Louise Weld
  Rev. J. Robert Horn
  Rev. Andrew Williams
  Rev. Mark Cooke
  Rev. Elizabeth Bumpas

Note: Much of this information is found on pages ix-xii, compiled by Dr. Daniel Ellis, in *Saint James' Sampler II*.

APPENDIX B

Priests Sent Forth from Saint James Church

Name	Date of Ordination
Rev. Stiles Mellichamp	1843
Rev. John Rivers	1956
Rev. Edmond D. Campbell	1965
Rev. Robert A. Horn	1982
Rev. Christopher Mercer Huff	1982
Rev. Jennie Olbrych	1986
Rev. Creighton Evans	1995
Rev. Louise Weld	2006
Rev. Craig Stephans	2010
Rev. Suzy McCall	2013
Rev. Martha Horn	2015
Rev. Elizabeth Bumpas	2016
Rev. Mary Ellen Doran	2017
Rev. Jeremy Shelton	2018

APPENDIX C

Saint James' Historical Records in the South Carolina History Room, Charleston County Library

In Charleston County's South Carolina History Room in the downtown library on Calhoun Street are archives entitled *St. James Episc., James Island/Register* with various dates extending over decades, beginning in the 1830s, all preserved on microfiche.

There, researchers can find seemingly countless details regarding "Communicants—How and Where Received" and "Memoranda"—sometimes information pertaining to Confirmation, marriage, removal, transfer, date of death, burial, etc. For example, a communicant might be removed because of moving to a different location or transferring to another church.

Baptismal records include the full name of the one being baptized, sex, parents' names, sponsors, date of birth, date baptized, place baptized, and the priest officiating.

Burial records often state the full name of the deceased, sex, age, last residence, date of death, cause of death, place of internment, date of burial, and the officiating minister's name.

The Canonical Marriage Register states the full birth names of the bride and groom, their ages, indication if the male is a bachelor or widower and if the female is maiden or widow, and sometimes the parents' names.

There is also a section entitled "Families with Appendix: List of Families" giving the relatives' names, residences, relationships to the head of the family, dates of births, and "memoranda" column for noting removals and transfers.

The slides contain decades of varied kinds of information. Some microfiche slides include copies of envelopes and letters, newspaper articles, and legal documents. Other notes record details about cemetery headstones (often stating who erected the stones), handwritten accounts of the names of those buried in family plots in the church's cemetery, and obituaries.

Some additional records, particularly of the first half of the twentieth century, list members in the Women's Auxiliary, their dues, expenditures, and donations. Readers can glean interesting information about the economy and priorities of these early years.

Some records are written with painstaking clarity in a calligraphy-style handwriting; others are not so legibly recorded. Some have strike-throughs and ditto marks; some are smudged with erasures and age; others might include details squeezed into blocks of the registrar or margins of records. Usually the minutes exhibit correct grammar, precise diction, effective sentence structure, and signatures of the recording secretaries. Of course, all are dated.

Decades of Saint James' vestry minutes are preserved on microfiche. (St. James Episc. Church, James Island, Vestry Minutes 1898-1975 SCHS 50-95 RNC) One of the oldest consists of merely an outline: "previous minutes, election of vestry and wardens, reports, unfinished and new business." In the succeeding decades—1910 and beyond—the minutes become much more detailed, often two or three pages per meeting. These handwritten notes often skip months or even years, perhaps due to less frequently held meetings compared to today's vestry meetings or perhaps to not being preserved. Mixed in with the vestry minutes are also minutes taken at annual congregational meetings.

Portions of meetings are, of course, summarized, portraying the intent of goodwill, a deep concern for doing the right thing for the church and community, the necessary frugality of the vestry, political mindset and current events of the times, and "character sketches" of priests and parishioners alike. These words bring to life these church leaders in the unique times in which they worshipped and served.

According to James T. Gallahorn, Saint James Vestryman, and Richard Cote, Historical Society, the following records of Saint James were turned over to the Historical Society of Charleston for micro-filming:

Sentence of Consecration	1802	1 page
Sentence of Consecration	1964	1 page
Register of Marriage	1831-1945	22 pages
Register of Baptism	1831-1900	26 pages
Register of Burials	1830-1954	16 pages
Parish Record	1898-1960	191 pages
Misc. Documents on Burials		17 pages

Parish Register	1959-1973	232 pages
Women's Auxiliary Records	1907-1956	108 pages
Vestry Minutes	1899-1946	180 pages
Vestry Minutes	1946-1966	475 pages
Vestry Minutes	1966-1975	470 pages

APPENDIX D

Historical Records Housed at Saint James Church

In the Parish House at Saint James are several three-ring binders that contain many primary sources regarding the history of the church. Documents include sermons; letters, cards, thank you notes, and other means of personal correspondence; newspaper articles; photographs, some of which are dated and labeled with parishioners' names; and contractors' bills and receipts.

On file are vestry notes and annual reports from the 1970s until the present day. As a means of protection, these are stored in Fire King file cabinets.

Also available are compiled records of Saint James' history. One includes a manuscript based on when Mr. Hinson, long-time member and vestryman, was interviewed; a multi-page manuscript was produced in 1888. Other historical records are comprised of pamphlets and booklets produced in various decades. In addition are a video made by a committee of parishioners in the mid-1980s and a transcription of its narration about the history of Saint James.

Three additional historical records housed at Saint James are leather-bound booklets entitled "Register of Baptism in St. James Church, James Island," (50-90) "Register of Marriages in Saint James Church, James Island," (55-91) and "Register of Burials in St. James Church, James Island" (#50-92), the numbers within parentheses coding the sections of the microfiche done in 1980 by the South Carolina Historical Society. Each booklet begins with 1830 or 1831 records, and although incomplete, they are significant, especially because the entries are recorded and signed in the handwriting of Rev. Paul Trapier, Rev. Cranmore Wallace, Rev. Stiles Mellichamp, Rev. A.E. Cornish, and Rev. H.C. Mazyck. The entries reveal details of the decades and verify other aspects of the church's and island's history.

The baptismal records portray much of the culture. One record from May 19, 1833 states, "Titus (a very old Negro slave of Josiah R. Harvey)—baptized in his master's house on James Island." Another record of baptism is as follows: "Christine and Robert (slaves of Josiah R. Harvey) aged about eight years and five years respectively—were baptized in the Episcopal Chapel at Johnsonville." A very sad record is that of December 25, 1837, which reads, "baptized privately (he being near death) the infant son of Mr. Ephaim Mikell Clark and his wife Susan Jane Clark—name Ephaim Mikell. This child died the following night."

Some of the marriage records extend up to 1945. One entry states, "Mr. Edward Peronneau was married in St. James Church March 13, 1834 to Mrs. Anna S. Parker "Nee" Desaure (sp?); the next ceremony was not performed here until the marriage of Priestly Cooper Coker to Lillie Baynard Lebby November 8, 1905 (71 years later) followed by the other sister— C. F. King to M.L. Lebby June 14, 1906." Some entries read, "married in house of her father [father's name] in presence of many witnesses." The marriage of two slaves was recorded: "Married August 10, 1846—Philandu to Jerimiah—servant of Dr. Mikell." The entries pertaining to the slaves often used the wording "servant of…" or "belonging to…"

The burial records are just as interesting. Phrases often included, "buried in yard of St. James," "service read at [name]'s residence," "service read at the house of [name,]" "service read at the home of [name] in Johnsonville, James Island." One cites Saint James Presbyterian Church as the burial site. Slaves' burials were recorded as "Harriet—servant of Capt. Bowman," "Maria—servant of Capt. John Rivers." Birth records were not always kept, so some death records would state "about 40 years," "about 92 years." Then others recorded longevity more accurately, such as "wife aged 17 years 8 months, youngest son about one year." Some indicate that burials were on family property: "buried at the family burial ground (Stiles Point)"

Parishioner Louise Morrison saved many of Saint James' Episcopal Churchwomen's (ECW) booklets from the 1970s, 1980s, and 1990s. These thirty-to-fifty-page publications document an annual theme, a calendar of events, fund-raising projects, service opportunities, financial reports, budgets, executive board members, by-laws, a directory of the female parishioners, prayer partners, and prayers. Others also include scriptural passages, goals, a memorial page, suggested readings, parishioners' poetry, organizations to which they contributed, a list of Saint James ladies living at the Bee Street Home, a parish calendar, and letters from the rector. Each has information about the three chapters: St. Anne's, St. Catherine's, and St. Martha's, which met at different times to accommodate different schedules. Each had its own officers, committee chairpersons, as many as thirty members, and unique undertakings. These booklets portray the interconnectedness and dynamic service of Saint James' female parishioners as well as detailed historical facts. The art on the covers is often a sketch of Saint James Church. Some covers have a circle surrounding the letters "ECW," a cross, and an upright, outstretched hand. The symbolism of this ECW Logo is explained as follows:

- Cross—our life in Christ and serving Christ in the world

- Circle—the hope for wholeness in our lives and for others

- The upward open hand—This receives the bread of life in the Eucharist, which gives us strength. The strength enables us, as members of the ECW, to extend our hand to help wherever we are needed.

Rev. Guerry contributed some notebooks containing various records:

- Letters, notes, cards, and personal correspondence

- Letters of transfer, letters of recommendation

- Rules for annual Sunday school picnics for Saint James and St. Johns (July 4, 1959)

- Booklet for the Church Fire Insurance Corporation (lists reproduction costs, objects of art, construction of building, etc.)

- Black and white photos of the fifth and sixth church buildings

- Thanksgiving Day program from joint Saint James and St. Johns worship service (November 28, 1957)

- List of ushers and their duties

- Church repairs, bills, loans, legal documents

- Newspaper clippings

- Treasurer's report (1954)

These sources have served as a basis for the details throughout this book and are often cited within the text as well as in footnotes and the bibliography.

Among the church's historical records is a clipping by John Woolverton entitled "Parish Archives: Basic Instructions for Beginning a Parish Archive" probably printed in the mid-1980s. In it he states, "You yourselves are [custodians not] of dead relics but of a living tradition which will help people get their bearing in an uncertain and risky world. Be an advocate of the many who have gone before and should not be forgotten…Saint James is above all a vital link between the tenacity of past generations, the creativeness of the present, and the high hopes of those still to take their places."

APPENDIX E

List of Saint James Vestry Members

The vestry and the rector are the official representatives of the parish and have charge of the temporalities—properties, revenues, policies, etc.—of the church. The following alphabetical list of names and dates is based on numerous records, such as vestry minutes and reports from annual congregational meetings. However, many extenuating circumstances may make this information incomplete or even incorrect, especially when one considers partial terms served, misinformation and conflicting data in original sources, historical interruptions in active worship at Saint James, variances in names (nicknames vs. birthnames, maiden vs. married names, "junior" vs. "senior"), vestry elections occurring different months of the year, undated resources, and human error on the part of the author. Although the typical vestry term lasts three years, vestry members elected in more recent years might appear to have served four; however, their terms began mid-year, followed by two full years, and then another half year, thus spanning across dates encompassing four years. "Junior and senior warden" attached to listed years indicates that the vestry member served in that leadership role but not necessarily the years the label follows or all those years. By some of the names the phrase "on first vestry" is written; this information was taken from "Historical Sketch of St. James' Parish James Island, South Carolina." These vestrymen served in the latter 1800s under the leadership of Rev. Trapier, but the source does not make clear the exact dates that they held their positions. The following list also includes information taken from a Saint James source entitled "List of Vestrymen of St. James' Church 1898 to Present Time [1973]."

Walter S. Ameika	1980-1982; 1984-1986; 1988-1990; 1992-1994
Jonathan J. ("Jon" and "JJ") Anderson	1991-1993; 1996-1998 (senior warden)
Lloyd M. Ash, Jr.	1970-1972; 1974-1975; 1976-1978; 1980-1982
Elise Badger	1991-1993
William ("Bill") R. Bailey	1957-1959; 1961-1963; 1968; 1974-1976; 1980-1982 (junior and senior warden)
Joni Wallace Banks	2008-2009
Robert Barber	1995-1997
Charilla T. Barham	1988-1990
Marie "Scooter" Barnette	2003-2006; 2009-2012, 2017-2020
Richard "Dick" Louis Bartels	2008-2011
Virginia Brown Bartels	2011-2014; 2018-2021 (people's warden)
James Swinton Baynard	1960-1961
S. Sandiford Bee	1913-1926
S. Stiles Bee	1927-1929; 1948-1950
Dr. Norman H. Bell	1994-1996; 1999-2000 (senior warden)
James F. ("Jim') Bennett	2007-2010; 2011-2014
Cosmo E. Brockington, Jr.	1946-1948; 1952-1954
Denis ("Corky") B. Brooks	1988-1990
William S. Brown	1962-1964 (junior warden)
Carlton "OC" Brummett	2015-2018
Bobbie Bryan	2005-2008
Katherine Burrell	1984-1986; 1990-1992
Dr. Victor ("Vic") G. Burrell, Jr.	1977-1979; 1981-1983; 1987-1989; 1993-1995 (junior and senior warden)

Richard Caldwell	1978-1979
Edmund D. Campbell, Jr.	1961-1963
Dr. William C. ("Bill") Carter III	1988-1990; 1992-1994 (senior warden)
Amy Case	2013-2016
Frank W. Clement	1928-1941
Frank W. Clement, Jr.	1950-1952; 1955-1957; 1964-1966 (junior and senior warden)
Samuel M. Clement, Jr.	1965-1967; 1973-1975 (junior warden)
Dr. Joel Cochran	2011-2014
Louis E. Costa	1972-1974; 1976-1978
Jack P. Cranwell, Jr.	1972-1974; 1976-1978; 1980-1982
David Cupka	1994-1996; 2000-2002; 2006-2009 (senior warden)
Kay H. Cupka	1997-1999
Seth Cutter	1976
Dr. Larry Daniel	2017-2019
Clark DeCiantis	2013-2016 (junior warden)
Pam Dickson	2014-2017
Joseph T. Dill	1898 (senior warden)
Keith Doran	2003-2006; 2007-2010 (junior warden)
Floyd I. Dovell, Jr.	1953-1955; 1959-1962; 1967-1969; 1972
James ("Jim/Jimmy") DuPre	1992-1994; 1998-1999 (junior and senior warden)
Susan DuPre	1990-1991
Mark Joseph Durinsky	2008-2011
Melissa Ward Durinsky	2002-2005

Dr. Barbara Edlund	2008-2011; 2014-2017
Bill Edlund	2007-2009; 2009-2012
Dr. David Egleston	1982-1984; 2008-2011
Frances ("Francie") Egleston	1989-1991; 1997-1999; 2005-2008
Anna ("Kitty") Swinton W. Ellis	1974-1975;1977-1979;1981-1983; 1986-1988 (senior warden)
Dr. D. W. Ellis	1898-1922
Dr. Daniel W. Ellis	1932-1946; 1956-1958; 1963-1965; 1967-1969; (senior warden and senior warden emeritus)
William ("Bill") Elmore	1994-1996
Ben English	2005-2008 (senior warden)
Charles "Sonny" Eppes	2015-2018
Mark Evans	2010-2013; 2016-2019
Noel Ferguson	2007-2010
Art Field	2001-2004; 2014-2015; 2018-2021
Prentiss Findlay	2012-2015
Randy Flanders	1984-1986
J. Wyman Frampton	1966-1968; 1977-1979
R. Frank Freeman	1972-1974
Robert ("Bobbie") E. Galbraith	1990-1992; 1997-1999; 2001-2004
James "Jim" T. Gallahorn III	1979-1980; 1981-1983
Royal ("Chip") H. Gibson	1985-1987
Edward L. Grimball, Jr.	1955-1957
Raymond F. Grimball	1946; 1954-1956
P. Maynard Grooms	1973-1975; 1978-1979

John W. "Slip" Haizlip	1987-1989
Mike L. Halsema	1996-1998 (senior warden)
Francis Motte Harleston	1959-1961; 1964-1966; 1969-1971 (junior warden)
Fred Hart	2006-2009
J. R. Harvey	(on first vestry)
Jack W. Henley	1948-1950; 1952-1954
Jack Henley	2015-2018
Susan Henley	1994-1996
John Hensel	2005-2008
Irvine Keith ("Ike") Heyward IV	1986-1988
Brent Hilpert	2019-2022
Tom Hilton	2012-2015; 2016-2019 (junior and senior warden)
J. B. Hinson	(on first vestry)
William G. Hinson	1898-1919 (senior warden)
J. Robert Horn IV	1975; 1976-1978
Artie Horne	2018-2021 (people's warden)
Benjamin S. Horne	1996-1998 (junior warden)
Jane B. Horne	1999-2001
Christopher Mercer Huff	1977-1979; 1980
William ("Bill") D. Huff	1995-1997; 1999-2001
John R. Jefferies	1947-1949
Daniel LaRoche Jenkins, Jr.	1951-1953; 1960-1962
Gordon H. Jenkins	1983-1985

Laurence L. Jenkins	1965-1967; 1968; 1971-1973; 1976-1978 (junior and senior warden)
Oliver ("Midge") Jenkins	1983-1985
W. R. Jenkins	1898-1905
J. R. Jervey	(on first vestry)
Gunnar Johnson	1974-1976; 1978-1980 (junior warden)
David ("Dave") Jordan	2004-2007
John Alexander Keith	1959-1961
Jimmie Ketcham	1983
Ann LaRoche King	1997-1999; 2001-2004; 2014-2017 (senior warden)
Mary Bailey King	1992-1994; 2012-2013
Thomas ("Tommy") P. King, Jr.	1970-1972
William ("Bill") Kitchens	1980-1982
Amy Knox	2009-2012
Harry E. Lawhon, Jr.	1948-1950
St. John A. Lawton	1898-1946 (junior and senior warden)
Winborn Lawton	(on first vestry)
Joseph Hinson Lebby	1926-1935
Ellen Leighton	2006-2009
Larry Lessard	1982-1984
Carl D. Lewis	1963-1965
George Lisle	2002-2005 (junior warden)
Frank E. Lucas	1965-1967; 1973-1975 (senior warden)
Julia Marshall	1993-1995

Teena Martindale	2003-2004
Bill McDaniel	2004-2007
Bruce McDonald	2008-2013; 2015-2018 (senior warden)
Rosalyn McDonald	2013-2016
William Ellis McLeod	1916-1917; 1938-1951; 1953-1955; 1957-1959; 1960-1963 (junior and senior warden and warden emeritus)
Lillian ("Lillie") McGougan	1978; 2001-2004
Henry B. McManus	1969-1971; 1974-1976; 1980; 1981-1983; 1985-1987; 1989-1991
W. Gresham Meggett, Jr.	1983-1985
Wilmer Gresham Meggett, Sr.	1946-1948; 1950-1952; 1954-1956; 1958-1960; 1962-1964; 1968 (junior and senior warden)
B. Stiles Mikell	1950-1952
Hinson L. Mikell	1942-1949; 1955-1957
William H. Mikell	1911-1951 (senior warden)
William H. Mikell, Jr.	1947-1949; 1951-1953 (junior warden)
Jay Millen	2017-2020
R. Eugene ("Gene") Miller	1977-1979; 1983-1984; 1985-1987; 1989-1990 (senior warden)
J. B. F. Minott	(on first vestry)
Joseph ("Joe") E. Moran	1998
Steve Morillo	1999-2001 (junior warden)
Eugene Clark Morrison, Jr.	1958-1960; 1965-1967; 1969-1971; 1980-1982; 1984-1986; 1990-1992; 1995-1997
Gene Morrison	2010-2013; 2016-2019
E. Michael Musgrove III	1974

Alexander S. Oswald	1920-1927
Cecil Oswald	1910-1932
Robert Paige	2012-2015
Doug Pait	2004-2007 (junior warden)
Paul S. Pearce	1949-1951
Paul Pennington	2019-2022
Philip D. Pinckney	1969-1971
Edward (Eddie) Porcher	1993-1995 (junior warden)
Edward P. Porcher	1941-1948
Joel P. Porcher	1970-1972; 1974-1975; 1976- 1977; 1980-1982; 1996-1998 (junior and senior warden)
W. Kenneth Powers	1951-1952
Allen Puckhaber	2014-2017; 2018-2019
William Rambo	1967-1969
Arthur Ravenel, Jr.	1952-1954
Arthur Ravenel, Sr.	1956-1958; 1970-1972
Anne Read	1991-1993
Jane Read	2006-2007
Thomas L. Read, Sr.	1969-1971; 1987-1989 (senior warden)
William ("Bill") D. Read	1999-2001
Thomas Rehm	2019-2020
William McLeod ("Mac") Rhodes	1982; 1986-1988; 1990-1992; 2003-2006 (senior warden)
Dr. Donald Riopel	1975-1976
Elias L. Rivers, Sr.	1898-1911

Elias L. Rivers, Jr.	1922-1945
John Rivers	(on first vestry); 1905-1941
J. R. Rogers	(on first vestry)
Patrick Ruppe	2019-2022
Shannon Sears	2013-2016, 2017-2020
Les Sease	2000-2002; 2004-2007; 2011-2014
E. Marshall Shingler	1957-1959
The Honorable William Henry Simmons, Jr.	1954-1956; 1958-1960; 1962-1964; 1968-1970; 1972-1974; 1986-1988 (junior warden)
Dr. Charles J. Smith	1959-1961; 1964-1966
Kersey Smith	1980-1982
Peggy Spell	2007-2010
Daniel "Dan" R. Stevenson	1998-2000
Ann Stirling	1993-1995 (senior warden)
Dr. Ashby Taylor	1991-1993
Cdr. Jack Thorp	1975-1977; 1979-1980 (junior warden)
Mary Townsend	1979-1981 (junior warden)
Matthew ("Matt") T. Townsend	1963-1965; 1968-1970; 1972-1974; 1989-1991 (junior and senior warden)
Mark VonAllmen	2010-2013
James "Jeb" E. Waterbury	1998-2000 (junior warden)
John ("Buddy") R. Watkins	1985-1987; 1989-1991
Glynn Watson	2002-2005
Robert ("Rob") Welch	1979-1981
Louise Weld	2002

David White	2009-2012 (people's warden)
Jenny White	1995-1997
Fred Whittle	2016-2020 (senior warden)
Frederick "Fred" C. Wichmann	1987-1989
John Wilder	2000-2002
Becky Williams	2000-2002
Edward S. Williams, Jr	1963-1965
Abram Wilson	(on first vestry)
Bonum S. Wilson, Sr.	1949-1951; 1953-1955; 1957-1959; 1961-1963; 1966-1968; 1971-1973; 1976-1978; 1980 (senior warden)
Bonum S. Wilson, Jr.	2003-2006 (senior warden)
William A. ("Billy") Wise	1980-1981; 1982-1984
Warren H. "Jack" Yeager	1973-1975; 1979-1981; 1983-1985; 1990 (junior warden)

INDEX

Egbert, Rev. John L., 46, 340

Egleston, Dr. David, 123, 167, 248, 356

Egleston, Frances "Francie", 123, 137, 149, 356

Ellis, Anna Swinton Welch "Kitty", x, 109, 110, 112, 123, 131, 151, 217, 218, 238-239, 279, 356

Ellis Creek, x, 4, 5, 26, 135, 188, 193

Ellis, Dr. Daniel Wordsworth, x, 2, 3, 6, 9-12, 15, 22-23, 26-28, 30, 34-35, 43, 45, 49, 61-62, 73-75, 80, 87, 89, 90-91, 94, 96, 99, 108-109, 123, 133, 238, 279, 356

Episcopal Church Women (ECW), 132, 137, 152, 180, 217, 218, 239, 261, 263, 264, 350, 351

Episcopal Diocese of South Carolina, 29, 41, 82, 180

Episcopal Youth Council (EYC), 96, 100, 104, 118, 125, 135, 137, 146, 151, 163, 180

Eppes, Charles "Sonny", 203, 356

Evans, Barbara, 206

Evans, Mark, 180, 280, 356

Evans, Jr., Rev. Vernon Creighton, 115, 184, 227, 231-232, 343

Faith in Action Fundraising Campaign, 154-150, 160

Felts, William "Will", 280

Field, Art, 155, 161, 206, 210, 258, 265

Fifties Plus Group, 263

Finch, Jr., Rev. Floyd W. , 152-153, 162, 225, 266, 279, 341, 342

Flip Flops and Faith Worship Services, 208, 261, 262

Florence Crittenton Home for Unwed Mothers, 127

Folly Beach (Island), 4, 56, 78, 137, 218, 251, 262, 263

Folly Road, 61-62, 64, 75, 77, 92, 105, 111, 238, 243, 272

Food Wall, 250

Fort Johnson Road, 5, 75, 154

Frampton, Creighton, 138

Frampton, Frances, 167, 211-212

Frampton, Jr., Wyman, 99, 128, 245, 356

Fresh Start, 254

Frontline Missions, 254, 255

Fuchs, Francis, 167

Gadsden, Bishop Christopher, 28, 29, 128

GAFCON, 179, 181, 211

Galbraith, Bobbie, 154, 155, 160, 162, 257, 356